D1518321

AMERICAN TRADE UNIONISM

AMERICAN TRADE UNIONISM

Principles and Organization

Strategy and Tactics

Selected Writings BY

William Z. Foster

INTERNATIONAL PUBLISHERS

NEW YORK

CONTENTS

Preface

This book consists of selections from my writings on trade unionism published in one form or another during the past thirty-five years. The period covered in these writings runs back, roughly, half a century. While not a formal history of trade unionism during this time, the book nevertheless throws much light on the major developments in the trade union movement. It particularly highlights the long struggle of the left-wing and progressive forces for improved trade union organization, policies, and leadership.

The period in question has been one of stormy and significant economic and political developments. American industry has expanded prodigiously and also has become highly monopolized. World capitalism has matured and entered into its final stage of imperialism and decline. Two world wars, fascism, mass pauperization, and endless class struggle have been expressions of this development of capitalism. The writings in this volume show how the American working class has reacted to this vital expansion and the decline of the world capitalist system.

While there have been other compilations of writings on trade unionism, I believe this is the first time that the policies, tactics, and role of the left wing during the past three or four decades have been recorded in a single volume. Written in the midst of the struggle, the material assembled here is itself part of the living record of the American trade union movement. For this reason, aside from omissions dictated by limitations of space, I have made no changes in the original text other than those of a minor and stylistic nature.

To facilitate the use of this book, it has been divided into four parts corresponding broadly to periods of development in our country's history and in the trade union movement. Such a chronological arrangement, it seems to me, has the advantage of bringing historical perspective and development to the study and evaluation of the major issues, policies and problems of the trade union movement. By referring to the index, the reader can single out for study the separate questions and individual topics as registered in the different periods covered by this book. Each selection is identified by the year in which it was written, while the source of the various items will be found in the reference list at the end of the book.

A number of selections, such as the chapter on the packinghouse campaign of 1917 and the steel strike of 1918, were taken from my book *From Bryan to Stalin* published in 1936 instead of from writings produced directly in connection with the events. The choice of the more succinct summaries provided by this later book was dictated entirely by the limitations of space. In this manner the extensive body of trade union material in the earlier volume, *From Bryan to Stalin*, now out of print, has been utilized and preserved in the present book.

For the same reason, the reader will find excerpts from my book *Misleaders of Labor* published in 1927 instead of from writings produced during the period under consideration. The bulk of the chapters, however, consist of pamphlets or articles written in the course of events under discussion. The last chapter, "Summary and Conclusions," was written especially for this book.

W. Z. F.

PART ONE

1. Early Days

I was born in Taunton, Massachusetts, near Boston, February 25, 1881. From the age of seven to ten I went to school, selling newspapers the while. But at ten, so meager was the family income, I had to quit school and go to work. My first job, in 1891, was with a sculptor.

This was the first of my twenty-six years' experience as a worker, an experience which took me into many industries, including chemical, lumber, metal, meatpacking, agriculture, marine transport, railroad, building construction, etc., all over the country from New York to California, and from Florida to Washington. I stayed two years with the sculptor, but the wages he paid were so low (from $1.50 per week for the first year to $2.00 for the second) that I quit him. I got a job at $3.00 a week at the local type foundry of Mackellar, Smith & Jordan, where I worked some two and a half years and learned much of the type-founders' trade. I began to follow with great interest and sympathy the many strikes and other struggles of the workers in this period.

The first strike in which I actually participated was that of the Philadelphia street carmen in 1894, when I was fourteen years old. The strike lasted only about a week, but it was very bitterly fought. I, together with other strikers and sympathizing workers, was clubbed and ridden down by mounted police at 15th and Market Streets in a vicious charge of these thugs against a peaceful parade of strikers. It was my baptism in the class struggle and it exerted a profound influence upon my general outlook.

The decade when I was a growing lad, from the middle eighties to the middle nineties, was one of active struggle by the workers. In point of militancy it was unequaled for the next twenty-five years.

9

This was the heyday of the Knights of Labor and the foundation period of the American Federation of Labor. Some of the greatest strikes in the history of the United States took place during this time.

This decade of extreme working class militancy was started off by the great eight-hour strike movement of 1886 centering in Chicago, which greatly stimulated the trade unions everywhere, and which resulted in the legal lynching of its militant leaders, Parsons, Spies, Fisher, Engel, and Lingg. Soon this historic struggle was followed by another almost equally famous, the Homestead strike of 1892, when the steel workers, fighting a losing battle against the growing steel trust, drove away the Pinkerton thugs* in armed struggle and seized the local steel mills, rifles in hand. Then, in May 1894, in the midst of the great industrial crisis of that time, the powerful strike of the American Railway Union took place, led by Eugene V. Debs, which was crushed by a combination of violence by the Federal government and treachery by A. F. of L. and railroad craft union officials. Meanwhile in the Rocky Mountain states, among the metal miners, the Western Federation of Miners, with William D. Haywood as its leading spirit, a whole series of the most spectacular and hard-fought strikes in American labor history were developing, many of them being armed conflicts of the workers against company thugs and state troops. And another famous movement of this period was Coxey's national march of the unemployed upon Washington, a movement that profoundly stirred the working class, stricken as it was by the huge wage cuts and unemployment caused by the prevailing economic crisis.

While the workers were thus resisting American capitalism so militantly, the small farmers of the Middle West were also in a high state of political discontent. There was also much discontent among the urban petty bourgeoisie, or small manufacturers, merchants, etc. They were feeling the crushing power of the growing trusts and monopolies. Already they had succeeded in having the Sherman Anti-Trust Law passed in 1890 in a vain attempt to stifle the growth of monopoly; their cup of unrest was also filled to overflowing by the deep industrial crisis of this period.

It was upon this general background of discontent of the workers, farmers and city middle class that the Bryan Democratic Party cam-

* The Pinkerton Detective Agency was the most vicious strike-breaking and labor-spy agency in the United States during the last half of the nineteenth century.

paign of 1896 developed. It originated in the Populist Party of the farmers, and the farmers remained the backbone of the movement, although large numbers of workers and city middle class elements also participated in it.

I was profoundly stirred by all these great events. Especially was I interested and aroused by the bitter strikes of the period. It is true that I knew of 1886 only from the older workers, but it was then still a strong tradition among them and I eagerly absorbed it. The American Railway Union strike of 1894 I remember quite distinctly, and I read with close attention the newspaper reports of the fierce strikes of the Rocky Mountain metal miners and also of the many struggles of the coal miners in the anthracite districts of Pennsylvania. My sense of solidarity with the workers was actively aroused. I followed with bated breath the march of "Coxey's Army," and on my way to work I used to linger around Coxey's Philadelphia recruiting office at 13th and Filbert Streets to read the displayed bulletins from all over the country as to the progress of the various detachments of the army of unemployed. When the movement came to its absurd anti-climax by Coxey's being arrested for walking on the Capitol lawn, it was for me a personal tragedy. But the greatest effect of all upon my awakening class feeling was produced by the great Homestead strike of steel workers. I was only eleven years old at the time but I remember how I shared my father's indignation at the sending of the Philadelphia National Guard regiments to Pittsburgh.

Forces were at work which were rapidly developing my native proletarian instinct into genuine class consciousness. It was fast outgrowing the petty bourgeois limits of the Bryan movement and was on the way to a revolutionary outlook.

My experience in industry was broadening. By the end of 1900 I had added to my previous jobs three years' work in the fertilizer industry, working in plants in Reading, Pennsylvania, and Jacksonville, Florida, where I had become a steam-fitter, stationary engineer and an expert fertilizer mixer. I had also worked in Florida peonage lumber camps, put in two months as a brakeman on the Pennsylvania & Reading railroad, and spent six months as a trolley car motorman on the Third Avenue line in New York City. It was at the latter occupation that I joined my first union, the Street Carmen. Conditions were abominable on the New York cars, the men being completely unorganized and the company arbitrarily dictating wage and working conditions. I decided to try to change all this. The result was that I was discharged for trying to organize the street carmen.

This whole process of disillusionment with capitalist economics, government, and religion was preparing me for my transformation into a socialist, which came with dramatic suddenness in the summer of 1900. I began to read socialist literature in earnest and to become better acquainted with the movement. In the fall of 1900 I was working in a fertilizer plant at Wyomissing, Pennsylvania, near Reading, when the elections came on. Eugene V. Debs and Job Harriman were the Socialist candidates. Although only nineteen years old and too young to vote myself, I walked six miles with another worker, my brother-in-law, George McVey, to "help" him cast his vote for the Socialist ticket. The same year I joined the Socialist Party, then just being formed out of the split-off from the Socialist Labor Party.*

From 1901 to 1904 my revolutionary development suffered a rude interruption. The two and a half years I had worked with lead in the type foundry as a child worker had undermined my health. The three years following in the fertilizer industry, where we usually toiled totally unprotected, in dense clouds of poisonous dusts, broke me down so that the doctors pronounced me a consumptive. I was in a fair way to go to an untimely grave, grinding out profits for employers, as vast armies of workers had done before me. So I quit my job, pulled up stakes and headed for the West. I hoboed my way.

Arrived in Oregon, I worked for a few months on the local docks and in neighboring logging camps and railroad construction jobs. Then, early in the winter of 1901 I shipped out of Portland on an old square-rigged sailing vessel. She was the *Pegasus,* a British four-masted bark, and bound around Cape Horn for Cape Town, South Africa, with a cargo of wheat. Thus opened my life as a deep-water sailor, my most interesting and unforgettable experience as a worker. During this time I sailed one and a half times around the world. All told, the voyage, counting considerable stays on the South African, Australian and South American coasts, lasted almost three years and covered some fifty thousand miles. It gave me a real taste of hunger, hardship, low wages, and danger, and it exposed me to the rawest and most callous exploitation. It helped very much to steel me in my growing revolutionary convictions.

* The Socialist Labor Party was organized in 1876, fusing the various socialist groups into a single party. The Socialist Party was formed in 1901, as a result of a split in the S. L. P. The new party also included other Socialist groupings in the middle west.

My last ship, the *County of Cardigan,* paid off at North Shields, England, and I took a steamer for Philadelphia. There I joined the Atlantic Coast Seamen's Union, intending to work as a sailor on the coast. But again I listened to the siren song of the West. Once more I hoboed it to Oregon, arriving early in November 1904, just in time to vote for Debs for President.

From 1904 to 1907 I worked in the Portland area and began to take an active part in the Socialist Party. I paid up my dues in the local branch and began to read the party literature.

During these three years I worked in many local industries characteristic of the Pacific Northwest: farming, logging, sawmills, building, metal mining, railroad construction, railroad train service, etc. I became a pretty typical Western floating worker.

I had secured a job as fireman on the Oregon Railroad and Navigation Company on the Portland-Umatilla division. After six months of this gruelling work I made an application to join the Brotherhood of Locomotive Firemen and Engineers, having decided to work up to an engineer. But then came the sharp industrial crisis of 1907, which swept me out of work and wrecked my plans.

During these several years my revolutionary understanding and enthusiasm were rising. I was a very ardent supporter of the Socialist Party, which was then torn by a bitter and growing internal struggle in the Pacific Coast states. Domination of the S. P. by middle class elements condemned the party to a policy of opportunism. The revolutionary worker members of the party deeply resented this petty bourgeois control and opportunist regime. I took an active interest in this factional struggle and at once found myself in the left wing of the party. All my experience and reading in the class struggle had tended to make a militant of me. I had learned the elementary lesson that the class struggle is indeed a fight. I was profoundly convinced that the reformist plan of gradually turning capitalism into socialism by a series of reforms was futile. So I joined definitely with the proletarian elements, who wanted to make of the Socialist Party a revolutionary organization.

The industrial crisis of 1907 uprooted me in Portland and, job seeking, I made my way to Seattle. Here I worked mostly as a building laborer and in the local sawmills during 1907-09.

When I arrived in Seattle the S. P. internal fight was already acute. The state organization was in the hands of typical opportunist groups. The majority of the party membership favored the left opposition.

The fight, centering around the main question of proletarian versus petty bourgeois control of the party, developed, with many ramifications, into a struggle for power.

The situation climaxed in the party state convention held in Everett early in 1909. The left wing refused to participate in the convention, withdrew its delegates, held its own convention and elected a state secretary. There were thus two socialist parties in Washington. Whereupon, the opportunist-controlled National Executive Committee of the Socialist Party pronounced the left wing convention illegal, recognized the right wing state secretary and gave the left wingers the option of rejoining as individuals. Few ever went back to the Socialist Party. At first we tried to keep going our version of the Socialist Party. But this policy could not continue, because there was a great disinclination to use the hated name of the Socialist Party. We had, therefore, to cast about for a new form of mobilizing our forces.

With the 1909 split on our hands in Washington, we had to make a decision as to our next step organizationally. Most of us, like left wingers generally in that period, were saturated with the semi-syndicalist theories of Daniel De Leon. But we finally decided not to join the Socialist Labor Party of which De Leon was the leader. Its crass sectarianism repelled us; we felt De Leon's dogmatic utopianism rather than analyzed it. We decided to form a new party, and we did.

After much travail, the new party was launched in Seattle on February 25, 1910. It called itself the Wage Workers Party. The organization was short-lived. The W. W. P. was a sort of hybrid between the Socialist Labor Party and the Industrial Workers of the World (I. W. W.), formed in 1905. There was no place in the class struggle for such an organization as the W. W. P., so it died as soon as it was born. The period from its formation to its collapse was only a few months. It got out only one issue of its paper, *The Wage Worker*. One of the active spirits in this movement was Joe Manley, later an active Communist trade union leader.

The W. W. P. was important in that it was one of the earliest crystallizations of the S. P. left wing, a forerunner of the big fight of 1912 and the eventual national S. P. split of 1919. It was a local skirmish in the world-wide fight of the revolutionary elements inside the S. P. against the reformist leadership.

I was not greatly enthused over the formation of the Wage Workers Party, and even while it was being launched I was turning my attention to the Industrial Workers of the World. Specifically, I went from Seattle to Spokane in the fall of 1909 to report the free speech fight there for Titus' *Workingman's Paper,* formerly the *Seattle Socialist.*

Immediately upon my arrival in Spokane I joined actively in this struggle. I heartily endorsed the splendid fighting spirit of the I. W. W., which contrasted sharply with the wishy-washy S. P. I was arrested and served two months. While in jail I joined the I. W. W. Upon my release I was placed at the head of the committee which negotiated the settlement of the struggle. This settlement resulted in an almost complete victory for the I. W. W.

It was chiefly disgust with the petty-bourgeois leaders and policies of the S. P. that had made me join the I. W. W. It was an easy step for me to conclude from the paralyzing reformism of the S. P. that political action in general was fruitless and that the way to working-class emancipation was through militant trade union action, culminating in the general strike. This conclusion was a serious error—confounding political action as such with S. P. opportunism, and thus casting aside the political weapons of the working class. It took me many years to correct this basic mistake.

I was also drawn to the syndicalist point of view by the influence of the militant I. W. W., and likewise as a result of the spectacular success of the General Confederation of Labor (C. G. T.) of France. This syndicalist organization was at that time conducting a whole series of local and national general strikes that were stirring the workers in every country. I decided to go to France and study French syndicalism at first hand. So, early in 1910, with a hundred dollars in my pocket, I hoboed my way to New York and soon landed in Paris.

I stayed six months in France and intensely studied the labor movement, gaining a speaking and reading knowledge of French. I was deeply impressed by a basic feature of French syndicalism, new to me and quite contrary to I. W. W. policy. This was the policy of militant workers fighting for their policies within conservative unions, rather than withdrawing from them and trying to construct new, ideal, industrial unions on the outside.

It seemed to me that this tactic and the whole theory of the militant minority were highly intelligent and far superior to the I. W. W. policy of building dual industrial unions and also to its naive theory that there were no leaders in the organization, all the members being leaders. I resolved to raise these two questions in the I. W. W. when

I returned to the United States, and the sequel showed that they were to play a very large part in my future labor activities.

From France I went to Germany, where I also stayed six months, incidentally learning the German language. My experience in Germany fortified my syndicalist opinions. The manifestly non-revolutionary Social-Democratic Party and the conservative mass unions and co-operatives under its control convinced me further of the necessity of a revolutionary syndicalist policy. Furthermore, the sectarian isolation of the German syndicalist union convinced me that by withdrawing from old unions, on the I. W. W. plan, they were simply turning the mass trade unions over to the deadly control of Carl Legien* and that good tactics required working within the mass unions. I was led to conclude that the policy of dual unionism was wrong not only in Germany, but also in the United States.

My scheduled six months' stay in Germany coming to an end, I was hastily picking up a reading knowledge of Italian and Spanish preparatory to spending six months each in Italy and Spain, when Vincent St. John, General Secretary of the I. W. W., cabled me to represent that organization at the meeting of the International Trade Union Secretariat (forerunner of the Amsterdam International) to be held in Budapest, Hungary, August 10 to 12, 1911. On my way, I attended the national congress of the German trade unions in Dresden, and saw Legien's iron-clad bureaucracy in action. As I was broke I had had to walk 150 miles of the way from Nuremburg to Dresden. At Budapest I received another cable from St. John to come home immediately to attend the forthcoming I. W. W. convention, which I did.

I arrived in Chicago in time for the sixth convention of the I. W. W., which was held in September 1911, and I at once took up the question of winning the I. W. W. for a policy of working within the conservative trade unions. I began an active campaign in favor of this fundamental change of policy, and won the support of Jack Johnstone, Joe Manley, Jay Fox, Sam Hammersmark, and a few other militants. The existing situation in the I. W. W. was favorable to our agitation. The glowing hopes of the 1905 convention had not materialized. The organization had gradually dwindled in numbers and influence—the convention had only 31 delegates. Ideologically the I. W. W. had narrowed down pretty much to a small group of hardboiled anti-political, anti-religious secretarians. Debs had quit it and

* Carl Legien was the reformist leader of the trade unions in Germany.

De Leon likewise, both having split off when the I. W. W. reje political action. Pessimism was rampant in the organization and question, "Why don't the I. W. W. grow?" was a live issue.

Meanwhile, however, an important event was developing that soon effectively crippled our budding agitation in the I. W. W. This was the famous I. W. W. Lawrence strike in January 1912, of 23,000 textile workers. It was hard fought, well-led, and resulted in a real victory for the workers. I. W. W. stocks went skyward again everywhere and it grew rapidly. Within a short period afterward, the organization conducted a whole series of important strikes in Paterson, Akron, Little Falls, Lytton, in the Mesaba iron range, the Washington lumber districts, etc.

This sudden wave of strikes, many of which won concessions, brought the I. W. W. to what Prof. Paul Brissenden calls its "crest of power."* Pessimism vanished and the I. W. W. militants were jubilant. St. John declared enthusiastically: "The victory in the Lawrence mills means the start that will only end with the downfall of the capitalist system." In such a situation our proposal to have the I. W. W. forces merge with the old trade unions fell flat. A new wave of dual unionist sentiment spread in all sections of the left wing. Only a few of us looked upon the current spurt of the I. W. W. correctly as but "a flash in the pan."

The revival of the I. W. W. dual union sentiment caused a change in our tactics. Our newly formed groups began to split off from the I. W. W. and to join the A. F. of L. to work there. The first to take this course was local Syndicalist League No. 1, in Nelson, British Columbia, which had been formed by Jack Johnstone. It was only a short while afterward until we had similar groups within the A. F. of L. in Kansas City, Omaha, Chicago, Minneapolis, Vancouver, B. C., St. Louis, San Francisco, Los Angeles, Seattle, Tacoma, Denver and several other cities in the Middle West and West.

As for myself, I paid my last dues to the I. W. W. in February 1912. I was working as a railroader and I joined the A. F. of L. union of my craft, the Brotherhood of Railway Carmen of America, in Chicago.

The few forces with which the new movement began its work came, as we have seen, almost entirely from the I. W. W. We had practically no contact with the left wing of the Socialist Party, which

* In reality, however, the I. W. W. reached a higher membership total in 1917, when it officially claimed 130,000 members.

was thoroughly saturated with I. W. W. dual union sentiment.
Our new movement was too weak to call a national conference or
convention. In agreement with the outlying groups, the Chicago local
league acted as the national center. It selected an executive board and
elected me as National Secretary. The organization was named the
Syndicalist League of North America, this title being chosen because
the League included groups in Canada and hoped to extend its activities also into Mexico.

The Syndicalist League of North America lasted two years, from
1912 to 1914. This was a period of growing struggle by the workers,
under the impact of the prevalent industrial crisis. The A. F. of L.
unions grew rapidly and conducted several important strikes; the
I. W. W. grew and led many struggles; the S. P. increased its membership from 41,479 in 1909 to 118,045, and in 1912 its vote was 900,000,
the largest in its history. And all this in spite of Theodore Roosevelt's
efforts to demoralize the toiling masses with his "Bull Moose"
campaign.*

Despite its considerable activities, the S. L. of N. A. did not succeed
in becoming a mass organization. Also, it never penetrated the industrial East, being almost entirely located in the territory west of
Chicago, the traditional I. W. W. stronghold. It was composed chiefly
of skilled workers, mostly native-born. No accurate statistics were
kept, but its actual membership of militants was estimated at not to
exceed two thousand, although the unions led by these militants easily
counted ten to twenty times that many workers. The League's influence, especially in view of its considerable press, was far greater than
its small membership would indicate. After two years of life the
S. L. of N. A. fell into decline. In the summer of 1914 its national
center was liquidated and the movement crumbled away into disconnected groups of militants working here and there in the trade union
movement.

The S. L. of N. A. program exhibited the basic flaw of the syndicalist movement in general; that is, it constituted a great over-sim-
plification of the workers' revolutionary problem in both theory
and practice.

---

* In 1912, Theodore Roosevelt, failing to get presidential renomination on the
Republican ticket, organized the Progressive Party which campaigned for a third
term for him on a liberal program, and which denounced both the Republican
and Democratic parties as machine-controlled. Roosevelt, however, was an aggressive representative of growing American imperialism.

Despite its short life, the S. L. of N. A. left its mark upon the left wing, however, and it must occupy an important position in American revolutionary history. It stands as the first organized effort of revolutionary workers to wrest the leadership of the trade unions away from their reactionary leaders. In this it represented a great step forward over the crude dual unionism to which the left wing was then wedded. The only earlier serious efforts by revolutionaries to win leadership in the trade unions was that of *Spies, et al,* in Chicago in 1886, and by the revolutionary pioneers in the early days of the S. L. P. But this was in the period before the left wing became afflicted with its long sickness of dual industrial unionism. The League led the first serious assault upon this paralyzing policy.

The failure of the S. L. of N. A. to establish itself permanently in the labor movement was a facer to our small group of syndicalists. It did not, however, shake our conviction that the prevalent left wing policy of dual unionism was wrong and very harmful. So, hardly had the S. L. of N. A. collapsed than we began to move to establish a new national organization. This effort crystallized in a conference held in St. Louis, January 17, 1915, consisting of a dozen delegates from Chicago, St. Louis, Omaha, and Kansas City. At this conference we set up the International Trade Union Educational League. Chicago was chosen as national headquarters; a small national board, with representatives from our four main points, was selected, and I was picked as secretary.

The I. T. U. E. L. was born a few months after the beginning of the World War, in the midst of the 1914-15 industrial crisis and just on the eve of the great war boom. It was a time of rapidly rising cost of living and of spreading discontent among the workers. The workers were in a militant mood, but their organizations were giving them no fighting lead and there were few struggles. The A. F. of L. unions were stagnant in the industrial crisis, the I. W. W. had declined after its upshoot of two years before, and the S. P. was still suffering heavily from the big split of 1912.

Objectively, the situation was favorable for I. T. U. E. L. work, which translated itself chiefly into efforts to organize the unorganized. But the I. T. U. E. L. never succeeded in developing into a national movement. I made a seven thousand mile agitation tour through the West in winter time, hoboing it as usual, trying to build the movement. Here and there local militants endeavored to set up groups. But without avail. The I. T. U. E. L. secured less spread nationally than even the S. L. of N. A. It finally simmered itself down pretty much into a local league in Chicago; a group, however, which was fated to play an important role in the general labor movement.

The reasons for the failure of the I. T. U. E. L. to grow were pretty much the same as in the case of the S. L. of N. A. There were the usual syndicalist weaknesses. Then there was the traditional left wing opposition to participation in the conservative trade unions. Although the I. W. W. was in a slump, dual unionism remained the unchallengeable and undiscussable gospel of the I. W. W., the S. L. P. and the left wing of the S. P. The dual union theory was at the time drawing sustenance from resentment against the deepening corruption in the A. F. of L. and its impotence in trustified industry, as well as from the rapid growth of the Amalgamated Clothing Workers, an independent union split-off from the United Garment Workers. Another factor that drove a wedge between the I. T. U. E. L. and the body of the left-wing forces was the right opportunist conception of syndicalism that we had developed. This clashed violently with the leftist, sectarian conceptions prevalent generally in the left wing and tended to further isolate our forces from the general revolutionary movement.

The Chicago group of the I. T. U. E. L., numbering about one hundred, was noteworthy because it was instrumental in setting on foot many militant movements and it was a prime factor in eventually making the Chicago Federation of Labor the most progressive labor council in the United States at that time. The Chicago F. of L. displayed its progressivism through its initiative in starting the great stockyards and steel industry organizing campaigns of 1917-19, its activity in the Labor Party movement, its support of the Mooney-Billings case, etc.

Through 1915 and 1916 we continued building up a strong I. T. U. E. L. delegation in the Chicago Federation of Labor. Our policy included a united front on many questions with the leading group in the C. F. of L. headed by President John Fitzpatrick. Although we considered John Fitzpatrick devoid of theoretical knowledge of the class struggle, we believed him to be an honest and courageous man who made the best fight he knew how for the workers.

The I. T. U. E. L. Chicago group took an energetic part in all the local strikes of the period. We came into sharp collision with the growing gangster control of the unions, making bitter enemies of the

Murphy and O'Donnell gangs and other forerunners of the lurid Al Capone era.

The I. T. U. E. L. also branched out nationally with its agitation. We sent many articles to the trade union journals embodying our viewpoint and we circularized thousands of local unions, pushing a distribution of our pamphlet, *Trade Unionism: The Road to Freedom.*

A very important action of the Chicago I. T. U. E. L. was to secure the adoption by the C. F. of L. of a proposal to form a Chicago Railroad Council, to be made up of locals of all railroad unions. The heads of the railroad craft unions fought this as a dangerous rank and file movement. In 1920 this Council led a national strike of 250,000 railroad shop workers.

1936

2. The Packinghouse Campaign

When the United States entered the First World War in 1917 I was working as a car inspector on the Soo Line in Chicago; for at the expiration of my year's term as business agent of the Railway Carmen, some time previous, I had refused the unanimous nomination of our thirteen locals for a second term and had gone back to work on the road. While I inspected freight cars I puzzled over what I might do to get some real organization work started. I felt quite helpless, I must say. Our I. T. U. E. L. was gone and there was I working twelve hours a day, seven days a week, and, consequently unable even to attend the meetings of the Chicago Federation of Labor, to which I was a delegate. Finally, however, one day as I was walking to work, and I remember well that it was July 11, 1917, it struck me suddenly that perhaps we could get a campaign started to organize the workers in the great Chicago packinghouses, whom the A. F. of L. had grossly neglected during many years. Except for the teamsters, they were then totally unorganized, their conditions were frightful, and the demand for workers was strong—a splendid opportunity for an organizing campaign. Perhaps the progressive C. F. of L. could be induced to give its support.

No sooner thought than done. That very night I took the matter up with the Chicago District Council of the Railway Carmen, which was led by former I. T. U. E. L. militants. Our craft is a prominent one in the packinghouse situation, because the refrigerator car, which we build, is the basis of that industry; so the Council readily endorsed my proposal. On the 13th, I was one of our committee to the meeting of the half-dead Local 87 of the bankrupt Butcher Workmen. We secured its reluctant endorsement, and on the 15th the two unions introduced a resolution into the Chicago Federation of Labor calling for a joint organization campaign of all trades in the local packing industry. The C. F. of L. unanimously adopted our resolution. Thus, only four days after the plan was born, the campaign to organize the workers of the great packing trust had got under way. From the outset, Joe Manley, Jack Johnstone and other left-wing trade unionists were very active in this movement.

On July 23, we formed the Stockyards Labor Council of a dozen local unions with jurisdiction over packinghouse workers, including Butcher Workmen, Railway Carmen, Machinists, Electricians, Coopers, Carpenters, Office Workers, Steam Fitters, Engineers, Firemen, etc. I was elected secretary and Martin Murphy, a rank and file butcher, president. Our working plan was that of a federation. We rejected the traditional left-wing policy of launching a new "one big industrial union," as such a dual union would have split our forces and wrecked our movement at the outset. We decided to move towards industrial unionism by setting up an industrial federation and by locking the various component craft unions so firmly together under one council, one executive board, one set of business agents, etc., as to create a firm front in the whole industry. The workers accepted this industrial plan readily, as their big 1904 strike had been completely smashed because of disunity and "union scabbing" among the several craft unions organized in the two separate, jangling councils. We infused our whole movement with the spirit of industrial unionism.

At the first meeting of the Stockyards Labor Council we decided to base our movement primarily upon the unskilled masses, that is, the foreign-born and Negroes, who made up a majority of the workers. The Negroes, of whom there were 12,000 among the 60,000 Chicago packinghouse workers, presented a thorny problem. Many of the skilled crafts, despite our best efforts, barred them, although the main union, the Butcher Workmen, admitted them. To complicate matters, we faced the open hostility of the Negro middle class elements, embittered by A. F. of L. discrimination. When we began our organization work we proceeded upon the policy of taking the Negroes into the big mass Butcher Workmen local unions, and we thought that we had thereby solved the problem. But at once the Negro leaders raised a shout that we were placing the Negroes into white unions where they would be a helpless minority and they demanded separate Negro unions. We naïvely agreed to this demand, whereupon, almost overnight, the cry of "Jim Crow" went along State Street with devastating effect. We eventually found a solution, however, by adopting the neighborhood principle, that is, by building mass unions in both Negro and white districts and having them open alike to Negroes and whites. This killed the Jim Crow issue and forced the corrupt elements among the Negro middle class elements, agents of the packers, to come out openly against our organizing campaign generally and to advocate a policy of scabbing. Such a proposal was easy for us to beat, however, and the sequel showed that we finally won over the majority of the Negroes and built up the largest Negro trade union membership ever organized in any American city.

But let me come back to the sequence of my story. Where were we to get organizers and money for our campaign? The A. F. of L. national office gave us not a penny and its local general organizer, Flood, was cynical and contemptuous. The ultra-reactionary Butcher Workmen officials, with a moribund union, looked upon us as upstarts and dangerous rivals, and extended us nothing but hostility. The preliminary work was done mostly on a voluntary basis by Jack Johnstone, myself, and other former I. T. U. E. L. militants. The C. F. of L. was friendly, but its initial financial help consisted in paying only the expenses of our first mass meeting. Upon the recommendation of the C. F. of L. and Railway Carmen's District Council, however, I was most reluctantly appointed by the Brotherhood of Railway Carmen of America General President Ryan as an organizer for a ninety-day period.* After we got well started and our movement looked promising, the C. F. of L. also put on Jack Johnstone as a paid organizer. Eventually, the Illinois Federation of Labor also gave us a couple of Negro organizers, and we scared up the help of occasional

* This finished for me ten years as a railroad worker, with service on many roads: Southern Pacific, Northern Pacific, Seaboard Airline, Chicago and Northwestern, Chicago Railroad and Navigation, Philadelphia and Reading, Spokane Portland and Seattle, Soo Line, etc., and in many capacities: fireman, brakeman, car repairer, airbrake man, car inspector, freight handler, railroad construction teamster, shop laborer, camp cook, etc., in all corners of the country.

Butcher Workmen and other craft union business agents. Beyond this, the movement financed itself and produced its own organizers.

John Fitzpatrick, President of the Chicago Federation of Labor, from the first was sympathetic to our campaign, but he was skeptical of its outcome, being afflicted with the prevailing pessimism in trade union circles to the effect that the packinghouse workers were unorganizable. But as our campaign began to get results he took a more active part, eventually becoming chairman of our national movement. His services were especially valuable in combating the disruptive tactics of reactionary A. F. of L. leaders and in carrying on the negotiations with the packers and the government.

AN AGGRESSIVE CAMPAIGN

We launched our organization drive with great vigor and directed our efforts at the five great Chicago plants of the biggest packers of the huge beef trust. The workers came in large numbers to our meetings to listen but, suspicious from long years of A. F. of L. betrayal and incompetence, few joined the unions. At the end of six weeks of intensive work we had organized only five hundred members. Fitzpatrick pronounced this result excellent, as no such showing had been made since the fatal strike of thirteen years before. But to me our progress was wholly unsatisfactory: the great packing industry could never be organized by such a one-by-one method. We simply had to find a way to start the workers into the unions *en masse*.

Our little militant leading group was determined that at all costs the workers must be organized, and we were prepared to use drastic methods to this end. We were proceeding on a militant strike policy which had nothing in common with the Gompers war-time "no strike" program and we were convinced that the workers were "strike minded" and would respond to our efforts if they saw a prospect for strike action in support of the demands (eight-hour day, right to organize, etc.) that we were popularizing.* Hence I proposed to our small leading committee a detailed plan whereby our 500 members, after good preparation and with the organized assistance of other industry militants, could be used to strike the great mass of 60,000 workers.

It was a very risky move, but I am still convinced it would have

* For a discussion of the policies of the A. F. of L. leadership during the first World War (1914-18), see pp. 26, 57-59 of this book.

succeeded had we tried it. The organizers agreed with my proposals but, as we were getting ready, fortunately we were able to find a surer way to bring the masses into action by a strike movement. Under the influence of our Chicago campaign and the generally favorable situation, local organizations and strikes had begun to take shape in various western packing centers. I, therefore, proposed the strategy of calling a national conference of packinghouse workers to prepare demands to be made upon the packers. The leaders of the Butcher Workmen, typical A. F. of L. reactionaries, smelling a possible strike, strongly disagreed with this proposal, even as they violently condemned our whole militant line. But fearing to be swept aside by the rising mass movement, they finally grudgingly agreed. Whereupon, over their protests, we gave the story to the newspapers, stating that the move for a conference would probably culminate in a big national packinghouse strike.

Next day, as I expected, the Chicago press bore great flaming headlines, "Strike Looms at Yards." And so it was in other packing centers. The whole packing industry seethed over the threatening strike.

The effect upon the discontented mass of workers was electrical. At last they saw the action they wanted, a chance to strike back at their exploiters. Then they fairly "broke the doors" down in joining the Chicago unions in masses. The feeble stockyards' organizations grew wildly. For example, the decrepit Local 87, Butcher Workmen, took in 1,400 members at its first meeting after the press announcement of the threatening strike. Likewise, the movement grew like a bay tree—in Sioux City, St. Louis, Fort Worth, Omaha, Kansas City, St. Joseph, St. Paul, Oklahoma City, Denver, and other big western packing centers. Tens of thousands streamed into the A. F. of L. locals. Our strategy had succeeded better even than we had anticipated. We were over the top in the organization of the great national packing industry, for years considered in trade union circles to be an utterly hopeless task. Meanwhile, we had joined the dozen co-operating packinghouse unions together nationally into a loose committee, of which John Fitzpatrick was chairman and I, secretary.

However, the packers had not been idle. At first, except for flooding our movement with spies, they had made no hostile move,* evidently believing that our campaign, like so many A. F. of L. "drives" in the past, would collapse of its own weight. But when they realized

* These spies were everywhere. For example, two of our three Polish and Lithuanian organizers in Chicago finally confessed being under-cover men.

we were making real headway, they became alarmed and replied with the usual open shop weapon of discharging active unionists. This discharge campaign spread far and reached its climax when Libby, McNeil and Libby, a Swift subsidiary, fired some fifty of its Chicago workers.

The policy of our militant organizers was to head towards a national strike of packinghouse workers. We figured that only by such a strike could the workers fully secure their demands and establish their unions. We were also convinced that the packers and the government never could stand a great packinghouse strike in war time, in view of the frantic demand for foodstuffs. So the packers' provocations fitted right into our strategy and we replied to Libby, McNeil and Libby by quickly taking a national strike vote, which was almost a hundred percent favorable. Then we began hasty preparation for a strike; but just at this juncture the A. F. of L. national leaders stepped in and steered the whole movement into the treacherous channels of a government mediation.

THE GOVERNMENT COMES TO HELP THE PACKERS

The Wilson administration, it will be remembered, to sidetrack the many strike movements and to prevent the extension of the trade unions into the open shop industries, had a policy of making government labor agreements for the duration of the war. Its Federal Mediation Commission was going about the country settling strikes on this basis. The A. F. of L. leadership was, of course, in full harmony with this anti-union policy.

Jack Johnstone, myself, and other packinghouse militants were against such government interference. Fitzpatrick also opposed the government's entering; but he had no confidence in a strike, whereas the whole strategy of Johnstone and myself was based on the need for a strike to force the packers by direct pressure to sign a union agreement.

But the A. F. of L. brought the government in, in spite of us. As a matter of routine we formally notified the A. F. of L. headquarters of our strike vote, whereupon, without notifying us, they promptly turned the matter over to the government. We were immediately infested with agents of the Federal Mediation Commission. Later, when I protested to Gompers about his bringing the government onto our necks, he lamely excused himself on the ground that he was not in his office when our telegram had arrived and that his secretary, Miss Le Gard, had referred it as a matter of course to the Department of Labor for mediation—an explanation which threw a bright light on the A. F. of L.'s war-time no-strike policy.

This A. F. of L. action upset our whole strike strategy. What was now to be done? Could we ignore the government mediators and strike anyhow? The cards were all stacked against such a course. The A. F. of L. leaders would be solidly opposed to it and so, likewise, would be the national officials of all the dozen federated unions in our joint movement. The great weakness of our Chicago Stockyards Labor Council, from first to last, was that, although it gave the whole stimulus and militant leadership to the national movement, the actual control of the international unions involved remained in the hands of reactionary A. F. of L. officials and, alas, we had no organized group of militants to link us up with the rank and file workers in the other packing centers.

About eighteen months after this, in the 1919 steel campaign, we faced a somewhat similar situation. Our committee then confronted a demand from President Wilson, Gompers, and a large majority of the leaders of the 24 steel unions that we should sidetrack our developing strike movement and put our trust in government maneuverings. We were strongly organized enough to defy this treacherous demand, however, and to go on with the great national strike. But in the packinghouse situation, with our new unions and our lack of national control, such a course would have been folly. So, yielding before superior forces, we had to enter, against our will, into the government mediation and to depend upon the growing strength and militancy of our movement to carry it on to victory in spite of its enemies, the packers, the government, and the A. F. of L. top leadership.

THE PACKING INDUSTRY ORGANIZED

After much jockeying around, we finally drew up an agreement with the Federal Mediation Commission in Chicago, in December 1917, which provided for the right to organize, set up shop committees, present grievances, attend union conventions, etc.; it further granted a 10 per cent wage increase, the principle of seniority in employment, no discrimination because of "creed, color, or nationality," display of piece work schedules, abolition of arbitrary discharge, abolition of compulsory benefit societies, establishment of proper dressing, lunch, and wash rooms, etc. Our other six major demands then went to Federal Judge S. Altschuler, administrator of the packing industry, for arbitration decision.

The national packinghouse arbitration proceedings, held in Chicago early in 1918, were highly dramatic. The five big packers, Armour, Swift, Morris, Cudahy, and Wilson, were represented by attorneys Meyer and Condon, and the workers were represented by Frank P. Walsh and John Fitzpatrick. For three and a half weeks we paraded witnesses on the stand—workers, economists, labor leaders (including Gompers)—giving publicity to the horrible working and living conditions of the packinghouse workers and the fabulous profits being made by the packers, Armour himself admitting a war profit of $40,000,000 in 1917. I must say that I took double pleasure in this exposure and discomfiture of the packers, for I personally had felt the lash of the hard conditions in the industry, having worked the winter of 1915 in the Swift & Company car shops for such miserable wages that I was too poor to buy an overcoat to shield me from the bitterly cold weather.

On March 30, 1918, Judge Altschuler handed down his award. With an eye on our militant movement and on the certainty of a national packinghouse strike in case of an unsatisfactory decision, he granted about 85 per cent of the unions' six demands. His award provided for another 10 per cent to 25 per cent wage increase, a basic eight-hour day with ten hours' pay, extra time for overtime, equal pay for men and women doing the same class of work, a guarantee of five days' work per week in slack seasons, and time off with pay for lunch periods in eight-hour shifts. The award was retroactive, the 125,000 workers of the five big packers receiving $6,000,000 in back pay, or an average of $40 per worker.

With enthusiasm the packinghouse workers greeted these terms as a great victory. They streamed into the unions all over the country and built solid organizations in every plant. Now our job of mopping up began. We made the hundreds of small packers sign the Altschuler award and then we carried the organization campaign into many subsidiary sections of the industry, such as retail butcher shops, the independent soap, washing powder, glue, canning, butterine, fertilizer, cooperage, etc., works. Besides this, many other local industries, such as machine shops, car works, etc., caught the contagion and were organized.

In Chicago, we had dozens of strikes in this follow-up campaign.

The most serious struggle was with the Union Stockyards and Transit Company. This powerful concern, owned by the great packers, received, fed and distributed the tens of thousands of animals arriving daily at the Chicago Yards. It is the nerve center of the local packing industry. Its autocratic head, a Mr. Leonard, refused to sign the Altschuler award, so we struck his 3,000 stockhandlers on an hour's notice. Instantly, the transfer of all cattle, sheep, and hogs stopped. Frantically, the packers wired all over the West to halt the shipment of stock. Johnstone, Murphy, and I were summoned to the downtown Department of Justice office, where we were threatened with jail for obstructing the war. But we stood our ground and insisted that the U. S. & T. Co. come to the unions' terms. Gradually, the huge packinghouses, cut off from supplies of animals, came to a standstill. The menace of a great packinghouse strike loomed. But, after a few days, the U. S. & T. Co. weakened and signed on the dotted line. It was a real victory and the oppressed packinghouse workers were jubilant.

The great stockyards organization campaign had by now achieved its major goal. The industry was thoroughly organized all over the country from top to bottom. More than 200,000 workers had come into the dozen federated unions. These included unskilled as well as skilled, immigrant workers and native-born, and fully 25,000 of the new members were Negroes. Many office employees also joined the organization and even the stockyards policemen formed a union. At last, the autocratic packers were compelled to meet with the workers and talk business with them, and especially they did not relish conferring with Johnstone and me.

The packinghouse victory marked a new high stage in American labor organization. It was the first mass production, trustified industry ever to be organized by the trade unions. And the victory was doubly significant in that it was accomplished by militant policies and on application of the industrial union principle, at least in a modified form. But, of course, the reactionary A. F. of L. bureaucracy learned nothing constructive from all this.

For us former I. T. U. E. L. militants the campaign had a very special significance. It was a glowing justification of our policy of working with the old trade unions, and it also showed what could be done on our theory of organizing the unorganized millions by militantly taking advantage of the war situation.

THE AFTERMATH IN THE PACKING INDUSTRY

It turned out that soon after Judge Altschuler's decision I left the packing industry to take up the big steel organizing campaign. But I cannot go on with that until I tell how the splendid organization of the packinghouse workers was eventually destroyed by the packers, with effective assistance of the A. F. of L. leaders. It is one of the most shameful stories of betrayals in American labor history.*

From the outset in 1917, the Gompersite officials of the Butcher Workmen, headed by Dennis Lane, a stockholder in a local packing company, did everything possible to sabotage the organizing campaign. Their aim was to destroy the Stockyards Labor Council with its splendid solidarity and its militant leadership. They wanted to wipe out its industrial union trend and re-establish the old, discredited craft system. So they fought to cut off its per capita tax from the locals; they demanded that each local have its own business agent, instead of our centralized system; they insisted that there be formed a second council, that is, a packing trades council of Butcher Workmen locals only. That was the fatal two-council system that had destroyed the 1904 strike and which, at the beginning of the Stockyards campaign, we had pledged ourselves never to reintroduce. They flooded the Chicago locals with "organizers" who, supported by every packer's spy and stool pigeon, fought for this splitting program. It was in the face of such disruptive tactics that we had to go on with our organizing work.

The fight became very bitter. Finally, Lane's crowd, in alliance with the notorious Simon O'Donnell gang of building trades thugs, decided to take over the Stockyards Labor Council by strong-arm methods. As an entering wedge, they tried to force us to seat one of their thugs as a delegate. We refused and for this I was slated to be "rubbed out," the notorious gunman, "Big Tim Murphy," openly threatening me. However, we were not helpless and we let it be known that if any "rough stuff" were tried we would know whom to reach and how. The Lane-O'Donnell plan fell through and we remained in full control.

In the first year after I left the packing industry the fight grew still more bitter. Two organizers were killed. My successor as secretary of the S. L. C., Jack Johnstone, one time, gun in hand, shot it

* See *Misleaders of Labor*, 1927.

out successfully with a gang of Lane's armed raiders who tried to seize the headquarters by force.

Lane, who controlled the official Butcher Workmen Union machinery outside of Chicago (our weak spot all along), finally organized a Chicago packing trades council. Only about 2,000 members joined it. He thereupon expelled 40,000 of his union's members who remained affiliated to the Stockyards Labor Council. The Chicago Federation of Labor protested against this outrage but was warned by Gompers to keep its hands off. Then other A. F. of L. union officials in the packing industry set to work to help Lane split up the packinghouse workers and destroy the industrial solidarity that had been the key to the great success of the movement. Finally, there were three councils: the Packing Trades Council, the Mechanical Trades Council and the Stockyards Labor Council. Besides, there were several unattached locals and large numbers of unorganized workers, demoralized by the A. F. of L. treachery. Similar disruptive tactics were used in other packing centers.

This went on for two and a half years after our big victory in 1918. By the fall of 1920, the former splendid organization was much weakened; so the packers, in step with the great post-war open shop offensive of the time against organized labor, set up company unions, slashed wages, and broke off all relations with the unions. The workers replied to these attacks by a national packinghouse strike on December 5, 1920. But though they fought heroically, they were defeated and their organization almost completely wiped out, a victim of the reactionary policies of the A. F. of L. If the Greens and Hutchesons of today wish to know one of the many reasons why the workers in the basic industries want no more of craft unions and are demanding industrial organization, let them observe the tragedy of the packinghouse 1917-1921 movement.

FROM MEAT PACKING TO STEEL

But let us come back to the events of 1918. With our theory that the main task was the organization of the millions into the trade unions and that at all costs the war-time demand for workers must be utilized to this end, we naturally sought to use the big victory in the packing industry as a point of departure for a new organization drive. I had no idea of settling down as a trade union official in the packing industry. After considerable thought, I decided to make a try at steel. The trade unions had conquered their first trustified industry, meat packing, and I was confident that, if they would only bestir themselves a bit, they could also win out in the greatest of all trustified industries, steel.

Therefore, even before Judge Altschuler had handed down his arbitration decision, being sure that he must grant most of our demands, I had written a resolution to have the Chicago Federation of Labor call upon the A. F. of L. to initiate a national organizing campaign in the steel industry along the general lines that had proved so successful in meat packing. However, for a couple of weeks I did not introduce the resolution into the C. F. of L. because of a curious reason. During our arbitration, the packers' lawyer, Condon, had dramatically declared that if Altschuler conceded our demands it would create a vast upheaval among workers in industry generally and that millions of them would go marching in to the bosses to make similar demands. Even as he was saying this I had in my pocket the proposed steel campaign resolution. So fearing that its introduction into the C. F. of L. might seem to Altschuler too much like Condon's prophecy coming true and thereby adversely affect his decision, I had to withhold it until after the judge's award.

Finally, on April 7, 1918, a week after Altschuler's decision, I introduced the resolution into the C. F. of L., signed by the Railway Carmen * and a dozen other metal trade unions. It called for a nationwide A. F. of L. joint campaign of all the unions having jurisdiction over workers in the steel industry. It was based on a broad industrial movement, from the coal and iron miners and the lake transport workers all through the industry to the men doing the last phases of finishing in the fabricating division of the steel industry and those who hauled the final products out on to the railroad main lines. Such a federated movement, as in the packing industry, was the most practical approach to be made to the necessary industrial form. The C. F. of L. adopted the resolution unanimously and the great steel campaign was on.

1936

---

* The Railway Carmen came into this campaign on the basis that there were scores of thousands of steel car builders in the great steel plants in McKees Rocks, Butler, Pullman, Johnstown, and many other plants. I was a member of this craft union.

3. The Great Steel Strike

The A. F. of L. leaders, with their "social peace" war-time policy, made no effort to organize the more-than-ripe basic industries. Indeed, they actually hampered such work. Sufficient proofs of this were the facts that I, a rank and file worker in industry, had to initiate the national packinghouse campaign, and that we faced A. F. of L. opposition from start to finish. The A. F. of L. leaders were even less interested in organizing steel. Again the vitally important work had to be started by myself, who was by this time a lesser official; and again, breaking through A. F. of L. sabotage, constituted the major problem in organizing the workers. The A. F. of L.'s reactionary attitude towards organizing meat packing and steel was characteristic of its policy in all the industries. What growth the unions made during the war time was mostly spontaneous, the work of rank and file militants.

A. F. of L. sabotage of the steel campaign began immediately after the Chicago resolution was adopted.* Our resolution asked the A. F. of L. to lead the work. But Gompers thought to liquidate the matter offhand by referring the C. F. of L. resolution to the approaching convention of the Amalgamated Association of Iron, Steel and Tin Workers (A. A.). He might as well have sent it to the United States Steel Corporation as the officials of this company-controlled union. Naturally, the A. A. convention evaded the whole business. But I was not to be sidetracked so easily, and I reintroduced the resolution into the C. F. of L. Here it was once more adopted and I was sent to the A. F. of L. convention in St. Paul, June 1918, as C. F. of L. delegate, to get action upon it.

What happened at the convention was a classic of A. F. of L. "organization" methods. Gompers let the resolution be adopted without change or opposition; for such resolutions make good reading matter for the rank and file. Besides there are better ways to get rid of unpleasant resolutions than by directly rejecting them. My resolution

* See page 32 of this book.

called for a meeting of steel industry delegates during the convention to start the campaign. So, after waiting a few days and no meeting being called, I became alarmed and, inquiring from Secretary Morrison, was informed that it would be held "in about six weeks." Time was the very essence of my organizing plan and delay would be fatal: we simply had to utilize the war situation if it was to succeed, and the war might end very shortly. I, therefore, protested to Morrison that this postponement was disastrous and in violation of the resolution, which very specifically provided for holding the meeting during the convention.

A day or two later, suddenly and without notifying me, an announcement was mumbled just before the convention's noon adjournment that the steel meeting would be held during the lunch recess. Think of it, a conference to organize the nation-wide steel industry of 500,000 workers squeezed into the lunch period, with the delegates hurrying out to eat before the afternoon session. Very clearly it was a deliberate attempt to kill the campaign. Despite my experience with A. F. of L. bureaucrats, I was shocked and astounded. I could see the steel campaign going to smash at its very start.

At the designated corner of the convention hall a number of delegates, on their way out to eat, stopped off, in curiosity mostly, to see what was going to take place. No Gompers or Morrison was there, and no one was in charge. I hastily called the "meeting" to order and organizer Tom Flynn got on a table and began a speech about the need of organization. I could see that lack of time made such a course fatal, so I interrupted Flynn and proposed that we only take the names of all present and call a meeting for the next night, over which we should invite Gompers to preside. Then we adjourned our lunch-recess steel organizing conference.

Now came the problem of getting Gompers to come to our meeting. That afternoon I informed him of what had taken place. The arch bureaucrat listened in a bored manner but he became furious when I invited him to the proposed meeting and refused point-blank. Evidently he had already had enough of this bothersome steel campaign which refused to be killed. Then I pulled the ace out of my sleeve. I showed him the list of officials (our knot of curiosity seekers) who had attended the steel "meeting," and I told him it was they who were inviting him. Then his tone changed and he grumbled out that "maybe" he would attend.

So Gompers was roped in for the meeting. Now it remained to

lasso the other necessary union leaders. To accomplish this I asked Gompers if he would make the announcement to the convention of the proposed steel meeting. "No! You do it!" he fairly yelled at me. So, that afternoon, I ventured to state to the convention that upon the request of Mr. Gompers I was authorized to invite all concerned to the steel conference, at which Gompers would be present. I could see Gompers getting purple as I said this. We had a good crowd, Gompers' name attracting them. Thus had succeeded my little strategy of netting Gompers by using the names of my "curiosity seekers" and, on the other hand, of drawing in many other officials by utilizing Gompers' name. By such a device did I literally have to trick the A. F. of L. leaders into this vital organization campaign. After this maneuver I felt as though I had been swimming in a sewer and future prospects for the work seemed most unpromising.

The principal thing our steel meeting did was to call a formal conference, to take place six weeks later. This was a deadly loss of time. The best organizing period American labor had ever known was fast slipping away as the war neared its end. Four months were criminally wasted, from the time I originally introduced my resolution on April 7, until the first real conference was to be held in August. Such delay can only be termed deliberate sabotage. At the St. Paul meeting, however, after much struggle, I managed to have the proposed conference scheduled for Chicago. I did this in the hope that thereby John Fitzpatrick (who was not at St. Paul) could be drawn into the work as A. F. of L. organizer in Chicago and thus help protect the sprouting campaign from the hostile reactionary bureaucrats.

THE CHICAGO CONFERENCE

The Chicago steel conference was held in the New Morrison Hotel, August 1-2, 1918. Representatives of fifteen international unions were present. When the meeting got down to business, the chairman, Gompers, turned to me and said: "Well, brother Foster, you have called us together; now what do you propose?" That was the "great" Gompers' approach to organizing the steel industry; he had brought no proposals whatever. So I proceeded to outline my plan, which can be summarized as follows:

There should be a whirlwind campaign of organization initiated at once and simultaneously in all important steel centers; this to be carried on jointly by all unions claiming jurisdiction in the steel industry. There should be used such methods as huge mass meetings, noted speakers, brass bands, parades, full-page newspaper advertisements, etc., to set the masses in motion. As financial means, I proposed that each union should assess itself 25 cents per member; and to begin building an organizing crew, that each union should delegate three or more organizers. To carry on the work all the unions should be closely federated, with a national committee headed by an A. F. of L. representative. The unions should establish a uniform small initiation fee. I calculated that with such a great drive, we could get the bulk of the steel workers under our leadership in about six weeks: that is, three weeks' time to assemble our money and organizers and three weeks to carry through a great series of three mass meetings in each town. These meetings, I figured, would give us such a grip on the masses of workers that we could at once send our committee to the steel trust, with an implied threat of a national steel strike if the committee were not received, a threat that we could enforce.

This plan for a great, swift, simultaneous organizing drive in all steel centers was realistic and practical. It conformed to the actual situation and to the potentialities of the unions. It offered the best possible way to arouse the steel workers' enthusiasm and to outwit the inevitable counter strategy of the employers. The workers were in a militant mood and would have surely responded in decisive masses.

My time schedule of six weeks was also strictly feasible; it had only taken us about nine weeks to get the great masses under our leadership in the packing industry and successfully to threaten a strike, and, in view of our riper experience, added prestige and greater resources, we could have done the job much quicker in the steel industry. This would have brought our movement to a head while the war was still on, and the government and the steel trust could not possibly have faced a war-time strike in this great munitions industry. Had my proposals been adopted we would have won through easily and definitely established the unions in the steel industry.

The plan of federating the unions was likewise practical. It was at that time the logical next step towards industrial unionism and the building of a single steel workers' organization. This was so because at that period there was little positive sentiment for industrial unionism in the A. F. of L. and it would have been utterly impossible to get the many craft unions to surrender their jurisdiction claims to the little, half-dead, corruptly led Amalgamated Association. The system of industrial federation was succeeding on the railroads and we had just won a great victory with it in the packing industry. It was a case of either a joint movement by the crafts or no campaign at all. I, of course, intended to try to push the crafts into an eventual general steel amalgamation if our campaign succeeded.

My financial plan was similarly feasible. All the larger unions were rich with the wartime flood of initiation fees and dues (my own union, the Railway Carmen, for example, had some $3,000,000 in its treasury). Each of them could have paid the 25-cent assessment from its funds without the slightest difficulty. Inasmuch as there were some 2,000,000 members in the 24 unions eventually affiliated to our steel campaign, this would have given us several hundred thousand dollars. I estimated that $50,000 would have sufficed to put on our great planned drive for six weeks.

The Chicago conference, however, made ducks and drakes of this whole realistic plan. All that remained when the unenthusiastic bureaucrats got done with it was the principle of a federated campaign. The conference set up the National Committee for Organizing Iron and Steel Workers, which eventually included the 24 unions of Iron Miners, Coal Miners, Steamshovelmen, Clay Workers, Quarry Workers, Seamen, Steel Workers, Stationary Engineers, Firemen, Laborers, Machinists, Railway Carmen, Blacksmiths, Coopers, Electricians, Boilermakers, Patternmakers, Bricklayers, Structural Iron Workers, Foundry Workers, Molders, Sheet Metal Workers, Steam Fitters, and Switchmen. The movement thus covered the whole industry from the workers who produced the raw materials to those who delivered the finished products to the railroads, but none of the unions had more than a handful of members in the great unorganized steel industry. Gompers assumed the chairmanship of the National Committee and I was elected secretary. (This was, like the secretaryship of the Stockyards Labor Council, for me an unpaid job, as I drew my wages from the B. R. C. of A. as a regular organizer.) My proposal for an immediate, huge national drive in all steel towns simultaneously was killed. The top A. F. of L. bureaucrats present listened fishy-eyed and with ill-restrained disdain as I outlined the sure victory that must come from such a national drive. Several of them took the floor and, treating my plans as purely visionary, absurdly proposed instead concentrating the work in one locality, even in one steel mill—"to show the workers what we can do and thereby win their confidence." Gompers listened impatiently when I proposed the 25-cent assessment. He did not even discuss it, nor did any of the others. It was simply ignored. Thus the vital assessment proposal went by the boards, and instead of the at least $50,000 indispensable, the 15 unions present voted the National Committee the ridiculous sum of $100 each; and in place of the crew of one hundred or more organizers that I held to be immediately necessary, a mere half-dozen were delegated to the work. As for the A. F. of L. itself, it neither gave nor pledged a dollar.

On the second day of the conference, after my proposals had been well knocked on the head, Gompers withdrew from the meeting to join his convivial building trades cronies in a nearby hotel. To preside in his absence he named John Fitzpatrick as the ranking Chicago A. F. of L. organizer. This, at least, was good; my strategy of getting Fitzpatrick into the campaign was succeeding.

I was deeply dismayed by the results of the Chicago conference, its defeat of my practical plan to organize the steel industry. It was pretty clear that the A. F. of L. leaders were not interested in organizing the steel workers. One would think, from the resources given our National Committee, that we were setting out to organize a bunch of peanut stands, instead of the 500,000 almost totally unorganized workers in the steel industry, American finance capital's chief open shop stronghold. It was such reactionary policies as these that cost the A. F. of L. the loss of 5,000,000 to 10,000,000 possible members during the war time. The final defeat of the steel workers sixteen months later was directly traceable to the rejection of my plan by the Gompers leadership at the Chicago conference.

THE ORGANIZING CAMPAIGN

I daresay that when the Chicago conference adjourned few of the labor bureaucrats attending it thought that much more would be heard from the annoying steel campaign. But we went ahead anyhow. However instead of a great, sweeping campaign, opened by a "national steel workers' week," with huge meetings, parades, etc., in 50 to 75 steel towns simultaneously all over the country, we had to confine our activities to the Chicago (Calumet) district. We at once began work in Gary, South Chicago, Joliet, and Indiana Harbor. As far as we could, we applied the methods that we had intended using nationally. But, of course, these local activities were only a pale imitation of what our planned great national drive would have been.

Nevertheless, we scored an immediate and tremendous success. In Gary, at our first meeting, 15,000 steel workers attended, and similar mass turnouts were had in the other three steel towns the same week. Steel workers poured into our unions, by thousands. At the end of a month's time we could, if necessary, easily have struck all these great Chicago district steel trust mills.

This was a brilliant demonstration of the correctness of my original plan. Without the least difficulty (had the trade union leaders so willed it) we could have accomplished simultaneously in every important steel town throughout the United States what we had done in the Chicago district. And the experience showed that we could have got the masses behind us in even less time than I had figured on. Had the Gompers leadership backed my plan with the necessary men and money (and they had plenty of both) our success in the Chicago district showed that well within the six weeks' time I had set we could have been knocking at Judge Gary's* door and threatening him with a national strike. With the war still on, such a strike movement could only have resulted in a victory for the steel workers. Rejection of my original plan was tantamount to a refusal to organize the steel industry.

But what a different prospect faced us now as we began to get under way. Our big successes in Chicago (although they failed utterly to arouse the enthusiasm of the A. F. of L. leadership) greatly alarmed the steel trust heads, who previously had not taken us any more seriously than had Gompers. So they set out to fight us relentlessly.

In the next months, lacking men and organizers, we laboriously spread our movement to other districts. We met the most skilled and ferocious resistance of the steel employers. To head us off they gave four successive national wage increases and finally the basic eight-hour day. A month after our Chicago success the war came to an end, and an industrial slump set in. The whole situation weakened our offensive, robbed us of the advantage of surprise, and the employers' counter-offensive against us correspondingly was greatly intensified. As we now slowly battered our way into one steel fortress after another we faced wholesale suppression of the right of assembly in the steel towns, our organizers were slugged and arrested and one, Fannie Sellins, murdered. Many company unions were organized to block us, 30,000 workers were discharged for union membership, Ku Klux Klan movements were fostered, elaborate spy systems were used against

* Judge Gary was chairman of the U. S. Steel Corporation.

us, etc., in short, we faced the whole battery of weapons of the great steel trust.

All these overwhelming difficulties would have been avoided, of course, by carrying through my original plan. Our work was now many times more difficult. But, of our multiplying difficulties, the most serious was the steady sabotage we suffered from within our own ranks, from the affiliated union leaders. They systematically and shamelessly betrayed the steel workers into the hands of the steel trust. The tremendous importance to the working class of organizing the steel industry, though it stirred the violent resistance of the capitalists, left the A. F. of L. leadership quite cold.

One of the gravest forms of this official A. F. of L. sabotage was the practice of the top leaders, with few exceptions, to stay away from the meetings of our National Committee and to delegate in their stead powerless local business agents. Thus they escaped giving support to the campaign, while at the same time making an appearance of going along with it. The consequence was that we were constantly strangled for want of resources and unity of action.

Gompers himself was the worst offender in this respect. He was actual chairman of our National Committee, but he never spoke at a meeting of steel workers in the whole campaign nor helped us raise a dollar in money or build a crew of organizers. And about the only way I could get him to come to our meetings was to call an occasional meeting under his very nose, in the room of the A. F. of L. Executive Council in Washington. And sometimes even then he evaded it. Gompers always pleaded lack of time. He found plenty of time, however, to spend several months in Europe helping rig up the infamous Versailles Treaty; he also found time to junket down to Mexico City to set up that tool of American imperialism, the Pan-American Federation of Labor, but he had no time for the steel workers, struggling so desperately to establish trade unions.

I remember that once, during a special crisis, for want of funds, organizers and more concerted action by the unions, I drafted a very strong letter urging all the affiliated union heads to attend our next National Committee meeting. Then J. G. Brown, our general organizer, went to Washington to get Gompers to sign it jointly with me. Very reluctantly he did so. Upon receipt of the letter signed by Gompers and myself, various steel union leaders called up "Sam" and inquired how about this letter, was it really so urgent, etc.? Whereupon Gompers told them that it was "all right, only a routine meeting." Result: the same old kind of meeting with nearly all the decisive leaders absent. Even Gompers himself did not come. With such a lead from Gompers, the various union heads felt quite safe in the neglect and betrayal that they perpetrated constantly against the steel campaign.

Gompers hung on to the chairmanship of our National Committee, usually commissioning John Fitzpatrick to serve in his place. Finally, on the eve of our big strike, he quit in order to free himself of responsibility, and definitely appointed Fitzpatrick as chairman.

The sabotage of the steel campaign by the top officials of the 24 affiliated unions is clearly revealed, beyond possibility of contradiction, by the financial figures of the movement in my final report. The total funds eventually contributed to our National Committee by its 24 unions were only $101,047. This starvation amount, which we painfully extracted from them over a period of many months, was supposed to finance a great nationwide organization campaign of 14 months' duration, and to feed and otherwise finance a three and a half months' strike of 365,000 steel workers. Actually, all things considered, as I showed in my book, *The Great Steel Strike and Its Lessons,* the steel workers financed their own movement with the funds they paid in as initiation fees and dues. And even this sum of $101,047, together with what the 24 unions themselves spent for their average of three organizers apiece, was more than offset by the huge sums, not less than $500,000, that we turned over to them and that was collected by themselves in initiations and dues from the steel workers. The unions were flush with money at the time and, had they been sufficiently interested, almost any one of them could, alone, have given more to our strike movement than all of them did together. The fact is that three needle trade unions, the Amalgamated Clothing Workers, the Ladies Garment Workers, and the Furriers, outside the steel industry altogether, donated a total of $180,000 to our strike relief fund, or almost double what the whole 24 affiliated steel industry unions gave during the entire 16 months' struggle.

The financial sabotage scandal reached its peak in the case of the ultra-reactionary A. A. of Iron, Steel and Tin Workers. This, the basic union in the industry, actually made a large surplus out of the campaign. From this union our National Committee, for all purposes, including strike relief, received only $11,811.81, although we had turned over to them more than $150,000 in initiation fees and they had collected probably twice as much more directly from the steel workers in initiation fees and dues. This union treasury showed a "profit" of $206,000. With this huge surplus the reactionary Tighe leaders bought, after the strike, a national union headquarters building in Pittsburgh.

As for the A. F. of L. itself, it raised no money whatever for the organizing campaign. When the strike came, we practically forced it to issue a general call for funds. This raised $418,141.14, but it was collected mostly by our steel organizers, the A. F. of L. officers making no effort. These were the only monies we received from the A. F. of L., and *they came fourteen months after the campaign had begun and six weeks after we had 365,000 strikers on the streets.*

However, despite all obstacles—the spy system, wholesale discharges of workers, wage concessions, company unionism, terrorism, suppression of civil rights, etc., of the steel trust and the deadly sabotage of the top union leaders—we finally managed, in the course of 14 months of bitter struggle, firmly to establish the unions in the many key plants of the steel trust in the main steel districts. My final financial report showed a minimum of 250,000 workers organized. There were probably many more than that. Our local staff of organizers could with justice make the proud boast that we had done the "impossible," organized the great mass of the workers in the steel industry. Where the A. F. of L. had failed utterly for 25 years we had succeeded. Labor had scaled the ramparts of the greatest of all open shop fortresses.

THE 1919 STEEL STRIKE

Then came the great steel strike, beginning September 22, 1919. Our committee had approached Judge Gary with our demands, but he refused to meet with us. Meanwhile, all through the industry a big offensive was on to smash our unions, over 30,000 of our members were already on the streets, discharged because of union activity. It was a case of either fight or die; we chose to fight.

In response to our strike call, 365,000 steel workers struck in 50 cities of ten states.* Almost every key plant of the U. S. Steel and big independents was paralyzed. The steel workers dealt a smashing blow at their giant enemy. The steel industry has never seen, before or since, a strike remotely approaching such magnitude and powerful effect.

The steel workers fought for the following demands: 1. Right of

* The Department of Labor figures said 367,000.

collective bargaining. 2. Reinstatement of all men discharged for union activities with pay for time lost. 3. Eight-hour day. 4. One day's rest in seven. 5. Abolition of 24-hour shift. 6. Increase in wages sufficient to guarantee an American standard of living. 7. Standard scales of wages in all trades and classifications of workers. 8. Double rates of pay for all overtime after eight hours, holiday and Sunday work. 9. Check-off system of collecting union dues and assessments. 10. Principles of seniority to apply in the maintenance, reduction and increase of working forces. 11. Abolition of company unions. 12. Abolition of physical examination of applicants for employment.

Needless for me to recapitulate; the strike was fought desperately by the steel corporations. The brave strikers had to face a reign of terror set up by armies of scabs, private gunmen, deputy sheriffs, police, and soldiers. Civil rights were completely suppressed in many of the key steel districts; a ferocious campaign of publicity was carried on against the strike all over the country. But worst of all was the sabotage within our own ranks. The persistent treachery of the top leadership now often reached the stage of strike-breaking: exemplified by the attempts of the A. A. to betray the whole movement for a separate agreement; the attempt of the Stationary Engineers to keep their craft at work, and, most disastrous of all, the refusal of the Railroad Brotherhoods to call out their men (who were organized but without union agreements) working on the highly strategic short roads connecting the steel mills with the mainline railroads; the failure of the A. F. of L. national office to rally the labor movement behind the steel strikers, etc.

COULD DEFEAT HAVE BEEN AVOIDED?

The heroism of the steel workers could not avail against all this hostile force. Twenty-two were killed, hundreds were slugged and shot, several thousands were arrested, and over a million and a half men, women, and children struggled and starved. But the great strike, although it eventually abolished the 12-hour day and caused many other improvements, did not win its major objective of unionization. On January 8, 1920, we called it off unconditionally. About 100,000 were still out, but the strike had lost its effectiveness. The bitter three and a half months' strike was defeated and the steel workers' new unions, built with such infinite difficulty, were smashed.

In the New York *World* of April 4, 1922, Gompers charged me with responsibility for the loss of the 1919 steel strike, as follows:

This is the same Foster, who in the face of definite information that the U. S. Steel Corporation was prepared for and wished a strike in 1919 and in the face of a request of the President of the United States that the strike be at least postponed, insisted on that disastrous struggle.

It took a lot of crust for one who sabotaged the steel campaign like Gompers did, to accuse me of wrecking the movement. But aside from that, at the outset let me say that I am proud to accept my full share of responsibility for the steel strike, even though it was lost. Never was a strike more necessary, more justified historically. To have accepted the proposed strike "postponement" that Gompers speaks of would have amounted to the rankest betrayal of the steel workers. His "postponement" was of a piece with his sabotage policy from the beginning of our campaign. The situation was as follows:

On September 11, just eleven days before our scheduled strike date, President Wilson gave a story to the press demanding a postponement of the strike until after the holding of his national industrial conference which was to begin on October 6, and which was supposed to establish industrial peace between capital and labor in the United States. Gompers, without consulting us, at once issued a public statement endorsing Wilson's demand to postpone the strike. Then, proving that there was a concerted movement among the top A. F. of L. leaders, there poured into our office a stream of wires supporting Wilson's and Gompers' stand from a majority of the union presidents who made up our National Committee. A few will suffice to show their trend:

I wish to be recorded as in favor of complying with the President's request.

W. H. Johnston, Pres., Int'l. Asso. of Machinists

Engineers will abide by suggestions of President Wilson that we delay action until after labor conference at Washington.

M. Snellings, Pres., Steam and Operating Engineers

The Executive Board of the Bricklayers, Masons and Plasters International Union desires action in steel strike postponed till after industrial conference in Washington.

Wm. Bowen, Pres.

It is our opinion that there should be no strike called until after the October conference.

J. R. Alpine, Pres., Plumbers and Steamfitters

A strike at this time would be very inopportune.

M. F. Ryan, Pres., Bro. Railway Carmen

It will be better to postpone the calling of the strike until after President Wilson's conference of October 6.

Wm. Atkinson, Acting Pres., Boilermakers

We oppose a strike in the steel industry until after the adjournment of the industrial meeting called by President Wilson.

J. Wilson, Pres., Patternmakers

Various other union presidents wired similarly, while the ultra-reactionary officials of the A. A. dodged about on the question, fearing openly to advocate postponement. The only presidents who definitely opposed halting the strike were those of the Blacksmiths and Mine, Mill and Smeltermen.

All this created a real crisis for us. The steel trust was violently attacking our unions and here we were confronted with a demand from the heads of the government and of the A. F. of L., backed by a majority of our committee, that our strike be called off. And worse yet, this demand was framed in such an insidious way as to make it appear that there was requested only a short postponement until "Labor's friend," President Wilson, could satisfactorily adjust the whole matter.

As for myself, I was entirely convinced that any postponement of the strike would be fatal. I had not the slightest confidence in President Wilson or his three-cornered conference of capital, labor and the public doing anything for the steel workers. A postponement of the strike would inevitably destroy the workers' confidence in our movement, throw the unions at the mercy of the vicious steel trust and smash the whole organization in a welter of confusion and wildcat strikes. Far better to take a fighting chance with our 250,000 and more organized steel workers. In any event, the best way to get consideration from the industrial conference was to confront it with a great strike.

But what could I do to hold fast to our strike date? To simply call together our National Committee would have been suicidal, as the majority were against the strike. Shortness of time also forbade any kind of a formal rank and file vote or national conference. So, upon my own responsibility, I wired and telephoned our field organizers, at least 95 per cent of whom were honest and wanted earnestly to have the steel workers organized, to express the opinions of their

local steel councils. Immediately, I received a flood of telegrams, showing an overwhelming mass demand to go on with the strike. Thus a
few of them:

Unless you call the strike before Friday morning we will be forced
to take matters into our own hands.

Gary and South Chicago Steel Councils in Joint Session

General committee of all unions at Bethlehem unanimously voted to
demand strike action by your committee.

Dave Williams, Organizer

We cannot be expected to meet the enraged workers who will consider us traitors if strike is postponed.

Organizers of Youngstown district

It is imperative that the strike be not postponed as the result will be a
demoralization of our forces and the creating of a situation that will be
positively dangerous.

*District Organizing Secretaries of Youngstown, Rankin,
Braddock, Homestead, Butler, Pittsburgh, Johnstown,
Wheeling, Steubenville, Buffalo*

Fitzpatrick, although he had little faith generally in strikes, agreed
with the field organizers' and my opinion that to postpone the strike
would be fatal. So we drafted a telegram to Gompers (which the
third member of our committee, the A. A. reactionary, Tighe, was
afraid not to sign) that "postponement would mean absolute demoralization and utter ruin for our movement" and demanded that the
strike go on as scheduled.

Thus, we confronted a head-on collision between the militant
masses of steel workers and the reactionary top union leadership
backed by the President of the United States. It all ended by Gompers
and company backing up. They simply did not dare to assume the
responsibility of openly destroying our movement and denying the
steel workers their only chance to win. So the great strike went into
effect, as scheduled, on September 22; but, needless to say, its chance
for success had been gravely injured by the Wilson-Gompers "postponement" maneuver, which alienated public sympathy.

The outcome of Wilson's national Industrial Conference showed
that we were quite right in not surrendering the steel workers' fate
into its hands. At this time the large employers were just launching
the biggest open shop drive in American labor history, the ferocious post-war offensive against the workers to strip them of the bet-

ter wages, shorter hours and union organizations they had built up during the war. Wilson's Conference,* dominated by the greatest capitalist interests, reflected this developing offensive and it was so reactionary that it immediately split over labor's proposal to grant the workers the elementary right of organization. Even the reactionary Gompers leaders had to walk out of the conference.

In going ahead with our strike we protected the workers' fighting chance, and we would have won the strike had it not been for the strike-breaking tactics of the A. F. of L. leaders. To have adopted the Wilson-Gompers "postponement" would have meant certain disaster, and the greatest strike-breaking shame the American labor movement had ever known.

If A. F. of L. leaders seek responsibility for the loss of the steel strike they need look no further than their own general offices. The true cause of the defeat was to be found in their reactionary attitude of indifference, sabotage, and strike-breaking towards the steel campaign from the beginning to the end. Had they adopted my original plan at the Chicago conference we could have won hands down, at most with a short war-time strike. But their policies of denying the movement the necessary organizers and money crippled the whole campaign and forced it into a period when the war was over, the acute demand for munitions had ended, an industrial slump was at hand, the government had abandoned its conciliatory attitude, and a great employers' offensive was under way. Nor could all the militancy and sacrifices of the steel workers in their bitterly fought organization drive and heroic strike overcome these obstacles, raised primarily through the sabotaging policy of the reactionary A. F. of L. leaders.

THE STRATEGY BEHIND THE STEEL STRIKE

Naturally, victory in the steel campaign would have given a tremendous impetus to the organization of the workers in all industries. With my appreciation of the importance of trade unionism, I was quite aware of the possibilities such a victory would open up and I based my general strategy upon them. When we won through in the packing industry I had been quick to take advantage of the stimulus it gave and to extend the campaign into steel; and if the steel campaign had been successful I was prepared to repeat this procedure and to branch out into a still more ambitious program.

* See pp. 60-61 of this book.

The capture of the main open shop fortress, steel, by the trade unions would have made easy the organization of many other industries. And my aim was to take advantage of such a situation by having the A. F. of L. launch a gigantic campaign of unionization simultaneously in all major unorganized industries. Concretely, I planned to propose that there be set up a big national committee, patterned after our steel committee, which should supervise the work of organization through sub-committees in each and every industry. I calculated that if we managed to defeat the steel trust we consequently would be able to line up the A. F. of L. for such a great organizing campaign and carry it through successfully in spite of all official sabotage. We would then be able to organize literally millions of workers and make real progress towards actually unionizing the working class as a whole. It was a bold plan but a feasible one, had the A. F. of L. leaders permitted the steel campaign to be won.

Such a great influx of members would, as I was quite consciously aware, profoundly change the character of the trade unions. Among the certain basic changes would be: (a) to shift the center of gravity from the skilled workers to the less skilled; (b) to break down the old system of craft unionism, and lay the basis of industrial organization; (c) to give the unions more of a class struggle policy and to broaden their social outlook; (d) to develop a more honest and progressive leadership. In short, I figured that such a great movement would go far towards realizing the plan which we had nourished for years—the transformation of the A. F. of L. into a progressive organization.

These tendencies were already clearly in evidence in the packing and steel campaigns, both movements were based primarily upon the unskilled masses, both were distinctly industrial unionist, both had a fighting policy, and both had developed a new anti-Gompers leadership.

It did not require any great brilliance to figure out the above major results of a victory in steel—that is, the organization of millions of other workers and the transformation of the A. F. of L.—and it is certain that the shrewd advisers of Gary and his powerful banker associates had more than an inkling of them. They doubtless realized that if we won the steel strike they would confront a rejuvenated and far more powerful labor movement; for which industry could resist unionization if steel were vanquished? That is why they fought the strike with such relentless fury.

Gompers, a keen old fox, also knew what the unfavorable implications to him of a victory in steel would be, and that is why he, too, sabotaged our struggle. He could plainly see all the industrial union tendencies developing in the packing and steel campaigns and he could not help but feel them as a growing menace to his whole regime. As for the question of a new anti-Gompers leadership, that matter actually broke out into the open and became a living issue.

One day George P. West, a well-known newspaper man, was in our Pittsburgh office. We had been quite friendly, and inadvertently, I hinted at the broader meanings of the steel campaign to the A. F. of L. West, giving me no inkling of his plan, sprang a "scoop" in the *Nation* of April 9, 1919. Dramatically, he pictured the menace the rising Fitzpatrick-Foster combination held for the declining Gompers-Morrison crowd and the transformation of the A. F. of L. Gompers was furious and demanded an explanation from Fitzpatrick. The latter called me up from Chicago.* We were in the midst of the organization campaign and an open fight would surely destroy it. So Fitzpatrick and I agreed to pooh-pooh West's story and let it go at that. But I was astonished and dismayed a few days later when I received a letter from Fitzpatrick containing a copy of his reply to Gompers, fantastically giving the latter vast praise for his "work" in both the packing and steel campaigns.

But Gompers and the other A. F. of L. leaders were not reassured by the apologetic letter of John Fitzpatrick. They only felt safe when the strike, with its radical leadership and, to them, threatening possibilities, was beaten. If these leaders, with few exceptions, sabotaged the campaign from start to finish it was because they, like Gary, had a vested interest that was in danger. All of which goes to show that the organization of steel and other basic industries is the task of the progressive wing of the labor movement and must be done in the face of reactionary labor leader opposition. This is as true in the 1936 steel drive of the progressive C. I. O. unions as it was of the 1919 steel campaign.

The organization of the steel industry was the most advanced point ever reached up to that time by the American trade union movement. The unions had deeply penetrated the greatest open shop industry. More was at stake in the 1919 steel strike than in any other in American history. The victory of this struggle, which the union

* During the steel campaign Fitzpatrick was located in Chicago, as president of the C. F. of L., while I headed the national organizing forces in Pittsburgh.

dership could have brought about, would have raised the whole
de union movement to a much higher level of strength and development. Its defeat, by the same token, was a big factor in intensifying
the oncoming heavy, employers' offensive and in deepening the reactionary trend in the unions during the following several years.

1936

4. The Basis of
American Syndicalism

The American labor movement has been long and deeply afflicted
with this anti-political syndicalism, very much more in fact than either
Germany or England, comparable industrial countries. Beginnings of
syndicalism were already to be seen in the great eight-hour movement
of 1886, with its general strike theories and anti-parliamentarism.
Many of the dual industrial unions of the next twenty years displayed
similar tendencies to exalt economic action and to play down political
action. But the syndicalist tendency received its fullest expression in
the organization of the Industrial Workers of the World, set up in
1905. A few years later came a lesser organization, the Syndicalist
League of North America. The long-continued hostility of the old
trade unions to working class political action was a product of the
basic forces that produced the general syndicalist trend.

The syndicalist tendency also showed itself very strongly in the
left wing of the socialist movement by trends towards anti-parliamentarism, glorification of the daily role of labor unionism, whittling
down the role of the party, theories of a trade union state after capitalism is overthrown, etc. The Socialist Labor Party and the left wing
of the Socialist Party collaborated in founding the syndicalistic I. W. W.
The three outstanding revolutionary leaders of the period displayed
strong syndicalist characteristics. Daniel De Leon was the theoretical
father of American syndicalism; Eugene V. Debs shared many of De
Leon's syndicalistic illusions; and William D. Haywood became an
outright syndicalist. A striking illustration of the power of syndicalist

tendencies in the Socialist Party was the fact that in the split of 1909 most of those leaving the party joined the I. W. W., and this was equally true of the far larger national Socialist Party split of 1912. In the big 1919 Socialist Party split that gave birth to the communist movement, the left wing was still afflicted with syndicalist tendencies and if it did not degenerate into outright syndicalism it was because of the presence of corrective influences which I shall consider shortly.

The persistent and widespread syndicalist tendency had its roots in basic American conditions, in a whole series of economic, political, and social factors, operating over a long period, European syndicalist influences being only a minor cause of it. These many American factors, by hindering the growth of class consciousness and checking the development of independent working-class political organization and activity, tended to restrict the struggle of the workers to the economic field and thereby to create the objective conditions favorable to the development of syndicalism.

There was, first, the more favorable economic situation which checked the class consciousness of the American masses. This was evidenced by such deterrent factors as the existence of plentiful government free land during several generations, the traditionally higher wage and living standards, the development of a very large and conservative labor aristocracy and corrupt trade union bureaucracy, the passage of large numbers of workers into the ranks of the petty bourgeoisie and many even into the big bourgeoisie during the long period of rapid industrial expansion, etc. These many economic factors tended powerfully to blur class lines, to create bourgeois property illusions among the workers, to stifle the class struggle of the masses and to predispose them to syndicalism.

Then there must be added the widespread bourgeois-democratic illusions among the masses, set up by the fact that the American bourgeois revolution accorded the workers a relatively high degree of formal democratic rights of free speech, free press, free assembly, the right to organize and strike, the right to be elected to any office, the fiction of legalized social equality, etc. These rights had been won by the workers many years before, and no longer provided the cause for acute political struggle. Thus, the American workers, unlike those of Germany, Austria, old Russia, etc., were not aware of burning, immediate political grievances sufficient to serve as the basis for a mass political party. The grievances that the workers had, and they were many and urgent, loomed up to them chiefly as economic, questions of wages, hours, working conditions, etc. In the given historical situation this is why the American workers have made their fight mainly on the economic field, why they were unable to build a mass socialist or labor party; and it formed an important basis for syndicalism.

A number of other important factors also tended to check the American workers' political activity as a class and to encourage syndicalism: the decentralized character of the American government, which scattered the political efforts of the workers; the presence of great masses of disfranchised immigrants and floating workers interested chiefly only in economic questions and subject to strong non-political and anti-political moods; the heterogeneous character of the working class—many nations, religions, traditions, etc.—which made class solidarity difficult; the notoriously corrupt American politics* which disgusted many workers with political action generally; the ultra-reactionary regime in the A. F. of L. which repelled revolutionary workers from the old unions; and, last but not least, the petty-bourgeois control and reformist policies of the Socialist Party which drove many workers (myself included) out of the party and into syndicalism, as we have seen in the splits of 1909 and 1912.†

All the foregoing factors constituted the native soil in which the persistent deviation, syndicalism, grew in the United States. But of themselves they only created the objective possibilities for syndicalism. The actual development of American syndicalism into a system was directly caused by another, a subjective factor, the theoretical weakness of the left wing. *This was the historical "left" sectarian tendency of not struggling against these anti-political forces, but of adapting itself to them and restricting its revolutionary struggle to the economic field.* There was no Lenin in America who could, in face of the many factors making against political action, hammer out a revolutionary political policy; nor was the American left wing even informed regarding Lenin's work. As we have already seen, the left wing's most outstanding leaders over a period of thirty years—De Leon, Debs, Haywood—could do no better than help it lose itself in the syndicalist swamp. Unfortunately I did my share to help increase the syndicalist confusion.

---

* This acute political corruption originated principally in the wholesale bribery of legislators in connection with the stealing of the public domain, one of the special features of capitalist accumulation in America.

† See pp. 14, 17 of this book.

Briefly, the main theoretical errors of the left wing which tended to the development of syndicalism were: (1) a great underestimation of the role of the party, especially by De Leon, which led straight to a repudiation of the party altogether by Haywood and other true syndicalists; (2) exaggeration of the role of labor unions and syndicalistic speculations of bringing about the revolution by utopian dual industrial unions; (3) misconceptions of the role of the state, especially the dictatorship of the proletariat, and also the elaboration of syndicalistic notions of conducting the future socialist society through a trade union state.

Although the syndicalist tendency persisted long and vigorously in the United States, it has finally shrunk to a very minor factor. This is because the theoretical confusion upon which it was based has been mostly cleared up. The experience of the Russian Revolution and the consequent popularization of Lenin's writings exploded the old-time American syndicalist fallacies by demonstrating in practice the revolutionary role of the party, the subordinate function of the trade unions, the nature of the dictatorship of the proletariat, etc. These basic truths, learned in the daily struggles, in the seizure of power and in the building of socialism in the U. S. S. R., were confirmed by the postwar revolutionary upheavals in Germany, Austria, Hungary, China, etc. The genuinely revolutionary forces in the United States were able to learn these lessons. Hence, with the organization of the Communist Party in 1919, which incorporated these fundamental political lessons in its program, American syndicalism suffered a mortal blow. The best revolutionary elements from the Socialist Party, Socialist Labor Party, I. W. W., Syndicalist League of North America, Anarchists, etc., rallied to the Communist Party. The anti-political I. W. W. began to shrivel up. Other factors greatly helped this theoretical clarification to hasten the decline of the I. W. W., such as its dual unionism, overestimation of spontaneity and underestimation of organization, decentralized form, overemphasis on antireligious propaganda, tendency to function more as a propaganda body and fighter for free speech than a labor union, placing of impossible demands in strikes, rigidity of tactics, sectarian refusal to learn from its own mistakes, and its counter-revolutionary attitude towards the Soviet Union, which alienated from it the most revolutionary workers. With the decline of the I. W. W. the syndicalist tendency generally passed rapidly into decay. And since that period the objective situation in the United States has also greatly changed;

the whole class struggle has become more political, all of which facilitates organized class political action by the working class and checks the syndicalist tendency.*

1936

5. The Trade Union Educational League

The loss of the 1919 steel strike upset my whole strategy. Gone was the plan for using this struggle as a springboard for beginning a general organizing campaign in all industries, and gone also was my hope of overthrowing the Gompers machine by the mass organization of the unorganized. But from our experience in the meat packing and steel campaigns two important lessons, aside from the major lessons of the great need for industrial unionism, etc., stood out sharp and clear for us as militants, and we proceeded to act upon them.

The first was that our policy of working within the conservative unions was fundamentally correct. A mere handful of militants had been instrumental in launching and leading movements that had organized over half a million workers—native and foreign born, Negroes and whites, skilled and unskilled, women and youth—in two of the most highly trustified industries in the United States. Furthermore, we had succeeded in directing these movements into elementary industrial channels, and the whole job had been done in the face of the crassest incompetence, indifference and down-right sabotage of the A. F. of L. leadership.

The second special lesson re-emphasized for us in meat packing and steel was that we had to have a left wing group, an organized militant minority. The loose united front we had made with the progressive elements, while correct in principle, was not enough. In both campaigns the lack of a strong left-wing organization had been a disastrous handicap to us, with the official union machinery as it was, in the hands of the reactionary top union leadership. In the packing industry we had suffered severely for want of an organized left-wing

* For a more extended discussion of syndicalism in the American labor movement, see my article in *The Communist*, November, 1935.

movement behind us. In the steel campaign, with a crew of about 150 organizers under our leadership, about half of whom were Socialists, Progressives, and Farmer-Laborites and other union militants, and including such old S. L. of N. A. fighters as Joe Manley and Sam Hammersmark, we were not so badly off as in meat packing. It was this instrument of rank and file control that had enabled us to defy the deadly demand of Wilson and Gompers that the steel strike be "postponed," that is, liquidated. But this organization also was insufficient.

Clearly, we had to build another organization. The old S. L. of N. A. and I. T. U. E. L. had gone on the rocks, it is true, but maybe we would have better success next time. With this general idea in mind, therefore, I resigned my position as B. R. C. A. organizer and secretary of the moribund National Steel Committee in January 1920, when the strike was finished. I was determined to go back to work on the railroad and to try again, as a rank and filer, to build an organized left-wing movement in the trade unions. After spending a few months writing my steel strike book, I tried to get a railroad job; but I found that I was black-listed at my trade in Chicago. I worked a short while on the C. F. of L. official paper, but gave this up and then found myself unemployed.

In the meantime Jack Johnstone, Joe Manley, some other Chicago militants and myself had been preparing the way for our new left-wing trade union organization. Finally, in November 1920, we launched it, a Chicago group of a couple of dozen members, and we called it the Trade Union Educational League. Again I was elected secretary.

THE OLD DISEASE—DUAL UNIONISM

Immediately, the newly-organized T. U. E. L. bumped against the same rock upon which its two predecessors, the S. L. of N. A. and the I. T. U. E. L., had been wrecked: the dual union attitude held generally by revolutionary elements. This seemed as strong as ever. During the packinghouse and steel campaigns the dual union illusion had been a great handicap to us. We simply could not induce the left-wing militants, of whom there were large numbers among the great masses of Polish, Russian, Lithuanian, and other immigrant workers, to participate aggressively in the two big organization campaigns. In the packing industry Jack Johnstone had spoken before left S. P. groups and fairly begged them to help him fight the Lane reactionary leadership. But in vain, the A. F. of L. was simply poison to them and they would have none of it.

In the steel campaign the situation was about the same. The dualist S. P. left-wing (out of which the Communist Party was then being born) assumed, except in one or two places, an indifferent and very unsympathetic attitude to our movement, while the I. W. W. and the S. L. P. denounced it in the sharpest terms. An example of the strength of dual union sentiment at the time was the clash we had with Eugene V. Debs in Youngstown. In 1919, in this great steel center, where the A. F. of L. had been badly discredited recently by betrayed strikes, we were having a desperately hard time to get the workers organized. Debs, then just on the eve of going to jail for his Canton anti-war speech,* was holding big meetings there and sharply assailing our movement with typical dualist arguments. This increased our difficulties and incensed our organizers, and I was made one of a committee of three to visit Debs to demand that he cease his attacks on pain of our making an open fight against him. Finally, he agreed to do this, but we could not induce him to tell the masses of steel workers who packed his meetings to join the A. F. of L. unions. Later on, however, when the big strike took place, Debs heartily endorsed it and sent me word from Atlanta penitentiary that if he were free he would be fighting shoulder to shoulder with us to win the strike.

By 1920, the I. W. W., the traditional hope of dual unionists, had heavily declined after its war-time spurt and had degenerated pretty much into a defense organization for its many political prisoners. But the dual union sentiment, nevertheless, fed upon a number of other independent industrial unions, all either very weak and some altogether fruitless, including the Amalgamated Food Workers, United Labor Council, etc. The main one of such unions was the One Big Union of Canada, which exerted considerable influence in the United States. After the turn of the century, Canadian rebels had not been so badly afflicted by dualism as the American left wing, and over a period of years they had won control of the whole union in the West and were rapidly securing influence in the entire Canadian trade union movement. But the dual union illusion finally caught up with them and their promising situation was wrecked by the launching of the

---

* Speech delivered at the State Convention of the Socialist Party of Ohio at Canton, June 16, 1918, for which Debs was sentenced to serve ten years in the Federal penitentiary.

ill-fated One Big Union in Calgary, on March 13, 1919. The O. B. U., by pulling the militants out of the old unions, as usual, left the reactionaries in complete control.

⇥Despite its long-continued lack of success, the dual union theory, however, still continued to exert a hypnotic effect over almost the whole American left wing. The I. W. W., fanatically dualist, would not even discuss the question of working within the trade unions, nor would the S. L. P., nor what remained of a left wing in the S. P. after the 1919 split. The nascent Communist movement, just born out of the S. P. in the shape of two Communist parties, was similarly dualist and endorsed the I. W. W. Even liberals and progressives, in the trade unions and outside, were also dead sure that nothing could be done in the old trade unions. I remember how, at a meeting of such liberal elements in New York in 1920, after my speech on the steel campaign, they scoffed at my proposals that revolutionists should give up their foolish policy of building dual unions and should concentrate upon work within the conservative trade unions.*

1936

6. The Post-War Attack on Labor

In the historic situation of the world war period all the class collaboration tendencies hitherto active or latent in the trade union movement came to a climax. The bureaucracy identified the interests of the workers completely with those of the employers. They degraded the trade unions into mere instruments of the capitalists. Whatever policy the capitalists outlined in the imperialist war the trade union leaders accepted as their own. When the policy of the government was "neutrality" none were more blatant neutralists than the bureaucrats. And when the capitalist class prepared to enter actively the imperialist war the trade union leaders began to cry out their support. Even before the United States actually began war on Germany the A. F. of L. bureaucrats gave assurance that the employers could depend upon the support of the unions. At a special conference, attended by

* For an evaluation of dual unionism see pp. 62-74 of this book.

the heads of all the important unions, held almost one month before the United States entered the war, a long patriotic declaration was adopted, containing the following:

But, despite all our endeavors and hopes, should our country be drawn into the maelstrom of the European conflict, we, with these ideals of liberty and justice herein declared, as the indispensable basis for national policies, offer our services to our country in every field of activity to defend, safeguard and preserve the republic of the United States of America against its enemies whosoever they may be and we call upon our fellow workers and fellow citizens in the holy name of Labor, Justice, Freedom and Humanity to devotedly and patriotically give like service.

A few months after the war began, the Gompersites, in order to check the left-wing agitation against the war, organized the so-called American Alliance for Labor and Democracy. Its declaration of principles begins:

The American Alliance for Labor and Democracy, in its first national conference, declares its unswerving loyalty to the cause of democracy, now assailed by the forces of autocracy and militarism. As labor unionists, social reformers and socialists, we pledge our loyal support to the United States Government and its allies in the present world conflict. We declare that the one overshadowing issue is the preservation of democracy, either democracy will endure and men will be free, or autocracy will triumph, and the race will be enslaved. On this prime issue we take our stand.

The resistance of the left wing was soon overcome. The overwhelming masses of trade unionists were duped into following the lead of the A. F. of L. officials. The latter then, cheek by jowl with the employers, plunged into every phase of war activity. They became members of all the committees, from the National War Labor Board down, created to further the war. They sent delegations to Great Britain and France to help force the reluctant masses into the war. Gompers blossomed forth as a great "statesman," the right-hand man of Wilson. On all sides the press and other capitalist institutions poured out flattery for the pliant labor leaders, who swallowed it greedily.

The employers, with a shrewd eye to eventual bitter struggles with the workers, demanded the establishment of class peace during the war period. This the lackey-like bureaucrats readily agreed to. Early in 1918 they worked out an agreement which was not only practically of a no-strike character, but which also laid other direct obstructions in the way of organizing the workers. One clause of this agreement runs:

In establishments where union and non-union men and women now work together and the employer meets only with employees or representatives engaged in such establishments, the continuation of such conditions shall not be deemed a grievance.

This was a guarantee of the status quo regarding the "open shop," and it was so understood by the various labor commissions. It was a direct bar to the unionization of the industries. The leaders of the workers also accepted it in that spirit. They did virtually nothing to organize the masses to defend their interests. They were interested only in winning the war. With the tremendous demand for labor it would have been quite possible with but little effort to sweep several million workers into the unions. Because this was not done the unions later had a bitter price to pay.

Notwithstanding sabotage and betrayal by the Gompers leaders in every angle of the war situation, the pressure from the masses for organization and better conditions was so great however that the unions began to grow and function. Thousands of workers were organized in the railroad, steel, packing, lumber, metal, textile, and many other industries. The membership of the A. F. of L. advanced from 2,371,434 in 1917 to 4,078,740 in 1920. The eight-hour day was established in many industries, working conditions were improved, and wages, especially of the unskilled, were sharply advanced.

The end of the war found the trade union bureaucracy living in a fool's paradise. Everything seemed very rosy to them. The unions were strong, established in many industries hitherto completely closed to them, and growing rapidly in spite of official sabotage. The leaders, flattered by the employers and tied up with them in a maze of governmental class collaboration schemes, believed that their ideal class peace was at hand. But these illusions were soon to be shattered. Speedily after the war the trade unions were to find themselves in death grips with a capitalist enemy more militant than ever, with American imperialism, nurtured and strengthened almost beyond recognition by the World War.

With its vast extent of territory, stretching from the Atlantic to the Pacific, containing the greatest body of natural resources of coal, iron, oil, lumber, etc., in the world, the United States, prior to the World War, was forging steadily ahead to its inevitable goal as a great imperialist power. Long steps in this direction were the seizure of Hawaii, Cuba, Puerto Rico, the Philippines, Guam, etc., and the opening of the Panama Canal, which gave the United States rich colonies to exploit and hegemony over Central America. The growth of its unparalleled industrial system was also laying the basis for America's world role.

The World War of 1914-18 enormously speeded up this imperialist development of the United States. America's war-stricken allies placed monster demands upon its industrial and financial resources. These responded with a flood of war supplies and capital such as the world had never seen before. With one great leap the United States, displacing Great Britain, became the industrial and financial leader of world capitalism.

Almost immediately after the war this robust imperialism came into open conflict with the antiquated trade union movement. The employers' objectives were to strip the workers of what advances they had made during the war period. They were determined to cut wages, and especially to destroy the unions, so as to secure for themselves greater profits and a free hand in the industries. This movement to "deflate" labor in the United States was part of the world effort of capitalism to stabilize itself after the holocaust of the war.

The main attack against the American workers was camouflaged with a remarkable smoke screen of class collaborationism. During 1919 a whole series of proposals were put forth to establish class peace, especially by church organizations, including such bodies as the National Catholic War Council, Federal Council of the Churches of Christ, Episcopal Joint Commission on Social Service, Baptist Social Service Committee, Presbyterian General Assembly, Methodist Episcopal Board of Bishops, Interchurch World Movement, etc. The general program of this widespread movement was for a class peace based upon mild social reforms and a recognition of the right of the workers to form trade unions. The objective results of the movement were to confuse the workers and to demobilize them before the impending capitalist attack.

As part of this class collaboration camouflage movement, President Wilson, on September 3, 1919, issued a call for a National Industrial Conference to assemble in Washington on October 6. It was to be made up of representatives of the employers, the public, and the workers. Its avowed purpose was "to discuss such methods as have already been tried out of bringing capital and labor into close co-operation." But before the meeting came together the storm broke. On September 22, 365,000 steel workers struck. The refusal of the October 6 conference to deal with the strike led to the withdrawal of the labor delegation and the break-up of the conference. The class war was on in earnest.

Then followed the greatest series of labor struggles in American history. During the next three years big strikes raged in nearly all the industries. Everywhere the employers strove to cut wages and to smash the unions; everywhere the workers militantly resisted, despite a weak and treacherous leadership. Bitter strikes were fought out in the coal mining, meat packing, printing, building, textile, shoe, marine transport, needle, lumber, and other industries. The movement climaxed in the great national strike of the 400,000 railroad shop mechanics in 1922.

The trade union leadership proved itself utterly unfit in the face of this bitter and sustained attack upon the workers. Its petty-bourgeois ideas of class collaboration, its antiquated system of craft unionism, and its obsolete strike strategy were worse than useless in defending the workers and their organizations from the aggressive attacks of the capitalists, made powerful through militant imperialism. Craft betrayal, in its worst forms, was practiced on every front. Consequently the unions suffered heavy defeats all along the line. In the steel, meat packing, lumber, and marine transport industries they were either completely or almost completely annihilated. The miners' union was seriously weakened, likewise the organizations in the printing, needle, shoe, building, and textile industries. The smashing of the shopmen's strike undermined the whole structure of railroad unionism. The A. F. of L. lost more than 1,000,000 members in the whole struggle and was driven from many key industrial positions. This period was marked with ferocious state persecutions of the left wing, many hundreds being jailed and deported. Taken together, the reverses in the various industries constituted the most disastrous defeat ever suffered by the American labor movement in its entire history.

In the midst of these historic struggles the left wing in the unions, organized in and around the Trade Union Educational League, and the Workers (Communist) Party, raised the slogan, "Amalgamation and a Labor Party." It proposed that the scattered craft unions be consolidated and the unorganized workers mobilized into powerful industrial unions. It demanded that the labor leaders break with the two capitalist parties and that the unions launch a labor party. It insisted upon a policy of militant struggle against the employers. This program took like wildfire among the masses. The workers were in a fighting mood. Over half of the entire rank and file of the A. F. of L. unions voted endorsement of the slogan, "Amalgamation and a Labor Party."

But the conservative leaders would have none of such a program. Amalgamation would jeopardize their sinecure jobs in the unions; the labor party would break their profitable alliances with the capitalist politicians, and the plan of militant struggle was contrary to their whole class collaboration ideology. Hence, through their autocratic control of the union machinery, they strangled the amalgamation movement; they sabotaged the labor party, and they embarked upon a program of systematic surrender to the employers. To make this surrender possible, they opened up a bitter persecution and expulsion of the left wing, designed to disconnect its militants from leadership of the discontented masses.

After the defeat of the 1922 railroad shopmen's strike the trade union bureaucracy took an orientation towards an elaborated and intensified class collaboration.

1927

7. Dual Unionism

The weakness of the American labor movement, its lack of social vision and its general backwardness politically and industrially, as compared with the labor movements of other countries, have long been a matter of common knowledge. It cannot be denied or disputed, nor do real labor students try to do either. Their aim is to explain it, to find out the reasons for the paradoxical situation of the world's most advanced capitalist country possessing such a primitive working class movement. Two explanations for this condition, widely accepted among labor men and students generally, are (1) that the influx of so many millions of immigrants, with their innumerable language, national, and religious differences, has enormously complicated the problems confronting the labor movement and hindered the work of unionization and education by bringing together a practically unorganizable mass in the industries, and (2) that the workers of America, because of the existence of the free land for so long and the opportunities presented by the unexampled industrial expansion, have been better able to make a living, and consequently have not felt the need for organization and a revolutionary spirit to such an extent as the oppressed workers of Europe. Or, in other words, that too many immigrants and too much prosperity are to blame for the extreme backwardness of organized labor in the United States.

FOREIGN-BORN AS MILITANTS

Regarding the first of the explanations: Although, undoubtedly, the presence of so many nationalities in the industries has worked against the formation of a labor party and makes the problem of union organization more difficult, it is by no means an insurmountable obstacle. The situation is not nearly so bad as it has been painted. The "unorganizability" of the foreign-born workers is a very convenient cloak for labor leaders to cover up their inefficiency and the weaknesses of an unfit craft unionism. The fact is, the immigrant workers are distinctly organizable, often even more so than the native Americans. This has been demonstrated time and again in strikes during the past ten years. In the big Lawrence textile strike of 1912 it was the immigrant workers, a score of different nationalities, who were the backbone of the great struggle. Likewise, in the packing house movement of 1917-21, the whole thing centered around the foreign-born, mostly Slavs. They organized the unions in the first place (the Americans quite generally refusing to come in until after a settlement had been secured), and they were the ones who made the final desperate fight. The same experience was seen in the great 1918-19 organizing campaign and strike in the steel industry.* Although in some mills there were as many as 54 nationalities, they joined hands readily and formed trade unions. There was much more difficulty in organizing the minority of native Americans than the big majority of heterogeneous foreign-born. And when the historic struggle with the steel trust came the foreign-born workers covered themselves with undying glory. They displayed the very highest type of labor union qualities.

* See pp. 21-50 of this book.

The majority of the membership of the United Mine Workers of America are foreign-born. Indeed, one can search the world's labor movement in vain to find a union with a more valiant record. But the best illustration of the organizability of the foreign-born is to be found in the clothing trades. In that industry the unions are made up of a general conglomeration of nationalities, principally Jews, Poles, Italians and Lithuanians. The American-born form but a small minority of the membership and almost nothing of the administration. Yet the unions, all of them, are miles in advance of the ordinary American trade union. In fact, they will compare well with the average European labor bodies. They are the one bright spot in a generally dismal movement.

Again it must be said that, although somewhat complicating the problems of the labor movement, the immigrant workers cannot be seriously blamed for its present deplorable condition. Intellectually they are radical and receptive of the most advanced social programs. If they, making up the bulk of the working forces in the great industries, have not been organized industrially and politically before now, it is immediately because of the utter sterility and incompetence of the Gompers regime.

PROSPERITY NOT A DETERRENT

To urge the comparative prosperity of the American working class as an explanation of the backwardness of our labor movement is just as futile as to blame it upon the foreign-born. The fact is that exceptional prosperity, instead of being a deterrent, is a direct stimulus to labor organization and radicalism. The workers progress best, intellectually and in point of organization, under two general conditions, the antipodes of each other: (1) during periods of devastating hardship, (2) in eras of so-called prosperity. When suffering extreme privation they are literally compelled to think and act, and when the pressure of the exploiter is relatively light, during good times, they take courage and move forward of their own volition. The static periods, when very little is accomplished in either an educational or organizational way, are when times are neither very bad nor very good. Then both factors for progress, heavy pressure and stirred ambitions, operate at a minimum.

The benefits conferred upon organized labor by "opportunity" and "prosperity" can be traced clearly in the United States. The West has always been the land of opportunity, the traditional place of labor shortage and high wages in this country; and likewise it has ever been the natural home of militant labor unionism and radicalism in general. It is in the East, where labor has been most plentiful, wages lowest, and opportunity scarcest for the worker of small means, that labor organization and revolutionary understanding have made slowest progress. By the same token, when hard times prevail over the country the labor unions become weak, and the workers, defeated, grow pessimistic and lose all daring and imagination. But when the hard times are succeeded by a wave of "prosperity" the workers' cause picks up at once; the unions, victorious, grow rapidly and, having had a taste of power, they are ready for further conquests. This tendency was well illustrated during the war and the boom time following it. Never were the workers more prosperous, never were wages higher, job conditions better, and working hours shorter than in this period. But the prosperity, instead of injuring the labor movement, gave it the greatest stimulus, physically and intellectually, in its history. The workers, acting as they always do under such favorable circumstances, poured into the organizations by hundreds of thousands. Then the latter, tremendously invigorated by this enormous influx of new strength and finding the capitalists' fighting ability greatly handicapped because of the labor shortage, insisted upon concessions and conditions such as they hardly dared dream of in pre-war times. A basic radicalism developed throughout the working class, not the classic Marxist understanding, it is true, but a closely related deep yearning and striving for more power over industry and society. Naturally enough also it was in 1919, when the railroad unions were at the very zenith of their power and influence, that they announced the Plumb Plan* to take the railroads out of the hands of their present owners.

The workers, particularly in a backward labor movement like ours, learn by action. It is just when they enjoy greatest power and well being, in times of presperity, that they are most stimulated to desire and demand more. Because this is the case, because the workers habitually take advantage of every lessening of the pressure upon them by expanding their organizations and increasing their demands, periods of abounding prosperity are periods of danger to capitalism. They are eras of genuine progress to the working class, even as are the times of unbearable hardships. The explanation that the backwardness of

* See pp. 260-80 of this book.

American labor is due to too much prosperity will not stand up. The workers as a class do not become enervated by prosperity, they are energized by it and developed into militancy. Because American workers have been comparatively well off is a reason, not that they should have a weak labor movement, but that their labor organizations should be powerful, even if not revolutionary.

The American labor movement is in its present deplorable backward condition not because of the reactionary influence of the immigrant workers, or because of the stultifying effect of a higher standard of living prevailing in this country. This is plain when a serious study is made of the matter. Under certain circumstances both of these forces, particularly the former, may exert a hindering influence on the development of labor organizations, but at most they are only minor factors. A deeper cause of the extraordinary condition must be sought elsewhere. And it is to be found in the fatal policy of dual unionism which has been practiced religiously for a generation by American radicals and progressives generally. Because of this policy thousands of the very best militants have been led to desert the mass of labor organizations and to waste their time in vain efforts to construct ideally conceived unions designed to replace the old ones. In consequence the mass labor movement has been, for many years, systematically drained of its life-giving elements. The effect has been shatteringly destructive of every phase and manifestation of organized labor. Dual unionism has poisoned the very springs of progress in the American labor movement and is largely responsible for its present sorry plight.

In order to appreciate the destructive effects of dual unionism it is necessary to understand the importance to labor of the militant elements that have been practically cancelled by the dual union policy: Every experienced labor man knows that the vital activities of the labor movement are carried on by a small minority of live individuals, so few in number as to be almost insignificant in comparison to the organization as a whole. The great mass of the membership are usually inactive in union matters.

This militant minority is of supreme importance to every branch of the labor movement. It is the thinking and acting part of the working class, the very soul of labor. It works out the fighting programs and takes the lead in putting them into execution. It is the source of all real progress—intellectual, spiritual, and organizational—in the workers' ranks. It is "the little leaven that leaveneth the whole lump." The militant minority, made famous by the Russian Revolution as the "advance guard of the proletariat," is the heart and brain and nerves of the labor movement all over the world.

The fate of all labor organization depends directly upon the effective functioning of these militant, progressive spirits among the backward and sluggish organized masses. In England, Germany, and other countries with strong labor movements the militants have functioned in this way. They have remained within the old trade unions and acted as the practical teachers, stimulators, and leaders of the masses there assembled. Consequently they have been able to communicate to these masses something of their own understanding and revolutionary fighting spirit, and to make their movements flourish and progress. But in the United States dual unionism for years destroyed this natural liaison between the militants and the masses, which is indispensable to the health and vigor of organized labor. It withdrew the militants from the basic trade unions, and left the masses there leaderless. This destroyed the very foundations of progress and condemned every branch of the labor movement—political, industrial, co-operative—to stagnation and impotency. Dual unionism, so to speak, severed the head from the body of American labor.

THE DUAL UNIONS FAIL

For almost thirty years the dual union program, as outlined by Daniel DeLeon, has wasted a prodigious amount of invaluable militant strength. Tens of thousands of the very best men ever produced by the American labor movement have devoted themselves to this program and have expended oceans of energy in order to bring the longed-for new labor movement into realization. But they were pouring water upon sand. The parched Sahara of dual industrial unionism swallowed up their efforts and left hardly a trace behind. The numerically insignificant dual unions of today are a poor bargain indeed in return for the enormous price they have cost.

Consider, for example, the Industrial Workers of the World. The amount of energy and unselfish devotion lavished upon that organization would have wrought miracles in developing and extending the trade unions; but it has been powerless to make anything substantial of the I. W. W. Today, seventeen years after its foundation, that body has far fewer members (not to speak of much less influence) than it had at its beginning. The latest available official financial reports show a membership of not more than 15,000, whereas in 1905 it had 40,000. Even its former revolutionary spirit has degenerated until the organization has now become little more than a sort of league to make war upon the trade unions and to revile and slander struggling Soviet Russia. The I. W. W. is a monument to the folly of dual unionism.

The One Big Union of Canada is another example of rebel effort wasted in dual unionism. Four years ago it started out with a great blare of trumpets and about 40,000 members. Its advent threw dissension into the old trade unions and shattered their ranks. They lost heavily in membership, the militants pulling out the more active elements on behalf of the One Big Union. Yet, today, this organization, despite the great effort put into it, has but an insignificant membership, not over 4,000 at most, and its constructive influence is about in proportion. It was a costly, ill-fated experiment, and in the main has played havoc with Canadian labor. The Workers' International Industrial Union, another universal dual union, has occupied the attention of the Socialist Labor Party's active spirits for fourteen years, but now it can muster only a few hundred actual members. Similar records of disastrous waste of militant effort are shown by the dozens of dual unions started in the various single industries, all of which literally burned up the energies of the militants. Except for those in the textile, food, and shoe industries, which have secured some degree of success, these dual unions have all failed completely. They have absorbed untold labor of the best elements among the workers and have yielded next to nothing in return. Dual unionism is a useless and insupportable squandering of labor's most precious life force. It is a bottomless pit into which the workers have vainly thrown their energy and idealism.

DEVITALIZING THE TRADE UNIONS

The waste of militant strength, caused so long by dual unionism, has reacted directly and disastrously upon the trade unions. For many years practically all the radical papers and revolutionary leaders in this country were deeply tinged with dual unionism. In their program the ideas of secessionism and progressive unionism were welded into one. The consequence was that as fast as the active workers in the trade unions became acquainted with the principles of revolutionary unionism they also absorbed the idea of dualism. Thus they lost faith and interest in their old organizations, either quitting them entirely for some dual union, or becoming so much dead timber within them. The general outcome of this wholesale turning away of the progressive minority was to divorce the very idea of progress from the trade unions. It nipped in the bud the growing crop of militants, the only element through which virile life and development could come to the old organizations. Dual unionism dried up the very spring of progress in the trade unions, it condemned them to sterility and stagnation. It was a long-continued process of slow poisoning of the labor movement.

A disastrous effect of this systematic demoralization and draining away of the militants is that it has placed the trade unions almost entirely under the control of the organized reactionaries. In all labor movements the unions can prosper and grow only if the progressive groups within them organize and wage vigorous battle all along the line against the bureaucracy. By its incessant preaching that the trade unions were hopeless and that nothing could be done with them, dualism discouraged even those militants who did stay within the unions and prevented them from developing an organized opposition to the bureaucrats. Poisoned by dual union pessimism about the old organizations and without a constructive program to apply to them, the militants stood around idly for years in the trade unions while the reactionary forces intrenched themselves and ruled as they saw fit. Because of their dualistic notions the militants practically deserted the field and left it to the uncontested sway of their enemies. If the American labor movement is now hard and fast in the grip of a stupid and corrupt bureaucracy, totally incapable of progress, dual unionism, through its demoralization of the trade union opposition, is chiefly to blame.

During the great movement of the packinghouse workers of 1917-21 the indifference of the radicals towards the old unions wrought particular havoc. A handful of rebels, free from dual union ideas, were primarily responsible for the historic movement. Soon they found themselves and the middle group in a finish fight with the conservatives for control of the newly formed unions. Occupying the strategic position in the organizations, especially in the Chicago stockyards, they begged the dualistic radicals, who worked in the industry, to come in and help them control the unions, offering to place them in secretary-ships and other important posts. Had this offer been accepted, it would have certainly resulted in the big packinghouse unions, then numbering over 200,000 members, coming entirely under progressive leadership. But so strong was the spirit of dualism at that time, in 1919, that the outstanding left-wingers would not participate constructively in the trade unions even under such exceptionally favorable circumstances. They refused the invitation with insults and contempt. The consequence was that the few militants within the old unions were swamped by the reactionaries, who soon wrecked the whole organization by their incompetence and corruption. It was a splendid opportunity lost. Similar opportunities existed in other industries. It is safe to say that if the radicals had been free of dual unionist tendencies during the war period and had been active in the trade unions, the great bulk of the working class would have been organized, instead of the comparatively few that were gotten together by the reactionaries, who controlled the unions.

DISRUPTION THROUGH SECESSION

Dual unionism's steady drain upon the vitality of the trade unions by withdrawing and demoralizing the militants piecemeal has been ruinous enough, but the many great secession movements it has given birth to have made the situation much worse. It is the particular misfortune of the American labor movement that just when some trade union is passing through a severe crisis, as a result of industrial depression, internal dissension, a lost strike, or some other weakening influence, the dual union tendency breaks out with unusual virulence and a secession movement develops that completes the havoc already wrought. Exactly at the time the militants are needed the most to hold the organization together is just when they are the busiest pulling it apart. In such crises those who should be the union's best friends become its worst enemies. This has happened time and again. During the past two years, for example, the longshoremen and seamen have had bitter experience with such breakaway movements. Both organizations had lost big strikes, and both were in critical need of rebuilding and rejuvenating by the progressive elements. But just at this critical juncture the latter failed, and, instead of strengthening the unions, set about tearing them to pieces with secession movements. Four or five dual unions appeared, and when they got done attacking the old organizations and fighting among themselves, all traces of unionism were wiped out in many ports. Similar attacks are now being directed against the weakened railroad shopmen's unions.

A great secession movement, typical for its disastrous effects, was the famous "outlaw" strike of the switchmen in 1920. That ill-fated movement began because of a widespread discontent among the rank and file at the neglect of their grievances by the higher union officials. It was a critical situation, but had there been a well-organized militant minority on hand the foment could have been given a constructive turn and used as a means not only to satisfy the demands of the workers but also to defeat the reactionaries. But the long-continued dualistic propaganda in the railroad industry had effectively prevented the organization of such a minority. Hence, leaderless, the movement ran wild and culminated in the "outlaw" strike. Then, as usual, the secessionist tendency showed itself and a new organization was formed. The final result was disaster all around for the men. The strike was lost, many thousands of active workers were blacklisted, the unions were weakened by the loss of their best men, and the grip of the reactionaries on the organization was strengthened by the complete breakup of the opposition. The loss of the "outlaw" strike of 1920 was one of the heavy penalties American workers have paid for their long allegiance to utopian dual unionism.

Typical of the ruin wrought by dual unionism was the movement that gave birth to the Canadian One Big Union in 1918. Freeing themselves for the moment from the dual union obsession, the militants had raised the banner of industrial unionism in the old trade unions, and the workers, seeing at last an escape from reactionary policies and leadership, responded *en masse*. Union after union passed into revolutionary control, and the movement swept western Canada like a storm. It seemed that finally an organization of militants, without which there could be no progress, was about to be definitely established in the trade unions. But just when the movement was most promising, the dualists got the upper hand and steered the whole business into the quagmire of secession by launching the One Big Union as a new labor movement. Havoc resulted. The new union, of course, got nowhere, and the old ones were split and weakened by dissensions and the loss of many thousands of their very best workers. But, worst of all, the budding organized minority within the trade unions was wrecked, and the organizations passed completely into the control of the reactionaries. The One Big Union secession set back the whole Canadian labor movement for years.

BREAKING THE WESTERN FEDERATION OF MINERS

One of the great tragedies caused by dual unionism was the smashing of the Western Federation of Miners. This body of metal miners, organized in 1893, was in its early days a splendid type of labor union. Industrial in form and frankly revolutionary, it carried on for many years a spectacular and successful struggle against the Mine Owners' Association. Brissenden says that its strikes in Coeur d'Alene, Cripple Creek, Leadville, Telluride, Idaho Springs, etc., were "the most strenuous and dramatic series of strike disturbances in the history of the American labor movement."* Time after time the miners armed themselves and fought it out with the gunmen and thugs of the mining companies. Their valiant battles attracted world-wide attention.†

But this great organization, unquestionably one of the best ever produced by the American labor movement, has long since been wrecked both in point of numbers and spirit. Insignificant in size, it also became so conservative as to be ashamed of its splendid old name. It is now known as the International Union of Mine, Mill and Smelter Workers. This pitiful weakening of the Western Federation of Miners was caused directly by dual unionism. Some detail is necessary in order to show how it happened.

To begin with we must understand that in its best days only a few of the W. F. of M. membership, not over 5 per cent at most,‡ were active and revolutionary. This small minority, highly organized, occupied strategic points of the union. Thus they were able to communicate something of their own revolutionary spirit to the mass as a whole. The organized rebels literally inspired the W. F. of M. to be a virile fighting organization.

In 1905, the W. F. of M. was one of the unions that formed the I. W. W. It remained part of that organization for about two years, when it withdrew. The militant elements, those who had made the W. F. of M. what it was, were bitterly opposed to the withdrawal.

---

* See Paul F. Brissenden, *The I. W. W.: A Study of American Syndicalism,* New York, 1920.

† The history of the Western Federation of Miners gives the lie direct to the argument that prosperity kills the militancy of the workers. That union was made up mostly of American-born workers and operated in what was then the most prosperous section of the country, the Rocky Mountain district.

‡ Estimated by Vincent St. John, former Western Federation of Miners militant.

For the most part they stayed in the I. W. W. and allowed the W. F. of M. to go its way without them. Hundreds of the best men, including such fighters as Bill Haywood, Vincent St. John, etc., deserted the old organization, either by quitting it altogether or by becoming negative factors in it. The passage of the W. F. of M. through the I. W. W. served to sift out the active workers, to rob the W. F. of M. of its very soul. The W. F. of M. went into the I. W. W., a revolutionary organization; it came out of it, if not actually conservative, then at least definitely condemned to that fate.

After the W. F. of M.'s withdrawal from the I. W. W., its militants, all become ardent dual unionists, declared war to the knife against the union. The organization which had previously absorbed so much of their unselfish devotion was thereafter the object of their bitterest attacks. Once the very backbone of the W. F. of M., the militants now became its deadliest foes. Under these circumstances it was not long until the degeneration set in which has reduced the once splendid Western Federation of Miners to its present lowly status.

Among others, the writer was one who pointed out the folly of rebels destroying an industrial union like the W. F. of M., simply because it had withdrawn from the I. W. W., and who urged that a campaign be started to take control of the union again. But the answer always given was that the Moyer machine, especially because it controlled the big Butte local union, was unshakably intrenched. And when it was proposed to capture the Butte local this was declared impossible. But the fallacy of this objection was made apparent in 1914 when, as a result of insupportable grievances, the rank and file of the Butte organization rose up, drove their officials from town and took charge of the situation. This put Butte, the citadel of the reaction, squarely in the hands of the militants. Had they but stayed in the W. F. of M. and carried on a campaign in the other locals the whole organization would have been theirs for the taking. But they were so obsessed with the dual unionism prevailing generally among rebels, and so blinded with hatred for everything connected with the A. F. of L., that they seceded at once and formed a new union. This went to smash, as such organizations almost always do. The only practical effect of the whole affair was to deal a death blow to the W. F. of M., already weakened and poisoned by the desertion of its former militants.

It is one of the saddest facts of American labor history that the Western Federation of Miners was finally destroyed by the very men who had originally built it and had made it one of the joys of the working class. What the Mine Owners' Association, with all its money and power, was unable to accomplish, the militants, obsessed by dual unionism, brought about with little or no difficulty. Their allegiance to an impractical theory has broken up all organization among the metal miners. And the ravages that were made upon the W. F. of M. have been visited to a greater or lesser extent upon every other trade union in the United States, for all of them have had to suffer the loss of their most active workers and to confront as bitter enemies those very fighters who should be their main reliance.

NEW REALISM vs. OLD UTOPIANISM

But the American labor movement is at last freeing itself from the dual union tendency which has sucked away its life blood for so many years. During the past eighteen months whole sections of the militants have undergone an intellectual revolution, repudiating their historic policy of building independent idealistic labor organizations, and turning with remarkable rapidity and unanimity to the work of revamping and revolutionizing the old trade unions. Practically every branch of the radical and progressive movements has been effected by this unprecedented tactical about-face. The Communist groups, *viz.;* the Communist Party, the Workers' Party, and the Proletarian Party, have been particularly influenced. Made up of elements to whom dual unionism was almost a religion for many years, they have now turned entirely against that policy and are working diligently within the old unions to revive and reinvigorate them. Quite evidently those parties are determined not to make the fatal mistake, which ruined the Socialist Party, of failing to establish their militants in the strategic positions in the organized masses. The Farmer-Labor Party militants, always active in the unions, have had their work clarified and intensified. The Socialist Party, the I. W. W., the One Big Union, and the various single industry dual unions have also been greatly affected by the new viewpoint. Large numbers of the most active spirits among the latter have come out openly for consolidation with the trade unions. It is the most complete change of tactics that has ever taken place in any country in the world in so short a time. Dual unionism has been dealt a death blow.

1922

8. Industrial Unionism

The new movement, as represented by the Trade Union Educational League, repudiates the conception, long a dogma of the dual unionists, that the trade unions are anchored to the principle of craft unionism and cannot develop into industrial organizations. As against the old idea that the inevitable industrial unions have to be created out of the whole cloth, by fiat as it were, the new movement holds that they are coming as a result of an evolutionary process, by a constant building, reorganization, and consolidation of the primitive craft unions. This conception is borne out by world-wide labor history.

In the development of industrial unionism out of the original unorganized condition of the working class, the labor movement passes through three distinct phases, which may be roughly designated as isolation, federation, and amalgamation. In the beginning the workers almost always organize by crafts. These primitive unions, knowing little or nothing of broad class interests, fight along in a desultory battle, each one for itself. This is the period of isolation, or pure and simple craft unionism. But after a greater or lesser period it finally ends. The crafts in the various industries, seeing that the employers play their organizations against each other and thus defeat all of them, learn something of their common interests and set up alliances among themselves along the lines of their respective industries. This brings them into the second, or federation, stage of development. Their evolution goes right on. For the same forces that necessitated the craft unions federating, eventually compel them to consolidate these federations into actual industrial unions. Thus they arrive at the final stage of amalgamation. The resultant industrial unions then pass through a similar process of integration. First they fight alone, then they strike up federations with allied industries, and finally they amalgamate with them. Industrial unionism comes, not as a new system suddenly applied to the labor movement, but as the culmination of a long and elaborate evolution from the simple craft unions to the complex organizations necessary for the modern struggle.

Practically all the great industrial unions in the world have been built by this evolutionary process. In England, the National Union of Railwaymen, the Amalgamated Engineering Union, the Miners' Federation, and the Transport and General Workers' Union are amalgamations of many craft and district unions. In Germany, the Metal Workers' Union, the Building Workers' Federation, etc., etc., were built up the same way from original craft unions. These big organizations, and dozens more in other countries, have all passed through the three stages of isolation, federation, and amalgamation. That is the normal mode of labor union progress. And despite the efforts of the dualists to prove them static and unchangeable, American trade unions are traveling the same evolutionary route that the foreign unions have taken, although very much slower and more laboriously. At present they are quite generally in the federation stage of development. That is the meaning of the many alliances among them—the railroad federations, the printing, metal, building, and other trades councils—that exist in the various industries. The task of the militants is to develop the trade unions into the next stage, amalgamation; to speed on the present natural evolution until these bodies culminate in industrial unions.

THE MILITANTS AMONG THE MASSES

The new movement now crystallizing in the Trade Union Educational League also differs widely in tactical conceptions from those of the dualists. The essence of the program of the latter was to set up labor unions upon the basis of their several political and industrial theories and then to try to educate a backward working class into joining them. This was a violation of the first principle of labor unionism. The workers organize in the industrial field not because they hold certain elaborate social beliefs jointly, but because through united action they can protect their common economic interests. Labor unions are built upon the solid rock of the material welfare of the workers, not upon their acceptance of stated political opinions. In the very nature of things labor unions at present must consist of the many sects and factions that go to make up the working class— Republicans, Democrats, Socialists, Communists, Anarchists, Syndicalists, Catholics, Protestants, etc., etc., The natural result of the dualists' attempt to organize labor unions around their theories was a whole crop of new labor movements. As fast as new conceptions, political and industrial, developed, their proponents organized separate labor unions to give expression to them. In some industries there were as many as five of these dual movements, each representing a different tendency and each engaged in the hopeless task of converting the masses to its particular point of view. Dual unionism, with its program of labor organization along the lines of fine-spun theory, not only devitalized the trade unions by robbing them of their best blood, but it also degenerated the revolutionary and progressive movement into a series of detached sects, out of touch with the masses and the real struggle and running off to all sorts of wild theories and impractical programs.

But the militants in the Trade Union Educational League rigidly eschew this sectarian policy. Their program is the very reverse, to keep the militants in the organized masses at all costs. Instead of setting up intellectual and organizational barriers and then coaxing the worker to break through them, they carry their propaganda right into the very heart of the workers' organizations and struggles. The League militants conceive the question of labor organization to be largely one of leadership, and they aim to secure the backing of the mass of organized workers by taking the lead in all their battles, by showing in the crucible of the class struggle that their theories, tactics, and organization forms are the best for the labor movement. Thus will be broken the grip of the reactionary bureaucracy who now stultify and paralyze the labor unions, and the control of these organizations thereby gradually pass into the hands of the militants who will stimulate and develop them.

In the past the militants have voluntarily isolated themselves from the organized masses, which was very convenient indeed for the labor bureaucrats. But now these active spirits fight desperately against such isolation. They realize fully that their place is in the big trade unions. And when the controlling reactionaries, who instinctively know that the rebels are dangerous to them only if in the unions, expel individuals and local unions, the latter must fight their way back in again. Such a policy however, does not mean that the old organizations must be maintained at any price. In extreme cases secession movements may be unavoidable because of the refusal of the reactionaries to obey the mandates of the rank and file. But when such splits occur the militants must have so maneuvered as to keep the mass of the membership on their side. Otherwise disaster will come upon them and the labor movement. The winning combination for the rebel movement, the typical situation that the Trade Union Educational League is trying to create everywhere, is for the militants to function aggressively as a highly organized minority in the midst of the great unconscious trade union mass. The heart of the League's tactical program is that under no circumstances shall the militants allow themselves to become detached from the unionized section of the working class. "Keep the militants in the organized mass," is the slogan of the new revolutionary movement.

THE AMALGAMATED CLOTHING WORKERS

An excellent illustration of the effectiveness of the "keep the militants in the organized mass" method advocated by the Trade Union Educational League was the birth of the Amalgamated Clothing Workers of America. Characteristic of their general misinterpretation of labor history in favor of their policy, the dual unionists have cited this powerful independent union time and again as the one convincing proof of the correctness of the dual union program, and few indeed have contradicted them. All of which qualifies the Amalgamated so much the better to show the difference in principle and results between the old and the new methods of the militants.

The Amalgamated Clothing Workers was not built by dual union methods. It developed out of the work of an organized minority within the old United Garment Workers. The traditional way of dual unionism, and the very essence of its program, is for the handful of militants to devise ideal unions, set them up in competition with the old trade unions, and to engage with the latter in an open struggle for control of the industry, a process which almost always results in simply stripping the old unions of their militants and leaving those organizations in the hands of the reactionaries. But nothing like that occurred in the case of the Amalgamated Clothing Workers. The militants in the men's ready-made clothing industry had no dual union.* They accepted as their organization the United Garment Workers of America, and they planned to make it into a virile fighting union capable of playing a worthy part in the class struggle. To this end they organized themselves, in harmony with League principles, to defeat the controlling reactionaries and to make their own policies prevail.

* The needle trades generally have been unusually free from dual unionism, a fact which no doubt has had a great deal to do with the advanced types of organization prevailing in that industry.

The struggle between the progressives and the reactionaries in the United Garment Workers went on for a number of years. The rebel elements, utilizing every mistake or crime of the officialdom, gradually extended their organization and influence with the rank and file. The sell-out by Rickert in the great Chicago strike of 1910 strengthened their grip. Then came the bitter New York strike of 1913, with its record of treason by the old officials. This was the final blow. On the basis of the resultant discontent, the militants, now organized nationally through a rank and file committee (exactly the same as the League is at present setting up in the various industries), elected an overwhelming majority of delegates to the approaching 1914 convention in Nashville.

This brought the situation to a crisis. The militants had the rank and file behind them, but Rickert, in a desperate attempt to save himself, ruled out enough of their delegates to leave him in control. At this all the rebel delegates withdrew and reorganized themselves into another convention. Then they gave an eloquent proof that they were not dual unionists. Even after Rickert's outrage they refused to secede, but claimed to be the genuine United Garment Workers. It was only when the A. F. of L. convention, shortly afterward, denied this claim and recognized Rickert that they launched out as an independent union.

To call such a proceeding dual unionism is nonsense. It had absolutely nothing in common with the customary dual union policy of sucking the militants out of the old unions. The very heart of the campaign cited, and the reason why it succeeded, was that it kept the militants in the organized mass and united them there so that they could beat the old machine. The split at Nashville was a minor phase. No matter whether it took place or not, the militants had won the rank and file. Regardless of Rickert's antics, the organized men's clothing workers had definitely accepted the leadership of the men who later made their organization such a brilliant success. Instead of being an endorsement of dual unionism, the rise of the Amalgamated Clothing Workers is a striking justification of the "stay with the organized masses" policy advocated by the Trade Union Educational League.

THE TRADE UNION EDUCATIONAL LEAGUE

The new movement of militants working within the trade unions is centering around the Trade Union Educational League. The working theory of the League is the establishment of a left bloc of all the revolutionary and progressive elements in the trade unions, as against the autocratic machine of the reactionary bureaucracy. Thus, in order that these various elements of the different political persuasions can co-operate together, the policy of the organization must be essentially industrial in character. Except for condemning the fatal Gompers political policy and advocating the general proposition of independent working-class political action, the League leaves political questions to the several parties. Its work is primarily in the industrial field.

At its first national conference, held in Chicago, August 26-27, 1922, the League laid out a broad revolutionary industrial policy, upon the basis of which it is uniting the militants and carrying on its educational work in the unions.

In a statement of its program and principle issued in February, 1922, the aims of the League are stated as follows:

The Trade Union Educational League proposes to develop the trade unions from their present antiquated and stagnant condition into modern, powerful labor organizations, capable of waging successful warfare against capital. To this end it is working to revamp and remodel from top to bottom their theories, tactics, structure, and leadership. Instead of advocating the prevailing shameful and demoralizing nonsense about harmonizing the interests of capital and labor, it is firing the workers' imagination and releasing their wonderful idealism and energy by propagating the inspiring goal of the abolition of capitalism and the establishment of a workers' republic. The League aggressively favors organization by industry instead of by craft. Although the craft form of union served a useful purpose in the early days of capitalism, it is now entirely out of date. In the face of the great consolidations of the employers the workers must also close their ranks or be crushed. The multitude of craft unions must be amalgamated into a series of industrial unions—one each for the metal trades, railroad trades, clothing trades, building trades, etc.—even as they have been in other countries. The League also aims to put the workers of America in contact with the fighting trade unionists of the rest of the world. It is flatly opposed to our present pitiful policy of isolation, and it advocates affiliation to the militant international trade union movement, known as the Red International of Labor Unions. The League is campaigning against the reactionaries, incompetents, and crooks who occupy strategic positions in many of our organizations. It is striving to replace them with militants, with men and women unionists who look upon the labor movement not as a means for making an easy living, but as an instrument for the achievement of working class emancipation. In other words, the League is working in every direction necessary to put life and spirit and power into the trade union movement.

1922

9. The Movement for Amalgamation and a Labor Party

Although the T. U. E. L. made its influence deeply felt in many of the struggles of the stormy days of the early 1920's, it scored its swiftest and greatest successes in its big triple drive for amalgamation, for a Labor Party, and for recognition of Soviet Russia. It conducted a nationwide offensive with all its forces for these three issues. The whole labor movement was shaken by its campaign. Great masses of trade unionists rallied to the T. U. E. L.'s slogans. More than one-half of the trade union movement openly supported one or all its three central demands. Within a few months the T. U. E. L. had made them the main issues confronting the A. F. of L. and Railroad Brotherhoods.

The huge response to these three T. U. E. L. slogans evidenced the existing wave of radicalization among the masses. The workers saw in industrial unionism through amalgamation the road to real unity and power, the way to organize the unorganized and to stop the disastrous situation of one group of unions in an industry working while the rest were striking, which had proved so ruinous in the recent great railroad, building, printing, and other strikes, and which was the outstanding weakness of the packinghouse and steel campaigns. The workers saw in the Labor Party an effective answer, on the one hand, to the broken promises and strike-breaking troops, courts, and police of the government, and, on the other, to the fatal non-partisan political policy of the A. F. of L. leaders. And in their wide demand for the recognition of Soviet Russia, the workers expressed their natural proletarian solidarity with the new Socialist Republic. In the T. U. E. L. campaign as a whole they saw the way opening to a more honest, powerful, and effective labor movement.

The organized forces behind this big T. U. E. L. movement took the form of a broad united front of left wingers and progressives. The Communist Party and the T. U. E. L. were the driving left-wing forces, while the progressives, chiefly the Fitzpatrick-Nockels Farmer-Labor Party group, co-operated sympathetically. It was essentially a continuation and growth of the combination that had carried through the packinghouse and steel campaigns. The movement centered in Chicago and the amalgamation campaign proper took its national impetus from the adoption by the Chicago Federation of Labor on March 19, 1922, of a resolution, presented by T. U. E. L. delegates, which, after reciting the tragedy of craft disunity, concluded as follows:

Resolved, that we, the Chicago Federation of Labor, in regular meeting, call upon the American Federation of Labor to take the necessary action toward bringing about the required solidarity within the ranks of organized labor, and that, as a first start in this direction, the various international unions be called into conference for the purpose of arranging to amalgamate all the unions in the respective industries into single organizations, each of which shall cover one industry.

Reactionaries, led by Vice-President Nelson, fought against this resolution, but were voted down by 114 to 37. Then followed a big national T. U. E. L. sweep under the slogan, "Amalgamation or Annihilation." During the next eighteen months the Chicago resolution was widely endorsed and the solidarity movement expressed itself in many get-together tendencies. Sixteen international unions, including the Railway Clerks, Railway Maintenance of Way, Iron Molders, Butcher Workmen, Typographical Union, Bakery Workers, Lithographers, Brewery Workers, Amalgamated Clothing Workers, Furriers, Amalgamated Food Workers, Bookbinders, Metal Polishers, Firefighters, Textile Workers, and Shoe Workers, voted outright for amalgamation; while the Ladies Garment Workers, Railroad Trainmen, Railroad Firemen and several other internationals voted for federation or partial amalgamation. Likewise, seventeen state federations of labor, including such important bodies as those of Pennsylvania, Ohio, Indiana, Michigan, Wisconsin, Minnesota, Oregon, Nebraska, Washington, South Dakota, Utah, Colorado, etc., adopted amalgamation resolutions. Besides this, scores of central labor councils and thousands of local unions took similar action. We were well within the truth when we declared at the time that more than 2,000,000 workers, or about one-half the organized trade union movement, responded to the T. U. E. L. amalgamation slogan. From Canada, Tim Buck reported: "Amalgamation resolutions have been endorsed during the past year by almost every kind of union in every part of Canada, including the Alberta Federation of Labor and seven of the largest central labor councils, or, all told, over 50 per cent of the members affiliated to the Trades Congress of Canada."

The campaign for the Labor Party was also very effective. The Labor Party movement had sprung up spontaneously at many points in the years 1918-20, especially in Minnesota, New York, and Chicago. But the poor showing in the national elections of 1920 had paralyzed the newly formed Farmer-Labor Party, and it lingered along, more dead than alive, under the control of the Fitzpatrick-Nockels C. F. of L. group. Then, in agreement with Fitzpatrick, the Workers Party and the T. U. E. L. began to push the Labor Party issue. Result: an upsurge that was even more extensive than the amalgamation movement. Many international unions, state federations of labor, central labor councils, and local unions voted for the Labor Party. During this campaign the T. U. E. L. put out a national referendum to 35,000 local unions on the Labor Party question and received over 7,000 endorsements, and doubtless many more locals endorsed it without notifying us. The Labor Party movement culminated in the Chicago, July 3, 1923, convention.

1936

10. Organize the Unorganized

The greatest and most pressing task now confronting the working class of America is the organization of the many millions of unorganized toilers in the industries. As things now stand the unions, A. F. of L. and independents together, comprise not more than 3,500,000 members out of a total of at least 25,000,000 eligible to join. Organized Labor controls only the barest fringe of the working class, the rest are helpless in the grasp of the exploiters. The great steel, textile, automobile, meat packing, rubber, metal mining, lumber, and general manufacturing industries are either completely unorganized or possess only the weakest and most fragmentary unions. Even in those industries where labor has some strength, such as coal mining, printing, building, railroading, general transport, clothing, leather, amusements, etc., the degree of unionism in no case exceeds 50 percent, and in most instances it is far less. This is an impossible situation. The handful of organized workers cannot accomplish anything substantial with such a gigantic army of unorganized arrayed against them. The further progress of the American working class, politically as well as industrially, depends upon the organization of the vast masses of unorganized workers into the trade unions.

The present time presents an exceptionally favorable opportunity to accomplish this great and indispensable task of organization. Labor is in big demand in nearly all the industries. The workers are in a militant mood and, if approached right, will organize readily. A well-organized campaign would sweep millions of them into the unions. But the present situation is not only a golden opportunity; it is also a warning. If labor neglects this splendid chance to organize the unorganized it will pay dearly for it in the near future. Our prevailing prosperity is only a passing thing. It cannot last long. A year or two at the utmost is its limit. Then, as sure as fate, will come one of the worst periods of depression that this or any country has ever seen. All signs are pointing that way. And when the inevitable industrial breakdown comes woe betide labor if it has not had the intelligence and initiative to strengthen its lines by organizing the unorganized. The unions will be crushed. The employers, balked for the moment in their "open shop" drive by the wave of "prosperity," will renew their offensive with redoubled vigor and will not rest content until they have smashed the backbone of the trade union movement. At its peril will organized labor neglect the present opportunity to organize the unorganized.

In this critical situation what are the trade union leaders doing to solve the great problem of organization? Practically nothing. They are drifting with the stream, little reckoning of the cataract ahead. As for the general officers of the American Federation of Labor, the ones who should take the lead in this situation, they exhibit their usual somnolent, paralytic front of stupid indifference. They let slip the golden opportunity of the war time without developing a general plan of organization or even coming to realize that one was necessary, so naturally nothing may be expected from them now. They and their alleged organizers are too busy playing politics and fighting "reds." They are worrying more about disciplining the Seattle Central Labor Council for its progressive stand than they are about organizing the oppressed slaves of the Steel Trust.

In the various industries the situation is not much better. With the exception of the clothing trades unions and the independents, little is being done. The leaders quite generally share the inertia and indifference characteristic of the A. F. of L. general office. In the coal mining industry the best use John L. Lewis can find for his organizers is to send them into the organized districts to play politics against officials who refuse to do his autocratic bidding. Ignoring the fact that the miners will surely have to make a desperate fight, nationally, within the next year or two to preserve their union and the advantages they have won through years of bitter struggle, he completely neglects the urgent task of organizing the hundreds of thousands of unorganized miners in the Alabama, Colorado, West Virginia, Pennsylvania, and other districts. In the steel industry the situation is even worse. There is the Amalgamated Association of Iron, Steel, and Tin Workers, with only 8,000 members out of some 500,000 in the industry. At its head stands "Grandma" Mike Tighe. So incapable and timid that he could not keep the steel workers organized even if a 100 percent organization were presented to him on a silver platter, all he can do in the present situation is to cringe before the autocratic steel barons to assure and reassure the world that his organization is the most conservative and respectable in the United States. Not a hand does he turn to organize the unorganized. Meanwhile the twelve-hour day prevails, to the eternal disgrace of organized labor. On the railroads the same stagnation exists. Demoralized by the fatal shopmen's strike, the leaders, instead of trying militantly to recover the lost ground, are busy violating their union constitutions and employing all sorts of desperate schemes to block the movement to amalgamate all the unions into one industrial body. In the other industries similar conditions prevail. The leaders are doing nothing to organize the workers.

There must be an end put to this situation. The labor movement must be roused to a realization of its duty and opportunity in the present period of "prosperity." This means that the militants must become active everywhere. They must build fires under the reactionary leaders and insist that a great campaign of organization be started. If left to their own devices these leaders will do nothing. They are hopelessly lost in the enervating swamp of Gompersism. There is not a breath of life or progress in them. They must be shocked into action. "Organize the unorganized," should be the slogan of every militant. The question should be raised in every local union, central body, state federation, and international union. Only in this way can some headway be made. Our leaders must be compelled to organize the masses. The compulsion must come from the militants, and if it is not forthcoming, nothing will be accomplished.

To build up the unions more is necessary than simply to whip up the unorganized masses to the tune of the old slogans. This is because the army of non-union workers have lost faith in craft unionism. They can see no sense in joining organizations which have proved incapable of withstanding the "open shop" drive. The railroad shopmen, for example, will never come back to their old unions, isolated as they are, since they have seen these organizations topple like a house of cards even though they were practically 100 percent organized. They have no desire to repeat such an experience. And the same thing holds true in most of the industries. Craft unionism has lost prestige irretrievably. It can never again rally the workers. There must be a new deal all around. Something has to be done to re-awaken the workers' hope and enthusiasm, killed by craft union failures. This means that we must raise the banner of industrial unionism, to be achieved through amalgamation. We must approach the workers with a newer and more powerful form of organization. Then, with hope revived, they will come to us in masses. Seeing another chance to effectively combat their oppressors, they will rally again. And they never will rally unless the newer form of organization is offered them. "Amalgamation and an organization drive," that is the slogan that fits our present needs. The whole labor movement should proceed on that basis: on the one hand to reorganize the craft unions into industrial organizations, and on the other, to sweep the masses into the re-organized unions.

Considering the reactionary type of our trade union leadership, it seems a far-fetched and impossible proposal to change the craft unions into industrial organizations and to put on a vigorous organization drive. Yet every intelligent worker knows that this is what must be done if the problem of organizing the unorganized is to be solved. In fact, it is exactly the plan that is being followed in England. In that country the leaders are conservative enough, God knows, but they have at least enough gumption to make some pretense of meeting the situation. The General Council of the Trade Union Congress (which is roughly equivalent to the Executive Council of the A. F. of L.) is conducting a double campaign of amalgamation and organization. It is at once holding amalgamation conferences between the unions in all the important industries and it is carrying on a nation-wide "Back to the Unions" drive in all the big industrial centers. Much progress is being achieved in both directions. It is exactly this kind of movement that is needed in America, only prosecuted more vigorously. What we need and must have is, on the one hand, amalgamation, and on the other hand, a great organization drive in all the industries. When will our reactionary leaders realize this patent fact? To wake them up and to stimulate organized Labor into undertaking this indispensable double campaign of amalgamation and organization is now the greatest task confronting the militants. The organization of the unorganized is the supreme problem of our times. Upon its solution depends the welfare, if not the actual life, of the whole labor movement.

1923

PART TWO

11. The Trade Unions and the Coolidge Prosperity Period

The era of the Coolidge "good times," which, including the few months of Hoover, lasted with but short breaks from the middle of 1923 until the October crash in 1929, was a period of difficult struggle and relative isolation from the masses for the T. U. E. L. It was a time of the least working class militancy and struggle in the history of the American labor movement and of the worst corruption and autocratic rule ever practiced by the reactionary trade union leadership. Naturally, the T. U. E. L. felt sharply the effects of all the prosperity illusions, expulsions, terrorism, etc., in loss of mass contacts and mass movements.

The basic cause of this great sag in labor struggle was the big upswing of American imperialism during this period. American capitalism made huge advances, economically and in international influence, the United States becoming the world's strongest imperialist power. Various factors combined to produce its great industrial development and, hence, its increased political power. Among them were the capital export of 20 billion dollar war and post-war loans, which enormously stimulated American production and exports; the capture of world markets from the crippled European powers; the introduction of a tremendous speed-up or "rationalization" of industry; the growth of the vast installment buying system; the industrialization and mechanization of agriculture; the expansion of the automobile and various luxury industries; the industrialization of the South, etc. Altogether it was an orgy of profit-making for the American employers who became the objects of envy and admiration throughout the world capitalist class.

During this period the government was starkly reactionary. Its general spirit was exemplified by the huge growth of armaments and military propaganda, the repeated armed invasions of Caribbean and Central American countries, the systematic enslavement of Germany through the Dawes and Young plans, violent hostility towards the Soviet Union, and by such developments as hostile labor legislation, execution of Sacco and Vanzetti, continued imprisonment of Mooney and Billings, unchecked campaign of lynching in the South, the Teapot Dome scandal,* the Scopes anti-evolution trial,† etc.

THE RATIONALIZATION OF INDUSTRY

In this era of wild profit-making and reaction, now looked back to by American capitalists as the Golden Age, the central aim of the employers was further to increase their swollen profits by the most intense speed-up of the workers. They vastly improved industrial technique, and to lure the workers into their speed-up trap they developed a whole series of tricky institutions, such as new fangled bonus and piecework plans, elaborate "welfare" systems, pseudo old-age pensions, employee stockbuying, etc.‡

All this was accomplished by oceans of slick propaganda, through every publicity channel of capitalism, to convince the workers that their interest resided in co-operating with the employers to increase production for minimum costs. This poison gas campaign took on wonderful aspects. The magic formula of "mass production and high wages" was alleged to bring not only better living standards now, for the workers, but also their final emancipation from capitalism. A whole school of bourgeois economists developed this speed-up propaganda into a system which I at the time called "capitalist efficiency socialism."§ For example, Thomas Nixon Carver argued that the workers with their high wages were gradually buying

* The fraudulent transfer of Federal oil lands during the Harding administration in 1922 in which several cabinet members were implicated.

† The trial of a school-teacher in Dayton, Tennessee for teaching the theory of evolution in which William J. Bryan acted as prosecutor.

‡ While the company unions fitted into this general scheme, they were somewhat in abeyance during this period. They had been organized as a bar to the spread of trade unionism in the war period, and as the strength of the trade unions declined after the big defeat of 1919-22, so also did the company unions stagnate. It was only upon the new trade union upsurge in 1933 that the company unions took on a fresh lease of life.

§ *The Communist,* March 1928.

up control of industry, Gillette glibly stated that this was leading to a co-operative commonwealth, Stuart Chase portrayed the social wonders to be achieved by rationalizing capitalist industry, Foster and Catchings outlined their miraculous theory of "financing the buyer," etc. Everything was lovely and the goose hung high. In short, American capitalism had cured its inner contradictions. No more industrial crises nor mass unemployment. Ford had superseded Marx. And the capitalists all over the world marveled at this wonder, lauded the American "new" capitalism and sought to introduce it in their own countries.

In reality, however, the great volume of the new wealth created in these years by the rationalization of industry poured into the laps of the insatiable capitalists. The workers got very little of it. From 1923 to 1929, output in industry increased no less than 29 per cent per worker,* and profits doubled and tripled, but average real wages advanced, according to reliable figures, not more than 4½ percent.† Also most of this increase went only to the organized skilled workers, especially through overtime, steady work, etc., and their standards rose considerably. There was widespread in this period what Marx called the "bourgeoisification" of the labor aristocracy. The unskilled masses, if not materially much better off, were also considerably bourgeoisified ideologically from the current intense rationalization propaganda. It was a time of the most extensive capitalist prosperity illusions ever known among the toiling masses.

Without delay, the A. F. of L. leadership fitted themselves into this entire capitalist speed-up, rationalization program. In fact, they turned the unions into mere instruments of the capitalists' production plans. On the altar of production for less costs they sacrificed hard-won union conditions, and they peddled away every illusion put forth by the rationalization wind-jammers, besides inventing many of their own. Cheaper production became their fetish and the only way to working-class well being.

This whole development the T. U. E. L. dubbed "the new orientation of the trade union bureaucracy towards intensified class collaboration" and "the company unionization of the trade unions." It was the traditional A. F. of L. class collaboration policy elaborated, theorized, and revamped to meet the latest needs of the employers.

---

* National Bureau of Economic Research.

† Paul H. Douglas, *Real Wages in the United States,* 1930.

The trade unions were reorganized on a basis of Fordism. The movement began at the very outset of the Coolidge prosperity period.

1936

12. Business Unionism

In many, if not most industries, employers sought to achieve their program by the traditional method of destroying all unionism among their workers. But in many important cases their tendency was to develop a maze of class collaboration arrangements which concentrated themselves around company unionism in the shops and employee stock-ownership schemes in the realms of finance. It is these new tendencies which we must examine here.

COMPANY UNIONISM

About 1913, many American employers, under the lead of the Rockefeller interests, departing from the traditional 100 per cent "open shop" policy of no organizations among their workers, began to establish company unions. Their program was to break the trade unions and to build company unions. Since then, especially during the war period, the company union movement has spread rapidly. Under a maze of forms (a recent survey showed 214 types among the existing 814 company unions) it has been established in many key and basic industries; including steel, railroad, textile, oil, lumber, packing, electrical, etc. It encompasses over a million workers, largely in such great plants as the Bethlehem Steel Co., Pacific (Textile) Mills, Pennsylvania Railroad, Westinghouse Electric Co., Elgin Watch Co., International Harvester Co., Western Union Telegraph Co., Eastman Kodak Co., etc. A list of the firms having company unions contains many of the greatest capitalist concerns in America.

In connection with the company union movement, either as direct parts of it or as related institutions, these employers usually have a whole array of welfare plans and programs, covering group insurance, old age pensions, sick benefits, housing schemes, education, sports, etc.

A prime purpose of the company union movement, with its welfare attachments, is to speed up the workers. Recently a production engineer said that the great industrial efficiency expert, Taylor, had failed to understand that it was necessary not only to develop the technical methods of efficiency in production but also to secure the workers' co-operation in their application. The company unions are designed to secure such co-operation, and undoubtedly in some instances they partially achieve this purpose. Their proceedings are saturated with propaganda and actions calculated to speed up the workers.

EMPLOYEE STOCK OWNERSHIP

A twin brother to company unionism, making for the weakening of the workers' opposition, ideologically and organizationally, to capitalist exploitation, is the many-phased movement of the employers to assemble and control what moneys the workers are able to save out of their meager wages. These worker savings they concentrate in bank deposits, life insurance, etc., but the most significant aspect of the movement is their stimulation of the workers to purchase stock in various industrial enterprises. Within recent years this stock-buying movement, under forced draught from the various corporations, has been widely extended.

Reformistic defenders of capitalism pounce upon this and declare that the workers are becoming capitalists and are buying control of the industries. At the head of these enthusiasts stands Thomas Nixon Carver, Professor of Political Economy at Harvard, with his recent book, *The Present Economic Revolution in the United States*. A few quotations from this work illustrate the lavish way these economists ascribe billions of dollars and far-reaching industrial control to the workers:

The only economic revolution now under way is going on in the United States. It is a revolution that is to wipe out the distinction between laborers and capitalists by making laborers their own capitalists and by compelling the capitalists to become laborers of one kind or another (p. 9).

There are at least three kinds of evidence that indicate roughly the extent to which laborers are becoming capitalists: first, the rapid growth of savings deposits; second, the investment by laborers in the shares of corporations; third, the growth of labor banks (p. 11).

The saving power of American working-men is so great that, if they would save and carefully invest their savings, *in ten years they would be one of the dominating financial powers of the world* (p. 118).

Carver's utopia glitters, but it is only dross. It cannot and will not work. The workers are not buying the industries, nor are they becoming capitalists. For one thing, a very large percentage of those listed as "employees" in Carver's calculations are company officials, who notoriously invest their savings in stocks of the concerns for which they work. Thus, if the U. S. Steel reports 47,647 stockholders out of about 250,000 employees it is safe to assume that the overwhelming mass of them are company officials, "white collar" elements, and the upper layers of skilled workers. The masses of workers are little touched by the movement, despite twenty years of active stock selling by the corporation. The same remarks apply to many other firms.

Boosters of employee stockholding grossly exaggerate both the number of such stockholders and the extent of their ownings. Thus W. Jett Lauck says: "Altogether the holdings of 6,500,000 employee stockholders amount to only $500,000,000, showing labor has made an absolute but not relative gain in corporate ownership."* This number of employee stockholders is ridiculously exaggerated. The total number of all stockholders in the United States, discounting duplications, according to U. S. figures, is 2,358,000 and of these hardly more than 500,000 can be classified as employees. But if Lauck were correct it would represent a holding of only about $75 apiece, which does not seem a very capitalistic figure. The Federal Trade Commission report on National Wealth and Income, based on 1922 figures, shows that only 75 out of 1,000 stockholders are employees, and that these own the even smaller percentage of only 15 shares out of each 1,000. Of the total stockholders, 53½ per cent receive only 4 per cent of all dividends paid. And Professor Carver's own figures, in the case of many big corporations, indicate clearly that the big stockowners are increasing their holdings at a manifold more rapid ratio than are the employee stockholders. Nevertheless, the illusions growing out of such propaganda as Carver's are dangerous.

Undoubtedly many sections of American skilled workers have been corrupted and "bourgeoisified" and some isolated sections of the unskilled and semi-skilled (Ford plants, Philadelphia Rapid Transit, etc.) have been somewhat affected by American imperialism through

* W. Jett Lauck: *Political and Industrial Democracy,* p. 109.

high wages and other concessions, but the lesser skilled do not share this "prosperity." They are living from hand to mouth. The mass of the workers cannot buy actual control of or even heavy interests in corporation stocks. Not even if they are forced to buy such stocks.* The workers have not got the money. Their wages are too low. In *Current History*, March, 1927, Mina Weisenberg says, "In 1923 and 1924 the real wages of unskilled workers were only 20 per cent higher than the 1913 average which was then considered insufficient for a decent living standard." U. S. Department of Labor statistics show that average wages for male adult workers in the United States do not exceed $30 per week. To speak of workers so underpaid finding a solution of their economic problems by buying the industries with their savings is ridiculous.

And what about periods of industrial depression when unemployed workers are forced to draw upon their scanty reserves? Mr. Carver blithely assumes that the present "prosperity" will continue, or even increase. This is a fallacy. Inevitably the United States, despite its present economic strength, will be undermined by the contradictions inherent in world capitalism, and plunged into recurring deeper industrial crises. At present capitalism in all important industrial countries, in order to extricate itself from its deep difficulties, is making frenzied efforts to speed up production, by the wholesale introduction of machinery and new processes and by driving the workers still faster. This is the so-called rationalization of industry movement. Its effects are enormously to increase production. In the United States since 1919 the output per worker in industry has increased 40 per cent. In 1925, with 385,000 less workers than in 1923 (who worked for 270 millions less in wages), one billion dollars more was added to the value of manufactured goods. The rationalization movement leads inevitably to a sharpening of class antagonisms at home and to an intensified struggle for the world market. Mass unemployment is an inseparable result of it. Germany with its intense rationalization of industry illustrates this strikingly. There wages are at a minimum, the working day has been lengthened to 9, 10, 12 hours, and chronic mass unemployment prevails. The United States, because of its favorable position, escapes for the moment the full harmful effects of the movement. But certain it is that in the near future far-reaching in-

* In many New England shoe factories the employers are compelling the workers to purchase shares in the companies or lose their jobs. This is the so-called "Golden Rule Plan."

dustrial crises and unemployment on a gigantic scale will confront the American working class. Then, not only will stock buying cease, but the workers who have stocks will tend to get rid of them. They will then be gobbled up for a song by the big capitalists. Significant is the fact that during the crisis of 1921-22 the percentage of U. S. Steel employees holding stock fell from 42 per cent to 16 per cent.* Undoubtedly the next industrial crisis will knock the bottom out of the employee stock ownership movement.

The workers, with such stock purchases as they are making, are not buying their way into control of the industries, despite the isolated instances of the Philadelphia Rapid Transit Co., where the "employees" own about one-third of the common stock; and the A. Nash Co. of Cincinnati, where they actually own a majority. Big capital, which is rapidly concentrating and organizing itself, is not weakened by the extension of petty capitalist holdings. In his book, *Imperialism, The Highest Stage of Capitalism,* Lenin, in dealing with the power of big capital to dominate petty capital, says:

The "democratization" of the ownership of shares, from which the bourgeois sophists and opportunist "would-be" Social-Democrats expect . . . the "democratization of capital," the strengthening of the role and significance of small-scale production, etc., is, in fact, one of the ways of increasing the power of financial oligarchy (p. 49).

The big capitalists are finding ways and means to control the capital being assembled by the employee ownership movement and to turn it to their own advantage. W. Jett Lauck says, "The extent of employee ownership of stock has increased but the degree of control exercised by employees is very small." Various barriers are raised by the capitalists against employees exercising any degree of control through such stock as they may purchase. They often confine stock sales to trusted ranks of employees, as for example the Bell Telephone Co., which sells stock to only 5 per cent of its employees. In many cases the amounts of stock per employee are also limited, as with the Consolidated Gas Co. of New York, which does not permit its employees to secure more than 20 shares each of $50 value. Corporations often control blocks of employee-owned stock through their officials, who are also "employees." The discharge power also rests in their hands with which to terrorize refractory worker stockholders, if necessary. The vast funds in the insurance and building loan associations, whose billions Mr. Carver would have the workers invest in

* M. Weisenberg: *Current History,* March, 1927.

stocks in their own behalf "any day they see fit," are of course safely in the hands of the capitalist bankers.

Carverism, supported by a widespread propaganda in the capitalist press, undoubtedly cultivates dangerous illusions among the workers even though the masses can buy no stocks. These illusions must be vigorously combated. The whole movement works out to the benefit of the capitalists by, on the one hand, giving them greater financial control and, on the other, by tending to confuse the workers and to weaken their organizations and struggles.

In the early stages of the company union and employee stock ownership movements the trade union leaders, despite their general tendencies towards class collaboration in all its forms, gave considerable opposition to these movements. They denounced company unionism vociferously and, to some extent, actually fought against it. Even as late as October, 1925, William Green, patterning after a previously published article in the September, 1925, *Workers Monthly,* organ of the Workers (Communist) Party, demanded that the workers capture the company unions and make them points of departure for movements to start real unions. This piece of copying *The Nation* dubbed "taking a leaf out of the book" of the left wing. The union leaders also, on many occasions, sharply condemned the practice of the workers buying stocks in capitalist industry. They still placed some reliance in the strike and the power of the unions as such.

But following the loss of the 1922 strike of the railroad shopmen, a radical change set in among the union leaders. Their new orientation, manifested by new and intensified forms of class collaboration, constitutes in reality a great surrender of the workers' interests by an acceptance of the employers' general programs of company unionism and employee stock ownership. This acceptance takes the forms principally (in addition to its more political aspects which will be discussed later) of the "company-unionization" of the trade unions and the establishment of trade union capitalism.

COMPANY-UNIONIZING THE TRADE UNIONS

In pressing for a docile working class, speeded in production to the limit, and controlled by the employers' agents, the capitalists are proceeding along two general routes, both leading to the same goal. They are not only organizing company unions directly out of the unorganized masses, but they are also systematically degenerating the trade unions in the direction of company unionism (when they do not smash them altogether). In this latter course they have the assistance of the reactionary labor bureaucracy.

Undoubtedly the employers are proceeding consciously to the company unionization of the trade unions. Many capitalist apologists are actually proposing the organizational as well as the functional consolidation of company unions and trade unions. In his recent book, *Political and Industrial Democracy,* W. Jett Lauck, bourgeois economist, says:

> It cannot be denied that shop committees and more extensive systems of employee representation are of fundamental importance, but they should be co-ordinated with regular unions. Not only industrial democracy and the co-operative spirit in industry will be thus better realized, but the greatest measure of efficiency and productiveness in industry attained.
>
> Co-operative relations between employers and employees can never be realized permanently by shop committees or systems of employee representation unless the labor union is adopted as the fundamental basis of procedure (pp. 82-84).

As we shall see, the trade union leaders have already proceeded far towards the functional amalgamation of company unionism, under the stimulus of the employers. Nor will they hesitate before a possible organizational amalgamation, unless checked by rank and file resistance. The Boot and Shoe Workers Union, now only a shade better than a company union, shows how far the leaders will go towards company unionism unless blocked by the workers' resistance.

THE BALTIMORE AND OHIO PLAN

Speed-up and no strikes—that is the demand of the employers upon their workers in this era of American world imperialism. That is the road to company unionization. The railroad union leaders, convinced after the loss of the 1922 shopmen's strike that they could not make even formal resistance to the powerful companies, were the first to surrender completely to this demand. They adopted as their working principle "co-operation" with the employers in production. They elaborated the B. and O. Plan. It was worked out by Otto S. Beyer, an efficiency engineer, and sponsored by William H. Johnston, former President of the International Association of Machinists. Johnson says of it:

The idea underlying our service to the Baltimore and Ohio railroad may be compared to the idea which underlies the engineering services extended to railroads by large corporations to furnish, let us say, arch brick, superheaters, stokers, or lubricating oils. The union members furnish their services to the best advantage of all. In response to the recognition accorded the union and by virtue of the agreement existing between the management and us it becomes peculiarly feasible for us to take steps between management and men and create as it were an all-pervading collective will for the major purposes of railroading, namely, efficient service to the public, a fair return to the investors, and adequate wages and steady employment for the workers. The legitimate, standard, genuine unions of the railroad shop mechanics are more than eager to offer the same positive cooperation to any railroad management which is intelligent enough and courageous enough to see the inevitable logic of events. I maintain that such a management would never again desire to see the affiliated shop unions effaced from its railroad.

The B. and O. plan involves abandoning all struggle against the employers. Says F. J. Cullum, a union official on the Canadian National Railways:

It is absolutely essential that there should be complete harmony among the members of the committee (B. and O. plan). There should be at no time a feeling that they belong to different groups, neither that one shall seek an advantage over the other.*

Railroad workers are already intensely exploited. Says Leland Olds in a recent Federated Press article:

According to W. H. Dunlap in the monthly review of the U. S. Dept. of Labor, the productive output of railroad labor in the United States has increased about 40% since 1915 and about 150% since 1890. . . . The increased productivity of railroad labor since 1920 is reflected in a drop of about 275,000, or 13½% in the number of workers employed.

The B. and O. Plan facilitates this increasing exploitation. The employers quite generally greeted it. After its adoption by the Baltimore and Ohio railroad it was installed upon the Chesapeake and Ohio, Chicago, Milwaukee and St. Paul, Chicago and Northwestern, Canadian National Railways, etc. It has also been introduced into various metal trades contract shops.

Under the B. and O. Plan the union officials help the employers to drive the workers. Recently on the Canadian National Railways at

* *American Federationist*, February, 1927.

Winnipeg, they presented the company, to be laid off, a list of men, some with from 12 to 17 years service, because they did not "co-operate" with the company.

The B. and O. plan has proved profitable for the employers. In 45 shops of the B. and O. R. R., according to a recent report, 18,000 efficiency suggestions were made by the men, of which 15,000 were accepted. Dividends of the B. and O. company amounted to 17 per cent for 1926, or almost double as much as in 1924. "Co-operation" of the workers with the employers in speeding up production was a big factor in producing these high dividends. No wonder that Willard, president of the road, glowingly endorsed the B. and O. plan in a recent speech before the National Civic Federation.*

As for the workers, they have had their pains for their trouble. They receive less for their work, by from four to six cents per hour, than the shop workers employed on the non-union Pennsylvania Railroad.

The ruinous effects of this intensive class collaboration policy of the railroad trade union leadership is exemplified by the Watson-Parker Law, lately adopted by Congress for the purpose of regulating wages and working conditions on the railroads. This law, undoubtedly the most vicious piece of anti-labor legislation enacted for many years, proceeds far towards the company unionization of the railroad unions. It emanated from the big railroad companies, the notorious union-crusher Atterbury of the Pennsylvania being its outstanding advocate. But it was enacted into law with the full support of the railroad union officialdom and the higher bureaucracy of the A. F. of L.

The Watson-Parker Law crystallizes the employers' program for hamstringing the railroad unions. It incorporates, with official labor's endorsement, many anti-labor features long bitterly resisted by the trade union movement. It virtually illegalizes strikes on the railroads and establishes compulsory arbitration. It opens the door wide to the development of company unions. It gives the reactionary Federal Courts the right to interfere in and regulate wage disputes between the railroad workers and the railroad companies. It cements the alliance, disastrous for the workers, between the companies and the union leadership, an alliance based on the surrender of the workers' interests. The Watson-Parker law registers the lowest point reached by American trade unions in their degeneration, brought about by joint

* This organization, now defunct, was a public propaganda body, an alliance between the big corporations and reactionary labor leaders.

action of the employers and reactionary union leaders, towards company unionism.

THE NEW WAGE POLICY

The interests of the imperialistic employers demand the most intense possible exploitation of the workers. The reactionary union leaders, chastened by the general defeat of the trade unions in the years 1919-23, and in their true role as "agents of the bourgeoisie in the ranks of the workers," yield to this demand and make haste to help the employers drive the workers at ever greater speed. Traces of this eventual development, now definitely crystallized under the name of "the new wage policy," were already to be found in the Portland convention in 1923. The 1924 convention of the A. F. of L. in El Paso specifically endorsed the B. and O. plan, and the 1925 convention in Atlantic City elaborated its underlying principle of "co-operation" with the employers to increase production into the fundamental policy of the official labor movement. The essence of the new wage policy, as stated by the A. F. of L. in 1925 is as follows:

We hold that the best interests of wage earners as well as the whole social group are served, by increasing production in quality as well as quantity, and by high wage standards which assure sustained purchasing power to the workers, and therefore, higher national standards for the environment in which they live and the means to enjoy cultured opportunities. We declare that wage reductions produce industrial and social unrest and that low wages are not conducive to low production costs. We urge upon wage earners everywhere: that we oppose all wage reductions and that we urge upon management the elimination of wastes in production in order that selling prices may be lower and wages higher.

Social inequality, industrial instability, and injustice must increase unless the workers' real wages, the purchasing power of their wages, coupled with a continuing reduction in the number of hours making up the workingday, are progressed in proportion to man's increasing power of production.

Some hailed this last paragraph as a radical advance for the A. F. of L. In reality, considering the lackey-like official practices under the new wage policy, it is no more than a platonic argument in favor of higher wages in return for more production.

The Atlantic City convention, as a means of putting its new wage policy into effect, proposed:

. . . a conference of organized labor, organized farmers, and trade associations under the direction of Secretary Hoover of the Dept. of Commerce. The purpose of the conference is to consider the elimination of difficulties preventing the constructive organization of industry.

In the furtherance of this policy the entire trade union leadership is carrying on an intensive propaganda. The union journals reek with class collaboration "co-operation." That hand maiden of the bureaucracy, the Workers Education Bureau, also does its share. The two outstanding champions are Green and Woll. They offer, in all keys and tones, unstinted "co-operation of the workers to intensify production, provided the employers will stop their union-smashing campaigns and permit the existence of degenerate unions. They especially claim that the employers can gain more in production through trade unions than through company unions. Their plan, in brief, is to scab the company unions out of existence.

Trade unions are increasingly basing their agreements on the "union-management co-operation" principles. In the anthracite coal regions, for example, this "co-operation" is being vigorously practiced. The employers are rapidly mechanizing the industry and are introducing the speed-up under various forms. In this they have the full support of the union officials. The conditions of the workers are sacrificed ruthlessly. Wide discontent prevails. But when this manifests itself openly the workers are told by both company and union officials that it is all necessary in the good cause of efficiency and "co-operation."

The "socialist" trade union leaders are fully in harmony with this entire company-unionization movement. In fact they and the progressives were pioneers in outlining many features of it. They developed the B. and O. Plan, and various phases of trade union capitalism. The extreme right wing has adopted it from them. Sydney Hillman, president of the Amalgamated Clothing Workers, contributed to the development of this ultra-class collaboration.

In the other needle trades the "socialist" leaders follow the same general policy. The great fight now raging between "rights" and "lefts" in the garment industry centers about the general company-unionization tendency, with the "rights" yielding to it and the "lefts" stoutly resisting it. For example, the recent cloakmakers' strike in New York turned around the demand of the employers for the right to " organize" their shops. That is, the employers wanted to secure the right arbitrarily to discharge yearly 10 percent of their employees. In this demand there is contained the whole company-unionizing tendency. Its effects would inevitably be to speed up the workers, to weaken their militancy, and to undermine the union generally. The "rights" proposed to concede this demand; the "lefts" categorically rejected it. Hence the bitter strike, with the "lefts" supported by the masses, on one side, and the "rights," backed by the employers, the press, the police, and the whole A. F. of L. bureaucracy, on the other. With the help of their "labor" allies, the employers won the right of re-organization.

The events in the needle industry epitomize the general struggle throughout the labor movement between the forces making for progress and those making for company-unionization. The difference is that the needle workers are more advanced and better able to voice their opposition than workers in other industries. Besides their industry is in a deep crisis. Everywhere the union leaders, co-operating with the employers, are driving the workers faster in production, weakening their organization, and generally laying the basis for eventual broad class upheavals.

TRADE UNION CAPITALISM

Through the B. and O. Plan and similar schemes the union leaders are adopting the company unionization program of the employers, and through trade union capitalism (labor banking, investment corporations, trade union insurance companies, etc.) they are accepting the whole program of employee stock ownership and "the workers becoming capitalists" theory behind it.

Listen to the voice of Professor Carver coming from the mouths of labor leaders. The August, 1925, *Brotherhood of Locomotive Engineers Journal* says:

Labor banking is the only revolution in the world worth a peck of beans. Its colossal possibilities become apparent when one considers that the total wage bill of the country is approximately one half of the 50 billion dollars financial resources of our 31,000 banks, and that the farmers' annual crops equal in value about two-thirds of the remainder. Once let a majority of the workers and farmers of America learn to concentrate their savings and their credit power in their own banks, and they can control the resources of the world's richest nation within one generation.

Says W. B. Prenter, then head of the B. of L. E.:

We set out with only one theory. That is the theory that in America there is no such thing as a working class as distinguished from a capitalist class. Men pass too readily from one group into the other to be tagged with class labels. . . . It is the Brotherhood's aim in its financial enterprises to show its members and workers generally how they can become capitalists as well as workers.*

In such poisononus propaganda lies the real danger for the workers. This tendency is most clearly expressed by the B. of L. E. officials, the outstanding and outspoken leaders of the trade union capitalism movement. Thus for example, in combination with the National City Bank, subsidiary of the largest bank in America, they bought $3,500,000 worth of bonds of the International Great Northern R. R. and sold them to their members. Said W. S. Stone of this deal, one of scores like it:

Ownership of a bond makes a man a creditor. We sold many of the Great Northern bonds to men employed on that railroad. Immediately each became concerned with the first concern of a creditor for his debtor—the debtor's solvency. Bonds bring a sense of responsibility and of security.

The labor banks, labor investment corporations, and trade union insurance companies, amassing large funds, must invest them. They do so by buying regular capitalist securities. This prepares the way for all the illusions cultivated by Carver and such capitalist propagandists that the workers can buy the industries. It also tends to paralyze the struggle of stock-owning workers against the employers by creating the false notion among the workers that because they have a thin scattering of company stocks, they have interests in common with their employers. It poisons the labor movement with graft.

The devastatingly destructive efforts of trade union capitalism upon the labor movement were amply demonstrated by the recent collapse of the B. of L. E. financial enterprises, which has given the trade union capitalism movement a staggering, if not mortal blow.

LABOR BANKING

Among American workers, especially the favored skilled trades, there are considerable numbers who, despite the average national weekly wage of only $30 for all categories of workers, manage to set aside certain amounts as savings from their wages. To some extent these savings are the equivalent of the state unemployment, old age,

*Saturday Evening Post, November 6, 1926.

sickness, and other insurance plans to be found in various European countries. Estimates vary as to how large is the aggregate of these savings annually. Guesses as to their amount range from several hundred million to several billions. Thus, Mr. Peter Brady, President of the Federation (labor) Bank of New York, makes the following fantastic and manifestly grossly exaggerated estimate in his speech to the British Labor Congress:

Each year $25,000,000,000 is paid in wages to our industrial workers and from $6,000,000,000 to $7,000,000,000 is saved in various ways. It is this huge sum which labor banks hope eventually to control.

The employers awoke first to the existence of considerable amounts of worker savings, and they organized strings of small savings banks, stock-selling schemes, etc., to get control of them for their own use. Now the trade union bureaucracy has learned of these funds and is proceeding to assemble them. This is the basis of trade union capitalism, expressed by labor banks, investment corporations, life insurance companies, etc. The foundation of the whole structure is labor banking.

At present there are 36 labor banks in operation. Their resources aggregate well on to $150,000,000. Pioneers in this movement were the Trade Union Savings and Loan Bank of Seattle (1918) and the Mount Vernon Bank established by the Machinists in Washington in 1920. The labor banks are organized by single national unions or by groups of local unions of various trades. The railroad unions are the leaders in this movement. The B. of L. E. owns twelve banks with total resources of over $50,000,000. The Federation Bank of New York has resources of about $12,000,000. Important links in the labor banking chain are the banks of the Amalgamated Clothing Workers and International Ladies Garment Workers Union in the needle trades.

The labor banks, although widely advertising themselves as "co-operative" in character, are manifestly not genuine co-operatives. Even those that have fallen entirely into the hands of the capitalists still call themselves "co-operatives." Control of the regular labor banks' stock is in the hands of the reactionary bureaucrats at the head of the unions. The same rule applies to all the modern trade union capitalistic institutions. Thus, for example, 51 per cent of the stock of the $10,000,000 B. of L. E. Investment Co. is held "by the union," which means by the already deeply intrenched reactionary upper leadership, while the rest is sold to the general membership and the public. These leaders, without check by the rank and file, use the bank funds to finance all sorts of capitalistic concerns, which they personally fatten upon. They are trade union capitalists. With the huge funds at their disposal they are building up a monstrous bureaucracy by debauching democracy in the unions, and are growing wealthy.

LABOR INVESTMENT CONCERNS

The labor bureaucrats, basing their activities upon the funds and general facilities of the labor banks, are organizing investment companies. These are all controlled by little cliques of leaders at the top of the unions, who engage in the wildest speculations. There are eleven of such investment corporations, with an aggregate paid-in capital of $34,000,000, besides a large number of separate enterprises, including office buildings, apartment houses, coal mines, etc. There are two general types of such institutions, (a) those organized privately by little groups of high union officials, (such as the Hobart-Stone $250,000 mail order house in Cleveland), and (b) those established by these officials in the name of their unions, (such as the Brotherhood Holding Co. of the B. of L. E.). The latter is the favorite form. It puts the full prestige of the unions behind the capitalistic enterprises and it does not lay too many obstructions in the way of the trade union leaders milking these concerns for their own benefit.

The Seattle labor movement during the war period took the initiative in this labor investment movement. Listman, Ault, and other local labor leaders organized a series of fly-by-night capitalistic concerns, such as "United Finance," "The Listman Service," "Class 'A' Theaters," "Padilla Bay Reclamation Co.," "Deep Sea Salvage Co.," "Consumers Co-operative," etc. They were of the privately controlled type and sold blocks of stock to the unions. All failed, entailing losses to the workers estimated at from $1,000,000 to $2,500,000.

The labor investment movement got well under way after 1922. It grew side by side with labor banking and the B. and O. Plan. As usual in trade union capitalism generally, the B. of L. E. is the most active union also in this phase. It controls 10 investment corporations with a combined capital of $27,000,000. It owns two great office buildings in Cleveland, and for a time held a controlling interest in the $40,000,000 Equitable Building in New York, long famous as the largest office building in the world and located in the heart of the

Wall Street financial district. It has heavy investments in banks, railroads, and various industries. Labor banks and investment companies put their money into all kinds of ventures, from building apartments to financing foreign loans.

TRADE UNION LIFE INSURANCE

An important form of trade union capitalism is trade union life insurance companies. Employees' group insurance stimulated this movement. The Portland (1923) and El Paso (1924) conventions of the A. F. of L. gave the first big impetus to this movement. Accordingly a meeting of representatives of fifty international unions was held in the offices of the A. F. of L. in July, 1925. The conference unanimously endorsed the plan of the unions going into the life insurance business.

Out of this conference was born the Union Labor Life Insurance Co., capitalized at $600,000. Matthew Woll is its head. It is dominated by a clique of ultra-right wing reactionaries, who hold the majority of stock firmly in their control. A few socialists and progressives are drawn to the leading committees in an effort to give the organization a mass appeal. There are a couple more of such companies already in the field: the John Mitchell and the Union Co-operative Insurance companies, the former specializing in insurance for miners and the latter for electrical workers. The railroad leaders proposed in 1925 to launch the American Endowment Corporation, to be headed by nine prominent railroad union leaders. These, with a strangle hold on the company control, were to receive half of the profits. Apparently this scheme has collapsed.

In organizing the trade union life insurance companies the bureaucrats are dreaming of billions of dollars of petty investors of which they hope to secure control.

There are other great insurance companies totaling additional billions. In a word, the plan of the bureaucrats is to compete with them and to cut into their rich field of operations.

Trade union life insurance, like other forms of trade union capitalism, works injuriously upon the labor organizations. It diverts their attention from the struggle and into capitalist enterprises. It poisons the organizations with an anti-working class ideology, and subordinates them organizationally to capitalist institutions. It corrupts the leaders, enriches them, and makes them less and less responsive to rank and file interests and control. It is a menace to the labor movement.

"THE HIGHER STRATEGY OF LABOR"

The class collaboration policies of the bureaucracy in the new orientation, the new American reformism, which is based upon co-operating with the employers to increase production and upon trade union capitalism, and which is a cessation of struggle against the capitalists, Professor Carver classifies as "the Higher Strategy of Labor." Apparently, according to him, the "lower strategy of labor" was when the labor leaders made at least some pretense at the defense of the workers' interests. The so-called higher strategy of labor was thus indicated by Warren S. Stone in the *World's Work,* November, 1924:

Organized labor in the United States has gone through three cycles (some of the unions are still in the second). The first was the period during which class consciousness was being aroused. . . . The second was the defensive struggle for the principle of collective bargaining. This was and is a period of warfare. . . . The third cycle or phase lies in constructive development towards a system of cooperation rather than war, and the most striking evidence of this phase is the labor bank.

The speeches of Green, Woll and other prominent reactionary union leaders, which are re-echoed throughout the entire trade union press, are saturated with these same ideas: that the crude, primitive, warlike days of labor are past and gone; that henceforth the workers will progress through "co-operation" with the employers and by saving their money. At Harvard University Green recently said:

The trade union movement has been passing through that period when physical controversies and the tactics of force were most effective; it is now in a period when its leaders must seek the conference room and there, by exposition and demonstration, convince conferees of the justice and wisdom of its position.

Before the Taylor Society in New York he said:

Labor realizes that the success of management means the success of labor. For that reason labor is willing to make its contribution to assist management and to bring about the right solution of problems dealt with by management. . . . The workers believe that through understanding and cooperation the best interests of all those associated with industry can be served.

In the *New York Evening Post,* January 3, 1927, he said:

Through our trade unions we are helping the workers in industry to become investors, to carry insurance, to assume a responsible part in industry and community life.

That is, teaching them to give up the fight, to accept the leadership and direction of the capitalists and to be content with whatever few crumbs the latter may deign to throw them from their over-loaded tables.

Matthew Woll, chief spokesman of big capital in the trade unions, accepts Carver's term "the Higher Strategy of Labor" and thus defines it in a recent number of *Iron Age:*

In its early struggles labor sought to retard, to limit, to embarrass production to obtain that which it desired. Now it seeks the confidence that it is a preserver and developer of an economic, industrial and social order in which workers, employers and the public may all benefit.

The so-called higher strategy of labor plays into the hands of the employers at every point. It is an invaluable aid for their speed up program. Already the workers are speeded to an impossible rate, and the pace grows faster. Thus, in 1926 the productive output of railroad labor per man was 40 per cent greater than in 1915, and 150 per cent more than in 1890.

In 1925 all production records of industry as a whole were broken, there being 6 per cent more production than in 1923, yet the number of actual workers was less by 4½ per cent than in 1923, and 7 per cent less than in 1919. Figures for 1926 will show similar tremendous speeding up.

The bureaucrats, with their theory of higher wages being possible only by increasing production, and their program of "co-operation" with the employers, are entirely in step with the latter's plans to exploit the workers to the limit.

In 1926 the capitalists reaped enormous, and in many cases, unprecedented profits. The railroads, typical of many industries, gained a larger net income, $1,232,000,000, than ever before in their history. Except in the cases of skilled workers, in some industries, wages have not advanced materially. The leaders, with their anemic policy, have made no struggle to improve conditions. Often wage cuts have been suffered, as in textiles, shoes, etc. Even as I write this the United Mine Workers, undermined and demoralized by the reactionary Lewis machine, are in a life and death fight against a cut in wages in the bituminous fields. Never did the workers receive a smaller portion of what they actually produce, and their share grows steadily less. In 1849 workers received 51 per cent of the value added to raw materials during the process of manufacture. In 1889 this had declined to 45 per cent, and in 1923 to 41 per cent. The "higher strategy of labor," with its policy of speed up and no struggle, will help sink this percentage still lower. The weak efforts of the leaders for the shorter work day and work week, affect only the skilled trades, and by no means offset the tremendous increases in efficiency of the workers, the chief advantage of which goes to the employers.

The new orientation of the trade union leaders towards intensified class collaboration, Mr. Carver's "higher strategy of labor," devitalizes the unions. Nothing is being done to organize the millions of unorganized, nor to consolidate the ranks of the antiquated craft unions. False illusions about the benefits of the capitalist system are instilled into the minds of the workers. Trade union capitalism brings the unions into poisonous contacts with the employers and still further corrupts the leaders. Nothing is done to break with the capitalist parties and to found a real party of labor. With a stagnant or declining membership in the strategic industries, the unions are not holding their own as against the employers. They are a diminishing factor in the life of the working class.

More and more the bureaucrats' tendency is to cast aside the strike as a weapon against the employers. Steadily the number of strikes diminish. In 1926 there were fewer strikes than in any year since the war time. The motto of the trade union leaders is "not strikes against the employers but co-operation with (surrender to) them."

In the days when the unions still possessed some militancy the conditions of organized workers always stood forth clearly as being far better than those of unorganized workers. But now in many cases union workers are employed under conditions little if any better than those of non-union workers. This is a deadly situation. The militant employers, with their Ford systems, Mitten plans, welfare work, voluntary wage increases, etc., are claiming on all sides, with a maze of statistics, that in many instances they have established as good or better conditions in their industries than exist in industries controlled by the unions.

The truth is, not that the "soulless" corporations are improving the conditions of the masses, but that the unions, with their corrupt and reactionary leadership, and their hopelessly antiquated policies, are failing to make an effective fight, either for the masses at large or their own membership.

Present day intensified class collaboration stifles the fighting spirit of the unions and saps their vitality. A widespread lassitude and indifference among the workers towards the unions is one of the most pronounced and significant characteristics of the present situation in the labor movement. In the recent survey by the Pennsylvania Federation of Labor to find out what is the matter with the unions, 22 of 26 officials replying stated that the general state of indifference now existing among the membership is greater than ever before.

Apologists for the bureaucracy have attempted to explain away this deadly indifference, this serious lowering of the organized workers' morale, by ascribing it to widespread prosperity among the workers, which they say makes a militant ideology and fighting policy impossible; to the popularization of motion pictures, the radio, and the automobile, which occupy the workers so that they do not attend meetings of their unions; to the growth of welfare systems in the industries, which tend to take away the fraternal features of the unions, etc., etc.

But such reasons are vain. The real cause is the declining role of the unions, under the new orientation, as fighting organizations. The leaders do nothing to stir the militant spirit and class enthusiasm of the workers. They fail to lead the unions in defense of the workers' interests; they resist every effort to develop the unions into organizations capable of coping with modern capitalism, they rigidly suppress all union democracy and poison the very class soul of the unions with capitalist economics. The widespread indifference of the workers towards the unions is an inevitable result of the prevailing intense class collaboration policies of the union officialdom.

Even before the development of the new orientation, beginning about 1922, the unions suffered from the class collaborationism of the leadership. But now the situation is worse. The bureaucrats are compromising the unions on all fronts, ideological and organizational. They are not successfully defending the workers' interests now, nor are they educating and organizing the workers for the great class struggles which must come at the end of the present period of industrial activity. On the contrary, the top leaders are striving to degenerate the trade unions into company unions, with the help of and under the pressure from the employers.

The great masses of workers, both organized and unorganized, live in hardship. They lack many of the real essentials of life, while on all sides they see the employers and their parasitic hangers-on rolling in wealth. They want better conditions and they display many indications that they are willing to fight for them. But to a very large extent their efforts to build real labor organizations and to wage aggressive struggles against the employers are defeated by the reactionary leaders, who play the game of the bosses. The liquidation of such chloroforming arrangements as the so-called "higher strategy of labor," the elaboration of a militant program of struggle, the modernizing of the trade unions organizationally and otherwise, the development of an honest and aggressive leadership;—are vital and inevitable steps in overcoming the present slump in the labor movement. They are essential to give expression to the workers' discontent and desire for struggle and in the development of a fighting organization representative of the workers' interests and capable of defending their interests.

1927

13. Wrecking the Labor Banks

The first crack in the illusory structure of "business unionism" came in 1927 with the collapse of the railroad labor banks.

The question of establishing a labor bank was first proposed to the B. of L. E. at its convention in 1912, but it was voted down. In the 1915 convention, however, the delegates voted to set up a bank to handle the union's growing funds. But the war situation prevented definite action until 1920, when the Brotherhood of Locomotive Engineers Co-operative National Bank was opened in Cleveland. Its popularity was instantaneous. A "miraculous flow of gold came in from every side." Within a couple of years its resources totaled $27,000,000.

Their appetites whetted by this golden success, the B. of L. E. officials, under the thumb of the tsar-like Warren S. Stone, launched headlong into a program of frenzied financiering such as has seldom been seen in this country. Declaring that it was as easy to operate a bank as to run a peanut stand, Grand Chief Engineer Stone proceeded to establish labor banks all over the country. All that was necessary was money to float them, then riches would come. The engineers scraped together their savings and, trusting their officials implicitly, poured their money into the various financial schemes one after the other.

In addition to the publicly listed institutions and investments, the B. of L. E. has or has had many other companies and interests which have more or less remained unknown publicly. For example, there was the investment in the Empire Trust Co. of New York, a $90,000,000 corporation. Stockbridge says that "It was not much less than a half interest." Besides, there were many side issues, where the officials plunged into various companies on their own account, drawing the membership after them, a case in point being the $10,000,000 Radio Corporation of which Stone was president.

All told, banks, investment corporations, real estate projects, industrial companies, etc., the financial enterprises of the B. of L. E. amounted to the imposing total of $100,000,000.

For a time everything went lovely. Fulsome praise was poured out upon Stone and his associates for their "wonderful" financial achievements. They were the idols of every labor bureaucrat who itched to get his hands on the workers' slim savings. The capitalists welcomed the whole development, which they were quick to see worked entirely against militant unionism. Stockbridge, in his enthusiastic article in the ultra-scab *Saturday Evening Post,* said: "Capital simply cannot afford to let the Brotherhood fail; it would be too serious a setback to the growing amity between capital and labor."

Wall Street opened its doors to Stone. Praise for him filled the capitalist press. He was the herald of a new day of no strikes and a docile working class. Stone declared that a new era had dawned for the labor movement. He divided labor history into three epochs. The first was the beginning of class consciousness and organization; the second was a general struggle for the right of collective bargaining, and the third, now beginning, is to be an era of co-operation with, rather than war against, the employers. Of the new development the most striking manifestation is the labor bank. This theory of Stone's, seized upon by Matthew Woll and other reactionary leaders, has been developed by them into the so-called "higher strategy of labor," the

theory that it is not necessary to struggle against the employers, but
to co-operate with (that is, surrender to) them.

In the midst of an atmosphere of wild promises of wealth and
power the B. of L. E. financial institutions developed. Stone became
absolute dictator. He reorganized the union on the basis of the new
conceptions. He made himself president at $25,000 a year, with almost
as much more in expenses. The financial side of the union became
dominant. The protective department, the section dealing with wages
and working conditions, was relegated to a minor phase of the union's
make-up and activities. The Grand Chief Engineer at the head of it
was reduced to fourth ranking officer.

The rank and file of the union for the most part were hypnotized
by Stone's "successes" and his sophistries. They believed his promises
of riches to be won in industry, in finance, in real estate. They gathered
together their hard-earned dollars and poured them unquestioningly
into his various enterprises one after another as they were launched.
So great was their confidence, for example, that only one circular
letter to the membership sufficed to sell the $1,000,000 capital stock of
the Brotherhood Holding Co. The other companies were similarly
accepted and financed. A deaf ear was turned to the more conscious,
more clear-sighted elements in the union who warned against these
developments. For the most part their warnings were scoffed at as the
complaints of incurable radicals altogether out of touch with the realities of life. The union lived in a golden dream.

The greatest financial disaster of the B. of L. E. was its vast land
speculation at Venice, Florida, on the Gulf Coast below Tampa. In
May, 1925, a month before he died, Stone informed the union leaders
that the union faced a deficit estimated at $6,000,000 in its failing
business enterprises. To recoup, the union leaders recklessly decided
to plunge into the wild orgy of speculation in Florida, which was then
at its height. . . .

The plan was a gamble and a quick get-away with a few millions
of easy Florida money developed into the proposition of building
Venice into a great new winter resort. Eventually 50,000 acres of land
were purchased. For the promotion of this scheme the B. of L. E.
Realty Co., capitalized at $1,000,000, was organized. Then a flood of
money was poured into it, from insurance and pension funds, from
the banks and investment companies, from the sale of stock to the
membership. All the tricks of the sky-blue real estate sharks were
used to inveigle the workers into this financial morass. Visions of wav-

ing palm trees, tropical breezes, golden strands, marvelous climate, incomparable fishing, hunting, and other features of a heaven on earth were spread before their eyes. "Come to Venice, the resort supreme on Florida's West Coast. There ten acres and independence await you," screamed the gaudy, multi-colored circulars with which the union members were deluged. All told, according to the Committee of Ten report, $16,000,000 was invested in Florida.

The building of Venice went ahead in an unparalleled maze of speculation, extravagance, and graft, when suddenly the bottom fell out of the entire Florida land boom. Real estate values fell to a half or a third of their former figures. The B. of L. E. was left holding the sack. The Florida scheme, in which hundreds of engineers had invested their last dollar, utterly collapsed. The very life of the union was threatened.*

A RUDE AWAKENING

The golden dream was now quite at an end. The disillusionment came during the B. of L. E. convention held in Cleveland from June 6 to July 21, 1927. The delegates got the shock of their lives. They suddenly discovered their union to be plunged into one of the greatest financial failures in American history. The vast network of banks and investment companies, which they had thought to be such a glowing success, turned out to be nothing but a ghastly ruin, the whole thing tottering on the brink of bankruptcy, with sheriffs knocking on the door and lawsuits menacing from all sides. Their trusted and "brilliant" leaders they found out to be charlatans and grafters when not incredibly stupid and incompetent. They learned that not only were their banks and other financial concerns broke, but also that the union funds were gutted, and that they, personally, could be held liable for millions of dollars squandered in the incredible financial debauch. They confronted a desperate situation threatening the very life of their organization. It was indeed a rude awakening.

Faced by this crisis, the deepest in the sixty-four years' history of the B. of L. E., the delegates practically turned the convention over to a receivership, the Committee of Ten with an attorney, Judge Newcomb, at its head, to find a way out of the shambles. Then for six and a half weeks, the longest convention ever held by the B. of

* This section on the Florida land scheme is taken from the author's book, *Misleaders of Labor*.

L. E., and at a cost of about $1,000,000, they struggled to rid themselves of the herd of financial white elephants thrust upon them by their leaders and to find a way to save their organization.

The loss from the many wrecked institutions runs into millions. No very definite totals were developed. The Committee of Ten submitted no general balance sheet. After studying the financial maze for several weeks Delegate Van Pelt of the Committee of Ten said (p. 1888),* "Does anybody know what we owe? Does the Committee of Ten know? Not by a damned sight." Some approximation of the loss can be made, however, from the emergency measures adopted by the convention to meet pressing obligations. First, the convention plastered a $4,000,000 mortgage on the two Cleveland office buildings; then it put on a $7,200,000 assessment on the membership. After all this, chairman Myers of the Committee of Ten said (p. 2061): "I want to say that at the end of two years the committee will be badly mistaken if we don't find ourselves with an indebtedness of approximately $8,000,000 hanging over us."

Thus the loss would be at least $19,000,000. And this does not take into account millions lost by members in buying stock for which the B. of L. E. cannot be made directly responsible. Delegate Merriman (p. 2015) even suggested a total loss of $30,000,000, and no one rose to contradict him. That the losses are huge, possibly as much as $20,000,000, was further indicated by the proposals of Mitten (to be dealt with later) which required that the B. of L. E. raise $25,000,000 to cover its bad investments. How hard the erstwhile rich union is hit was indicated by a statement of Delegate Huff, a Financial Trustee (p. 1983), "On July 19th we owed $300,000 to the Corn Exchange Bank in New York and we didn't have a thin dime to pay it with."

Business institutions wrecked, union finances gutted, officials discredited, themselves tricked and robbed, the union itself menaced—it was not a beautiful picture for the delegates. Judge Newcomb rubbed more salt into their wounds when he pointed out that the individual union members were responsible for all the bankrupt institutions in which the Brotherhood held a majority of the stock or where it had guaranteed the investments and loans.

One thing the delegates learned—that they have had a sufficiency of trade union capitalism. All voiced that sentiment. It would have taken a brave "labor-banker" to face that disillusioned and enraged body of engineers and spin to them the fairy tales, formerly gospel

* Page number in printed convention proceedings.

in the organization, about labor becoming capital and the workers winning a competence by investing in labor banks and similar concerns. Even the most reactionary of the leaders had to yield to the spirit of disgust towards labor financiering that animated the rank and file. Delegate McGuire of the Committee of Ten sounded the keynote when he said (p. 2002):

I have been giving all my time for several weeks to studying this problem and it has resolved itself into three or four words, and they are: "Get out of it, and the quicker you get out of it, why the better off you will be."

The leaders who managed to save their skins in the house cleaning which took place all came forth, for convention purposes at least, as strong opponents of trade union capitalism and its works. They tried to get a fresh hold upon the rank and file by capitalizing the indignation and resentment in the latter's hearts. Thus, Assistant Grand Chief Engineer Edrington, himself all involved in the financial disasters, put into voice the determination of the body of delegates when he said (p. 2132):

I hope to see the day come when we can forget about investment companies, holding companies, realty companies . . . and get back to the old Brotherhood as a labor organization.

THE HARMFUL EFFECTS

Labor banks and similar institutions divert the attention of the unions away from their proper functions as organs of direct struggle against the employers and turn their activities into enervating and corrupting capitalist business channels. The real tasks of building the unions and defending the workers' interests are forgotten. Thus Grand Chief Johnston said correctly (p. 2133) "Ninety per cent of our time has been spent discussing the financial activities and no time has been given to the Brotherhood." Such neglect saps the unions at their very foundations.

The misdirecting of the unions into capitalistic business draws them inevitably, or rather their leaders, into the most demoralizing alliances with the employers. The B. of L. E. banks and investment projects are tied up with all sorts of labor-crushing capitalists. Inevitably the union leadership thus falls under the control of these enemies of the workers and does their bidding. Thus we see such shameful spectacles as Warren Stone endorsing, in 1924, the great multi-millionaire labor exploiter, Coleman du Pont, as a "friend" of labor in the Delaware senatorial elections. Thus we see the union leaders cheek by jowl with the great Wall St. capitalists, as in the Equitable deal. And so long as the union engages in capitalistic business, just that long the employers will control the various banks. Significant was it that at the B. of L. E. convention the choice presented was whether to turn the banks, etc., (and with them a large share of union control) over to the Mitten capitalists or to the Newcomb capitalists.

Trade union capitalism inevitably cultivates among the workers demoralizing illusions that the workers, by thrift and the investment of their funds in capitalistic stock, can actually buy control of the industries. This is a rank fallacy. The great masses of workers, with the exception of some categories of favored skilled workers who can lay aside a few dollars of savings in this period of "prosperity," live at the poverty line. The average weekly wage of adult male workers is only $29. What can the workers save on such wages? What little money the workers are able to set aside is largely the equivalent of the unemployment, old age, and sick benefits the European workers receive from their governments. American workers are very much unprotected by social insurance. They are compelled, as individuals, to make provision for old age, sickness, and unemployment. The theory that workers can become capitalists is a delusion and a snare for the workers. It prevents the workers from building militant labor organizations, industrial and political.

Not only the locomotive engineers, but all of organized labor should learn from the bitter experiences of the B. of L. E. trade union capitalism, its institutions and its false theories which are widespread in the labor movement. And they tend in the same general direction as in the B. of L. E. towards the spreading of class collaboration illusions, the further corruption of the leaders through speculating, graft, destructive alliances with the capitalists, and to the general weakening of the labor movement. Although not so dramatically evident as in the case of the B. of L. E., similar disintegrating tendencies are at work in the labor banks, investment corporations and trade union life insurance companies of other unions (see for example the collapse, through "frozen assets," of the Philadelphia and Pittsburgh labor banks). The situation is so dangerous that even the ultra-reactionary A. F. of L. Executive Council has had to issue a sharp note of warning against it. In the report to the 1927 convention of the A. F. of L. in Los Angeles, the Executive Council said:

> Experience in this field has now sufficiently cumulated to make a solemn warning imperative. Great care and sound judgment should be exercised before labor unions and members of labor unions put their money into labor bank promotions, or into investment companies. . . . Since the recent development in the B. of L. E. financial activities, more and more attention is being directed to the manner in which labor banks are financed and conducted. . . . In our judgment the time has come to stop expansion in the field of labor banking until experience with those labor banks already organized shall have been critically studied and evaluated.

This cautious statement admits the deep crisis in the trade union capitalism movement. But it does not indicate the remedy. The way out is not for the unions to try the hopeless task of seeing to it that their banks and investment companies are honestly and efficiently run. The evil goes much deeper. The whole system is wrong, in theory and practice. The theory of labor becoming capital is false, and the practice of the unions to build labor banks and investment companies is wrong.

The unions must cut loose from the labor banks and their destructive influences and be redeveloped as fighting organizations. Not the gathering together of the workers' dimes by the trade union capitalist institutions and the cultivation of illusions that the workers can buy their way out of wage slavery, but the building up of the workers' organizations, by organizing the unorganized, by amalgamation, by democratization, by adopting a militant policy of struggle, by launching a labor party—that is what the labor movement needs. The B. of L. E. financial debacle dealt a heavy blow at trade union capitalism. If considerable portions of the workers can get even an inkling of the lessons of this important event, the harsh experiences of the B. of L. E. will not have been in vain.

At the time the champions of "business unionism" were peddling their disastrous illusions to the workers, the T. U. E. L. was pointing to such real tasks of the labor movements as organizing the unorganized.

1927

14. Corruption and Autocratic Control in the Unions

The "new orientation" is accompanied by more traditional forms of betrayal. In the industries the reactionary trade union leaders sacrifice and compromise the workers' interests retail and wholesale in innumerable ways. They confine the unions chiefly to skilled workers, in many cases refusing to recognize the unskilled workers, and trading off their interests for the sake of the skilled. Often they transform the unions into job trusts, charging extravagant initiation fees, and barring from membership, with one device or another, many workers of their own trades. All too frequently they actually sell out strikes for cash. They discriminate against Negroes, women, and the youth in the industries and in the unions. Often they also first drive the workers into outlaw strikes and dual unions by neglecting their interests, and then, with the aid of the employers and the state, ruthlessly smash such movements. They wipe out all semblances of democracy in the unions. For fear of losing their jobs they refuse to amalgamate the weak craft organizations into industrial unions. To further the interests of their respective craft unions at the expense of other workers they engage in deadly and stupid jurisdictional wars. They often go over to the bosses' organizations after they lose their official union positions and use the knowledge, skill, and prestige that they gained in the ranks of the workers against the unions. All of which policies, neglect, and treachery constitute, in plain English, flagrant and far-reaching betrayal of the workers.

An especially disastrous form of working class betrayal is union scabbery, that is, where the leaders keep one or more unions in an industry at work while others strike. This degrading practice of union scabbery, which is more prevalent in the United States than in any other country, has lost the workers hundreds of strikes and has spread incalculable demoralization in their ranks. In numberless cases where, for example, the machinists struck, the union boilermakers stayed at work, where the carpenters went out the organized bricklayers remained at the job, where the longshoremen tried to tie up the docks the union sailors manned the ships loaded by scabs, where the printers struck the pressmen stayed at work, and where the railroad firemen declared a strike the engineers stuck at work and helped the employers break it, and vice versa, in practically all the industries. And, of course, there is also endless scabbing between the industries—the railroad workers haul coal produced by scab miners, the miners produce coal for scab railroads, scab steel mills, etc. The trade union leaders have done nothing to check this shameful system of mutual betrayal by the unions. On the contrary, their system of leadership being based upon it, they have clung to it and bitterly resisted every effort of the rank and file to force a consolidation of the labor organizations and to develop a real solidarity of labor.

And, finally, there is the utter and shameful betrayal exemplified by the labor detective, the undercover man of the employers. Mulhall exposed many of these degraded creatures who are often degenerate trade union officials. Sydney Howard and Robert W. Dunn, in their book, *The Labor Spy,* show how the whole contemptible system works and paint graphic pictures of many of these sorry heroes. The corrupt practices which flourish unchecked in the unions contribute largely to producing these labor spies, who, well placed and influential, infest the trade unions in astonishing numbers. When a trade union official takes money from a capitalist politician for misleading the workers in election times, or when he accepts a bribe from an employer for calling off a strike, and great numbers have done and are doing both, he is on a toboggan of corruption which may easily carry him to the very lowest depths of treachery to the working class, even to actually spying.

TRADE UNIONS AND GRAFT

Towards all this corruption and graft the general policy of the leaders in the trade unions has been to pass it over in silence. The false argument is made that if it is exposed it will injure the labor movement. This idea is carefully propagated by the reactionary officialdom, and large numbers of the rank and file are deceived by it. As for the grafters themselves, they interpret this policy of silence as giving them a free hand to carry on their destructive activities.

Rarely has the labor bureaucracy itself taken the initiative in exposing the corrupt leaders. Usually this is done by the left wing.

Sometimes even the employers expose them. After they have been exposed the unions sometimes expel them. Otherwise the whole practice of grafting on the workers and employers is tolerated and condoned. The disease of corruption goes on untreated. A search of the *History, Encyclopedia, and Reference Book of A. F. of L.,* brings forth on page 161 the following lone action taken on the question of bribery by the A. F. of L.:

Bribe-taking—(1903, p. 202) An isolated case of bribe-taking does not warrant the conclusion that dishonesty on the part of the officers of organized labor prevails. On the contrary, we are convinced that the representatives of organized labor are by far the most reliable, honest, and trustworthy of any walk of life.

The reason for this failure to attack the grafters is plain. The right-wing machine in the A. F. of L. bases itself, and has for a generation, upon the most corrupt and reactionary elements in the labor movement. One-third of the entire membership of the A. F. of L. belong to the building trades unions, where corruption is at its worst. Their delegations at A. F. of L conventions are solidly reactionary. Their leaders, in combination with the bourbon heads of the printing trades and the miners unions, form the body of the reactionary A. F. of L. bureaucracy.

Gompers always protected the grafters. He himself apparently did not take money from the employers, nor did he accept their many offers of political positions. He got his reward for his treason to the workers by being maintained as president of the A. F. of L., where he basked in friendly publicity and lived as a wealthy man. All the worst labor fakers gave him their active support. For years it was axiomatic that the more of a labor faker the more of a Gompersite. "Skinny" Madden, Sam Parks, Simon O'Donnell, Frank Feeney, Robert Brindell, Matthew Woll, George L. Berry, *et al,* were Gompers' bosom friends and co-workers. On their kind his rule was based.

Whenever and wherever building trades fakers were exposed Gompers never failed to defend them to the last. Likewise in other industries. In the 1920 convention of the A. F. of L., Mahon, head of the Street Carmen's Union, was accused correctly by the Detroit Federation of Labor of running an "open shop" sheet metal works in Detroit. But the charges were smothered and Mahon was whitewashed. Characteristically, Gompers, in his book, *Seventy Years of Life and Labor,* thus defends the traitorous conduct of the steel workers' leaders, Jarrett, Bishop, Weihe, Nutt, and others, in going over to the employers, saying:

It was not that they were corrupted, but they were weaned away; the organization paid them very meager salaries, less indeed than that of a first-class man in the industry. (Vol. I, p. 340.)

Is graft diminishing in the building trades? This is a difficult question. Some factors appear to make against it in its old forms. The employers, becoming constantly more trustified, have less and less need of the trade union leaders' co-operation for the maintenance of hard and fast local monopolies of labor and material which exclude outside competition. And it is upon such illegitimate co-operation that the typical building trades graft system is largely based. Moreover, the growing strength of the employers, and the breaking down of the skilled trades through specialization tend to weaken the position of the building trades unions and to make it somewhat more difficult for the venal officials to carry on their traditional policy of wholesale plunder.

But, whether increasing or decreasing, the building trades graft is practiced on a wide scale and it poisons and demoralizes the whole labor movement.

BOURGEOIS LABOR LEADERS

There is a strong tendency, universal in capitalist countries, for the trade union leadership to develop certain group interests of its own antagonistic to those of the workers. The leaders tend sharply, by their manner of living and by their general outlook, to become to all intents and purposes a section of the lower middle class.

The labor official of today, with his private fortune, fancy automobiles, aristocratic apartments, and extensive business interests, is a very different type from the men who laid the basis of our trade union movement. Debs thus describes the pioneer trade unionist:

The labor agitator of the early day held no office, had no title, drew no salary, saw no footlights, heard no applause, never saw his name in print, and fills an unknown grave. The labor movement is his monument, and though his name is not inscribed upon it, his soul is in it, and with it marches on forever.*

Mother Jones, champion of the workers, makes this comparison:

* *Eugene V. Debs: His Life, Writings, and Speeches,* p. 125, 1908.

Many of our modern leaders of labor have wandered far from the thorny path of these early crusaders. Never in the early days of the labor struggle would you find leaders dining and wining with the aristocracy; nor did their wives strut about like diamond-bedecked peacocks; nor were they attended by humiliated, cringing servants. The wives of those early leaders took in washing to make ends meet. Their children picked and sold berries. The women shared the heroism, the privation of their husbands. In those days labor's representatives did not sit on velvet chairs in conference with labor's oppressors; they did not dine in fashionable hotels with the representatives of the top capitalists, such as the Civic Federation. They did not ride in Pullmans nor make trips to Europe.

The rank and file have let their servants become their masters and dictators. The workers have now to fight not alone their exploiters but likewise their own leaders, who often betray them, sell them out, who put their own advancement ahead of that of the working masses.*

In 1887 Parsons, Spies, Engel and Fischer, breathing the spirit of the pioneer American labor movement, went bravely to the gallows. They were of the type described above so eloquently by Debs. Their fighting spirit and self-sacrificing devotion still live in the left wing. But the official labor leaders now know it no more, except to hate it and to crush it. The modern top trade union leaders are pampered servants of capitalism, well-paid betrayers of the working class. Their aims and ideals have been divorced from those of the rank and file; their prime purpose is to advance their own interests regardless of those of the workers. That is why, as William E. Trautmann once said, "They have made America the land of lost strikes."

This conservative trade union leadership, seeking first of all to protect its fat sinecures, has distinct group, if not class, interests in conflict with those of the workers. The rank and file want the amalgamation of their unions because it would strengthen them for struggle against the employers; the officials oppose it because it would, by upsetting the present balances of power and by possibly cutting the number of jobs, knock some of them out of their well-paid positions. Likewise these misleaders of labor oppose the formation of a labor party because it would compel the severance of their present illicit alliances with the capitalist parties and force them into the hard task of building up a mass party of labor. They reject a policy of militant struggle against the employers because all their group interests lead them to develop friendly relations and collaboration with the exploiters

* *Autobiography of Mother Jones,* p. 40, 1925.

of the workers. Between the interests of the mass of American organized labor and those of their leaders a vast chasm yawns.

Naturally the well-paid trade union leaders exert every effort to retain their positions, against the strivings of other hungry office seekers and in the face of rank and file revolts. Michels, in his *Political Parties,* explains in great detail the many devices used by Social-Democratic bureaucrats to maintain themselves in office during the days before the World War: making themselves technically apparently indispensable, transforming temporary positions into permanent ones, playing themselves up in the organization press and playing down their opponents, exploiting the loyalty of the masses for men who have long served as their officials, making concessions to rival leaders and broadening the bureaucratic base to accommodate them, manipulating the finances in various petty ways, developing a rigid centralism, overstepping the mandates of the rank and file, and generally playing upon the weaknesses inherent in every democratic mass organization of workers.

But American trade union leaders use not only most of the tricks that Michels touches upon but many more of which he never dreamed. To hang on to their jobs they appeal to the gun and knife, they make open alliances with the employers and the state against the workers, and they ruthlessly suppress democracy in the organizations. Many of their methods are more akin to those of fascism than to legitimate labor unionism. And more and more such methods are also being applied in other countries.

With the developing of the new American reformism, that is, the orientation of the labor bureaucrats towards intensified class collaboration, their methods of hanging on to control of the union become more drastic and desperate. As the leaders drift to the right and enter more and more into "co-operation" with the employers inevitably they more flagrantly sacrifice and betray the interests of the rank and file. Consequently widespread discontent develops in the many unions, especially in those containing masses of semi-skilled and unskilled. The membership begins to listen to the voice of the left wing. Therefore, the bureaucrats, in order to avoid disaster to themselves through rank and file revolts, must crush by force the left wing, which leads these revolts, and which they cannot defeat in free debate before the workers. To fight back the growing discontent no means are too drastic for them to use; none are impermissible, even to actually destroying the unions. The bureaucrats sharpen up and use with added vigor all the traditional means of autocratic control, and they invent new ones.

SUPPRESSION OF UNION DEMOCRACY

To control the unions the reactionaries have built up many powerful bureaucratic machines. These are constructed upon various lines. The A. F. of L. itself is ruled by a well-knit clique, the foundations of which were laid by Gompers. The great power of Gompers and his extended control were due in very large part to the policy he followed of closely protecting the craft autonomy and reactionary practices of the international unions affiliated to the A. F. of L. He was an inveterate enemy of all tendencies to centralize power in the hands of the A. F. of L. proper. He jealously guarded the "rights" of the bureaucrats of the respective unions, except where he helped some powerful union to put pressure on a small one. Thus they came to look upon him and to organize around him as a "safe" man, as one who would not permit the central mechanism of the labor movement to infringe upon them. His policy was centralization of the individual international unions and decentralization of the A. F. of L. itself. He grew strong personally by keeping the A. F. of L. weak and unprogressive. He was a king enormously popular among his nobles because he allowed them to do as they pleased in their respective domains.

In the various International Unions there exist many established cliques, formed for the purpose of offsetting democratic checks and for controlling the official positions. Usually these groups, without formal names or organization, are simple understandings of the bureaucrats to stick together. They use the union funds freely to advance their clique interests. Occasionally these groups take on definite form. The "Wahnetas" of the Typographical Union are perhaps the best example. This reactionary group, with scores of nuclei throughout the country, was organized to control the Printers' Union, and it succeeded well until the opposition built the still better organized "Progressive Party."

Often cliques build themselves around fraternal orders, such as the Masons, Elks, etc. The Catholic Church also has its organized following in many unions, especially among the higher ups. The responsiveness of the A. F. of L. to the Catholic Church program is one of the reasons why Catholic unions were never built in this country. Formerly the Socialist Party had many groupings in the unions. But now, when its grip on the unions is restricted to the needle trades, the Daily *Forward* machinery is the basis of its organization. The recently formed "Committee for the Preservation of the Trade Unions" was an attempt of the Socialist Party to rebuild its groups throughout the labor movement. In view of the many groups and cliques of the reactionaries, which universally finance themselves with the unions' money, it comes with poor grace from them to make their present big outcry at the formation of rank and file groups by the left wing.

To maintain themselves in office and to defeat rank and file control, the corrupt bureaucrats systematically seek to destroy the convention as a democratic instrument in the unions. Many are their devices, and as the bureaucracy drifts to the right and rank and file revolts become more intense, these devices grow bolder and more fascist-like.

The A. F. of L. convention is the classical illustration of a labor gathering in which the rank and file have no say. The delegation is made up almost entirely of upper bureaucrats. For example, the United Mine Workers (U. M. W. A.), representing some 300,000 workers, has eight delegates. These usually consist of the president, vice-president, secretary, and five district presidents of the organization. The rank and file are completely shut out. The same system prevails in almost all of the other international unions. The only place a worker gets a look in at the A. F. of L. convention is as a stray delegate from a federal labor union or petty central labor council. Such a convention, completely in the hands of the corrupt bureaucracy, is a fortress of reaction.

In the international unions various schemes of disproportionate representation are used to disfranchise the majority of the membership. For example, at the recent convention of the I. L. G. W. U., the Sigman machine held a majority of delegates although the opposition represented two-thirds of the entire union membership. Thus, at this convention the right wing per capita tax proposal for 15 cents carried by a vote of 146 delegates representing 15,832 actual members against 114 delegates representing 34,762 actual members. Approximately this same vote prevailed throughout. It was manifestly a minority-ruled convention. Sigman formerly controlled the New York Joint Board, the heart of the union, by a similar jugglery. The "lefts" controlled four big locals with a membership of 36,000, for which they had 20 delegates; whereas the "rights," who controlled a number of smaller locals totaling only 20,000, had 38 delegates. After the bitter Joint Action Committee fight in 1925, which defeated Sigman, partial proportional representation was introduced in the Joint Board. The "lefts" secured a majority. Similar "democracy" prevails in the other socialist needle unions.

The reactionaries at the head of the Amalgamated Association of Iron, Steel, and Tin Workers control that organization by means of a lot of nondescript delegates from little locals all over the country, many of them merely on paper. The usual thing at its conventions is for the progressives, coming from the larger locals and representing a majority of the membership, to find themselves very much in a minority. George L. Berry, like the heads of many other unions, uses this same system of basing his control upon the small town locals. When the convention assembles, Berry, in the orthodox manner of Hutcheson and others, makes his control doubly sure by appointing all the convention committees. In fact, he appoints many of the delegates as well.

Not content even with such means of control, the bureaucrats in many unions seek systematically to have fewer and fewer conventions. The Hod Carriers have had only two conventions since that union was organized in 1903. Formerly the Carpenters held conventions annually, now they hold them every four years. Almost every international has its conventions at greater intervals than formerly. A favorite method to eliminate conventions is to make them so costly, by paying the big delegations extravagant per diem expenses, that the union, with its regular funds, cannot afford them. Then when the rank and file vote on the holding of a convention they also have to vote an assessment on themselves to finance it. So they usually vote "no convention." The cost of the Railroad Brotherhoods' conventions runs up as high as $1,000,000. The officials take care also to see that the conventions degenerate into pleasure junkets, with constant rounds of entertainments, so that there will be little thought of constructive work by the delegates. Thus many an opposition movement has been defeated.

The conventions of the United Mine Workers are tragic examples of the suppression of union democracy. Lewis' task always is to build up a convention majority from a union membership which is from 60 per cent to 75 per cent against him. To do this he packs the conventions shamelessly. He brings in the "payroll" vote, at least 300 delegates, from far and wide. Then he rigs up delegates from hundreds of "blue sky" locals. At the 1927 convention he had 166 delegates from West Virginia, where the union had only 337 actual members. Delegations from other districts were similarly packed. Opposition delegates, especially the capable speakers, were ruthlessly ruled out. Speakers were terrorized by professional gunmen. If in spite of such precautions a majority does vote against Lewis in a convention he brazenly ignores it. At the 1924 convention he did this four times.

When it comes to stealing elections Tammany Hall politicians are no more brazen than the trade union bureaucrats. Every conceivable form of fraud is practiced. Many a reactionary leader has thus "saved his bacon" from an aroused rank and file.

In the recent national election in the Carpenters Union, Hutcheson canceled many votes to build up a majority against Brown and Rosen. The recent Machinists' national election was also marked by gross frauds. And the only way Jensen could elect himself head of the Chicago Carpenters District Council in the recent election was by arbitrarily throwing out the vote of one local union. The opposition had no appeal except either to the reactionary Hutcheson or to the capitalist courts, both equally hopeless. "Umbrella" Mike Boyle varies such methods by falsifying the voting machines borrowed from the city by the union. In the 1924 elections in the Bookbinders Union the official figures gave Reddick the election over Haggerty by 5,575 against 5,117. It was later proved in court, however, that Reddick had stolen enough votes in Local 25 of New York alone, not to mention others, to swing the election. Reddick is a crony of Berry's. One practice of reactionaries is to evade inconvenient elections altogether by having themselves elected for life. "Skinny" Madden started this. William Near of the Chicago Milk Wagon Drivers and many other reactionaries are continuing it by electing themselves heads of their unions in perpetuity.

In the unions of highly skilled workers the reactionaries "get by" easier in elections and do not usually need to use the grossest frauds. It is especially in the organization of semi-skilled and unskilled that such methods are found at their worst. The Miners Union is the horrible example. Thus during the 1926 elections in Kansas, Howat, who had 90 per cent of the miners behind him, was simply removed from the ballot by Lewis and votes cast for him were not counted. Farrington was brazen in Illinois. He stole votes right and left. At one local union meeting, backed up by his strong-arm men, he boldly declared:

I do not give a damn whether you vote for me or not. As long as I carry a card in the Miners' Union I'll be President of District 12.

In the 1926 election in District 5, Pittsburgh, the opposition candidate, Siders, was clearly elected. But Fagan, the Lewis man, blithely stole the election by padding the returns and by voting non-existent "blue-sky" locals. Such corruption is, of course, always sustained by the International office if appeal is made against it.

But the election frauds reach their climax in the national elections in the Miners Union. In earlier years John H. Walker, at the time a Socialist, several times was robbed of the election. Alex Howat was also beaten by the fraudulent casting of more than 50,000 votes in the semi-organized districts. After the 1924 convention Lewis officially claimed to have defeated Voyzey, a rank and file Communist miner, by a vote of 134,000 to 66,000. Wholesale frauds were practiced by Lewis. Voyzey was undoubtedly elected. Lewis has never ventured to issue a tabulated report of the vote, as required by the union constitution.

The 1927 miners' election exhibited similar frauds. Lewis officially claimed 173,000 votes as against 60,000 for Brophy. This would make a total of 223,000 votes cast for an actual membership of 273,000, a manifest fraud, as returns from hundreds of locals, assembled by the left wing, showed that not more than one-third of the miners actually voted. Lewis stole votes wholesale, both for himself and from Brophy. In District 30, Kentucky, which has no actual dues paying members, 2,686½ votes were reported cast for Lewis and none for Brophy, a clear steal. In District 31, West Virginia, with an average of 377 dues payers, 14,000 votes were stolen for Lewis. In District 19, Tennessee, with only 482 real members, 3,962 votes were reported for Lewis and 15 for Brophy. In the Pittsburgh district one-third of the locals voting have no existence except on paper. In all the other districts similar large scale vote padding and stealing went on.

Brophy, like Voyzey, was certainly elected. Lewis, holding onto the power Mussolini-fashion, refuses to yield to majority votes. He has killed the one time firm opinion of the left wing that the referendum election is a specific cure for autocratic union control.

When labor union bureaucrats find themselves, in spite of all their tricks of control, confronted with definite instructions to apply militant and progressive policies, they unhesitatingly violate the mandates of their rank and file, trusting to the general inertia of the mass to escape punishment for their treachery. The history of the labor movement is full of such instances.

During 1922-24, the great T. U. E. L. movement for amalgamation swept through the trade unions. Seventeen state federations and nine international unions, besides scores of central bodies and thousands of local unions, adopted resolutions calling upon the A. F. of L. Executive Council to hold conferences to lay the basis for amalgamation. The Council blithely ignored the whole demand, though it represented more than half of the entire labor movement.

A case in point during the big amalgamation drive occurred in the Railway Carmen. Lodge 299 of Minneapolis submitted for referendum a proposition to commit the union to amalgamation. The proposal was regular in every respect, having ten times the required number of local union endorsements. It would have carried overwhelmingly if the rank and file had been allowed to vote on it. But the national officials swept it aside with a technical objection and refused to let the members vote on it. Thereupon Lodge 299 resubmitted its proposition with at least twenty times the required endorsements. This time the officialdom suppressed it without any excuse, refusing to send it out for a referendum vote, although the constitution gives them no option but to send out all such proposals. Result: the proposition was strangled.

At the 1923 convention of the A. F. of L. fully 50 per cent of the delegates came from unions which, during the prevailing great progressive stir among the workers, had voted for amalgamation, the labor party, and recognition of Soviet Russia. Yet all three of these measures were voted down practically unanimously at the convention. In the same way the railroad union bureaucrats ignored and defeated the demand of two-thirds of their membership for the amalgamation of the railroad unions following the disastrous 1922 railroad shopmen's strike. When Simon O'Donnell was defeated in his union as delegate to the Chicago Building Trades Council, of which he was president, it was, under the constitution, tantamount to his removal from office. But his building trades clique quickly adopted a rule that it was not necessary to be a delegate in order to be president of the Council. Similar instances of violation of constitutions and rank and file mandates could be cited indefinitely.

The trade union leaders are wide awake to the value of the labor press as an instrument for the propagation of their reactionary doctrines and the perpetuation of their personal power. Consequently it is a settled policy of theirs to reduce the various trade union papers, which once made a real show at freedom for rank and file expression, into mere house organs to advance the fortunes of the particular ruling cliques. In many unions there is not even a semblance of press freedom. Ideas and programs not acceptable to the dominant bureaucrats are unceremoniously thrown into the waste basket. Oppositional movements are almost completely barred from expression in such journals. Often even official action by big sections of the organizations does not suffice to break the embargo. This suppression of free rank and file expression in the union journals is one of the greatest bars to the progress of the labor movement.

As the trade union bureaucracy drifts more to the right it fights ever more viciously to prevent the left wing from mobilizing the discontented rank and file against it. Therefore the reactionaries apply constantly more drastically the foregoing autocratic methods of control and in the growing struggle against the rank and file upheavals new dictatorial methods have been added. Most of these have originated in the "socialist" needle trades unions, where the fight between the "rights" and "lefts" is sharpest.

One of such relatively new schemes is the arbitrary disfranchisement of the opposition. In the reactionary Boot and Shoe Workers Union the practice has long been followed of placing rebellious members in the so-called "local O," where they have no rights of voting or attending union meetings. But it remained for the needle trades leaders to bring this system to its maximum. In all the needle unions, they have reduced many left wingers to a state of semi-membership, denying them many of the constitutional rights of the union. Especially is this method used during elections. Scores of times the controlling bureaucrats, with the most trivial excuses or with none at all, have simply refused to place left wing opposition candidates on the election ballot. This nefarious practice is being adopted by the reactionary leaders of many other unions, especially among the miners, where it was used extensively in many districts during the recent elections.

The favorite method of the reactionaries, however, is outright expulsion of left-wing leaders from the unions. In earlier years American labor bureaucrats often brutally applied the expulsion policy. But it was usually in some such local affair as the wholesale expulsion of the New York carpenters in 1916 by Hutcheson. It remained for Sigman of the I. L. G. W. U., patterning after the methods of the Amsterdam International, to introduce in our trade union movement the use of expulsion as a settled policy against political opponents in the unions. He began his expulsion campaign in 1923, in co-operation with the *Forward* machine in New York. Hundreds were driven out of the unions in various cities. This culminated in 1925 in the expulsion of the entire executive boards of the three big locals, Nos. 2, 9, 22 with about 35,000 members. Result, a mass uprising, the formation of the Joint Action Committee of the expelled bodies, and the temporary defeat of Sigman and his expulsion policy.

In the needle trades the expulsion campaign has reached its high point. Sigman of the I. L. G. W. U., partially recovered from his defeat of two years ago, and supported actively by the A. F. of L. leaders, the employers, the police, and the press, has arbitrarily expelled some 40,000 members of the New York Joint Board. This splits his union and threatens it with destruction. It is deadly to the workers' organization and to union conditions in the shops. The bosses have slashed wages on all sides. Following the suicidal policy of Sigman, the leaders of the Furriers' Union, who are mere catspaws of the employers and of Woll and Green, have expelled the New York Joint Board of their organization. It has some 10,000 members, or three-fourths of the membership of their entire union. Wholesale expulsions are also being prepared for other cities. The two expelled Joint Boards, banded together under the "Unity Committee," are now fighting for readmission into their unions. The slogan of the right wing A. F. of L. leaders and their "socialist" allies is to get rid of the left wing even if the unions concerned are destroyed in the struggle. The very life of unionism in the needle industry is at stake in this desperate effort to suppress union democracy and to force the workers back under the arbitrary dictation of the reactionary leaders, which means under the control of the employers.

A form of terrorism now at high pitch in the trade union movement is the so-called "red baiting." Red baiting consists of terrifying the ideologically backward union membership with frightful stories of the "red menace" and thus stampeding them into supporting the reactionaries. The extent to which this is practiced and the means used to accomplish it are almost unbelievable. Soviet Russia, bolshevism, communism, boring from within—these are magic words in the mouths of the labor fakers. Around them they build plots and sinister conspiracies at which even a white guard propagandist would shamefacedly blush. Systematically, they play upon the weaknesses of the workers, their religion, patriotism, and petty bourgeois notions generally. Russian gold, to hear the reactionary union leaders tell it, flows freely in the dastardly attempt of the left wingers to destroy all that is good and holy in society.

Practically all trade union journals and conventions, from the A. F. of L. down, now have as regular features such slanders. The reactionaries first picture a terrible red menace and then, identifying all progressive proposals with it, scare away the more timid delegates. They make, in the minds of many, such elementary issues as amalgamation, the labor party, and the organization of the unorganized, synonymous with bolshevism. Result, the right wing delegates are whipped into a fascist-like frenzy and are made ready for any violence, such as the mobbing of Joseph Manley, A. Wagenknecht, and others at the Scranton, 1923, convention of the anthracite miners. The middle group, or progressives, usually wither under the fiery blast. One of the most deplorable features of present-day trade union conventions is that these "progressives," terrorized by the attacks of the reactionaries, commonly vote against such issues as the labor party, amalgamation, etc. Lacking the courage and aggressiveness to bring in such measures themselves, the progressives are afraid to vote for them when the left wing proposes them, for fear of being identified with the Communists.

These misleaders of labor do not hesitate, however, when hard-pressed, to proceed to much more violent methods. American trade union bureaucrats, especially in the building trades, stand quite apart from union leaders in any other country in the use of physical force to control the workers' organizations. Their methods often approach those of the Italian fascists. Chicago offers classical examples. Crime here takes on a terror and violence without a parallel in any other American city. The spectacular gun fights and murder campaigns between the bootlegging gangs, which, carried on with machine guns, armored cars, bombs, and other implements of modern warfare, have cost the lives of about two hundred men in the past two years, are typical of the ruthless spirit of such elements.

The reactionary Chicago labor leaders are saturated with this same reckless violence. The union official positions are rich prizes. They mean wealth and power to the corruptionists, and the latter do not hesitate before the most violent means in order to secure and hold them. Consequently there has developed a regular school of labor gunmen, typified by such elements as Madden, Enright, Murphy, and scores of others. For many years these toughs, with their body-guards and armed cliques, have terrorized numerous Chicago unions. The wars between these gangs for control have been many and mur-derous. During the past twenty years scores of men have been killed in such union feuds, some being secretly assassinated, and others shot down in open fights in saloons and union halls. Seldom are these reactionary leaders punished for such crimes, so powerful are their connections with corrupt politicians. The armed cliques of reaction-aries war against each other for control of the unions, but they always unite when they are confronted with an upheaval among their rank and file. They have made democracy a farce in many Chicago unions. And what is true of Chicago unions in this respect, is true likewise, to a lesser degree, of unions in all big industrial centers.

A few typical incidents from scores of such in Chicago's lurid inner-union feuds illustrate the methods of these gunmen. Thus the killing of Charles Victor a few years ago at the Painters District Council, by T. Shepler, a bureaucrat-gunman. Said the *Chicago Day Book* of the fight:

Shortly before the meeting adjourned Victor jumped on his chair and fired at Shepler. The rush and shouts of the men trying to escape from the hall almost drowned the fusillade of shots. Shepler stood up. His gun, which had been hanging in a holster on his belt, flashed. Victor tottered and fell headlong from the chair. Blood gushed from his mouth. He shivered and lay still. Shepler sat down heavily. When the police arrived Victor was dead. At the Iroquois Hospital Shepler was found to be shot in the right arm and leg. Another bullet gashed the left side of his head.

Thus operates democracy among the Painters, Gompers style. Here is how the reactionary Teamsters Union Officials settle their disputes, as reported in the *Chicago Tribune,* January 13, 1921:

South Chicago teaming concerns were under heavy police guard last night following a pitched battle between members of two rival teamsters' unions at Ninety-fifth street and Escanaba avenue early yesterday morning. The battle, during which more than 200 shots were fired, was fought from eight automobiles. Several men are said to have been wounded in the engagement but they were spirited away by their companions in auto-mobiles and their names were not learned. "No truce" has been adopted as the slogan of both sides and sluggers were being recruited last night by both unions.

Or take a commonplace note from Cleveland labor history: On May 31, 1924, as W. M. O'Brien, second international vice-president of the Sheet Metal Workers, and J. Nester, business agent of the Sheet Metal Workers, in company with other officials, were leaving the union meeting the automobile in which they were riding was bombed by opposing factionalists. Nester was killed and O'Brien was maimed for life. It was never learned who did this job.

The New York "socialist" needle trades unions, like many other New York unions, are also infested with such terrorists. Many of them are connected with the criminal underworld gangs, headed by "Little Augie," Jack Noy, "Frenchy," etc. Usually these plug uglies first established connections with the needle unions during the strikes, because instead of developing the militancy of the strikers themselves in such struggles, the right wing officials commonly called upon the gangsters to man the picket lines. This enabled these corrupt elements to worm their way into the unions, and often into official positions. Their influence upon the unions has been poisonous.

With the development of the present struggle between the right and left wings in the New York needle trades unions the reactionary officials have called into their service all these gangster connections. These, with full police protection, are carrying on an open terroristic campaign, slugging pickets, terrorizing meetings, and beating up left wingers. At times the conflicts between the opposing forces take on the aspects of pitched battles.

The widespread use of such reactionary control methods by the labor bureaucrats gives the lie effectively to those apologists who assert that the reactionary A. F. of L. officialdom is a true reflection of the backward rank and file in the unions. These misleaders are by no means the free choice of the organized workers. To a very great extent they force themselves upon the unions by means of selling out the unskilled, accepting assistance from the employers and the state, and by the arbitrary suppression of union democracy.

For the time being, with the industrial crisis not yet very keen and masses of workers somewhat lulled by relatively steady work during the capitalist "prosperity," these autocratic methods of control stand the reactionary bureaucrats in good stead and make it very difficult for the left wing and progressive forces to unite the rank and file for effective action against their false leaders and the employers. But ample experience has demonstrated that despite all this terrorism and suppression of democracy substantial results can be achieved in educating and organizing the masses and the basis can be laid for real progress in the unions. And as the industrial crisis sharpens and the working masses are forced to lower living standards such autocratic methods will be less and less effective. The rank and file, driven to revolt by hard economic conditions and an awakening class consciousness, will break through every autocratic restriction laid upon them by their misleaders and will build their unions into the militant, powerful organizations that they should be.

1927

15. Labor and Politics

From the very beginning the progressives fell into step with the new class collaboration movement of the bosses and A. F. of L. top leaders. In fact, they became its most skilled and enthusiastic leaders and they were its instructors to the Gompers-Green bureaucracy. It was the progressives, Johnston and Beyer, who originated the B. & O. plan. Johnston, Stone and Hillman were the outstanding champions of the demoralizing labor banking movement, which I christened "trade union capitalism" and which dovetailed into the whole class collaboration movement. And Stone and Hillman were among the chief theoreticians of the "Higher Strategy of Labor." This theory was thus stated at the Philadelphia convention of the Amalgamated Clothing Workers:

We have our problems and fortunately it is not necessary to apply the weapon of the strike for the solution of many of them. We have passed in our industry from the days of the jungle into an era of civilized ways of dealing with employers.

PROGRESSIVES AND SOCIALISTS SUPPORT
CLASS COLLABORATION

The Socialists were equally ardent supporters of the B. & O. plan, labor banking and the class collaboration movement generally. Many of them hailed it as the road to socialism. Abe Cahan baldly repudi-

ated Marx as outmoded and the Socialist Party struck out all reference
to the class struggle from its membership application forms. Its attack
against the Soviet Union was redoubled. Internationally, the Socialists
were no less enthusiastic about the class collaboration developments.
The British Labor Party, German Social-Democracy, in fact the whole
Second and Amsterdam Internationals joyfully hailed capitalist rationalization and the "new capitalism." They spun many tricky theories
about its developing into an "organized capitalism," a "super-imperial-
ism," that was evolving directly into socialism. Henry Ford became
the Messiah of the international socialist movement.

The American socialist-led unions, mostly needle trades, became
practically indistinguishable from ordinary A. F. of L. unions. They
practiced class collaboration intensely in all its newer forms, they were
infested with gangsters, democracy was practically unknown among
them, and they pushed the expulsion campaign against the left wing
to further limits than any other unions in the United States. Moreover,
their leaders, dropping the last vestiges of the traditional Socialist
opposition, became part and parcel of the reactionary A. F. of L. ruling
clique. On this phase let witnesses friendly to them testify:

> After the world war the socialist boring-from-within policies and tactics
> were completely reversed. . . . Instead, they aim to sue for the confidence
> and good will of the entrenched labor leaders. . . . The new political
> alignment of the Socialists with the administration forces marks the end
> of their leadership of the opposition in the labor movement.*

> The Socialists gave up their policy of militant boring-from-within and
> sought to win the confidence of the A. F. of L. administration.†

The role of the progressives during this period merits closer examination. Dropping all pretense of struggle, these vacillating elements
fitted themselves entirely into the new intensified class collaboration
and speed-up policies of the bosses, and indeed became their most
ardent champions. The first of the progressives to so hoist the white
flag were the right wing elements. These, grouped around the railroad
unions, were organized in the Conference for Progressive Political
Action. The Socialist Party was also an active factor in this organization. The C. P. P. A. contained about 3,000,000 organized workers
and farmers. These masses clearly wanted a labor party, but their

---

* D. J. Saposs, *Left Wing Unionism*, pp. 37-39, 1926.
† D. M. Schneider, *The Workers (Communist) Party and the American Trade Unions*, p. 21.

progressive leaders, after talking radically about a labor party during the period of sharpest struggle after the war, sensed the new turn of events towards class collaboration, and therefore ran the whole movement into the ditch. At the Cleveland, December 11, 1922, conference of the C. P. P. A., they definitely repudiated the plan of forming a labor party, indorsed the A. F. of L. non-partisan policy and, making complete peace with the A. F. of L. leaders, they soon set sail together for the LaFollette fiasco of 1924. The right wing progressives then completed their surrender by unceremoniously dumping overboard their Plumb Plan of government railroad ownership, canceling their inter-union solidarity agreements and soon becoming the very leaders in the developing movement for intensified class collaboration.

The left wing of the progressives, the Fitzpatrick Farmer-Labor Party group, with whom the T. U. E. L. and Workers Party (the name of the Communist Party at that time) were co-operating, held out several months longer against the new conservative trends in the labor movement, but they also finally went to the right. Fitzpatrick had denounced the Cleveland decisions of the C. P. P. A. as rank betrayal of the labor party movement and had formally agreed with the Workers Party to call a national convention in Chicago, July 3, 1923, at which a new labor party would be launched, provided there were at least 500,000 workers represented. The Workers Party was officially invited to attend the convention, and it accepted; but the Socialist Party, which followed the line of the right progressives into the camp of LaFollette and intensified class collaboration, declined the invitation. It was in the months preceding this 1923 convention that the T. U. E. L. and the Workers Party campaign for the labor party took on its broadest mass character.

Meanwhile, the Gompers leaders, strengthened by the rising wave of prosperity, the growth of class collaboration policies, the decline in the workers' fighting spirit, the spread of prosperity illusions among the toilers and the collapse of the C. P. P. A., felt themselves able to begin to put pressure on the Fitzpatrick-Nockels group. In June, 1923, therefore, they cut off 50 per cent of the Cleveland Federation of Labor's monthly subsidy and threatened to reorganize the C. F. of L. if it did not break its alliance with the Communists and stop agitating for amalgamation, the labor party, and Russian recognition. This coercion had an effect and the C. F. of L. leaders began visibly to lose interest in the coming labor party convention.

When the July 3 convention assembled there were present some

600 delegates representing over 600,000 organized workers and farmers, besides several important unions (A. C. W. and others) that sent observers. From the start it was evident that the Fitzpatrick group wanted to break its relations with the Workers Party, although, only shortly before, they had specifically invited it to the convention. They hemmed and hawed with various maneuvers to this end; finally, on the last day of the convention, submitting a proposal to exclude the Workers Party on the grounds that it advocated the overthrow of the government and asking all present except the Workers Party to affiliate to the old moribund Fitzpatrick Farmer-Labor Party. The convention delegates (of whom only a very small minority were Communists) roared disapproval of this course, and by a vote of 500 to 40 established the originally planned Federated Farmer-Labor Party, of which Joe Manley was elected secretary.

Whereupon Fitzpatrick and a handful of delegates walked out of the convention. Nearly all of his customary supporters, however, including such veterans as Alex Howat, Duncan McDonald, Mother Jones, etc., indorsed the Workers Party line in the convention. They could not see the consistency of Fitzpatrick's first condemning the C. P. P. A. a couple of months earlier for not seating Workers Party delegates and denouncing it as a scab organization for not launching a labor party and then, suddenly switching front, taking essentially the same course himself in this big convention. Although supported by only a few delegates, nevertheless the Fitzpatrick walkout became a real break. The capitalist papers helped it decisively by yelling "split" in a thousand headlines all over the country.

This split, combined with the general trend of the A. F. of L. and organized farmers towards the candidacy of LaFollette, prevented the growth of the newly organized Federated Farmer-Labor Party, and it perished after a twelve months' lingering existence. The Fitzpatrick Farmer-Labor Party also soon died out, with its leaders turning back more and more to the A. F. of L. non-partisan political policy.

Fitzpatrick has many times since bitterly attacked the Communists for the July 3 split. But this is not in accordance with the facts. The main responsibility lay with himself. We simply stuck to the plan we had definitely agreed upon with Fitzpatrick before the convention, of forming a new, federated party. It was he who directly caused the split, in his eagerness to break with the Communists and to put himself in tune with the strong conservative trends developing at the time in the trade union movement.

The worst that we can be fairly charged with was an error in tactics. As I have pointed out, Fitzpatrick and his group, feeling the upswing of prosperity and the growth of class collaboration, were at the time retreating rapidly to the right under Gompers' fire. This trend on their part was clearly demonstrated afterwards by Fitzpatrick's giving up the labor party movement altogether and reverting back to the A. F. of L. non-partisan policy, by abandoning amalgamation, and by becoming a bitter enemy of the Soviet Union. He also became an ardent advocate of all the subsequent A. F. of L. schemes of intensified class collaboration. Our failing was that we should have realized more clearly all this rightward trend and, instead of holding Fitzpatrick to his pre-convention agreement, made the greatest compromises in order, if possible, to avoid such an open and sharp break.

The whole history of the next several years showed, with the progressives generally gone far to the right and becoming the leaders of the class collaboration movement, that the Workers Party and T. U. E. L., with their class struggle policy, were bound to have the greatest difficulty in carrying on any joint struggle whatever with them. Nevertheless, we should have fought more skillfully against the split. As it was, the split developed in the worst form, dramatically and around such a major issue as the labor party. The sequel showed that the Chicago split cost the Workers Party loss of contacts with many important farmer-labor militants in various sections of the country. It shattered the united front combination that had done such effective work in the meat packing and steel campaigns and in the amalgamation, labor party, and other movements and that held promise of important future activities.

THE A. F. OF L. COUNTER-OFFENSIVE

The Chicago split in the united front between the Communists and left-progressives was manna from heaven to the threatened Gompers leaders, and they accepted it as a signal for a big offensive against the T. U. E. L., the Communists and progressive movements generally. The first serious clash came at the Illinois Federation of Labor convention in Decatur, September 10, 1923, at which I was a delegate. This was said to be the largest state federation convention ever held in the United States, the A. F. of L. having made a big mobilization of its forces to defeat us. Gompers had sent out a special letter condemning us and delegated Matthew Woll to lead the fight against us.

The battle centered around the question of amalgamation, and it was a hot fight. The Fitzpatrick Farmer-Labor Party delegates, very bitter at us for the Chicago split, joined forces openly with Woll, signed his statement condemning amalgamation and helped vote down their own C. F. of L. amalgamation resolution. Result: amalgamation was defeated by a four to one vote, whereas three months before it would have been adopted by the same delegation with an overwhelming majority. This was the first time the A. F. of L. leaders had been able to defeat amalgamation in any state federation convention and their jubilation knew no bounds.

Just at this critical time, with the Gompers machine managing to get on the offensive against us, the Socialist needle trades union leaders taught the right reactionaries a new trick in how to fight militant unionism. In the International Ladies Garment Workers, where our movement was very strong, they began a campaign of expulsion of T. U. E. L. members in Chicago, New York, and elsewhere. They backed this up by suppressing free speech in the union and infesting it with professional gangsters.* To the Socialist old guard leaders, to Sigman in person, therefore belongs the shame of having initiated into the United States the reactionary policy (which they copied from their parent Amsterdam International) of expelling workers from labor unions and their jobs because of their political opinions. An attempt was made to give a color of justification to such expulsions by the absurd charge that the T. U. E. L. was a dual union.

The reason for this ruthless attack was that the Socialist leaders were extremely antagonistic to us. They were allied tightly with the Gompers' bureaucracy and following out its whole class collaboration policy.

The Gompers clique were quick to follow the lead given by the old guard Socialist trade union leaders and they proceeded to adopt the expulsion policy generally. They were determined to exterminate all rank and file opposition to their ruinous collaboration policies. They dramatized the expulsion policy at the Portland, 1923, A. F. of L. convention, where with bell, book, and candle, they demonstratively

---

* In Chicago, during a large protest meeting in Carmen's Auditorium against these outrageous expulsions, a notorious gunman suddenly appeared from the fire escape and fired three shots into the meeting in my direction while I was speaking. A disastrous panic was narrowly averted. We protested to Debs against this outrage and against the whole I. L. G. W. U. expulsion policy. Debs claimed he could do nothing about it and he refused to take up the battle against the reactionary Socialist Party old guard.

expelled from the convention William F. Dunne, T. U. E. L. national committee member and regularly elected delegate of the Silver Bow (Butte), Montana, trades council. The T. U. E. L. was officially branded as a dual union and a call was issued for war against the Communists in the unions. And although the majority of the organized workers had voted for amalgamation, a labor party, and Russian recognition, and the bulk of the organizations were definitely committed to one or all three of these issues, the reactionary leaders almost unanimously voted them all down, the labor party vote, for example, being 25,066 to 1,895. This most reactionary convention then capped its destructive work by adopting as labor's "constructive program" the new schemes of class collaboration which were well-nigh to destroy the unions during the next six years.

Never was there a more flagrant violation of trade union democracy than the actions of the Portland A. F. of L. convention, one of the last attended by the arch-reactionary Gompers before his death. The misleaders of labor served notice that henceforth there would be war to the knife against the T. U. E. L., the Communists, and every sign of militancy in the labor movement, and there was. After Portland, expulsion from unions and jobs, backed by gangster control and suppression of trade union democracy, became the official weapon against the militant opposition. The A. F. of L. leaders demanded that the Cleveland, Minneapolis, Detroit, Seattle, and other central labor unions expel all Communists and T. U. E. L. members, on pain of losing their charters. Then most of the international unions adopted the same policy, the socialist-controlled needle trade unions outstripping all others in this reactionary campaign, wholesale expulsions in the needle industry even reaching the total of tens of thousands of workers in certain cases.*

In the early stages of the expulsion drive the T. U. E. L. held its second national conference in Chicago, September 1, 1923, with 143 delegates from 90 cities, including three from Canada and one from

---

* Among the many militants expelled in this several years' long period of expulsions was myself. The usual expulsion method was to use little or no formality, but with me the following "diplomacy" was applied by the Brotherhood of Railway Carmen's Association leaders: When, as usual, I submitted my dues by mail to Chicago to my local (I lived in New York) I was notified that upon instructions of the National Office I should take a withdrawal card. I refused to do this, whereupon my dues in money was returned to me without explanation. I sent it back again, demanding dues stamps. No answer. Then, at the end of three-months, I was notified that I had been dropped for nonpayment of dues. Thus ended sixteen years of membership in that union.

Mexico. The convention took steps to speed up its three major campaigns, and worked out concrete plans for partial and complete amalgamation in the most important industries. It also proposed to fight the growing expulsions by mass demands for reinstatement in the unions. But it was unable to find effective means to consolidate its loose mass movements in the face of the developing offensive of the Gompers bureaucracy.

Under the pressure of the fierce attack of the top union leadership, in many cases supported by the bosses and the police, and under the influence of the growing "prosperity" and class collaboration, the T. U. E. L. forces in the unions were soon driven back. Hundreds of its best fighters lost their key union positions and also their jobs in the industries. Reaction and autocracy grew everywhere, and the movements for amalgamation, the labor party, and recognition of Soviet Russia suffered a heavy decline. In this time also, the workers' militancy fell off greatly. Gradually, the work of the T. U. E. L. in general slowed down and lost in mass volume. Its militants found themselves largely cut off from the organized workers. Thus there entered the period of partial or relative isolation of the T. U. E. L. from the masses, a situation which was to last more or less as long as the Coolidge "prosperity" era.

1936

16. The Work of the Trade Union Educational League

The T. U. E. L. could not entirely escape the wave of pessimism and inaction that affected the working class during the Coolidge prosperity period. The combined effects of the bourgeoisification of the skilled workers, the poison propaganda of class collaboration, the turn of the progressives to the right and our split with them, and the barbarous expulsion policy and gangster control of the unions, definitely weakened the T. U. E. L.'s offensive in support of its three great issues of amalgamation, the labor party, and recognition of

Soviet Russia, and prevented it from passing from the agitation stage into concrete action and results. T. U. E. L. work was forced to take on more of a local or partial character than its big sweeping movement of 1922-23.

The T. U. E. L. found itself in relative isolation from the masses in this period. Nevertheless, in the Coolidge period the T. U. E. L. did manage to conduct a number of broad united front struggles. One of the more important of these was in the Carpenters' Union led by M. Rosen and N. Kjar. This union's leadership, corrupt and autocratic, followed the usual policy of intensified class collaboration and backed it up by expelling many militants in Chicago, New York, Los Angeles, etc., in some cases with police help. The T. U. E. L. fight reached its high point in the union elections of 1925, when Rosen, an avowed Communist, received, even according to the falsified official election returns, 9,014 votes against Hutcheson's 77,985.

More effective, however, was the T. U. E. L. fight in the Machinists Union, led by A. Overgaard. William H. Johnston, the head of this union, was the first sponsor of the B. & O. plan and the organization was saturated with the new forms of class collaboration. Big discontent existed among the rank and file at the bad union conditions. Johnston tried to quell this by expelling Overgaard and many other militants in Toledo, Chicago, etc. As a result of the T. U. E. L.'s fight against the B. & O. plan, expulsions, etc., the left wing at the Detroit, 1924, International Association of Machinists convention polled 44 votes against the administration's 107. In the ensuing 1925 union election, the T. U. E. L. made a united front with the progressive Anderson group against the expulsion and class collaboration policy of the union leaders. Even from the official election returns it was clear that the united front slate had won, but the so-called progressive, Johnston, according to the prevailing union officials' practice, did not let that detail worry him. He proceeded to steal the election, announcing the doctored returns as: Johnston 18,021, Anderson 17,076.

The T. U. E. L., in the Coolidge years, conducted many other struggles against class collaboration in the various internationals, locals, and central labor bodies. But its main fights occurred in the mining, textile, and needle industries. In these three industries special conditions prevailed. First, foreshadowing the eventual general crisis of American industry, they were all greatly depressed from overproduction, with accompanying unemployment, low wages, and bad union conditions. And, secondly, the workers in these industries were especially rich in fighting traditions, so they responded more readily to T. U. E. L. leadership.

IN THE MINING INDUSTRY

Throughout almost the entire Coolidge period, the coal industry was in depression. This, part of the world coal crisis, was caused by over-development during the war, a high state of competition, mechanization of the mines, use of oil, water power and other substitutes for coal, etc. Result: chronic mass unemployment and gradual worsening of wages and working conditions even several years before the 1929 general crisis. The miners' position was made worse because the Lewis administration of the U. M. W. A., which in those years followed a typical conservative course, proved to be unable to alleviate these evil conditions. Consequently, the miners were deeply discontented and much inclined to hearken to the T. U. E. L. program.

From its outset, the T. U. E. L. had a strong following among the miners. As we have seen, it defeated Farrington's attempt in Illinois to disrupt the 1922 national strike. It also took a prominent part in the fight against the expulsion of Alex Howat, militant president of the Kansas miners, a fight in which Lewis was once defeated by a convention vote of 977 to 866.

On June 2-3, 1923, in Pittsburgh, the T. U. E. L. miners met and formed the Progressive International Committee of the U. M. W. A., with 25 delegates present, including Howat. Tom Myerscough became its secretary. This conference adopted a program of nationalization of the mines, labor party, amalgamation, organize the unorganized, recognition of Soviet Russia, alliance between miners and railroaders, six-hour day, national agreements only, against dual unionism, for democracy in the union, etc. At this conference it was reported how the T. U. E. L. had prevented a split of 40,000 miners in the anthracite. Lewis replied to this conference by making membership in the Communist Party or T. U. E. L. an expulsion offense and, in the next period, by systematically expelling hundreds of militants.

The first big clash with the Lewis machine came in the union elections of 1924. On the basis of its Pittsburgh program, the progressive U. M. W. A. Committee put up as its candidate for president, George Voyzey of Illinois, a Communist miner. Although he was but little known, vast masses of miners voted for him. The final official returns gave Lewis 136,000 and Voyzey 66,000. We charged fraud and asserted that Voyzey had actually been elected.

Things went from bad to worse in the U. M. W. A. The coal crisis deepened, the bosses redoubled their attacks upon the workers on all fronts, the U. M. W. A. administration ruthlessly expelled militants throughout the organization. At that time Lewis himself was a prominent figure in the Republican Party and many of his organizers and district presidents were tied up with employers' associations and all kinds of conservative organizations. The union was shot through with the prevailing ruinous union-management co-operation. Consequently, the union crumbled and fell to pieces in many districts, including Middle Pennsylvania, West Virginia, Maryland, Iowa, Missouri, Kansas, Oklahoma, Alabama, Canada, etc. In 1925, the powerful Pittsburgh Coal Company repudiated the Jacksonville agreement, went open shop, and threw down the gantlet of battle to the U. M. W. A.

In this grave crisis the T. U. E. L. forces raised the slogan, "Save the Union." They demanded that there be a vigorous organization campaign started in the South and other unorganized districts and that the anthracite miners unite their forces with the bituminous miners for joint action in the life and death struggle ahead. The T. U. E. L. built up a broad united front with non-Communists and created a national Save-the-Union Committee, with branches in many localities. During this campaign I spent five months on the road doing organizing work. In the union elections ensuing, this committee put up a united front "Save-the-Union" election ticket, headed by John Brophy, former president of District 2. Lewis violently opposed this entire development with further expulsions, suppressions of union democracy, etc. When the election returns were issued they gave Lewis 173,323 and Brophy 60,661. We protested these figures, claimed gross frauds in many districts, and asserted that Brophy had been cheated (by padding Lewis' vote and reducing Brophy's) of 100,000 votes and thereby of the election.

The next U. M. W. A. convention, late in 1926, presented a sorry picture. The Jacksonville agreement was about to expire, the union faced a desperate struggle, and no real preparations had been made for it. Widespread discontent at Lewis' leadership existed in the union. But the T. U. E. L. united front forces could accomplish nothing at the convention. Lewis had solid control, based chiefly on large numbers of office-holder delegates from the organized territory. The left-progressives also charged that there were hundreds of delegates from "blue-sky" locals in the many disorganized districts where the district provisional administrations were appointed by the U. M. W. A. Board. Lewis ruled the convention with a strong hand and defeated every proposal of the opposition. Evidently the U. M. W. A. was in very bad shape and threatened with disaster.

On April 1, 1927, with the Jacksonville agreement ended, the union found itself on strike, or practically locked out, in all the unionized northern bituminous fields. The miners fought bravely, and the Communist Party and T. U. E. L. threw all their forces into the desperate struggle. We organized mass picketing and set up a relief system under the leadership of A. Wagenknecht. As for the U. M. W. A. officialdom, it seemed paralyzed and disorganized. Characteristically also, the top A. F. of L. leaders in Washington, lost in their dreams of prosperity through the speed-up and class collaboration, were oblivious of the vital importance of this most crucial strike and raised for the miners only enough funds to pay their strike relief rolls for one week.

The organized left-progressive bloc did much to stiffen the ranks of the miners, and so well did the strikers fight that on April 1, 1928, a full year after the strike began, they were still standing solid in all the key union districts notwithstanding extreme starvation, neglect, and police terrorism. On this date, the Save-the-Union movement held a national conference in Pittsburgh. Present were 1,125 delegates, representing approximately 100,000 miners from all over the country. The conference decided to strengthen the strike by stiffening up the picket lines and by extending the fight, first, into the important Western Pennsylvania and West Virginia fields, and, finally, into the anthracite districts. In consequence, a revival of picketing took place and 19,000 unorganized miners soon struck under T. U. E. L. leadership in nearby Fayette and Westmoreland counties.

But the great strike was already defeated and we could not revive it. The formal end came when the union signed a separate agreement in Illinois, and the miners who could get jobs draggled back to work in the other districts. The big battle was lost. The U. M. W. A. had been practically wiped out of its remaining strongholds in Western Pennsylvania, Northern West Virginia, and Ohio. The vast bulk of the soft coal fields were now open shop. At one blow the miners lost wages and conditions and the union that had taken thirty years to build up. The U. M. W. A. ceased to be a real power in the bituminous districts, and by this fact organized labor in general suffered one of the greatest defeats in its history.

IN THE TEXTILE INDUSTRY

The textile industry, like coal mining, was in a state of depression from overproduction for several years before the 1929 crisis. Again like mining, its bad situation was a part of a world-wide crisis in that industry. Unemployment, low wages, and excessive speed-up were the lot of the oppressed and impoverished textile workers. Only about 5 per cent of the 1,000,000 textile workers were organized, and these solely in the North, the South being totally unorganized. The principal unions were the United Textile Workers, the American Federation of Textile Operatives, and the Associated Silk Workers, the two latter being independent unions. The leadership of these unions was saturated through and through with the current speed-up, class collaboration schemes, and worked diligently with the employers to intensify the exploitation of the workers. The three unions were inert and paralyzed, valuable only to the employers to help drive the workers faster and faster in production.

Among the textile workers, who have good fighting traditions, there was much unrest and the T. U. E. L. had worked among them since 1922. Its general program condemned B. & O. plan-ism and company unionism, and called for a fighting policy, for honest leadership, amalgamation, and organization of the unorganized. It proposed a united front between the squabbling unions pending amalgamation. It organized local groups in the unions and set up united front mill committees in the mills, made up of representatives of the various unions and the unorganized. The T. U. E. L. textile section held two national and several local conferences. It did much local organization work and exposed the fallacies of class collaboration at all times.

The first big T. U. E. L. mass movement among the textile workers was the Passaic, New Jersey, strike of 1926. The T. U. E. L., under the name of the United Front Committee of Textile Workers, began activity in Passaic right after the 10 per cent wage cut of October 1925. The United Textile Workers and the other textile unions were practically non-existent in Passaic, so the U. F. C. began recruiting members and forming a union, intending later to join the A. F. of L. Soon 1,000 had affiliated, and on January 25, the U. F. C. committee presented demands to the Botany mill to rescind the wage cut, for time and one-half for overtime time and no discrimination against union workers. The company replied by discharging the whole committee of 45. Then the 5,000 Botany workers struck and spread the fight to the other mills, soon involving 15,280 workers and tying up the whole Passaic textile industry.

The strike was stubbornly fought on both sides. It lasted for eleven months. The bosses used the police, the courts, citizens' peace committees and every method of strikebreaking and terrorism; the workers replied with heroic solidarity and tireless endurance. This very militant and dramatic strike of the impoverished textile workers attracted broad working class sympathy all over the country; while the A. F. of L. officialdom, saturated with class collaboration poison, viewed it with ill-disguised hostility. Senators, governors, mayors, lawyers, philanthropists, etc., galore, took a hand in trying to "settle" the bitter struggle.

By terrorism and duplicity the bosses were unable to break the strike so, after six months of it, in July, they decided on a maneuver to defeat the workers; they announced that they would deal with the strikers provided the Communist leadership was removed and the strikers were affiliated to the U. T. W. To agree to take out the mass leaders was a difficult condition for us, but the strike was in a hard situation; so, refusing to let the issue of communism stand in the way of a settlement, we called the bosses' bluff and withdrew the official leader of the strike, and we also affiliated the workers to the U. T. W.

The employers, seeing that their maneuver had failed, then stated they would not deal with the A. F. of L. either. In consequence, the strike dragged on, bitterly fought (under our leadership—the U. T. W. doing nothing) until December 13, when the big Botany Mills capitulated to the union by restoring the wage cut, agreeing not to discriminate against union members and recognizing grievance committees. The other mills soon followed suit. Thus ended almost a year of struggle. It was a hard-won, if only partial, victory, but it produced little tangible results in organization. The union, weakened by the long struggle and neglected by the U. T. W. conservative McMahon leadership, was unable to follow up with a vigorous campaign for organization and against blacklisting.

The Passaic strike was very important. It stood out like a lighthouse in the midst of the prevailing fog of class collaboration in the A. F. of L. It was also the first mass strike in this country led independently by Communists. It strengthened the resistance of the textile workers all over the country and was a stimulant to the whole revolutionary movement. But, perhaps, most important of all was the influence this strike had, as we shall see, on changing the policy of revolutionary trade unionism in the United States.

IN THE NEEDLE TRADES

In the Coolidge "prosperity" years the needle industry, suffering like mining and textile from over-development and extreme competition, experienced difficult and depressed conditions. Heavy unemployment became more and more chronic, and the "busy" seasons grew shorter and shorter. As in all industries, the employers drove through with a rationalization program, speeding the workers by every known device.

The Socialist top leaders of the unions in the industry dovetailed their policies to fit into this speed-up program of the bosses. In no other American industry was the class collaboration "union-management co-operation" so highly developed as in the needle trades. The Socialist leaders joined hands with the technicians of the employers in putting through a whole series of "minimum standards of production," piece-work systems, wage cuts, etc. In some cases, with their own efficiency experts, they actually took over the technical management of the speed-up; in others they even financed bankrupt employers with the savings of workers collected in their labor banks. No other unions went so far as they in the speed-up, and none proceeded to such extremes to suppress the opposition by abolishing union democracy, by expulsions, blacklisting, and gangster tactics.

The needle workers, the most revolutionary in American industry, revolted in large masses against the worsening of their unions and conditions through this misleadership. They accepted the T. U. E. L. and built its needle trades section into a powerful united front movement, with at one time at least 100,000 workers directly following its lead and many more under its influence. This mass revolt developed in all sections, especially in New York, the main center of the industry. The chief points in T. U. E. L. policy were: against class collaboration and for a policy of class struggle, against gangsterism and corruption and for union democracy, for amalgamation of all needle unions into one industrial union based on the shop delegate system, for the labor party, recognition of Soviet Russia, affiliation to the Red International of Labor Unions, release of political prisoners, etc. Besides these general demands, the T. U. E. L. groups had specific programs for each union in the industry.

The bitter fight took on much the aspect of a political struggle between the Communist Party and the Socialist Party. On the one side, were the C. P. and T. U. E. L., backed by huge masses of discontented workers, and, on the other, the S. P. and union bureaucracies, supported chiefly by skilled workers and actively aided by the bosses, the A. F. of L., the capitalist newspapers, Tammany Hall politicians, and often even by the police. Never in any American unions had there been such a widespread and relentless internal fight.

The struggle reached its most acute stages in the International Fur Workers Union and the International Ladies Garment Workers Union. In the Amalgamated Clothing Workers conditions were as bad as in the other unions. The T. U. E. L. fought to put the Amalgamated on a class struggle basis and it had many successes; but our movement, principally because of poor leadership, did not take on the sustained mass character that it did in the I. F. W. U. and I. L. G. W. U. In the Cloth Hat, Cap and Millinery Workers International Union, the left wing also developed a strong movement which was influential in the life of the union, but it was not able to win control of the organization or of its large strikes away from the class collaboration leadership.

To give a detailed picture of the long and complicated struggle of the T. U. E. L. in the needle trades would run far beyond space limitations here. The student can find the main facts in Jack Hardy's book, *The Clothing Workers*.* Here all I can do is to touch upon the high points of the struggle in the two unions where it was the keenest, the Fur Workers and the I. L. G. W. U.

In the I. F. W. U. the Kaufman bureaucracy, reactionary and autocratic, early followed the I. L. G. W. U. method of breaking the opposition to the speed-up by expelling militants out of the union, blacklisting them from the shops, and ruling the union by gangster methods. At the union meetings dissenters were slugged, Ben Gold, the T. U. E. L. fur workers' leader, being dangerously stabbed. The T. U. E. L. was condemned as a dual organization and membership in it pronounced sufficient cause for expulsion. But the mass opposition movement grew, nevertheless, as official mismanagement forced the workers' conditions from bad to worse. The struggle culminated in the May 1925 elections, when the T. U. E. L. forces, setting up a

* Published by International Publishers. 1935.

united front with the "middle" group, won control of the Furriers New York Joint Board, the bulk of the whole international union. Gold became head of the new local administration.

In February 1926, over 12,000 New York furriers under Gold's leadership went on strike with a central demand for the forty-hour week. The ensuing seventeen-week struggle was one of the hardest fought in the history of New York. The workers not only had to battle large numbers of professional scabs and gangsters, but also the right wing leaders of the International Union sabotaged the strike shamelessly. When it finally looked like victory in spite of all, these people brought in William Green, and together they made an agreement with the bosses behind the local leadership's back for a 42-hour week. Then they tried to stampede the strikers to return to the shops. But the workers stood firm, rejected Green's settlement, carried on their strike for several weeks longer, and finally won the forty-hour week. It was a slashing victory, a splendid example of effective strike leadership and a sharp repudiation of the whole A. F. of L. no-strike policy.

The right wing Socialist labor leaders, and especially Green himself, were greatly compromised by these events. These people especially feared the stimulating effect of this splendid strike upon the discontented masses throughout the needle trades. So they redoubled their attacks upon the union's left wing leaders. They shouted red revolution, charged Gold with mishandling the union's funds, using violence in the strike, bribing the police, violating the union constitution, etc. Then an A. F. of L. "investigation" committee, composed of the ultra-reactionaries M. Woll, E. McGrady, J. Ryan, J. Sullivan and Hugh Frayne, with the co-operation of the Socialist Party, the bosses, newspapers, etc., proceeded to reorganize the New York Joint Board by expelling its members, "dissolving" its four locals, and setting up new unions. This action forced the great mass of furriers outside the A. F. of L., where they remained under left leadership and in the sharpest struggle until unity was achieved seven years later.

The struggle in the I. L. G. W. U. was no less bitter and protracted. Again, only its bare outlines can be given here. In the I. L. G. W. U. the outstanding left united front leader was Joseph Boruchovich. This union suffered acutely from the prevalent "union-management co-operation" schemes, gangsterism, suppression of democracy, etc. Especially vicious was the expulsion policy. The T. U. E. L. forces fought in all garment centers against these conditions, but the fight climaxed in New York, where the masses gave the left wing militants a ready ear.

The first major clash came in 1925. After three years of struggle the T. U. E. L. had built up a left united front leadership in locals 2, 9 and 22, comprising about 70 per cent of the New York Joint Board, backbone of the international. Whereupon President Morris Sigman on June 11, seizing upon the absurd pretext that the Communist *Freiheit* editor, M. Olgin, had spoken at the locals' May Day meeting, arbitrarily expelled the whole regularly elected 77 executive board members of the three locals as Communists, which amounted to expelling some 35,000 members. This provoked an explosion of indignation in the industry. The "Joint Action Committee" was set up among the expelled locals, a bitter struggle ensued, and after sixteen weeks of it, Sigman had to give in and reinstate the expelled locals and executive boards.

This was a big left-wing victory and it mobilized at least 75 per cent of the whole I. L. G. W. U.'s membership behind the T. U. E. L. militants. The left wing united front won control of the New York Joint Board. Similar victories were had in the Chicago Joint Board and in local unions in many centers. But the "old guard" Socialist Sigman administration managed to retain control at the Philadelphia, November 1925, convention of the union by reason of the prevailing system of "paper locals" and disproportionate representation. Thus Sigman had on his side 146 delegates representing 15,852 members, while the opposition, representing 34,762 members, had only 114 delegates. With the convention thus packed, Sigman ruthlessly steam-rollered the left wing proposals. This provoked a crisis and the outraged opposition delegates left the convention in a body, determined to launch a new union.

The convention left much bitterness in the union. The next big struggle between the conservative administration and the T. U. E. L. united front developed during the strike of 35,000 New York cloakmakers, beginning July 1, 1926, which was led by the left wing New York Joint Board. Again, as in the Furriers' strike, the right wing leadership sabotaged the struggle. And again, seizing a favorable time when the strikers were exhausted by the long fight, the Sigman leadership, although they had regularly spoken for and endorsed the strike at its outset, suddenly on December 13, denounced it as illegal, took over the negotiations with the bosses, referred the whole matter to arbitration and ordered the cloakmakers back to work. Unlike in the

Furriers' strike, the lefts were unable to defeat this maneuver by mobilizing the strike-tired workers, so the strike was lost and the workers' conditions were slashed by the arbitration board. It was a big defeat for the workers and the T. U. E. L.

Sigman, with A. F. of L. and S. P. support, then intensified his offensive against the T. U. E. L. by expelling the New York Joint Board, and several of the big New York locals. Similar action was taken in Chicago and other left strongholds. Then, aided by the pressure of the bosses' blacklist, the I. L. G. W. U. leaders proceeded with a campaign of re-registering expelled workers into new local unions. Like other reactionaries in similar situations, the I. L. G. W. U. leaders showed that they were ready to wreck the union rather than allow it to pass under left leadership.

As the result of Sigman's splitting policy at least 35,000 workers now found themselves expelled from the I. L. G. W. U. Thus of the Furriers and the I. L. G. W. U., altogether some 50,000 workers had been ousted from their unions and the A. F. of L. They, therefore, linked forces in a joint action committee to continue the struggle for trade union unity through reinstatement, for democratization of the A. F. of L. needle unions, and against the rapidly worsening economic conditions of the needle trades workers.*

1936

17. The Question of the Unorganized

The question of organizing the many millions of unorganized workers is the most vital matter now before the American labor movement. The future progress of the working class depends upon the solution of this great problem.

The organization of the unorganized is a life and death question for the labor movement. To bring the millions into the unions is

* Subsequently these workers organized an independent union. At the time of the formation of the C. I. O., the ladies' garment workers returned to the I. L. G. W. U. The fur workers joined the C. I. O., developing and expanding their union into the present International Fur and Leather Workers Union (C. I. O.) with 100,000 members.

necessary not only for the protection of the unorganized workers, and to further class ends in general, but also to safeguard the life of the existing organizations. Many of the trade unions are now under such heavy attacks from the employers that their very existence is threatened. These struggles can be resolved favorably to the workers only by drawing to their support the great mass of unorganized.

The Miners' Union is a case in point. The bituminous coal industry is shifting from the organized fields of Illinois, Ohio, Indiana and Pennsylvania, into the southern unorganized districts, with consequent heavy unemployment among the union miners. The coal operators are taking advantage of this fact by smashing the union in the organized districts. Unless the southern fields are unionized, the United Mine Workers of America is doomed.

To a greater or lesser extent similar menacing conditions exist among the unions of Railroad Workers, Metal Workers, Needle Workers, etc. They are not only seriously weakened, but they cannot even exist with such large sections of their industries working under non-union conditions.

The organization of the unorganized masses will mean a tremendous step forward to the general revolutionizing of the labor movement. At present the unions have only 3,500,000 workers out of a total of at least 20,000,000 who are organizable. Doubling or tripling the total number of organized workers will, merely by the increased weight of organized labor alone, enormously enhance its power and stimulate all its institutions.

But, bringing the masses into the unions means much more than simply to add them numerically to the number of organized workers. Far more important will be the consequent changing in the composition of the unions and the shifting of their centers of gravity into the heavy and key industries.

The overwhelming bulk of the unorganized masses are semi-skilled and unskilled. They are the most proletarian and revolutionary section of the working class. Of the 3,500,000 organized workers, fully one-half are highly skilled. They dominate the whole movement and color it and restrict it with their craft prejudices and petty bourgeois conceptions. A great influx of the at present unorganized semi-skilled and unskilled workers will drown out these unhealthy tendencies and start the movement in the direction of revolutionary development. The newly organized workers, with no craft interests to preserve, will tend strongly in the direction of industrial unionism—the organization of the unorganized will mean a great surge forward towards the amalgamation of the existing organizations.

It will also mean a powerful development of the labor party movement, partly through the increased class consciousness given to the movement by the addition of the masses of semi-skilled and unskilled, partly because of the intensification of the class struggle accompanying the organization of the unorganized, and partly because the increased size of the labor movement will furnish a better foundation for the labor party—where the unions are only skeleton in form, the existence of a powerful labor party is almost out of the question.

Also, the very progress of bringing the millions of semi-skilled and unskilled into the unions will provoke a whole series of struggles against the employers and will enormously increase the militancy of the labor movement. The present epoch of militancy and class conscious development in the British movement was hastened very much by infusing into the old conservative skilled workers' craft unions many hundreds of thousands of semi-skilled and unskilled workers. And a similar result will be produced on the unions in the United States by bringing in the unskilled.

A further vital consideration is that the organization of the unorganized masses will tend to revolutionize the labor movement by establishing its foundations in the basic and other important industries. At the present time the trade unions are strongest in the lighter industries, such as building, printing, clothing, etc. Where they touch the basic industries, as on the railroads and in the coal mines, they are either confined largely to the skilled workers, or their hold on the masses in general is weak.

The big industries present a deplorable lack of trade union organization: railroads 35 per cent, coal mining 40 per cent, general metal 5 per cent, general transport 10 per cent, metal mining 5 per cent, steel 3 per cent, textiles 10 per cent, leather 15 per cent; while practically no organization exists at all in the meat packing, automobile, electrical supplies, lumber, agricultural machinery, etc. A trade union movement so weak in the big and basic industries of the country cannot possibly make an effective struggle against capitalism. The firm establishment of the unions in these industries by organizing the great masses will enormously increase the strength of the labor movement and throw it at the very heart of capitalism. It will imbue the entire organization with a new understanding and a new fighting spirit.

The organization of the unorganized is of tremendous importance to the left wing. It tends to revolutionize the labor movement, to make it more responsive to left wing slogans, and to create generally a more favorable situation in which the left wing can operate. Moreover, in the organization process, by taking an active lead in the campaign, the left wing will win direct leadership over large sections of the newly organized masses, for whoever organizes the workers leads them. It will also give the left wing invaluable experience in mass work and leadership. We must realize the vital importance of the great campaign of organization and the leading role the left wing has to play in it.

The present period presents an exceptionally favorable time to bring the unorganized masses into the unions. Industry is going ahead at a relatively high rate. The workers are bitterly exploited, their standards of living are not advancing. In fact, in many industries such as textile, mining, shoe, in spite of the prosperity of the employers, the workers are facing wage cuts. There is much discontent in their ranks. The situation is ripe for a great drive for organization. The present period of "prosperity" cannot last indefinitely. Already there are signs of its weakening. We must take the fullest advantage of the situation now. The workers are in a mood to organize. We must take the lead and show them how.

Failure of the unions to strengthen their ranks now by the inclusion of vast masses of the unorganized will expose them to the most deadly dangers in the slack industrial period that is not far ahead, when the employers will renew their "open shop" campaign of destruction against the unions with redoubled vigor.

The Trade Union Educational League is fundamentally correct when it places as "point 1" in its program of action the initiation of a general campaign to organize the millions of unorganized workers.

THE LEFT WING MUST DO THE WORK

The organization of the unorganized millions of workers is primarily the task of the left wing. There is no other section of the labor movement possessing the necessary courage, energy, and understanding to carry through this basic work. This is a prime lesson that T. U. E. L. militants must understand.

The three general groups in the trade union movement play essentially the following roles in the gigantic task of organizing the unorganized masses: The left wing militantly leads, the progressives mildly support, and the right wing opposes.

The left wing alone has a realization of the tremendous social significance of the organization of the unorganized. It speaks primarily in the name of the unskilled and semi-skilled who make up the mass on the outside of the unions, and it habitually leads a militant struggle to unionize them. It is the champion of industrial unionism and the labor party, the fate of both of which is bound up in the general question of organizing the unorganized. It realizes that only when the great masses are mobilized in the unions can effective assaults be made against capitalism. Hence, it is the life of every organizing campaign, and it must be such, whether these campaigns are carried on through the medium of the existing trade unions, or by the launching of new organizations.

The progressives primarily represent the skilled, and, to a certain degree, the semi-skilled workers. They usually mildly favor and support general campaigns of organization. They have some appreciation of the importance of bringing the masses into the unions, but they have not the necessary understanding and militancy to do the actual work. They must be stimulated into action by the left wing.

They lack the leadership to map out and carry through the broad, daring campaigns necessary for the organization of the masses in American industries. They fear the militant and desperate strikes which must accompany such campaigns. They are class collaborationists, they are afflicted with many of the craft prejudices and much of the conservatism of the right wing. But, under the pressure of the left wing, they can be pushed into doing effective organizing work.

The essential form of an organizing committee or movement under present conditions in the American labor movement is a united front between the left wing and the progressives, with the left wing functioning as the driving force.

The right-wing controlling bureaucrats are the real stumbling block to organization. They fear that the organization of the unorganized masses of semi-skilled and unskilled will overwhelm the organized skilled workers. The bureaucrats want to maintain craft lines and craft interests, in wage scales, in organization forms, and in various other ways, and they know that the influx of the unorganized mass will tend to wipe out these special interests. They know that the struggle to organize the unorganized will compel the skilled workers to abandon their class collaboration policies, and they fear it will force them into fights against the employers that will jeopardize their craft organizations and preferred wage scales.

They know that with the mass organized, the skilled workers will not be able to trade so successfully at the expense of the unskilled workers, as, for example, the Railroad Brotherhoods and many other unions are now doing. The right wing bureaucrats fear the unskilled will flood the unions and capture them from the skilled. They dread the influx of the mass because it means a general disturbance of the equilibrium in the organizations, the rise of new leaders, and probably their own displacement. They sense the general revolutionizing effect of the influx of semi-skilled and unskilled workers into the unions, and they shrink from it.

Hence, the right-wing bureaucracy is ordinarily opposed to the organization of the unorganized, except along their narrow craft lines, where they often display organizing activity. Their policy is to set up bars against apprentices, against helpers, and to develop their unions into job trusts. They concentrate in certain industries easy to organize, such as the Electrical Workers' Union, confining itself principally to the building trades; the Metal Trades Unions, specializing on the railroads, while they neglect other industries "hard" to organize.

Even when driven into organizing campaigns by pressure, the right wing bureaucrats refuse to lend them real support. At best they then only trail along. Their policy is one of sabotage. They are affected by a hundred petty craft considerations, and they raise innumerable technical and other objections in order to hinder the organizing work. Often they co-operate with the employers to prevent organization. They usually will accept mass organization if it is "handed to them on a silver platter" by the left-wing organizers, but they will not go out and fight for it. They are lazy, unimaginative, corrupt, and petty bourgeois. The left wing must consider and deal with them as a major obstacle in the work of organizing the unorganized.

It would be a grievous error, however, to conclude from the foregoing that the right wing can block the organization of the unorganized by the trade unions and that nothing can be done in these bodies. A whole series of organization campaigns by the trade unions belie this pessimism. The impulse of the labor movement to expand into a real mass and class organization is very powerful. Where there is an insistent and intelligent demand from the combined left wing and progressives, the right wing can literally be driven into organizing campaigns. This is what was done to Gompers and the presidents of the various internationals in the steel and packing industry campaigns.

And on the railroads the more progressive elements were responsible for the organization of hundreds of thousands of the unorganized during the war period.

The right-wing bureaucrats find it exceedingly difficult to fight directly against the demand for organization. Their method is mostly indirect. They commonly adopt organization resolutions, presented by the more progressive elements, and then sabotage them to death. They do lip service to the organization of the unorganized and then prevent it in practice. The American Federation of Labor has adopted, from time to time, resolutions for the organization of every industry in the country, and immediately after the conventions has promptly forgotten all about them.

In the struggle against the right wing over the question of organizing the unorganized, two principal dangers confront the left wing, both of which must be guarded against. The first is a pessimistic conclusion that the trade unions cannot be stimulated to do organization work. The second, the other extreme, is a naive, over-optimistic belief that the right wing will put into effect the adopted resolutions calling for the organization of the unorganized.

Both of these tendencies block real organization work. The proper policy in the trade unions is for the left wing to enter into alliance with the progressive elements, to force the adoption of programs of organization, and then themselves to do the actual work of organizing, in spite of the sabotage of the right wing. The theme of this chapter is correct; upon the left wing rests primarily the burden of organizing the unorganized.

THE A. F. OF L. AND INDEPENDENT UNIONS

A most important question for T. U. E. L. militants to understand in order to carry through successfully our work of organizing the unorganized is our relationship to the A. F. of L. and Independent unions. Our goal must be to build mass labor organization of the workers, and to bring or maintain these unions in affiliation with the general labor movement, the American Federation of Labor. This involves the two-sided policy of: (a) stimulating the existing unions into organizing campaigns; and (b) forming new unions in industries where there are no unions or where the existing unions are hopelessly decrepit. The two evils we have to guard against are, on the one side, the devil of dual unionism, and, on the other, the dogma of unity with the old trade unions "at any price."

The advantages of bringing the newly organized workers into the existing labor movement are manifest, save in certain exceptional cases. In most instances positive and direct support for these workers in their initial crucial struggles is gained by such affiliation. But even where this is not the case, there are certain negative advantages of affiliation to the A. F. of L. For one thing, the workers are shielded from the disastrous attacks of the bureaucracy, which are always leveled against dual unions. To a certain extent, also, the conservative name of the A. F. of L. saves the workers from the attacks of the employers and the state, even though their policies be as militant as those of any independent union.

But perhaps the most important asset of affiliation to the A. F. of L. is the feeling of the newly organized workers that they are connected with the mass labor movement of the country. This ordinarily gives them far greater confidence and staying power. It is a feeling they do not acquire in independent unions. Among a certain section of unorganized workers there is a deep hostility towards the American Federation of Labor. The T. U. E. L. militants must not allow themselves to be dominated by this antagonism. They must and can liquidate it wherever the interests of the workers dictate that they shall be affiliated to the A. F. of L. unions.

In the industries where there are no A. F. of L. unions our course is clear. We must form new unions and bring them into affiliation with the broad labor movement as quickly as practicability permits. Or if there be independent unions in such industries we must give them our active support and work for their affiliation to the A. F. of L. In those fields where the I. W. W. functions more or less effectively, as for example, among the lumber, general construction, and agricultural workers, we must support it.

In industries where there are A. F. of L. unions, but where these unions are so weak and decrepit, with corrupt leadership, hidebound agreements, etc. that it is impossible to stimulate them into the necessary activity to mobilize the mass militant organization campaigns or to defend their interests in strikes arising therefrom, our problem is more complicated. There the advantage of affiliation may easily be outweighed by the disadvantages. Such situations raise the question of independent unionism in its most intricate form. In spite of our most urgent desire for unity with the general labor movement, we will often, under these circumstances, be compelled to form independent unions.

But wherever we form such new unions, whether because there are no A. F. of L. unions in the field or because those that may exist are absolutely decrepit, we must from the outset follow a program for the affiliation of these unions to the A. F. of L. We must be keenly on our guard not to get into a dual union position, by declaring against the A. F. of L. in principle or by permitting an open warfare to develop against it. Experience teaches us that dual unionism means sectarianism, isolation from the broad labor movement, and eventually disintegration. One of the outstanding contributions of the Communist International and the Red International of Labor Unions to the labor movement was their categoric condemnation of dual unionism.

Dualism must be fended off by a two-sided policy of: (a) teaching the membership of the new unions from the start that their place is in unity with the mass of workers in the A. F. of L.; and (b) to begin a series of maneuvers to get into affiliation with the A. F. of L.

Such a policy is bound to be successful. On the one hand it checks the dangerous and ever-present spirit of sectarianism, and, on the other hand it either leads to amalgamation and affiliation, or it gives the new union many of the advantages of affiliation by breaking up the official bureaucratic opposition. When per-capita-tax-hungry trade union officials see a fat independent union that wants to affiliate to their organization, they are much inclined to look upon it with some degree of friendliness and tolerance, even though, for the time being, they are afraid to accept its affiliation. Negotiations for affiliation by independent unions give them standing in the broad labor movement by making that movement understand that the new union feels itself to be a part of the main body of organized labor. This, in turn, strengthens the rank and file of the new union by a knowledge of the general friendliness of the mass labor movement.

But while militantly propagandizing amalgamation and maneuvering for its accomplishment, the new unions must make every effort to work in harmony with the old unions by the initiation of joint organization campaigns, by assisting them in their strikes, etc. Its aim must be generally to create a spirit of friendly co-operation which shall culminate in an amalgamation.

Where independent unions have been set up, and especially where there are already existing A. F. of L. unions in the field, our greatest danger comes from a dual union tendency to repel the old organizations and to maintain an independent existence of the new union. This bases itself upon various illusions and wrong policies, such as utopian hopes for the future of the new union, underestimation of the power and importance of the old unions, the tendency to seek reasons to quarrel with the old unions rather than to co-operate with them, neglect of amalgamation and maneuvers to bring about a consolidation, the presentation of impossible programs as the basis of amalgamation or affiliation, etc.

This whole dual union tendency must be relentlessly combated and the policy pursued of coming more closely into cooperation and affiliation with the old unions. The T. U. E. L. militants must also guard against the opposite tendency of making affiliation with the old unions a fetishism, or developing a "unity-at-any-price" program. Such a policy is wrong and might easily do big damage by resulting in a surrender off-hand of the leadership of strikes, organizing campaigns, and new-formed unions to ultra reactionary leaders who would destroy them.

Often these leaders will propose such terms of affiliation as to make their acceptance tantamount to the sacrifice of the interests of the workers. We must fight for affiliation to the A. F. of L. unions, but we also must fight for honest and militant leadership, and mass industrial organization. Our growing left wing leaders must be provided a place to function in the unions, and above all, at this stage, we must retain the initiative in carrying on the great work of organizing the unorganized.

In working out propositions of affiliation, or operating within the trade unions, these ends must not be lost sight of. One of our most delicate tactical problems will be to judge when we can best further these ends by affiliation to the existing unions, and when it will be necessary to form or maintain independent organizations.

But again I emphasize, the greatest danger that the left wing confronts in such situations is the persistent dual union tendency to pull away from the old unions and to establish new and independent organizations which isolate our forces from the main body of organized workers.

Under the general head of left-wing relationship to the old unions must be considered the problem presented by the jurisdictional claims of these organizations. First, the question of open jurisdictional fights. In many cases left wingers, taking the points of view of their respective craft unions, become deeply immersed in the jurisdictional quarrels of their organizations, with the result that their arguments and programs are almost indistinguishable from those of the ordinary craft unionist. This is fundamentally wrong. We must rise above such petty, shortsighted quarrels and base our policy upon the interests of all the workers in the totality of the unions involved.

Then there is the situation, common in many industries, where a score of unions, most of them with little or no organized membership in the industry, claim jurisdiction over the workers of their respective trades in the industry. The left wing cannot support such ridiculous jurisdictional claims, nor can we wait until these reactionary unions decide to amalgamate with stronger and more basic unions in the industry. Sometimes it will be necessary, in such situations, for the left wing to ignore the claims of these dog-in-the-manger unions, and support the basic unions at the expense of the weaker ones.

Thus, for example, in the steel industry, we must at this time insist that the Amalgamated Association of Iron, Steel & Tin Workers take in all workers in and around the steel mills, regardless of the claims of a score or more of other unions for certain categories of these workers. Also, in the metal industry generally, we must more and more apply such a policy with regard to the Machinists' Union.

In thus precipitating amalgamation from the bottom, and the realignment of the unions according to industrial lines, we must, however, take care not to provoke open jurisdictional struggles between the unions.

In the general problem of our left-wing attitude towards the A. F. of L. and the independent unions, the T. U. E. L. policy must be: In industries with strong unions, we shall build up these organizations; in industries with no unions or with incurably decrepit unions, we shall form independent organizations and then affiliate them, or seek persistently to affiliate them to the A. F. of L. This is the basic program which the necessities of the present situation dictate.

METHODS OF ORGANIZATION

In the United States, the task of organizing the workers is an extremely complicated and difficult one. The situation in the industries is not uniform. In industries that are competitive in character, especially where there are established unions or where the workers have a tradition of organization, unions and efforts to organize them are tolerated, or at least not violently persecuted.

In other industries, where the organization and tradition of unionism are weak, and the employers, highly organized, are applying a militant "open shop" policy, the unions are ruthlessly crushed and attempts to establish them are met with an iron repression. This situation necessitates upon our part two general kinds of organizing work, open and secret. Let us first discuss "open" organization work.

It is possible to carry on "open" trade union organization work in many industries such as on various railroads, in half organized northern coal fields, in the unorganized sections of the building, needle, culinary, and printing trades, and in the general mass of small metal and other competitive industries, where the employers are not strongly organized. In such situations are commonly found trade unions, however weak. Wherever "open" trade union organization is possible, the task of the left wing consists, for the most part, in stimulating the existing unions into carrying on open organizational campaigns among the workers by mass meetings, individual solicitation, etc.

To develop this activity of the old unions necessitates a variety of means. Every phase and stage of the movement must be stirred up on the organization question. In every local union the question of organizing the unorganized must be made a burning one, and committees established to unite the workers. Between the local unions of one craft, or among those of several crafts in one industry, joint organization campaigns can be established. The Central Labor Councils can also be stirred into action.

A number of years ago the A. F. of L. used to promote in the various cities what were called "Labor Forward" movements. In these all the unions of a given city rallied for a general organizing campaign, many internationals sending in organizers to assist. Often good work was done. The "Labor Forward" type of movement should be revived. Likewise the international unions, especially at their conventions, can be energized into making national organizing campaigns in their respective jurisdictions, either alone or in co-operation with related unions.

In all this stimulation of the trade unions it must never be lost sight of, however, that the left wing must lead in the actual work of organizing. Simply to pass resolutions calling for organization, and then to leave the matter to the officialdom, is futile. Their policy is to let such resolutions die a quiet death. They cling desperately to old forms and practices. They have to be crowded into action.

The left wing and the progressives must follow up their resolutions by demanding the formation of large organizing committees through which they can carry on actual work of organization. Such committees must know how to force through the necessary reductions of initiation fees, and generally to remove the many barriers which the reactionary leadership has raised against the organization of their fellow workers. They must also know how to mobilize the full financial resources of the unions and to bring the general membership into the organization work. Such organization committees offer splendid opportunities to bring forward the whole T. U. E. L. program and to mobilize all the progressive elements in the unions against the right wing bureaucracy and the employers.

There are many other industries, on the other hand, such as steel, textile, rubber, southern coal fields, on many railroads, etc., etc., where unionism has been eliminated and where "open" organization work is practically impossible because of the terrorism of the employers. In these "closed" industries, we must adopt "secret" or indirect methods of organization.

A most important consideration in these "closed," unorganized industries is the fact that the left wing must take the initiative in the organizing work to a far greater extent than in the "open," semi-organized industries. Usually there are no unions at all in the "closed" industries to be stimulated into action and upon whose resources the left wing can draw. The reactionary leaders refuse to tackle these tough industries. Consequently the left wing has to depend primarily upon its own resources and upon its own direct initiative in launching and carrying through the organization campaigns.

In the industries which are "closed" against trade unionism by the terrorism of the employers, our basic method for organizing work must be "secret" or indirect in character. It is true that upon occasion, as in the big organizing campaign among the steel workers in 1918-19, such gigantic efforts can be put forth directly so that the workers can be openly mobilized in spite of the most violent opposition by the employers. The left wing must seek to develop such broad, sweeping, "open" campaigns. But they are the exception. Most of the work in these industries will have to be done on a relatively small scale, which means more or less "underground."

For a long time the trade unions have used "secret" methods of organization in such instances. But their efforts have been crude and ineffective, being usually merely the quiet recruiting of members into local unions which are spy ridden, ordinarily dead of dry rot, of repression by the employers, or through premature strikes. The left wing will have to be far more skillful in "underground" trade union organization. It must utilize the most diverse forms of proletarian organization in order to secure a basis for the establishment of unions, or for the launching of strike movements which will eventually result in building unions.

One form of organization which must be utilized for this work is the company union. Company unions flourish especially in those industries "closed" to trade unionism. The left wing must carry on a policy of working within these organizations where they have any degree of mass participation, with the ultimate aim of destroying them and building trade unions.

We must raise economic demands of the workers in these organizations in order to expose their nature as instruments of the employers and to crystallize the discontent of the workers. We must participate in the plant elections in order to sharpen and clarify the struggle of the workers against the employers, and to place our men in strategic positions. At the company union conventions, especially on the railroads, the question of trade unionism can be raised effectively.

The experience during the movement of the steel workers, in 1918-19, when many company unions were captured from the employers, as well as the experience among many other groups of workers show clearly that these organizations can be utilized for the launching of movements among the workers which culminate in the destruction of the company unions and the formation of trade unions.

Another form of organization valuable for organizing in the "closed" industries is the various workers' clubs and fraternal organizations in the industrial towns. Made up for the most part of unskilled, foreign-language speaking workers, they readily adapt themselves to supporting drives to organize the local industries. Under cover of these clubs general organizational propaganda can be successfully carried on and committees formed to lay the first foundations of trade union organization for the various factories. In the textile industry, particularly in Passaic, Lawrence, etc., their value has been demonstrated. They are to play an important role in the organization of the great masses of workers.

The left wing must follow a policy of establishing such workers' clubs and fraternal organizations and of winning over those already in existence, especially in cities dominated by one or two industries. This does not mean, however, the inauguration of a campaign to use such clubs as organizing instruments generally in the industries where there are unions. Wherever it is possible to organize openly and directly into the trade unions, we must by all means utilize the opportunity.

The shop branches of the Communist Party are an organizational form of great importance in the organization of the unorganized workers. These branches, distributed widely through the industries and built upon the basis of the respective factories, will prove invaluable contact points for the starting of broad movements for the launching of strikes and the establishment of trade unions. Their factory papers will arouse and educate the workers, giving voice to their demands, organizing the resistance to the company unions, and generally preparing the ground for trade unionism.

The shop committee movement will also be used very profitably in the organization of the workers in the "closed" industries. Among the unorganized workers this movement consists in the formation of committees, more or less informal, representing the workers, department by department and factory by factory. It carries on a struggle for the demands of the workers and for their recruitment into trade unions. The value of the shop committee movement among the unorganized has been demonstrated in the textile industry. In the struggle to organize the unorganized it will play an increasingly important part.

Under certain circumstances, all these various forms of proletarian organization, such as workers' clubs, fraternal organizations, shop branches, shop committees, etc., can be joined together, in united front movements, facilitating the creation of open trade unions. Even the representatives of company unions should be admitted to such united front committees unless there are special reasons for excluding them.

All these proletarian organizations will play a big part in the organization of the workers in the "closed" industries. They will also serve to a certain extent in other industries where the employers are not so hostile but where the workers are simply lethargic. Yet they offer no royal road to organization. Upon occasion the employers will fight them bitterly. They will discharge the workers for militant activities in company unions; they will clean out the shop committee men; they will fire workers for membership in clubs that are showing a tendency towards trade unionism; they will fill all these institutions with detectives. Nevertheless, we must utilize them. They offer the means for a flank attack against the employers, which is necessary considering the weak forces of organized labor in the "closed" industries.

In its organization work, the left wing must aim to work in the "open." When this cannot be done, we must work "underground." The question of determining just how far we can work in the "open" and how much we will have to use the indirect method will prove one of the most delicate problems we have to solve in our organization campaigns.

ORGANIZATION AND STRIKES

The organization of the unorganized on any considerable scale in American industry inevitably precipitates hard-fought strikes. Organization campaigns are the first phase of bitter struggles between the workers and employers over questions of wages, hours, working conditions, and the right to organize.

In most industries the acute phase of the struggle, the strike, comes quickly. Usually, when an organization campaign begins, the employers take the initiative and try to nip the movement in the bud by militantly attacking it. But even if they do not follow this course, the workers themselves will soon precipitate the strike struggle by raising their demands against the employers. This basic connection of strikes with organization movements is a foundation fact. All our strategy in the campaign to organize the unorganized turns around it.

The first consideration is to center our campaigns of organization around the economic demands of the workers. The unorganized workers have very little understanding of or desire for trade unionism as such. It is only the advanced elements who appreciate the real value of organization. When the masses join unions it is in the hope of securing immediate satisfaction for their burning grievances. They want unions directly for what they can get through them from the employers, and usually they will not wait long for results. Therefore, we must make the fight for the workers' demands the basis of all our tactics in our organization work, bringing in our general left-wing program as the struggle develops.

A glaring weakness of conservative trade unionists in attempting to organize the unorganized is their failure to take into consideration this fact, that the mass of workers have organized themselves in order to fight immediately for their demands. The conservatives stress the purely organizational side too much and the struggle side too little. They ignore the urgency of the workers' demands. They assume that the mass of workers understand the general value of trade unionism as such. They proceed upon the basis that the workers can be brought into the unions slowly, man by man, and then held there and disciplined indefinitely until the great mass is organized, when, sometime in the distant future, perhaps demands will be made on the employers for better conditions.

Such a theory is of course absurd. It always fails in practise, a case in point being the fiasco of the recent A. F. of L. organization campaign in the steel industry.

The future trade unions of the great unorganized industries will be born in the heat of the struggle against the employers over the demands of the workers. The organization campaign which does not voice the demands of the workers and envisage an early struggle in defense of them is doomed beforehand to failure.

The nature of the workers' demands are determined by the state of the industry and the moods of the employers and workers concerned. In periods of slackened industry, with the employers on the offensive, the fight of the workers in their present stage of ideological development will be to maintain existing standards, to struggle against wage cuts, lengthening of the work day, etc. In periods of "prosperity," the workers will fight for better wages, shorter hours, etc. But, in any event, in good times or bad, the struggle for organization must center around the defense of the workers' pressing demands. The workers are especially militant in fighting against reductions of their living standards. The fight against wage cuts is one of the very best issues upon which to organize the workers and to bring them into struggle against the employers.

Organization campaigns in American unorganized industries are preparations for strikes. They are a struggle for position between the employers and workers in the big battle that is soon to come, the strike over the establishment of better conditions. It is in this sense that such campaigns must be conceived and carried through.

To prevent the organization of their workers, the employers have a whole arsenal of weapons which they use with skill and ruthlessness. When modern employers cut wages they commonly slash one group of workers at a time, thus breaking up the solidarity of the workers, instead of using the old-time method of making broad-sweeping wage cuts in all departments simultaneously, which united the workers. This canny policy makes the work of the organizer difficult.

The employers also fight the introduction of trade unions by setting up company unions. And when actually confronted with militant organizing campaigns, they try to break them up by granting wage increases, discharging active workers, forcing premature strikes, abolishing free assembly in their company towns, etc. In the steel campaign of 1918-19, for example, the steel trust, to head off the movement, conceded the workers several increases in wages and established the basic eight-hour day, while at the same time carrying on a policy of terrorism against the unions and the workers who joined them.

The T. U. E. L. left-wing militants must learn to defeat this anti-union strategy of the employers by the development of a thorough-going strategy of organization in support of the workers' economic demands. The very heart of this strategy is: (a) our organization work must be carefully planned; (b) it must embrace the widest possible scope of workers in each case; (c) it must be accompanied by an inspiring propaganda.

One of the greatest weakness of conservatives in trade union organization work is their policy of dabbling. They simply drift into their campaigns, haphazard and planlessly, wherever some local stir wakes them up a bit. Their efforts are mostly confined to a local and craft basis, with consequent failure. The method of the general office of the A. F. of L. itself is typical. It has never followed a thought-out plan for the organization of the workers. It simply sends its organizers around, hither and yon, wherever strikes happen to develop, and these organizers handle such strikes without regard to the situation in the industry as a whole. This is a policy of following the masses, not leading them.

The left wing must depart radically from such a primitive policy, which is totally unfitted for modern American industry. When we get into an organizing campaign in a given locality or industry, we must do so on the basis of a careful analysis of the whole situation. And we must make a determined effort for the utmost mobilization of our forces for the struggle. We must actually lead in the organization work.

Moreover, when the left wing undertakes an organization campaign it must be made as broad and sweeping as possible. Our aim must be for the organization of the whole industry, and all our strategy must go in that direction. Craftism and localism are totally out of place and must be fought. In most cases, as at the present time in the railroad industry, we will, by analysis, ascertain the opportune time for the organization of the masses and we will work for the necessary nationwide campaigns.

But where we are caught napping, so to speak, by sudden local strike movements of workers in national industries, we must immediately undertake to spread these movements out on a national scale. The trustified state of American industries prevents a successful fight being made on a local scale except in the most favorable and unusual circumstances.

It must be our special endeavor in all these campaigns to win over and develop the youth, who are the bridge to and uniting force between the masses of foreign-born workers and the American workers.

We must also accompany our organization work with a militant educational propaganda. We must learn to raise not only the economic demands of the workers, but also learn to fire the workers with the spirit of revolutionary enthusiasm. Strikes offer ideal opportunities to point out to the workers the full political consequences of the class struggle and to awaken their class spirit and consciousness. One of the failures of conservative trade unionism is its almost total lack of vision. It fails to arouse the fighting spirit of the workers, which can only be done by militant propaganda.

Successful trade union organizers must be masters of strike strategy. One thing they must know is how to deal a blow at the employers opportunely. The left wing must learn to hit the employers when they are least able to stand it, and to deliver the attack with a maximum force. The employers are wide awake to this danger and follow the counter policy of trying to force the workers into premature struggles.

This was the policy of the steel trust in the 1918-19 campaign. Gary tried to compel the steel workers to strike in certain localities before the national organization had been completed, by discharging thousands of them. His aim was to demoralize the movement before it got well started. We bitterly resisted this tactic, forcing the attacked points to stand fast under the severest pressure until we could mobilize the rest of the steel workers to support them. Thus we gained most precious time in which to organize. Nevertheless, Gary did succeed in precipitating the strike before we were fully prepared for it.

On the basis of a careful analysis of the state of the industry and of the condition of the workers' forces, the left wing must learn when to strike and when to organize. Nothing is more disastrous than ill-timed strikes and organization campaigns, which needlessly victimize the workers and break their spirit.

Left-wing organizers must learn every phase of the art of mobilizing effectively the masses in struggles against the employers. They must know how to dramatize their strikes and to make them spur the class instincts not only of the workers involved, but of the whole working class. They must understand how to mobilize public sentiment behind their cause, and especially to enlist the support of the trade union movement. They must be experts in the collection and distribution of relief. They must understand the technique of mass picketing and the application of the boycott. They must at all times display unfaltering personal courage.

They must know how to build their trade unions among the inexperienced workers during the strike, and how to take advantage of such big struggles as that in Passaic by organizing the masses in surrounding industries and localities who are inspired by the struggle. In short, they must be practical strike leaders in order to be effective organizers, and to do this they must take an active part in all the struggles of the workers.

The question of organizing the unorganized becomes daily more pressing. The T. U. E. L. and the left wing generally have a central part to play in the great developing movement for organization. This part we can play effectively if we will bear in mind the few general principles of organization elaborated above, namely, that the left wing must lead in and do the burden of the organization work, that we must avoid isolation from the organized masses and be prepared to utilize every form of proletarian organization in the "closed" industries to further the establishment of unions.

We must study carefully the state of the industry and the condition of the employers' and the workers' forces, base our organization campaigns upon the economic demands of the workers and at all times keep the fight focussed on these demands, plan our organization campaigns carefully and thoroughly mobilize all our forces to put them into execution, extend our scope of activity over the greatest possible extent of workers, strike the blow at the opportune time, demoralize the enemy, rouse public sentiment, develop the utmost fighting spirit in our own ranks by our invigorating propaganda, and follow up our victories to the limit by organizing all the workers shaken into action by our big strikes and struggles.

The left wing must take the lead in the organization of the unorganized millions. This is an historic necessity of the situation. We must not falter or fail at our task. It is a time for intelligent, courageous, militant action.

1925

18. The Trend Toward Independent Unionism

Since 1912, the T. U. E. L. and its predecessor organizations, the S. L. of N. A. and the I. T. U. E. L., had carried on a stout fight against dual unionism; but now in the latter Coolidge period—1926-29 —forces were at work that were gradually pushing the T. U. E. L. towards a partial policy of independent unionism. Indeed, there had long been a potential base for such unionism in the great masses of deeply exploited, unorganized workers in the mass production, trustified industries which the A. F. of L. had been unable and unwilling to unionize. This was true, in spite of the fact that such dual organizations as the I. W. W., the W. I. I. U., etc., because of their ultra-revolutionary programs, hostility to A. F. of L. workers, and general sectarian practices, were never able to build any independent unions on a permanent mass basis among the huge numbers of unorganized. The general course of events in the post-war Coolidge years had tended greatly to strengthen this potential basis for independent unionism and finally to put before the revolutionary movement as a living issue the question of forming new unions. Let us cite four of the general forces tending to produce this result, as follows:

1. There was the narrowing down of the A. F. of L. base in many industries during the great post-war employers' offensive, including the complete wiping out of its unions by strikes in the steel, lumber, and meat-packing industries, the crushing defeat of the railroad unions in 1922 with a loss of several hundred thousand members, and the eventual breaking down of the U. M. W. A. in the bituminous fields; besides, there was a serious weakening of the unions in various other industries, including building trades, marine transport, printing,

needle, textile, food, shoes, etc. In consequence of these strike defeats, the worst in our labor history, the numerical strength and strategical position of the A. F. of L. had been greatly weakened and the percentage of unorganized workers much increased. Especially the A. F. of L. had lost great masses of unskilled workers and tended to become more and more an organization of the skilled labor aristocracy.

2. There was the adoption by the A. F. of L. of its no-strike, "union-management co-operation," "higher strategy of labor" program. This policy of class collaboration, by distorting the unions from their basic role as fighting organizations into adjuncts of the employers' production speed-up, killed the militant spirit of the unions and inflicted upon the labor movement a disastrous dry rot. As a result of it the unions, during the Coolidge "prosperity" years, were not only not able to recover their losses in the big post-war strikes, but as we have seen, for the first time in history, had steadily declined in strength and influence. The A. F. of L. became less able than ever to defend its own members' interests and to organize the unorganized.

3. There was the expulsion of large numbers of militant and revolutionary workers from the trade unions, a fact which robbed these organizations of their best elements and hastened their decline. In consequence of these expulsions, the T. U. E. L. militants, largely outside, found it very difficult to work within the A. F. of L. unions, which, to make matters worse, were gangster-ridden and bereft of democracy.

4. There was a new and growing tendency among the organized and unorganized masses to fight, exemplified by such bitter, hard-fought strikes as the Passaic textile workers, the New York fur and cloakmakers in 1926, the national U. M. W. A. strike of 1927, the Boston shoe workers' strike, the New Bedford textile strike, and the great 1929 strikes of textile workers in Gastonia, Elizabethton, and many southern towns. This developing strike movement could not be stimulated, developed and led to victory by the corrupted leaders of the half-dead A. F. of L. unions, with their no-strike policies, but was in every instance directly sabotaged by them.

All these factors combined showed a definite decline of the A. F. of L. unions in strength and fighting ability. Their heavy loss of members and spirit-killing class collaboration, the mass expulsions, and the growing urge for organization among the unorganized, all worked together to prepare the ground for independent unionism. Especially, in the three major fields of T. U. E. L. activity—mining, textile, needle—the basis for new unions was definite and strong.

In the mining industry the bituminous section of the U. M. W. A. had been wrecked, the militants stood expelled in great numbers and the miners, with long organization experience, were bitter against the U. M. W. A. and definitely disposed to form a new union. After the disastrous 1927 strike this tendency manifested itself by the growth of a whole series of spontaneous local dual organizations in Canada, Colorado (I. W. W.), West Virginia (Keeney), Illinois (P. M. A.— 1932), Oklahoma, the anthracite districts, etc. A general outcropping of new unions was taking the place of the collapsing U. M. W. A.

In the textile industry, the tendency towards independent unionism took a somewhat different course, but the general direction was the same. The U. T. W. and the other textile unions, containing only 5 per cent of the workers, were paralyzed by the intense class collaboration practices of the period and were both unable and unwilling to respond to the demands of the discontented workers in the industry for a fight in behalf of their demands. The result we have seen in Passaic where the T. U. E. L., in spite of its intense anti-dual union attitude, was compelled to form an independent union in order to organize the workers.

In the needle trades the course towards independent unionism was again somewhat different, but none the less sure. The reactionary course of the union leadership, the steadily worsening economic conditions, the expulsion of almost 50,000 militant workers, all created a growing mass demand in the industry for a new, fighting industrial union.

But the T. U. E. L., traditional fighter against dual unionism, strongly resisted these mass demands for new unions. In the mining industry, for example, at the big April 1, 1928, Save-the-Union Pittsburgh Conference, representing 100,000 miners, there was a strong trend to launch a new union, but it was defeated by the T. U. E. L. and Communist Party opposition. Most of the above-mentioned new unions in the mining industry were initiated by Socialists and other non-Communists. In the textile industry in Passaic, even after the T. U. E. L. had been compelled to form a new union, we were opposed to its independent existence and proceeded to affiliate it to the torpid U. T. W., this, indeed, being our line in all industries where we built new unions among the unorganized. And in the needle trades it was the T. U. E. L. that was responsible for stopping the split at the Philadelphia convention of the I. L. G. W. U. and for generally having the masses of expelled workers adopt the policy of fighting for reinstatement in their old organizations.

Just in the midst of these developments, on December 3-4, 1927, the T. U. E. L. held its third national conference in New York, whither the organization had just removed its headquarters from Chicago. There were 297 delegates, of whom 107 were from the needle trades. In total they represented a following estimated at 300,000, or about 10 per cent of the trade union movement. The conference clearly realized the menace arising from the smashing of the A. F. of L. in many industries, its failure to organize the unorganized, its fatal no-strike, class collaboration policy, and its reactionary trend in general. It stated that the unions were in full retreat before the employers' economic, political and ideological offensive and declared that the very existence of the trade unions was endangered. But it did not understand these developments as laying the basis for independent unionism. On the contrary, the whole orientation of the T. U. E. L. third conference was towards the A. F. of L., it directed all its efforts to an intensification of the fight within the old unions against class collaboration, for trade union democracy, for the organization of the unorganized, for the labor party, for unemployment insurance, against trade union capitalism (labor banking), against racial discrimination, for world trade union unity, etc. It called upon the many expelled workers to fight for reinstatement into their former unions and it put forth as a central slogan, "Save the Trade Unions."

1936

19. The Trade Union Unity League

The T. U. E. L. began its reorientation in policy towards independent unionism during the middle of 1928 by the organization of new unions in the three industries where it had its most substantial forces: mining, textile, and needle, and where, because of wholesale expulsions, decline of the A. F. of L. unions, etc., conditions were ripest. The first of these unions to be set up was the National Miners Union at its convention in Pittsburgh, September 1928. The miners were badly disorganized after the loss of the great 1927-28 strike and only some 15,000 joined the new organization. The second union established was the National Textile Workers Union, in New York, September 1928, with about 5,000 members. Then came the Needle Trades Workers Industrial Union, founded in a convention representing 22,000 workers in New York, January 1929. All these membership figures are only approximate, as the dues systems were as yet poorly organized.

THE FOUNDING OF THE T. U. U. L.

The T. U. E. L. held its fourth national conference or, more properly, convention, in Cleveland, August 31-September 1, 1929. There were present 690 delegates from 18 states, including 15 delegates from the Pacific Coast. Of these, 322 delegates came from the three new industrial unions then comprising approximately (probably an excessive estimate) 57,000 members; 159 delegates from left-wing groups in trade unions; 107 from small groups in unorganized industries; 18 directly from A. F. of L. locals with 2,855 members; 40 were members of the T. U. E. L. National Committee and 44 fraternal; 64 were Negroes, 72 women and 159 youths. The average age of the delegates was only 32 years.

The convention reorganized the T. U. E. L. and changed its name to the Trade Union Unity League. This was in conformity with the new tendencies in our movement, which were enthusiastically supported by the big convention delegation. The new constitution provided for three types of national organization: (a) industrial unions, (b) industrial leagues, and (c) trade union minority groups.

(a) The national industrial unions, adapted in form to the conditions in each industry, were based upon the principle of "one shop, one industry, one union"; they were departmentalized, corresponding to the important subdivisions of their industries; they had autonomy to elect their own officials, set their dues rates and initiation fees, work out their detailed programs and union agreements and conduct their own strikes, subject only to general T. U. U. L. control; an important feature was their youth sections. (b) The national industrial leagues were industrial unions in embryo; they were loose national groupings of local unions, shop committees, and individual workers. Bodies not yet strong enough to function as unions, their dues were set and their general activities supervised by the T. U. U. L.

National Executive Board. (c) The national trade union minority groups were a continuation of the old T. U. E. L. national industrial sections working within the conservative unions. Where A. F. of L. and T. U. U. L. unions existed in one industry the T. U. U. L. union was connected with the T. U. U. L. minority in the A. F. of L. to secure joint action.

Locally, the T. U. U. L. assumed a variety of forms, including local industrial unions, local craft unions, shop committees, initiative organizing groups, and left-wing trade union groups. All these were linked together into city-wide Trade Union Unity Councils. There was also provision for state Trade Union Unity Councils, although none ever developed.

THE PROGRAM OF THE T. U. U. L.

The Cleveland convention organized the T. U. U. L. into a new trade union center. But the convention did not set up a general system of dual unionism. It declared against a policy of individual withdrawals or petty splits from the A. F. of L. and it proposed to form new unions only where the A. F. of L. unions were decrepit or non-existent. It also warned repeatedly against slackening the work inside the A. F. of L. The *Program* said:

The new Trade Union Unity League has as its main task the organization of the unorganized into industrial unions independent of the A. F. of L. At the same time it organizes the workers within the reformist unions. It unites politically and organizationally the unemployed with the employed.

Except for these important new union developments, the convention continued and developed the general policies of the old T. U. E. L. It was distinctly a left convention. There were present but few outstanding trade union progressives. This was not remarkable, because at this time, the highest point of the Coolidge boom, the progressives were quite generally very enthused over trying to save the working class by the A. F. of L. union-management co-operation (B. & O. plan) method of speeding up production and they rejected the T. U. U. L. line of militant class struggle as naive and outmoded.

The convention made a head-on collision against the whole A. F. of L.-employer schemes of intensified class collaboration, B. & O. plan, the "higher strategy of labor," new wage policy, labor banking, etc. "The heart of the convention was the struggle against capitalist rationalization and all its evil consequences of speed-up, unemployment, accidents, occupational sickness, low wages, etc." * The convention declared for a militant strike policy. Its program was based on the class struggle and its central slogan was "Class Against Class." The convention's main decisions were sloganized as follows:

Build the Trade Union Unity League, fight against imperialist war, defend the Soviet Union, fight against capitalist rationalization, organize the unorganized, for the seven-hour day, five-day week, for social insurance, for full racial, social, and political equality for Negroes, organize the youth and the women, defeat the misleaders of labor, for world trade union unity.

The convention paid much attention to questions of industrial unionism, strike strategy, and the organization of the unorganized; it directed T. U. U. L. attention more sharply to the basic unorganized industries; steel, automobile, chemicals, agriculture, etc., and to work in the South; it discussed at length the problems of building shop committees in the mass production, trustified industries, and how to defeat the bosses' spy and blacklist systems; it worked out the application of the united front, especially between employed and unemployed, and between the A. F. of L. rank and file and the members of the T. U. U. L. unions; it stressed the policy of independent leadership by the workers, as against their reactionary union officials. The convention also paid much attention to the special problems of Negro, youth, and women workers, questions which had been largely neglected in the early days of the T. U. U. L.; it declared its solidarity with the oppressed workers in the colonial and semi-colonial countries; it warned of the danger of imperialist war, especially war against the Soviet Union. With no illusions as to the extent or continuance of the "prevailing prosperity," the convention adopted a demand for federal social insurance, based on full wages for all workers incapacitated through unemployment, sickness, accident or old age. The convention also modified the former T. U. E. L. attitude towards the labor party; in view of the prevailing reaction in union official circles, it declared for participation in the labor party only where it was actually a party in the hands of the workers. In the 1932 elections the T. U. U. L. and its unions supported the Communist Party ticket, as the T. U. E. L. had done in 1924 and 1928.

1936

* *Labor Unity*, September 14, 1929.

20. The Organization of Negro Workers

One of the most important features of the Trade Union Educational League convention to be held in Cleveland on June 1 and 2 will be the large delegation of Negro workers present. To organize the Negro proletarians, to draw them into the main stream of new revolutionary industrial union movement will be a major objective of the T. U. E. L. convention.

Of all the shameful treason to the working class committed by the misleaders who head the old trade unions, none has been more disastrous than their systematic betrayal of the Negro workers. It has long been the policy of the employers to draw a line between white and black workers, to set one group against the other in order better to exploit them, to cultivate the worst forms of race prejudice among the whites. They have deliberately and systematically discriminated against the Negroes, giving them the worst work, the lowest wages, and subjecting them to the most brutal repression.

Were the A. F. of L. leaders imbued with even a semblance of real working class spirit they would take it upon themselves as a first and basic task to defeat the plans of the employers by organizing the Negroes and by mobilizing the whole labor movement behind their elementary demands. But they refuse utterly to do this. On the contrary, true to their role as agents of the bourgeoisie in the ranks of the workers, they fall in line with the program of the employers and join hands with them to oppress the Negroes. They cultivate race chauvinism among the whites, they prohibit Negroes from joining the unions, they co-operate with the employers to keep the Negroes at the poorest paid jobs. All this constitutes one of the most shameful pages in American labor history.

But the T. U. E. L. convention represents the revolutionary forces that will stop this historic treachery. The convention will be made up of a body of workers of both sexes and all nationalities, of Negroes who understand and dare to strike a blow in behalf of themselves and their class, and of whites eliminating all white chauvinism from their ranks, recognize the Negro workers as class brothers and who will fight with and for them all the way to the end for complete social emancipation. The T. U. E. L. convention will have more significance to Negro workers than any other trade union gathering ever held in this country.

Negroes constantly take on more importance as a force in industry and as a potential factor in the trade union movement. During the past dozen years hundreds of thousands of them have poured into the mills and factories. For the most part they are going into the key and basic industries, coal, railroads, steel, meat packing, etc., exactly those industries that play the most decisive role in the class struggle. In a recent number of the Red International of Labor Unions bulletin occurs the following statement quoting Carroll Binder regarding Negroes in the industries of Chicago in 1929:

Thirty per cent of the labor force in the Chicago packing industry is colored; the Corn Products Company, which employed only one Negro eight years ago, today employs 350, or twenty per cent of its working force. Beavers Products—65 per cent. The American Hide and Leather Co. was the first tannery to use Negro workers; now all the tanneries use large numbers of them. The foundries and laundries are heavy employers of Negroes. Eleven per cent of the employes of the Pullman Car shops are Negroes. Negro women compose forty per cent of the workers in the lamp shade industry. About twenty per cent of the 14,000 postal workers of Chicago are Negroes. . . .

The great importance to industry and the class struggle of this constantly increasing body of Negro workers cannot be too much stressed. It is the special task of the T. U. E. L. to organize them as part of its general work of organizing the unorganized. This can only be done in the face of studied opposition of the A. F. of L. leaders working hand in glove with the employers.

But in order that the necessary progress shall be registered by the T. U. E. L. convention in the organization of the Negro workers real work must be done by the left forces between now and the convention. Special committees must be established in the various important industrial centers to prosecute this particular task. These committees, together with the general organizing forces of the T. U. E. L., must establish contacts with the Negroes in all the important industrial plants and draw them into all the shop committees, T. U. E. L. groups, and other organizations formed as a basis for the convention. In every delegation from every industry where Negroes are employed, there must be a heavy percentage of these wor' included. There especially must be a large delegation of Negro work ers from the coal and iron mines, the steel mills, fertilizer works, railroads, the cotton and tobacco plantations, and other industries of the South. The real mass character of the T. U. E. L. convention will be measured pretty much by the number of representative Negro workers present.

The Negro workers are good fighters. This they have proved in innumerable strikes in the coal, steel, packing, building and other industries, despite systematic betrayal by white trade union leaders and the presence of an all too prevalent race chauvinism among the masses of white workers. They are a tremendous source of potential revolutionary strength and vigor. They have a double oppression as workers and as Negroes, to fill them with fighting spirit and resentment against capitalism. It has been one of the most serious errors of the left wing to underestimate and to neglect the development of this great proletarian fighting force.

Let the T. U. E. L. convention therefore be a great mobilization center for the Negro workers. There must be present Negroes from all the important plants and localities. Such a delegation, upon which the success of the convention depends, can and will be assembled. The T. U. E. L. convention will be a revolutionary signal and inspiration to the masses of Negro workers, exploited and oppressed in the mills, mines and factories of American imperialism.

1929

21. Demoralization and Decay

▬ As a matter of fact, the "new" capitalism was only the "old" capitalism in a fresh guise. The boasted rationalization of industry could not and did not cure the great inner contradictions of the capitalist system, the contradiction between the social mode of production and the private ownership of industry, and the conflict between the rapidly increasing producing power of the toilers and their lagging purchasing power, which are the basic causes of the recurrent industrial crises. On the contrary, rationalization only intensified these fatal contradictions, the huge development of the productive forces during that period greatly hastening the whole system forward to the devastating international crash of 1929. Even a glance at the pages of Marx would have exposed this inevitable outcome. The whole rationalization business was a classical example of the "suicide economics" of capitalism.

The much-advertised paradise for the workers never materialized. During the Coolidge period, as we have already remarked, the workers as a class got very little out of the vastly increased wealth that they produced, and their very efficiency was rushing them on to the later holocaust of unemployment and mass starvation. What the workers did get in the Coolidge period, however, was the gravest demoralization, both ideological and organizational. Confused by the bourgeoisification of their upper ranks of skilled workers, they lost much of their fighting spirit. Never in the history of the labor movement were strikes so few and trade union morale so low.

For the first time in their entire existence the trade unions failed to grow during a period of prosperity. On the contrary, they actually lost members.* With a relatively good demand for labor power, it should have been an easy matter to organize large numbers of workers. But the unions had all the vitality sucked and beaten out of them by the rationalization campaign, with its accompaniments of speed-up, no strikes, surrender of union conditions, suppression of democracy, gangster control, expulsion of militants, and capitalist "prosperity" propaganda.

The Socialist Party, saturated with class collaboration, dwindled away in influence and membership until in 1927 it had no more than 7,425 members. The Farmer-Labor Party movement also practically disappeared, except in Minnesota, where it had become an established party. The I. W. W. and such independent unions as the Amalgamated Food Workers, all of which had become penetrated with Coolidge prosperity illusions and lost their former militancy, declined heavily in membership and influence.

The Coolidge era was the period of the deepest confusion and demoralization in the history of the American working class. The

---

* A. F. of L. reports show the membership figures practically stationary from 1923 to 1929. But these statistics are illusory, because during this time, many unions, notably the U. M. W. A., lost heavily in members, but kept up their per capita tax in order to maintain their voting strength in A. F. of L. conventions.

class collaboration poison was eating the very heart out of the labor movement. And upon this scene of working class paralysis the capitalists and their hangers-on could and did look with smug satisfaction. Thoughts of industrial crisis and strikes, not to speak of revolution, were far from their minds where America was concerned. They were drunk with power and prosperity. Their great enemy, the proletariat, seemed to be hopelessly drugged into insensibility and bound hand and foot by its official leaders. But they were living in a fool's paradise, as the next few years showed.

1936

PART THREE

22. The A. F. of L. and the Economic Crisis

Less than two months after the Trade Union Unity League convention, the great 1929 world industrial crash took place. The dizzy financial structure of American capitalism collapsed. The intense rationalization of industry and agriculture that was to herald the dawn of universal prosperity had resulted in a huge market glut, a great overproduction which the impoverished and robbed masses could not buy back and which could not be disposed of abroad. Industry swiftly fell off about one-half and wages were slashed on all sides. Agricultural prices dropped about 60 per cent and land values declined accordingly. The army of unemployed leaped from the 3,000,000 of the so-called good times to the unheard-of total of 17,000,000 in 1933. Poverty, destitution, and starvation gripped the toiling masses all over the country. The boasted "new capitalism" was giving a graphic illustration of the fact that it was only the old capitalism after all and that, as such, it was hopelessly involved in the worldwide decay and decline of the capitalist system.

The onset of the terrific crisis created consternation among the trade union and Socialist Party leaders. Tumbled in ruins overnight were their glittering dreams of the "new wage policy," the "higher strategy of labor," "organized capitalism," and all the rest of their speed-up, class collaboration, prosperity fantasies. The labor movement under their leadership had been demoralized and confused and the workers poisoned and disorganized by the long-continued, class collaboration, no-strike, B. & O. plan propaganda; the unions were weakened by loss of members, suppression of democracy, and the expulsion of their best fighters. Hence, as a result of these destructive policies, when the test came, under the shattering blows of the crisis, the masses were quite unprepared to defend themselves and their official leaders knew no other policy than one of precipitate retreat.

Consequently, during the first three and a half years of the crisis, until Roosevelt's New Deal, the great mass of the workers did not develop any real resistance, while the employers brutally shoved the burden of the crisis upon them and their families by mercilessly slashing their wages and reducing living standards generally. And the trade union leaders, by their surrender policies, actually helped the employers in this savage attack. Through this period of wholesale worsening of the workers' conditions there were fewer strikes than there had been for many years previously. In 1930, for example, there were only one-tenth as many strikes as in the corresponding crisis year of 1922.

The situation in Chicago was typical of that prevailing throughout the entire United States. Despite the fact that the workers of that city had many militant traditions and strong labor unions and fully 50 per cent of industrial workers were thrown out of work and the rest had their wages cut from 20 per cent to 50 per cent, there was not a single strike of any importance whatever in the first three years of the crisis. Unrestrainedly, the capitalists gloated over the widespread working class demoralization, the logical result of long years of A. F. of L. policy. Their publicists hypocritically declared that it indicated a great harmony between capital and labor, and they slobbered over the workers' "patience" and "loyalty" in facing the trials of the crisis. The capitalists, in their need, were indeed making effective use of their "labor lieutenants," the craft union leaders.

This period was one of the most shameful in the whole wretched history of the A. F. of L. policy. Every major step of the employers to save themselves at the workers' expense actually had the A. F. of L. leaders' direct or indirect support. These misleaders lulled the workers' vigilance by repeating all of the capitalists' underestimation of the crisis and ballyhoo about prosperity being "just around the corner." Hardly had the crisis begun when President Hoover, on November 11, 1929, called a national industrial conference of employers and trade union leaders, presumably to maintain wage standards. At that time wages were already being slashed in the unorganized mass production industries, and the purpose of the Hoover conference was manifestly to hog-tie the trade unions by a no-wage-cut-no-strike illusory agreement until, the masses of unorganized having their wages cut, it would be relatively easy also to reduce the rates of the trade union workers. Instead of adopting a militant strike resistance against the developing wave of wage-cuts at the very start of the crisis, as the T. U. U. L. urged, Green and the other A. F. of L. leaders served as bellwethers to draw the masses into Hoover's trap.

Thus, by their Hoover agreement, the A. F. of L. leaders threw the unorganized workers at once to the wage-cutting wolves. The wage slashing went ahead full blast in the trustified industries, the betrayed and demoralized workers being unable to resist; and meanwhile both Hoover and Green brazenly asserted that there had been no wage reductions. Finally, when the unorganized workers were "deflated," inevitably it came the turn of the organized workers to be slashed. Whereupon, the trade union leaders, reflecting the capitalists' interests, became ardent wage-cutters themselves, actually arguing that since wage-cuts had gone into effect in the unorganized industries now the organized workers had to accept reductions. So union after union accepted one cut upon another without the slightest resistance. What wage-cutters the leaders became was well illustrated when Matthew Woll hailed the acceptance of a 10 per cent wage reduction by the railroad unions without a strike as one of the greatest industrial achievements in the history of the country. In the needle trades the Socialist leaders also followed the general A. F. of L. policy of retreat. Never before in an economic crisis had the American working class taken wage-cuts lying down, as the great struggles of the 1890's and 1921-22 eloquently show.

Because of this aid from their A. F. of L. "labor lieutenants," the capitalists were able to put through their huge wage-slashing campaign without serious working class resistance, except what was developed by the weak T. U. U. L. unions. But the betrayal of the workers' interests by the A. F. of L. leadership reached its greatest depths in the case of the hungry millions of unemployed. Hoover's plan to handle the question of unemployment (and this was the plan of finance capital) was two-fold: First, a policy of share-the-work (or share-the-poverty), which meant to force the great body of workers on to short time and correspondingly reduced wages; and, second, a policy of treating unemployment relief as a matter of local charity and no concern of the Federal government. It was a most brutal program of organized mass starvation.

To their shame it must be said that the A. F. of L. leaders fitted themselves also into this outrageous assault upon working class living standards. They became the greatest champions of Hoover's "stagger plan" of sharing work and they were fanatical antagonists of unemployment insurance. With incredible brass and stupidity, they denounced the "dole" as "subsidizing idleness," "degrading to the dignity of the American working man," and "a hindrance to real progress." They declared that unemployment insurance meant the ruin of the trade unions and the downfall of civilization. In short, they used all the current arguments of big capital against feeding the starving masses. For this reactionary stand, the A. F. of L. won glowing praise from the Wall Street rulers of America. At the Boston, 1930, A. F. of L. convention, Hoover, together with many generals, bishops, capitalists, American Legion officials, etc., joined with Green, Woll, Frey, and others in repudiating unemployment insurance and denouncing the Communists who were so persistently fighting for it all over the country. And while the A. F. of L. leaders thus basked in the praise of the enemies of the working class, millions of unemployed workers and their families were sinking deeper and deeper into destitution and actual starvation.

THE T. U. U. L. IN THE CRISIS

The onset of the industrial crisis came as no surprise to the Communist Party and the T. U. U. L. They had long understood the temporary character of the "prosperity," and foresaw its inevitable crash. While the trade union and Socialist leaders were singing the praises of capitalist industrial rationalization in the Coolidge period, the Communist Party and the old T. U. E. L. had been warning the workers of the bitter reckoning to come. And as the crisis developed, the T. U. U. L. and the Communist Party undertook to mobilize the workers for the struggle against the growing capitalist offensive against mass living standards. They conducted many strikes and developed a strong campaign for unemployment insurance and relief; besides, they carried on many other militant activities, such as support of the struggling farmers, the veterans' bonus campaign, the student movement, the Mooney and Scottsboro cases, etc. It is an incontestable fact that during the crisis, up to the New Deal period, the only serious resistance made by the workers and other toilers against the monstrous mass pauperization was that organized and led by the Communist Party and T. U. U. L.

The employers and the government countered this left wing militancy with a policy of ruthless brutality. In most industries known membership in the T. U. U. L. was a signal for certain discharge and blacklist. T. U. U. L. strikes were fought by the employers ferociously. Its strike committees were raided and their members jailed; pickets were viciously slugged, shot, gassed, and arrested. Innumerable injunctions were issued against the red unions by the courts.* In several states T. U. U. L. unions were declared illegal. In Brooklyn agents of the Department of Labor intimidated employers and warned them not to make agreements with the T. U. U. L. organizations. And the same department, under the infamous labor traitor William N. Doak, deported hundreds of militant workers, including many T. U. U. L. union officials, often to fascist countries. Especially vicious were the government attacks upon the T. U. U. L. unemployed demonstrations, its answer being the club, the revolver, tear gas, the charge of mounted police, the prison. And the A. F. of L. and old guard Socialist trade union leaders condoned all these attacks upon the T. U. U. L. and other militant forces by the combined bosses, police, gangsters, etc.

In this T. U. U. L. baptism of fire hundreds of workers were beaten up, jailed, deported. Many also were killed. The Labor Research Association listed 23 workers killed in T. U. U. L. struggles from September 1929 to March 1933. Among these were eight killed in strikes, including Ella May Wiggins in Gastonia; Steve Katovis in New York; Harry Simms, Young Communist League and National Miners Union organizer, in Kentucky, etc. There were 15 killed in unemployment demonstrations, including five in the famous hunger march on the Detroit Ford plant March 7, 1932; three Negro workers shot down in a Chicago anti-eviction fight on August 4, 1931, and so forth.

THE STRUGGLE OF THE UNEMPLOYED

During the period of the crisis, up until the beginning of Roosevelt's term, the T. U. U. L. devoted its major activities to organizing and leading the starving multitudes of unemployed. Its organization was the National Unemployment Council.

The T. U. U. L. made the central issue in this work the demand for Federal unemployment insurance at the expense of the government and the employers, and on the basis of the average wages of employed workers. Its demands were in line with the T. U. U. L. convention

* At a local T. U. U. L. conference in New York in 1931, the Food Workers Industrial Union displayed 110 injunctions issued against its New York strikes.

resolution on social insurance and it crystallized them eventually in legislative form in the Workers Unemployment Insurance Bill (H. R. 2827). The T. U. U. L. also fought for every form of unemployment relief, including local cash relief, public works at union wages, against evictions, for free food for school children, etc. It organized the workers into block, neighborhood, city and national committees and councils, on a non-dues-paying basis. Its major method of struggle was the mass demonstration; but it also carried on intense work for relief of individual cases. It ruthlessly exposed all the many false charity schemes of the period, miserable substitutes for effective insurance and relief. Central in its strategy was the linking up of the struggles of the unemployed with those of the employed.

A very important feature of the T. U. U. L. unemployed work was its support of the left-wing A. F. of L. Committee for Unemployment Insurance and Relief, headed by Louis Weinstock. This rank and file body carried on a wide agitation in the trade unions for unemployment insurance and relief and against the reactionary Green policies of stagger plan, local charity relief, expulsion of unemployed from the unions for non-payment of dues, etc. At a government hearing in Washington, in February, 1934, Weinstock testified that more than 3,000 A. F. of L. unions had endorsed the workers' bill, H. R. 2827. The work of this committee was largely responsible for forcing the A. F. of L., at its 1932 convention, to reverse its reactionary attitude and to give at least lip service to unemployment insurance.

The National Unemployment Council, jointly with the Communist Party and T. U. U. L., was the first to take up the fight for the unemployed, the A. F. of L. openly supporting Hoover, and the Socialist Party toying about with every capitalist fake charity scheme (thus Norman Thomas joined over the radio with J. P. Morgan in support of the delusive "block-aid system") and only beginning to organize the unemployed two years after our forces had blazed the way. Consequently, great masses of workers rallied to the leadership of the Unemployment Council movement. Under the slogans: "Don't Starve, Fight" and "Work or Wages," it conducted many militant national demonstration struggles. The first of these was the famous one of March 6, 1930, which brought some 1,250,000 workers into the streets, including 110,000 in New York, 100,000 in Detroit, etc. This demonstration definitely raised the issue of unemployment insurance to the level of a living national, political question. In New York, with huge masses of unemployed and with the bourgeoisie in a panic of fear, the situation became very tense just prior to March 6. A few days before this date, Matthew Woll, openly co-operating with the police, lyingly announced far and wide through the press that the T. U. U. L. had received $2,000,000 from Moscow to stage the demonstration. Police Commissioner Whalen forbade the proposed march to City Hall and mobilized the 18,000 police and 7,000 firemen of Greater New York to prevent it. Union Square was saturated with police and the nearby buildings bristled with machine guns. We attempted to march nevertheless, whereupon the police charged upon the forming procession and clubbed it to pieces, injuring many workers. The workers' committee, including Robert Minor, Israel Amter, Harry Raymond and myself, were arrested and sentenced to three years in the New York County penitentiary, of which sentence we served six months apiece, except Raymond who did ten months. The rest we did on parole.

Besides this fight, the National Unemployment Council, with the full support of the Communist Party, T. U. U. L., and the Young Communist League, etc., carried through many other national unemployed demonstrations, hunger marchers, mass delegations and conventions. Three times there were national petitions of 1,000,000 or more signatures presented to Congress. Some of the more important of these big movements were the National Unemployed Convention in Chicago, July 4, 1930, with 1,500 delegates; National Unemployment Insurance Day, February 25, 1931, with 400,000 demonstrators; and February 4, 1932, with 500,000 demonstrators; the National Hunger March of December 7, 1931, with 1,800 delegates to Washington; the second National Hunger March of December 6, 1932, with 3,000 delegates and an estimated 1,000,000 participants in various cities; the big national demonstration upon Roosevelt's inauguration day, March 4, 1933. The T. U. U. L. also actively supported the famous veterans' bonus march to Washington in 1932, which was driven out of the Capitol by Hoover at the point of the bayonet. The call for this march was issued by the Workers Ex-Servicemen's League, headed by Emmanuel Levin, although the movement took on such a swift mass character that it largely escaped W. E. S. L. control.

But the main field of T. U. U. L. unemployment struggle was in the various localities. Here the Unemployment Council conducted numberless city and state hunger marches, anti-eviction fights, unemployed conventions, etc. Nearly every industrial center saw such activities. The demonstrations were extremely militant, usually facing violent attacks from the police. Altogether, they were a powerful force in compelling the reluctant city authorities to grant relief to the starving masses. To take only a few from many such examples; during the fall of 1932, the city council of St. Louis decided to cut 17,000 families off the relief rolls, but the Unemployed Council, by a vast and militant demonstration, forced the immediate abandonment of this barbarous proposal; in Chicago in the summer of 1932, the Unemployment Council, in a united front with the Unemployed Citizens League by great mass movements, defeated a projected 50 per cent cut in relief. Similar results were achieved in dozens of other cities by the policy of militant mass struggle.

In developing this great fight of the unemployed, the Communist Party, the T. U. U. L., and the Unemployment Council, wrote some of the finest pages of struggle in American labor history. The movement was a definite force in saving the masses from actual starvation and eventually compelling federal relief measures on a large scale. It was in brilliant contrast to the deeply reactionary policy of the A. F. of L. and the vacillating, dabbling attitude of the Socialist Party.

After its reorganization at Cleveland the T. U. U. L. broadened its strike activities. The continued decline and decay of the A. F. of L. in the early crisis years widened the base for independent unionism in the industries generally throughout the country and it threw ever greater burdens of leadership upon the militant unions. But the T. U. U. L.'s greatest field of struggle still remained the mining industry. Here the T. U. U. L. conducted several big movements in the crisis period up to the Roosevelt administration. The most important of these was the National Miners Union strike during the summer of 1931 in Western Pennsylvania, Eastern Ohio, and Northern West Virginia. Embracing 42,000 miners, it was the largest strike ever led by a militant union in the United States.

1936

23. The New Deal

When Roosevelt was inaugurated President on March 4, 1933, the American capitalist system, once world-boasted as crisis-proof, was in a chaotic, panicky situation. It was experiencing the world economic breakdown worse than any other country. Every bank in the country was closed, industry was paralyzed, domestic and foreign trade had fallen by 50 per cent, about 17,000,000 workers walked the streets unemployed, hundreds of thousands of farmers had lost their farms, millions of small bank depositors had been robbed of their funds, vast numbers of the middle class had had the mortgages on their homes foreclosed. The disillusioned and discontented masses were stirring aggressively; the whole country was full of militant hunger demonstrations of unemployed, bonus marches of war veterans, farmers' strikes, etc., and on all sides the masses talked angrily, if confusedly, about taking drastic action if measures were not adopted at once to relieve them of the intolerable starvation and pauperization that had engulfed them.

This threatening situation threw into the ranks of the American capitalist class the greatest fright it has ever known. Their writers and other spokesmen loaded the press and the air with pessimism, fear and lugubrious forecasts. Finance capital—the great bankers and industrialists—realized that if they were to hang on to their rich rulership of society something must be done to prop up the collapsing capitalist system and to allay the swiftly mounting mass radicalization. Manifestly the crude and brutal Hoover policy of simply pouring billions of relief into the coffers of the banks, railroads, etc., and letting everybody else go broke and starve was heading capitalism straight to disaster. New measures must be taken and that swiftly. The "something" that finance capital decided upon to save their capitalist system was contained in Roosevelt's "New Deal."

The sum up of the New Deal, as expressed by its score of alphabetical laws and bureaus, was a greatly increased centralization of the Federal government and its intensified intervention in economic life along the following main lines: (a) pouring of government billions into the banks, railroads, etc., to save them from threatening bankruptcy; (b) raising of the price level through inflation (devaluation of the dollar, immense bond issues, etc.), code price-fixing, and organized restriction of agricultural and industrial production; (c) liquefying of billions of dollars of the banks that were frozen in unpayable mortgages on farms and homes by extension of payment periods on these mortgages; (d) "priming the industrial pump" and easing the workers' unrest by large government capital investments in public works; (e) tinkering up by law the worst breaks in the capitalist banking and credit systems, including supervision of the stock exchange, sale of foreign bonds, etc.; (f) intensified struggle for world markets—bigger navy, air fleet, army, new tariff agreements, etc.; (g) throwing a bone to the starving masses of unemployed and aged by allotting them a niggardly Federal relief and skeleton pensions; (h) granting of rights of the workers to organize into labor unions; (i) organized subsidies to farmers for reducing production.

By its heavy government spending and minor sops to the masses, the New Deal, in substance, was a shot in the arm, a doping of the economic system out of its deepening crisis. It was calculated to preserve the capitalist system by relieving somewhat the economic and mass pressure. The center of it, the National Recovery Act (N. R. A.), was contrived in Wall Street and was first enunciated by the U. S. Chamber of Commerce. Many capitalist theoreticians hailed it as the beginning of fascism. To call the New Deal socialistic or communistic is nonsense; it had nothing in common with either.

THE UPHEAVAL OF THE WORKING MASSES

It is the proud and not altogether unwarranted boast of the New Dealers that they have saved the capitalist system, at least temporarily. At the time I write these lines, July, 1936, the same finance capitalists who heartily supported the New Deal at its outset are now fiercely attacking it and their Supreme Court is busy knocking out its N. R. A.'s, A. A. A.'s, etc., one after the other. But if these capitalists take such a hostile attitude now towards the New Deal it is only because they believe they are over the worst of the crisis, that the New Deal has exhausted its benefits for them, and that fresh policies of a more reactionary character are necessary. They want to take away even Roosevelt's few concessions to the impoverished masses of workers, farmers and lower middle class.

The workers believed the promises of Roosevelt and, as Jack Stachel said, "took seriously the statement that they had the right to join unions of their choice." So, after the beginning of the New Deal and continuing all through 1933, 1934, and to a lesser extent, 1935, they developed a great surging mass organization and strike movement, one of the most tempestuous in the history of the American working class. It was a huge spontaneous outburst, an explosion of proletarian wrath against the rapidly rising cost of living, long years of low wages, unemployment, inhuman speed-up, and autocracy in industry. It also revealed a growing lack of faith in the capitalist system as a whole. The big strikes of 1919-22 were defensive actions of organized workers under employer attacks; but the 1933-35 upheaval was basically a militant and powerful counter-offensive of the unorganized masses. One of the most striking features of the whole movement was the solidarity of the unemployed with the strikers and their refusal to be strike-breakers. With surprise and dismay the capitalists, who for a dozen years past had been complimenting themselves on the decline of working class militancy, watched the great toiling masses bestir themselves and launch this historic strike movement. They developed a great distaste for this whole phase of the Roosevelt New Deal.

When the N. R. A. was instituted on June 13, 1933, there was already a gradually mounting strike wave under way. The first effect of the N. R. A. was to halt this for a while, and to turn the budding strike movement into a general campaign of union building, the workers relying upon the promises of the government and A. F. of L. officials to secure redress of their grievances. But the movement soon passed out of this stage of naive hopefulness. The employers were establishing starvation minimum codes, militantly resisting the spread of the unions, building company unions on all sides, while the government and A. F. of L. policy was only one of rosy assurances to the workers. Sensing the situation correctly, and realizing that they must fight, the masses burst into a broad strike movement in the last half of 1933 "to help Roosevelt enforce the N. R. A." against the employers, as was said widely by the workers at the time. Strikes raged in coal, steel, copper, automobile, textile, needle and many other industries.* The incom-

* It is significant that this strike wave was least effective in those industries where the A. F. of L. antiquated craft union system was most intrenched: railroad industry, metal trades, building trades, food trades, printing industry, amusement trades, etc. The main force of the upheaval was among the unorganized and in those unions more approximating the industrial form and where left-wing influence was greatest.

plete U. S. Bureau of Labor statistics show there was a total of 812,000 strikers in 1933, as against 242,826 in 1932.

With the turn of 1934, the strike movement took on greater volume, the number of strikers for that year amounting to 1,353,608. But more important, the multiplying strikes were of a far greater militancy and a deeper political significance. This was because early in the course of the New Deal, finance capital had made it clear that it was continuing its traditional opposition to the unionization of the open shop basic industries, and the government also soon showed that it would not insist upon such unionization, despite its apparent sympathy towards trade unionism. That is why the several conciliation boards set up by the government in industries where the workers were developing strike movements invariably demoralized the new labor unions by yielding to the company unions. The estimates of the growth of company unionism under the New Deal range from 1,000,000 to 3,000,000.*

As the New Deal codes developed it became more and more clear, therefore, that the government's policy, especially in the unorganized basic industries, despite its liberal phrases, led to company unionism, starvation wages, and long hours. Without fully realizing the implications of this situation, large masses of workers nevertheless began to sense the elementary truth that if they were to secure the right of organization and relief for their grievances under the New Deal they would have to do as the T. U. U. L. was urging: write their own codes on the picket lines. Hence, the big strikes of 1934 bore increasingly the character of struggles against the N. R. A.; against its $12.00 to $15.00 minimum wage scales, for the right to organize and against company unionism, against the ruinous delays, fake elections, and equivocations of the various N. R. A. bodies set up by the Roosevelt government with the help of the A. F. of L. leadership.

The strikes of 1934 to 1936 took on the most acute political character of any in the history of the United States. Against the violent opposition of the A. F. of L. leaders, the political mass strike, long a cardinal point in the Communist Party's agitation, became an established weapon of the American working class. The workers fought with splendid heroism and solidarity in the face of the government, tricky union leaders, and an unprecedented use of troops, police, gunmen, and vigilantes against them. The great battles of Toledo, Milwaukee,

* *The Monthly Labor Review* (U. S. Dept. of Labor) of October 1935, in its study of company unionism, states that in the industries examined, 64 per cent of all existing company unions were established during the period of the N. R. A.

Minneapolis, San Francisco, Terre Haute (1935), Pekin (1936), the huge national 1934 textile strike, the national coal strike of 1935, and many other struggles of the period constitute one of the brightest pages in our labor history.

THE T. U. U. L. IN THE 1933 STRIKES

The T. U. U. L. did not confine itself to issuing manifestoes calling upon the workers to strike. On the contrary, from the outset, in 1933, it launched all its unions and leagues and minority groups, into the surging battle. Its program of struggle found response among the militant, discontented masses. Thus, despite its relative weakness, the T. U. U. L. was able to play a very considerable role in stimulating the big struggles and in directing the fighting masses along the path to victory.

Through this eventful period the T. U. U. L. was capably led by Jack Stachel, who had been elected assistant secretary in Decerber 1931. During the 1932 election campaign, as the Presidential Candidate of the Communist Party, I suffered a severe heart attack in the midst of a five months speaking tour and I collapsed in Moline, Illinois, on September 8. For many years I had overworked myself. Besides carrying on much strike and other intense activities, I had made a dozen national speaking tours of 100 to 150 meetings each, several of them on the hobo, in addition to making innumerable shorter tours. These trips had taken me repeatedly into every state and important city in the country. But in the 1932 campaign the pitcher went once too often to the well. Result, a smash-up: angina pectoris, followed by a complete nervous collapse that kept me in bed for five months and made my life a literal torture, day and night, for over two years. It is only now that I am recovered enough to begin slowly to work again. My best work has been always as a mass organizer during big strikes and other struggles, but it was my doubly bad fate to be laid up helpless all through the bitterly fought mass strikes under the New Deal.

T. U. U. L. ACHIEVEMENTS AND SHORTCOMINGS

During the six years of their existence the T. U. U. L. unions developed a substantial resistance to the wage-cutting, starvation offensive of the employers. In the early and difficult Hoover years of the crisis, while the A. F. of L. was submitting unresistingly to the workers' wages being slashed and was allowing the unemployed to be forced down into utter pauperism, the T. U. U. L. unions, supported militantly by the Communist Party, held aloft the banner of struggle. Their leadership of the unorganized into struggle was a decisive factor in winning a measure of relief for the starving jobless, and their militant strikes not only placed a serious hindrance in the way of the wage cutters, but also served as a powerful stimulus to the huge labor battles soon to occur under the New Deal. And when the big strike struggles developed in 1933-34, the T. U. U. L. was a real factor in furthering the organization and militancy of the workers.

The T. U. U. L. unions, however, did not succeed in building up powerful organizations numerically. This was largely because of the extremely difficult conditions under which they worked—blacklists, police raids, court injunctions, deportation of leaders, etc. A factor also in many cases was weak organization work. The unions' membership was loose and subject to violent fluctuations, hence exact estimates of their numerical strength were difficult to make. Their mass influence, however, extended far and wide beyond the concrete limits of the organizations. In the middle of 1934, the T. U. U. L. reached its maximum trade union organization, with approximately 125,000 members. This was aside from approximately 150,000 members reported for the National Unemployed Council in 1933 by its secretary, Herbert Benjamin.

In the earlier stages of its work, the T. U. U. L. developed a number of secretarian weaknesses which injured its general efficiency. The first was a tendency, under the fierce attacks from its many enemies, to develop its union programs upon a too advanced militant basis and to identify the organizations too closely with the Communist Party. This, of course, had the effect of checking the growth of the organization by making difficult its contacts with the more conservative workers and by narrowing down the T. U. U. L. united front with the progressives. It was a departure from the original plan for the independent unions, which called for programs not so sharply militant, but more of a broad united front character.

The second serious weakness of the T. U. U. L. in this period was the beginning of a tendency in the direction of dual unionism, the traditional weakness of the American left wing. The basis of this was the deplorable situation in the A. F. of L.; its lassitude in the face of the employers' attacks and its rapid decline in strength and influence. This tended to make the T. U. U. L. neglect the work in the old unions, to concentrate on the new unions, and to establish new unions in some cases when it would have been more practical to have worked inside the A. F. of L.

During 1929-32 the A. F. of L. was indeed in a critical position and showed many signs of disintegration. It was reaping in full the bitter crop of misleadership that its reactionary leaders had long been sowing. During the war-time these leaders had stupidly thrown away an unprecedented opportunity to organize many millions of workers; then in the great 1919-22 post-war offensive of the bosses they had, by their policy of craft scabbery and retreat, made labor suffer the biggest defeat in its whole career; they had followed this up during the Coolidge "prosperity" years, which could have been spent successfully organizing the workers, by adopting the infamous B. & O. class collaboration schemes which devitalized and paralyzed the whole labor movement; and finally, when the crisis came upon them, craft union leaders walked right into Hoover's wage-cut, starve-the-unemployed murderous policy. The general result was utter stagnation in the A. F. of L. unions, whose membership fell from 4,078,740 in 1920 to 2,126,796 in 1933, and the growth of a widespread belief that the A. F. of L. was definitely in decline.*

When the Cleveland T. U. U. L. convention laid down the policy for the independent unions it proposed, first, that the new unions might be affiliated to the A. F. of L. under conditions in which militant policy and leadership were assured; and, second, that work within the A. F. of L. unions should be continued and intensified. But under the pressure of the struggle and in view of the reactionary and brokendown condition of the A. F. of L., with its no-strike policies, its hidebound unions slowly crumbling and its membership dispirited and demoralized, the T. U. U. L. tended to deviate from its originally correct line in both of these important essentials of organization policy. It began to stress independent unionism somewhat too much. On the one hand, it abandoned the policy of conditional affiliation of the new unions to the A. F. of L. and tended to develop the T. U. U. L. as a rival trade union national center, and, on the other hand, it decidedly slackened its work within the A. F. of L. unions, although every state-

---

* This 1933 figure is far too high, as many of the unions were maintaining their regular per capita tax payments to the A. F. of L. for convention voting purposes, although they had actually suffered huge membership losses in the crisis. It is, therefore, doubtful if the A. F. of L., at its low point in 1933, had more than 1,500,000 actual members.

ment of T. U. U. L. general policy stressed the necessity for such activity.

With regard to the latter point: the most important work done by the T. U. U. L. in the old unions during this period was through the A. F. of L. Committee for Unemployment Insurance, which I have previously noted. Besides this, there was little more than rather desultory activities in the railroad, needle, mining, building, printing, metal, and shoe craft unions. The consequence was a great weakening of T. U. U. L. influence in the A. F. of L. unions. One sign of this was that leadership of the industrial union movement in the A. F. of L., traditionally led by the left wing, passed over automatically to John L. Lewis when he began his agitation for industrial unionism. Another result of T. U. U. L. neglect to work within the A. F. of L. unions was to give a stimulus to the growth of the Conference for Progressive Labor Action, an organization which, made up chiefly of lower trade union functionaries and intellectual dilettantes and headed by A. J. Muste, of Brookwood Labor College, tried to occupy the place once held in the craft unions by the old T. U. E. L. But this opportunistic organization failed and it finally merged into the Trotskyist Workers Party.* We have seen, however, that with the new situation, the T. U. U. L., following its true line of unity, resumed in full its work within the A. F. of L.

The life of the T. U. U. L. showed that its policy of independent unionism was basically correct and historically justified under the given conditions. This is true in spite of the incorrect tendency, already indicated, to distort in some cases that policy in the direction of dual unionism. The T. U. U. L.'s program of class struggle, industrial unionism, organization of the unorganized, trade union democracy, unemployment insurance, equal rights for Negroes, fight against fascism and war, etc., were also fundamentally correct and corresponded to the true interests of the working class. The T. U. U. L. unions and organizations of unemployed were a real force in the class struggle during the Hoover period and they took a very militant and effective part in the big strike upheavals of 1933-35. The sectarian weaknesses above noted, however, operated to considerably lessen the T. U. U. L.'s potential influence, both within the trade unions and in the independent union movement. But, as we have seen, the great sharpening of the workers' fight in the strike period under the Roose-

---

* In my pamphlet, *Little Brothers of the Big Labor Fakers*, (1931), I have analyzed the Muste movement.

velt New Deal soon caused a drastic change in the policy of the T. U. U. L., so that once more its main stress was placed upon work within the reformist unions. All factors considered, the T. U. U. L. represented a necessary and correct stage in the development of the American labor movement.

1936

24. Industrial Unionism

The present great and ever-growing demand within the A. F. of L. for industrial unionism is not the first such demand. The unions were being enfeebled right along by the effects of craft unionism. As far back as 1903, reactionary old Sam Gompers himself said that "scarcely an affiliated organization is not engaged in a desperate fight with one or more other unions," and that unless they changed their course the unions would destroy one another.

Such self-destruction—in the face of the ever-increasing attacks on wages and conditions by the employers who were steadily growing stronger, integrating mines, mills, and plants into giant holding corporations with billion-dollar financial interests, taking control of the main industries through subsidiary corporations and seats on boards of directors—such self-destruction was tragic. Trade union members who had sacrificed, and were willing to sacrifice considerably more, for their unions began to press hard for a change in the structure of the A. F. of L. away from the hide-bound craft lines, on the basis of plant and industrial unions.

In the years immediately after the first World War, when the big corporations, bloated with war-time profits, began to launch plans to take away the hard-fought gains made by organized labor during the war, the craft form of unionism was more seriously than ever before felt to be a handicap for the workers. The Thirty-ninth Annual Convention of the A. F. of L. in 1919 found the craft union leaders hard pressed by the demand for industrial unionism. In the great 1919 strike wave, craft unionism was the main cause of the loss of strikes, as it was in the ensuing railway and printing trades strikes. In 1922-24 agitation, led by the Communist Party and the Trade Union Educational League, for amalgamation of the craft unions into industrial unions assumed large proportions, especially making itself felt at the Forty-third annual convention of the A. F. of L. in 1923.

In the following years, the deadly toll of craft unionism began to be felt so sharply that no one could fail to notice it. As a result of the warfare between craft unions, the no-strike policy, the policy of playing ball with the employers, the policy of expulsion of members who had the guts to say what they felt on the union floor, the membership of the A. F. of L. declined from its highest point of 4,078,740 in 1920 to about two and a half million in 1929.

The result was that at the 1929 annual convention a resolution was introduced for the appointment of a committee of fifteen to formulate a plan for reducing the number of international unions and for consolidating them. The stodgy craft union leaders succeeded in voting down this expression of the sentiment of more and more of the membership. The craft union leaders reaffirmed the Scranton Declaration of 1901 as the expression of the A. F. of L. policy—on the principle of the fellow who says, "What was good enough for my great-great-grandfather is good enough for me."

The fight for industrial unionism in this period was guided by the fighting left-wing groups in the various A. F. of L. unions, marshaled by the Trade Union Educational League and by the Communists whose aim in the trade unions was to lead the workers in the struggle for industrial unionism, amalgamation of the various crafts in each industry, rank-and-file control of the unions, a policy of real struggle against the employers for improvement of wages and conditions instead of boot-licking on the part of the top leadership of the A. F. of L. These fighting groups formed influential movements for amalgamation in the railroad industry, the metal trades, the building trades, etc. Later, when the fighting independent unions of the Trade Union Unity League were formed on an industrial basis, the example they set of solidarity in strike action, of rank-and-file control of the unions, of a policy of fighting the bosses for what the workers wanted instead of trying to lick their boots—this example had a great effect on the A. F. of L. membership in increasing their disgust with the results of the craft union policy.

When, for the sake of the unity of the working class, the Trade Union Unity League dissolved its unions, its members entered into the unions of the A. F. of L., and brought to the welcoming A. F. of L.

membership the fruits of their experience in hard-fought struggles against the employers. Inside the A. F. of L. they continued to be among the staunchest fighters for industrial unionism, for trade union democracy, and for a policy of struggle against the employers, instead of the collaboration of the top leaders with the employers.

However, never before has the struggle for making the A. F. of L. into a powerful, unified weapon against the employers' attacks been so great as now. And here are the reasons for the intense seething going on in the A. F. of L., with the eyes of the entire working class on the struggle for a powerful A. F. of L. based on industrial unions.

For one thing, following the introduction of the N. R. A., the craft union policy was shown up by the great upheaval of the workers during the 1933-34 strike movement and the great desire for unionism expressed the determination of the American working class once and for all to take a fighting stand against the repeated wage cuts, loss of conditions, layoffs, etc. This time, the workers in the big mass production industries—aluminum, automobiles, rubber, steel, for example, who had been absolutely ignored by the craft-ridden A. F. of L. leadership—determined to take matters into their own hands, and organized hundreds of locals by themselves. They took part in some of the best-fought strikes ever known in American history. In most cases where the craft unions showed any interest at all in these workers, it was either to try to settle their strikes behind their backs or to come in during or after the strikes and attempt to split up these fighting, industrial locals among themselves. The great fighting spirit of the workers following the N. R. A. showed that if the A. F. of L. had had a policy of industrial unionism and a policy of struggle against the employers, from ten to a score of millions of these workers could have been organized, so anxious were they to fight and to have the benefits of trade union protection.

For another thing, company unionism began to grow by leaps and bounds, under Roosevelt, and the craft union policy could do little against it in the industries where it was especially rampant—steel, radio, electrical apparatus, oil refining, chemicals, automobiles, etc. In these industries the only A. F. of L. organizations which existed, if there were any, were a few small crafts, like bricklayers in oil refineries, or a molders' local here and there in an electrical apparatus plant, and the like. It is significant that an industrial union like the United Mine Workers of America was able to lick the company unions to a frazzle in nearly every case, organizing nearly 500,000 miners into an industrial union.

Then, fascist tendencies, like the Liberty League,* Coughlin, Hearst, blue, black, brown and many other colored shirt movements began to raise their ugly heads, one of their avowed aims being to smash trade unionism, as the fascists had done in Germany, Italy, and Austria. What chance has a trade union movement, enfeebled and torn asunder by craft unionism and weakened by an anti-struggle policy—what chance has such a trade union movement against fascist movements which can develop into organizations as powerful as in Germany, Italy, and Austria, if the working class does not unite to stop them? This fact set millions of workers thinking, and that is one of the big reasons why the demand for industrial unionism has become greater now than ever before.

To the three and a half million workers inside the A. F. of L., and to the nearly 30,000,000 other workers watching them in their fight for industrial unionism, it is a bread and butter proposition. The protection of powerful unions, industrial in form, democratically controlled, with a policy of fighting the bosses with a determined front, would mean not only a halt to the attacks of the employers, but a chance to take the offensive and get back what has been taken away from the workers in the shape of wage cuts, hacking away at conditions, etc.

The rumbling in the ranks of the A. F. of L. that foreshadowed the present big fight for industrial unionism was felt at the 1934 convention of the A. F. of L., held in San Francisco (the scene, a few months earlier, of the historic general strike). At that convention fourteen resolutions for industrial unionism were introduced. In an attempt to stave off the revolt they felt coming, the A. F. of L. Executive Council pretended to agree to allow the unions in at least a few of the mass production industries—automobiles and rubber—the status of international industrial unions. As for taking any steps toward industrial unionism in general, that was strictly taboo to these gentlemen. They were forced to talk glibly of organization campaigns for the steel, auto, and other mass production industries, which they later never even attempted to carry out. Instead of organizing the steel industry, they allowed the Mike Tighe machine to expel those leaders

---

* The Liberty League was organized by financial and industrial interests for the defeat of President Roosevelt in the 1936 elections. It was a reactionary anti-labor combination representing what Roosevelt called the "economic royalists."

and locals of the Amalgamated Association of Iron, Steel, and Tin Workers who wanted the campaign for organization of the steel industry carried out. Instead of organizing the mass production industries they busied themselves after the 1934 A. F. of L. convention in scrambling to divide among the craft unions whatever organization the workers themselves had been able to bring about in the mass production industries.

THE COMMITTEE FOR INDUSTRIAL ORGANIZATION

The 1935 convention in Atlantic City showed that a great movement for industrial unionism had begun to sweep through the ranks of the A. F. of L., a movement of such determination that international union leaders like John L. Lewis, president of the United Mine Workers; Charles P. Howard, president of the International Typographical Union (a craft union); Sidney Hillman, president of the Amalgamated Clothing Workers; David Dubinsky, president of the International Ladies Garment Workers Union; Thomas P. McMahon, president of the United Textile Workers; Harvey C. Fremming, president of the Oil Field, Gas Well and Refinery Workers; Max Zaritsky, president of the Cap and Millinery Department, United Hatters, Cap and Millinery Workers Union; Thomas H. Brown, International Union of Mine, Mill and Smelter Workers, and other higher officials found it a good idea to become leaders of the movement for industrial unionism.

Lewis and Howard led a powerful minority at the Atlantic City convention in the fight for industrial unionism in the mass production industries. A minority report signed by five members of the Resolutions Committee, including Howard, Dubinsky, and Lewis, pointed out that "the time has arrived when common sense demands the organization policies of the American Federation of Labor must be molded to meet present-day needs." Showing that in its 55 years of existence the A. F. of L. has enrolled only about three and a half million members out of thirty-nine million organizable workers, the minority resolution stated that "we refuse to accept existing conditions as evidence that the organization policies of the American Federation of Labor have been successful."

The resolution further stated that "in those industries where the work performed by a majority of the workers is of such nature that it might fall within the jurisdictional claim of more than one craft union, or no established craft union, it is declared that industrial organization is the only form that will be acceptable to the workers or adequately meet their needs." The resolution went on to show how fears of jurisdictional claims dividing the workers and preventing their unity had prevented organization of these workers to any large extent.

The minority resolution on industrial unionism was defeated at the craft-dominated A. F. of L. convention by 18,025 votes against 10,924. About a month after the convention, in November, 1935, a Committee for Industrial Organization was formed, with Lewis, Howard, Hillman, Dubinsky, McMahon, Fremming, Zaritsky, and Brown as its members and John Brophy, of the United Mine Workers, as its director. Its aims were to "bring the unorganized into the American Federation of Labor . . . by carrying on education within the Federation for industrial unionism, in order to win over a majority, and by giving advice and help to groups of newly organized workers in mass production industry."

The enemies of industrial unionism among the craft union leaders made no attempt to deny any of the arguments that crafts were disappearing; that mechanization, specialization, mass production in industry as it is today make industrial unionism necessary; that the trustification of industry has placed enormous power into the hands of the bankers and capitalists who control the major industries, and that a system of unionism which divides the workers, as does craft unionism, is ineffective against such enormous power. They are not able to deny that craft unionism has been responsible for the scabbery of union against union, for bitter fights over jurisdiction between unions, paralyzing the trade unions in face of the sweeping attacks of the employers.

The majority report of the Resolutions Committee at the Atlantic City convention could only answer the arguments against craft unionism made by the industrial union advocates, by reindorsing the craft unionists' declaration at the San Francisco convention in 1934 to the effect that "Experience has shown that craft unionism is most effective in protecting the welfare and advancing the interests of the workers. . . ."

The craft union leaders do not come out with the real reasons why they want to hang on to the craft union system. They are afraid, for one thing, that by bringing into the A. F. of L. the masses of unorganized, and unskilled workers, and through industrial unionism they will lose control of the unions and will have to give place to more progressive leaders. They are afraid they will lose their fat-salaried positions. They are afraid the nice friendships they have built up with open-shop employers, bankers, and corrupt labor-hating politicians of the Republican and Democratic parties might be cut off if the unions became unified, fighting organizations. These are the reasons why they do not want to organize the millions of unorganized—their interests are not with the working class, but on the bosses' side of the fence. The A. F. of L. Executive Council has even rejected the offer of $500,000 made by the Committee for Industrial Organization to aid in organizing the steel workers!

There remained only one other answer for the craft union leaders. And that answer they gave when William Green and the Executive Council, unable to meet the strong arguments of the Committee for Industrial Organization, ordered the C. I. O. to disband on pain of severe action. Reports are that the Executive Council will go to the length of splitting the A. F. of L. by expelling those unions which support the committee. Yes, these so-called labor leaders would split the A. F. of L. rather than adopt forms and methods which would unify the working class by enabling the A. F. of L. to organize the big majority of the unorganized.

The arguments of the Lewis industrial union bloc are powerful, and none but the blind or those who wilfully refuse to see the 30,-000,000 American workers organized can fail to support them. But arguments like these should be followed to their logical conclusion, which the Committee for Industrial Organization fails to do. It does not see that the question of industrial unionism affects not only the mass production industries, but every industry, for craft unionism has paralyzed the trade union movement in all industries. The C. I. O. does not see that without a fighting policy by the A. F. of L. and without trade union democracy, industrial unionism would be weakened as a weapon against the employers' attacks.

TRADE UNION DEMOCRACY

The Lewis industrial union bloc also as yet has not been able to see as far ahead as growing sections of the rank and file membership of the A. F. of L. as to the true implications of the fight for industrial unionism. The members of the Committee for Industrial Organization see the fight only as a question of a change in structure of the A. F.

of L., and, at that, as a change in structure only for a part of the A. F. of L. (only where the mass production industries are concerned). But they do not see, as the great masses of the rank and file do, that hand in hand with the fight for industrial unionism goes the need for genuine trade union democracy, which means the holding of conventions regularly by all the unions, freedom of discussion for all members of the unions, the democratic election of all officers, the right of all members of the unions to run for and hold offices, the right of all A. F. of L. members to hold any political belief they desire, the use of democratic methods so that the membership can decide on all questions affecting the unions they sacrifice so much for. It means cleaning house in the unions—doing away with all forms of racketeering and gangsterism which still hold sway in many sections of the labor movement.

The leaders of the industrial union bloc themselves now feel the results of high-handed bossism and lack of trade union democracy in the way in which Green and the Executive Council refuse, because they are unable, to argue the question of industrial unionism in any logical way, but resort instead to the method of autocracy, ordering the Committee for Industrial Organization to disband; resorting to threats, hinting at expulsion of those unions fighting for industrial unionism; sending letters, as Green did, to 1,354 local and federal unions directly affiliated to the A. F. of L., to all state federations and to 730 central labor bodies, ordering them not to have anything to do with the perfectly legal Committee for Industrial Organization. This is the same sort of tactic which is used against Communists and other fighting elements in the trade unions (and which Lewis himself has used repeatedly in the U. M. W. A.) because they speak out for a policy of struggle for the unions.

Because there is no real trade union democracy in the Carpenters Union, for instance, the fighters for industrial unionism saw the spectacle of Hutcheson, the leader of the Carpenters Union, speaking and voting at the 1935 A. F. of L. convention against industrial unionism in the name of 200,000 carpenters, even though he was speaking and voting against the real wishes of his members.

The union leaders who are at the head of the fight for industrial unionism can see attempts at discussion in favor of industrial unionism being choked off by gag methods in the craft unions. There is little question but that the bulk of the craft union membership would vote overwhelmingly for industrial unionism if given the chance. If the fight for industrial unionism is to be won, it must be carried into every craft union, and the members of the craft unions must be shown a real example of genuine trade union democracy by the industrial unions which make up the Committee for Industrial Organization. If, for example, at the 1936 convention of the industrial United Mine Workers of America, John L. Lewis had been one of the strongest supporters of the right of the miners to elect their own district officials, what a further strengthening of the fight for industrial unionism that would have meant!

John L. Lewis further weakened the fight for industrial unionism when he nominated the reactionary clique headed by Green back into office at the 1935 A. F. of L. convention. As long as this clique heads the A. F. of L., every real attempt to organize the unorganized will be seriously hampered, for the Green clique does not want to organize the unorganized.

The Committee for Industrial Organization bases its fight for industrial unions, and correctly so, on the fact that this will unify the ranks of the working class and will enable the A. F. of L. to organize the 30,000,000 unorganized workers in the United States. But these workers, so desperate, are raring to go for real struggle against the employers, as was shown on innumerable occasions in the past few years, when they struck without waiting for the sanction of the leading officials, when these officials refused to give such sanction, or when they struck on numberless occasions spontaneously. The Committee for Industrial Organization must come to these unorganized workers, offering them an A. F. of L. policy of class struggle, a policy of fighting for the workers' demands. By failing to see that the fight for industrial unionism is closely connected with the need of a class struggle policy, the C. I. O. greatly weakens the struggle for industrial unionism.

The masses of workers in the A. F. of L. not only want, through industrial unionism, to make the A. F. of L. a solid, united weapon against the bosses' attacks, but they want an end to the policy of class collaboration, of friendship for the bosses on the part of the A. F. of L. leaders instead of a fighting policy.

1936

25. The Renaissance of the American Trade Union Movement

For many years the conservatism of the trade union movement in the United States, represented chiefly by the American Federation of Labor, has been world-notorious. The A. F. of L. leaders, open defenders of capitalism, have opposed even the most opportunist forms of Social-Democracy, considering the Second International "too revolutionary" for their affiliation. They have fought against the formation of a labor party, their policy being to keep the workers affiliated to the big capitalist parties. They have clung to the antiquated craft union system in a country of trustified industry and mass production. They are indeed "labor lieutenants of the bourgeoisie." The general effects of their regime of corruption and class collaboration have been to render the American working class almost powerless: the workers have no mass political party of their own and their trade unions, largely composed of skilled workers, include hardly more than 15 per cent of the organizable workers.

At bottom, the causes for this ultra-conservative trade unionism were to be found in a number of economic, political, and social factors, including the relatively favorable economic position of the large labor aristocracy; the presence of millions of immigrant workers of many nationalities with different social and cultural traditions; the passage of many workers into the ranks of the petty bourgeoisie and some even into the capitalist class during the period of rapid industrial expansion, etc. All these factors tended to check the growth of class consciousness among the workers, to stimulate petty-bourgeois illusions among them, and to prevent the growth of powerful trade unions, a mass working class party, and a revolutionary perspective.

Now, however, the picture is rapidly changing in the United States. Seven years of crisis and depression, with semi-starvation and with the employed workers suffering heavily reduced living standards, with the growth of an incipient fascist reaction, etc., are having profound effects. The working masses are rapidly becoming radicalized. They are beginning to cast off their capitalistic illusions and to develop a more militant spirit. They are at last taking up seriously the questions of building a powerful labor movement and developing class political action. In short, the American trade union movement is at a turning point; it is breaking with its old conservative past and is crossing the threshold of a new era of progress.

THE RISE OF THE C. I. O.

The center of this new trade union renaissance is the Committee for Industrial Organization (C. I. O.). The C. I. O., headed by John L. Lewis, is composed of fifteen unions with some 2,000,000 members. It was formed about a year ago with a program of organizing the armies of unorganized workers in the mass production industries into industrial unions. The actual establishment of the C. I. O. did not take place until after Lewis had fought for two years to induce the A. F. of L. itself to undertake this work. Lewis himself has a very conservative background, but he saw the necessity for industrial unionism. His proposals, however, were rejected by the craft union reactionaries—Green, Woll, Frey, Wharton, Hutcheson, etc.—who dominate the Executive Council of the A. F. of L. The Lewis forces then launched the C. I. O. and began this fundamental organization work themselves, meanwhile maintaining their regular affiliation with the A. F. of L.

In the intervening months since then the C. I. O. has been signally successful in its organization work. In the automobile industry, in February of this year, the C. I. O. carried on a strike against the giant General Motors Corporation, involving 150,000 workers. This was followed by another strike of 70,000 against the Chrysler Company. Both were sit-down strikes (occupation of the factories) and both were won, forcing the automobile kings to grant many economic concessions and, for the first time, to recognize trade unionism in their plants. The Auto Workers Union grew almost overnight from a skeleton organization to a union of 300,000 members and it is still rapidly expanding.

This great success of the C. I. O. in the automobile industry was even surpassed by its victory in steel. After a several months' organizing campaign, and right upon the heels of the General Motors strike, the C. I. O. forced the great moguls of the United States Steel Corporation to meet with Lewis and agree to recognize the C. I. O.

steel workers' union. This union has also leaped from almost nothing to an organization of at least 300,000 members and is still growing swiftly. The powerful General Electric Company was also compelled to sign an agreement with the rapidly developing C. I. O. radio and electrical workers' union.

Besides these notable victories, the C. I. O. has won strikes and is conducting big organizing campaigns in a number of other industries, such as glass, shipbuilding, rubber, oil, textile, etc. The successes in auto and steel have created a veritable fever of organization and struggle among the workers in various industries. Most of the many strikes taking place are of the sit-down type and are extremely militant in character. The workers, fresh from their victory over the Landon-Hearst reaction in the November elections, are in a fighting mood and ready for vigorous action. The C. I. O. struggles are also favored by the improved economic situation and by the tolerant attitude of the Roosevelt government toward the trade union organization of the workers in the mass production industries.

In the many C. I. O. organization campaigns and strikes, the Communists are playing an important role, co-operating freely with the C. I. O. Especially is this true of the auto and steel industries. In the vital General Motors strike the Communists were an important factor and this was also true in the bitterly fought strike of 40,000 marine transport workers (A. F. of L.), the winning of which stimulated the workers' fighting spirit generally.

THE SPLIT IN THE AMERICAN FEDERATION OF LABOR

The reactionary leaders of the A. F. of L., fearing for the safety of their fat jobs and their corrupt regime, are bitterly fighting against the advance of the militant C. I. O. No sooner was the C. I. O. formed, early in 1936, as an organizing committee than the A. F. of L. Executive Council condemned it as a rival, dual organization. Then, a few months later, the Executive Council, in flagrant violation of the A. F. of L. constitution and in the face of a great mass protest of trade unionists generally, arbitrarily suspended the C. I. O. unions from A. F. of L. affiliation. The Tampa convention of the A. F. of L. in October, 1936, made up principally of craft union bureaucrats and in which the C. I. O. unions were denied the right to vote, confirmed the suspension of the C. I. O. unions.

The Communist Party had played a very active part in mobilizing the trade unionists against the suspension of the C. I. O. unions by the A. F. of L. Executive Council and it now also took up the cudgels against the splitting action of the packed Tampa convention. The Communist Party put out the slogan "Keep the split from spreading." It called upon the workers to refuse to suspend the C. I. O. locals from the city and state central labor councils, and thus to keep the movement intact at the bottom in spite of the split among the officialdom. The Communist Party also outlined a policy for reuniting the warring groups under the banner of the A. F. of L.

Realizing the mass resistance to their splitting policy, the Executive Council reactionaries did not dare at that time to order the local councils to suspend the C. I. O. unions. Thus was presented the peculiar situation of a split at the top of the labor movement and unity in its basic organs. This unity at the bottom was highly favorable to the C. I. O. as it was thus enabled to go ahead with its organizing campaigns in auto and steel unmolested by local A. F. of L. sabotage. In fact, the friendly co-operation of many A. F. of L. city labor councils was of great, if not decisive, importance in the crucial General Motors strike.

Deeply alarmed at the significant General Motors strike, the A. F. of L. Executive Council renewed its splitting offensive. President Green of the A. F. of L. denounced the strike as an outlaw affair, he condemned the sit-down tactics as illegal and imported from Moscow, and he repudiated the victorious strike settlement as a defeat and a betrayal of trade union principles. Later Green issued an instruction to the city central labor councils to unseat delegates of C. I. O. local unions and he has already revoked the charter of one council of the very many such councils that have refused to obey his splitting orders.

Meanwhile, the C. I. O. has not taken these blows lying down. The miners' union (C. I. O.), of which Lewis is president and Green was a member, expelled Green as a strikebreaker and a traitor. The C. I. O. locals and sympathizers are resisting Green's suspension order in the local labor councils and the C. I. O. has announced that it will issue charters for new councils where its locals are expelled. Meanwhile the C. I. O. has redoubled its organizing efforts in steel, auto, oil, textile, and many other industries.

Thus the situation now is that Green wants the split and is doing all possible to deepen it, while Lewis with his supporters growing rapidly both inside and outside the A. F. of L., is resisting the disruptive efforts of Green.

The C. I. O. and the A. F. of L. now practically constitute two distinct national trade union centers. The split, although steadily deepening, is, however, not fully completed. The C. I. O. unions are not yet officially expelled from the A. F. of L. (their status is one of suspension), and, besides this, the trade union movement still remains united at the bottom, in the city and state labor councils, to which the C. I. O. unions, in the main, are still affiliated. And there the situation stands at the present time of writing, the end of March, 1937.

THE RELATION OF TRADE UNION FORCES

As between the C. I. O. and the A. F. of L., the C. I. O. is numerically considerably the strongest, although its forces are not yet fully consolidated. The A. F. of L. claims a total membership of 3,586,567. But from this figure must be deducted over 1,000,000 C. I. O. members who have been suspended and who have since hugely increased their numbers. Besides, there are several unions in the A. F. of L. (printers, lumber workers, fur workers, etc.) totaling at least 200,000 members, which would promptly quit the A. F. of L. and join the C. I. O. if called upon to do it. Besides this, the C. I. O. has a tremendous body of active sympathizers in the A. F. of L., several hundred thousand at least. Not counting its large general following in the A. F. of L., the C. I. O. has now at least 2,000,000 actual members and it is growing with extreme rapidity, because of its successful organizing campaigns in auto, steel, textile, etc. Actually, therefore, the C. I. O. is numerically larger than the A. F. of L., and this factor daily grows more favorable to the C. I. O.

The C. I. O. is also far more strategically situated in industry than is the A. F. of L. The main strength of its fifteen affiliated unions lies in the basic and mass production industries—coal mining 500,000; auto 300,000; steel 300,000; textile 90,000; oil 80,000, and some 300,-000 in the rubber, electric, aluminum, metal mining, shipbuilding, and other industries. Besides this, the C. I. O. has a solid bloc of 400,000 members in the clothing industry. On the other hand, the A. F. of L. finds its chief strength in the lighter, non-trustified industries, and especially among skilled workers and government employees. Its main force is the building trades, 700,000 members. The other important industrial positions of the A. F. of L. are some 400,000 shop, trade, and office workers in the railroad industry (the running trades are in independent unions) and a strong organization in marine transport, although the great bulk of these workers are open supporters of the C. I. O. and will eventually probably join it.

The advanced position of the C. I. O. over the A. F. of L. also expresses itself in a variety of other ways. It is based on the principle of industrial unionism, while the A. F. of L. still clings to craft unionism; it is developing a new and progressive leadership, as against the hardboiled reactionaries of the A. F. of L.; it is awakening the political consciousness of the workers and arousing their militancy; whereas the reactionary A. F. of L. leaders have always been a brake on the class development of the workers.

Thus the C. I. O. is superior to the A. F. of L. numerically, in strategical position and in general political tendency. It is the most decisive of the two national trade union centers and it represents the broad path along which American labor needs to progress. When the A. F. of L. reactionaries rejected the C. I. O. program and suspended the unions they signed their own political death warrants as the major leaders of American trade unionism.

The split in the American labor movement raises sharply the question of establishing trade union unity. The big employers are quite alert to use the right-wing A. F. of L. against the progressive C. I. O. In the auto and steel industries they worked openly with bosses against the C. I. O., even offering to furnish leadership to the company unions to beat the new industrial unions. Hence, the workers need imperatively to put an end to such a menace by moving toward the achievement of trade union unity.

In the eventually unified trade union movement the C. I. O. forces and policies will doubtless play the central role. In fact, the fight for unity resolves itself into a matter of extending all possible support to the new C. I. O. center, while at the same time developing a movement looking toward the uniting of all the unions in one general federation.

Of first importance is to give the maximum possible support to the C. I. O.'s campaigns to organize the millions of unorganized workers. Success in this vital work is the dynamic factor in the whole situation, the key to the future development of the American trade union movement.

Also, every effort should be put forth to keep the Green reactionaries from further splitting the trade unions. Especially important in this respect is it to encourage the widespread refusal of the A. F. of L. city and state labor federations to carry out Green's order to exclude the C. I. O. delegates. This refusal, where successful, has the effect of keeping the labor movement intact at the bottom and of throwing the rebellious local federations definitely into the orbit of the C. I. O.

It would seem necessary also to contemplate the eventual holding of a well-prepared national union convention, called by the C. I. O., the A. F. of L. and the independent railroad unions to unify the whole labor movement. And in the meantime, so far as possible without deepening the split, the C. I. O. should consolidate its forces, both outside and inside the A. F. of L.

Of course, the Green reactionaries will bitterly fight this great unity movement as long as they can. But unless the writer is greatly mistaken, they face in the C. I. O. a mass movement that they cannot beat down. The handwriting is on the wall for them and their reactionary regime; the American labor movement is going to experience a New Deal of its own.

The basic significance of the broad organizing campaigns of the C. I. O. is that the American workers are finally beginning to organize as a class, both economically and politically. Heretofore the A. F. of L., with its narrow craft unionism and its anti-working class political policies, has definitely hindered such class organization. The class unionism of the C. I. O. is rapidly changing the make-up and outlook of the trade unions.

The advance of the C. I. O. is already resulting in vast changes in the labor movement. It is producing a new and progressive labor leadership; it is developing the new trade union form, industrial unionism; it is applying new tactics, the sit-down strikes; it is extending trade unionism into new fields, the basic trustified industries; it is winning real victories. Instead of the defeats and weak compromises of A. F. of L. craft unionism, it is rousing the militancy of the working class generally and dealing heavy blows at the A. F. of L. theories and practices of class collaboration.

The C. I. O. is also advancing the working class in politics. It displays many progressive political tendencies; it has a sharp and growing anti-fascist, anti-war trend; it was a powerful factor in defeating the Landon reaction in the November elections; it presses Roosevelt from the left and as it organizes the left-wing in the Democratic Party it is driving in the direction of a farmer-labor party; it strongly supports the trade union organization of Negroes; its leaders, unlike those of the A. F. of L., are not carrying on slander campaigns against the U.S.S.R. and the Communist Party. In short, around the C. I. O. are grouping the major mass forces that should, with effective leadership, eventually crystallize into a great American People's Front.

The C. I. O. has already forced a sharp change in the traditional anti-trade union policy of finance capital. Hitherto, the big trust magnates enforced their infamous open-shop policy in the mass production industries. But the C. I. O., by its big organizing campaigns and aggressive strikes, has broken this down, shattered the company union system and compelled the reluctant big capitalists to recognize the C. I. O. unions in the strategic auto, steel and electrical manufacturing industries.

It would be idle, however, to think that finance capital will tamely submit to the advance of the militant C. I. O. unions. Already their publicity agents are singing praises of "strikeless England," and are advocating that various methods of state incorporations, semi-compulsory arbitration, strike right limitation, etc., be enacted so as to hamstring the American unions somewhat as was done to the British unions after their betrayed national general strike. They will doubtless try to make a bargain with the C. I. O. upon some such class collaboration basis.

The big employers are also maneuvering for a more favorable time to smash violently the new unions if they cannot otherwise destroy their effectiveness. In fighting the C. I. O., the employers now face the triple handicap of a militant working class, a rising economic situation and the policy of the Roosevelt government. But they expect all this will soon change. For one thing they expect a fresh economic crisis within a year or two, and they hope either to defeat Roosevelt or to "take him into camp" by an agreement with him. In any event, we may be sure they are biding their time for a good opportunity to castrate or destroy the C. I. O. unions.

1937

26. Steel Strike Strategy

When organized labor goes into such an important strike as that evidently now looming in connection with the organization of the steel industry it must proceed with a definite strike strategy, based upon a realistic measuring of the balance of the opposing class forces and modified from time to time as changing circumstances dictate. We may be sure that the employers, in their fight to preserve the open shop, which is worth billions to them in extra profits, are going ahead with a highly developed strategy.

In the following pages, therefore, I shall undertake to outline some of the major principles of a sound strategy and tactics for the steel workers' struggle; to develop a line of policy that is realistic and justified by the present economic and political situation and by the general relation of forces between the capitalists and the workers. The leaders of the C. I. O. and the Steel Workers Organizing Committee are, of course, experienced strike leaders, and it is not for me to instruct them in strike strategy. There remains, however, the task of putting into popular form the principles of strike strategy and strike organization in this very vital situation.

In the development of any severe strike struggle between the workers and their employers the following general propositions, among others, should be constantly borne in mind.

First, the cultivation of a firm ideological solidarity in the ranks of the strikers. The bosses, proceeding from the traditional exploiters' principle of divide and conquer, constantly attempt to split the workers along lines of skilled and unskilled, Americans and foreign-born, Negroes and whites, men and women, employed and unemployed, adults and youth, Catholics and Protestants, radicals and conservatives. This danger is especially acute in struggles in the boss-ridden steel industry.

In 1919, the employers and their tools tried with all these means to pit one section of the workers against the other and they may be depended upon to do so again in 1937. As against these disruptive moves, the workers' leaders must counter by a loyal defense in the interests of all these various groups, thus making them all feel that they have everything to gain from the success of the general movement.

They must focus the attention of the masses primarily upon the immediate economic and political demands of the steel workers and reject all reactionary efforts to divert the workers' attention into abstract discussions of race, religion, policies, etc. Especially there must be no boss-inspired Red-baiting allowed to take root in the steel workers' movement and to disrupt its forces. The steel campaign can be a success only if the maximum possible ideological solidarity of the workers is achieved and maintained.

Second, another important consideration in the question of developing a successful strike strategy is the careful cultivation of a high morale among the strikers. This is very necessary in fighting such a vicious combination as the steel trust, and morale building must be gone about systematically. The achievement of the ideological solidarity previously discussed is an important element in developing a good morale among the workers, but it must be supplemented by various other factors, including persistent education of the masses regarding the strike situation and the political meaning of the struggle, by cultivating mass participation in strike activities and democratic control of the strike, by exercising a determined and reliable leadership, by a firm but not mechanical discipline, an effective dramatization of the struggle, good strike organization, etc.

Third, a further elementary question of good strike strategy is to proceed upon the general principle of the offensive. Workers, like soldiers, fight best on the attack. A defensive strike is a losing strike. The steel workers should never allow themselves to be put on the defensive. Every halt must be utilized to organize a new attack and every attack by the employers or the government must be offset by some form of renewed counter offensive. Only when workers are completely defeated is such a policy not possible. The steel workers must know how to guard their strike reserves and to draw upon them when a new forward movement is necessary. The present economic and political situation greatly favors a policy of the offensive.

These elements of strike strategy—a firm ideological solidarity of the workers, a high morale in the strike, a strike that proceeds upon the principle of the offensive—must be constantly borne in mind in developing every stage of the coming struggle. But there are many other principles of strike strategy, no less important, which I shall now proceed to discuss in some detail.

A unified command is a fundamental principle of strategy in all strikes, as well as military operations. What is involved in it is the unified action of the fighting forces. Failure to achieve such a unified strike leadership, principally through craft divisions, has cost the workers many a bitter defeat. Especially is a unified command and real solidarity of the workers necessary to beat the open shop kings in the steel, auto, rubber, oil, etc., industries.

The industrial form of the C. I. O. unions conducting the struggle in these industries lays a solid foundation for a unified command and the vital strike unity. Nevertheless a danger threatens from the craft union leaders of the American Federation of Labor. These reactionaries, although they themselves for years have done nothing to organize the mass production industries, are extremely antagonistic towards the Committee for Industrial Organization doing the job. They assume a dog-in-the-manger attitude. It is more than likely, therefore, that they will inject themselves into the situation and try to inveigle a fringe of the skilled workers into their many disconnected craft unions. At the moment I write these lines they are following such a strike-breaking policy in the General Motors auto strike.

Such an action would be a crime against the steel, auto and other workers, as it would seriously split their ranks and weaken their fighting force. But no one familiar with the shady history of the reactionary A. F. of L. leaders need be surprised to see them adopt such a disruptive course. They have done it time and again in strikes of independent unions. The danger is all the greater inasmuch as the trust magnates, happy to see the workers dissipate their strength fighting each other, always greet and encourage the craft union leaders in their splitting tactics.

The introduction of craft unionism into the mass production industries by the A. F. of L. leaders should be resisted militantly by every progressive force in the whole labor movement as a strikebreaking policy. This resistance should be supported by an aggressive campaign to educate the unorganized masses as to the historical failure of craft unionism in the mass production industries, and by a call to these workers not to join the craft unions but to affiliate themselves with the C. I. O. industrial unions.

If, nevertheless, the craft unions should succeed in getting into steel by the time the strike takes place, they must be dealt with on a united front basis, and unity of action sought in this manner. They should be drawn into the strike on a full co-operative basis with the industrial unions. This means that they ought to be allowed and induced to send regular delegates to the strike committees, and likewise to their sub-committees for relief, defense, publicity, etc., and that they should also participate in the mass picketing and other mass strike activities. The craft leaders would object to this, so it would have to be done over their heads by direct appeal to the membership. Only in the unlikely event, however, that the craft unions should become real factors in the steel industry would it be practical to make the resultant trade union agreement of a joint character signed by other unions as well as the Amalgamated Association.

In the developing great strike movement there must be prevented at all costs the shameful but all too common spectacle of union strike-breaking, that is, of one or more unions striking while the others work. The solidarity of labor demands that the craft unions stay out of the mass production industries and leave the field to the industrial unions. For them to enter these industries at this time could serve the interests of no one but the great trust magnates and reaction generally.

A good military strategist never forgets his main objective, although bad leaders often do. He refuses to allow himself to be diverted from his goal by the feints and tricks of his opponents. And so it is with the labor strategist; he, too, must always keep his major objective in mind. He must constantly be on the alert to keep the employers from sidetracking his whole movement into the fatal swamp of delay, disintegrations and betrayal. Especially is such vigilance necessary when the enemy is the powerful and resourceful steel trust.

Up till the present time the central strategy of the steel corporation has aimed at destroying the steel campaign by giving niggardly wage increases to the workers and by cultivating the company unions, although their great plant supplies of tear gas, machine guns, and other deadly weapons show that they are preparing for drastic violence. The employers have been unable as yet under the present circumstances to employ the widespread discharge of workers, suppression of free speech, terrorism of workers and organizers, etc., with which they opposed the organizing campaign in 1919.

As soon as the movement of the steel workers approaches the point of mass action we may expect that the steel barons will go into the next stage of their anti-union strategy, not only by using more terroristic methods, but also by having recourse to the policy of seeking to divert the whole thrust of the union away from the companies and into a hopeless morass of governmental committees, court action, time-killing mediation, etc. The first real test of the steel workers' strength and strike strategy will come when they have organized the bulk of the workers and they serve their demands upon the Iron and Steel Institute for a conference to work out a national trade union agreement for the steel industry. It is at this point that the steel companies will attempt to paralyze or kill off the workers' movement by bogging it down in a swamp of disintegrating maneuvers.

This is when the workers must be most acutely on guard and when they have to persist most determinedly towards their central objective of forcing concessions directly from the employers. The steel workers must not trust their cause into the hands of the Roosevelt government. The government is allied with many great capitalist interests, and it cannot be depended upon to force the steel trust to make a settlement favorable to the workers. Especially must the steel workers beware that Roosevelt's "era of good feeling" policy does not result in some sort of a compromise disastrous to their movement. If Hearst and other labor haters are enthusiastic over the so-called "era of good feeling" it is because they see in it a possible means to check the workers' advance to trade union organization and better living conditions.

Still fresh in the minds of the workers are the maneuvers by which the Roosevelt government, the courts and the A. F. of L. leaders killed off the Weirton steel strike and also the devious means by which they ruined the powerful movement of the steel workers in 1934, the one being sidetracked into endless court actions and the other getting lost in the trickery of a board set up by Roosevelt. These defeats of the steel workers through the Roosevelt government are in line with those of the workers in the automobile and other industries during the days of the N.R.A.

Such experience must serve as lessons to the steel workers in their present developing struggle. Towards the Roosevelt government their attitude must not be one of naive reliance, but of mass pressure to preserve civil liberties in the steel areas and to force the steel trust to yield to the demands of its workers. The steel workers must not let their movement degenerate into mere court actions to defend their right to organize, or long-winded government-controlled elections supposedly to learn whether or not the Amalgamated Association has the right to represent the steel workers. These questions must be settled by pressure against the employers and, if necessary, by mass strike action.

The central aim of the movement should be a direct settlement between the unions and the employers, and every step taken must be directed to accomplish this end. The steel workers should not enter into arbitration proceedings or other settlement maneuvers engineered by the government unless their major demands have been conceded.

Should the employers fail in their inevitable attempt to liquidate the steel workers' movement through government or court action, or through some such phony arbitration as employers have so often defeated workers in the past, then in all likelihood they will set out to beat the C. I. O. and the Amalgamated Association in an open strike struggle. Just what kind of a fight they are getting ready to make may be gathered from the fact that they are now storing up their plants with machine guns, rifles, tear gas, etc., and are even drilling their thugs in preparation for a fierce strike. The steel workers, therefore, must base their plans upon the practically certain prospect of a great strike against the steel corporations.

The perspective of a huge national strike confronts the workers' leaders with the necessity of bearing closely in mind another basic principle of strategy, that of mobilizing a full sufficiency of forces to achieve their objective. A good strategist never sends a boy to do a man's job. This strategic principle may be illustrated by an old-time circus story: A boss canvasman was explaining to a visitor how vitally important it was that the cook-wagon should arrive early on the circus lot in order that the men could breakfast, or else they would not put up the big top.

Said he: "No cook-wagon, no breakfast; and no breakfast, no work," and he explained, therefore, that they always used the precaution of having eight of the strongest horses to pull the cook-wagon over the muddy roads.

"But," inquired the visitor, "suppose the roads are so poor that your eight horses can't pull the cook-wagon, what then?"

"Oh, then," said the circus boss, "we put on more horses, and if they can't do the job we get out old Babe the elephant, to push it from behind."

"Still," persisted the visitor, "suppose the roads are so terribly bad that even all these horses and old Babe together can't haul the cook-wagon through the mire, how about that?"

"Oh, hell," declared the boss with finality, "we just put on more horses and more horses. The damned cook-wagon simply has to go through."

It is in this spirit of unconquerableness that the workers' leaders must face the eventuality of a national steel strike. They must be prepared to throw more and more forces into the struggle until finally they budge the "immovable" steel trust. The steel campaign must come through and that is all there is to it. Nothing will be handed to the workers gratuitously, either by the bosses directly or by the government. All they will get is what they are willing and able to fight for. The key to the winning of the movement of the steel workers is the greatest mobilization of labor's forces ever made in the United States.

Another major strategic consideration that must always be borne in mind in strikes is that of dealing the blow at the best time and place. The enemy must be hit both at the proper moment at its most vulnerable spot. The steel workers, if they keep this point clearly in mind, are in a splendid position to win.

The C. I. O. plans to have the majority of the steel workers organized by the middle of February, 1937, after which the demands of the workers will be submitted to the American Iron and Steel Institute and a conference insisted upon. This is a practical schedule and it climaxes the steel movement at a most favorable moment. Undoubtedly by the date set the great majority of the workers can readily be organized. Then, allowing a few weeks for preliminary negotiations, the steel situation should come to a head somewhere about the end of March.

This is just the time (March 31) when the national agreement of the 500,000 bituminous miners expires. From a strategic standpoint obviously the correct thing to do is to link the struggle of the steel workers with that of the bituminous coal miners, and possibly also of the anthracite miners, thus developing a broad movement of about a million coal miners and steel workers. This appears to be the aim of the C. I. O. and, if so, it is sound strategy. The interests of these two basic sections of the workers are bound up together. They have largely the same forces of massed financial capital to fight, and there is every reason why their fight should be combined into one general movement against the closely allied steel and coal corporations.

A joint strike of the one million steel workers and coal miners would exert a tremendous power. It would bring to a standstill the two most basic industries and tie up other industries far and wide. It would constitute by far the greatest strike in American history. In view of the favorable situation in industry, with production rapidly rising, the combined coal miners and steel workers would probably be able to secure victory, forcing the open shop kings, for the first time, to treat their workers like human beings. But labor should "make assurance doubly sure" by hooking still more horses to the cook-wagon if need be. There must be contemplated the extension of the strike struggle among the vast armies of workers in the automobile, rubber, and heavy metal and electrical fabricating industries, and also further, if necessary.

MASS PRODUCTION INDUSTRIES

The C. I. O. is now conducting organization campaigns in these mass production industries. In the present situation, so very favorable for organization work, its campaigns can and should be speeded up so that the unions involved (which, as they are led by the C. I. O., would not have to depend upon the reactionary leaders of the A. F. of L.) can also present their demands to their employers by the end of March, if not sooner. The entrance of the workers in the auto, rubber, aluminum, and other highly vulnerable and closely interlinked mass production industries simultaneously or at approximately the same time into the struggle would enormously strengthen the whole movement. Such a movement in the key industries would constitute a most effective co-operation of the strategic principles of opportune time, key place, sufficient power, etc. While each of these great groups of workers has its own demands, the entire movement should be co-ordinated around the central strategic task of winning the demands of the steel workers. This main objective especially must not be forgotten in whatever settlements are arrived at in the various industries.

It may turn out in reality that the steel workers, coal miners, automobile workers, etc., will not actually co-ordinate their national movements—the auto workers especially are running ahead and developing a great national struggle of their own. Possibly, in view of labor's present extremely favorable position, these great groups, acting separately, may achieve their major demands. It is also possible, although most unlikely, that they can secure their demands without great strikes. Nevertheless, the foregoing proposed line of strategy, the linking of these big movements, with steel as the center, is basically correct. It would be a tremendous manifestation of labor's power. It is the best course to be followed under the present circumstances, the policy that would insure the workers' victory most quickly and completely in these industries and open the doors the widest for a general advance by labor on all fronts.

Every conservative and reactionary influence will be exerted to pre-

vent the steel workers, miners, and other key workers from acting
jointly and will seek to defeat or half defeat them one section at a
time. It is, therefore, the great task of the progressive forces to do all
possible to link the steel, coal, auto and other workers into one great
united front fighting movement against massed financial capital.

To what extent it will turn out to be possible to call into action
labor's heavy first line reserves, both to win their own demands and to
achieve victory in the steel struggle, remains to be seen. But one thing
is clear; whether the steel workers strike alone, jointly with the miners,
or in combination with other industries, at least they must have substantial support from the railroad workers. The latter must refuse to
haul raw materials into, or finished products out of, the steel mills. If
the conservative leaders of the railroad brotherhoods do not agree to
prohibit the hauling of cars in and out of struck mills the rank-and-file
railroad workers must be organized not to go through the picket lines
into the mills and all this in spite of the wage concessions that the companies are evidently preparing to give them to lull their fighting spirit.
Failure of support from the railroad workers in this elementary respect
was a basic cause for the loss of the 1919 strike and it must not be
repeated.

Organized labor must be prepared, if necessary, to support the approaching steel strike by strike action far and wide in many other industries. At all costs the steel workers' struggle for organization must
be won. The fate of the trade union movement is bound up with the
steel workers, whose movement must needs be carried through to
victory.

A national strike of steel workers, and especially a great combined
strike of workers in steel, coal, and other industries, would be highly
political in character. It would become immediately the central political issue of the country. No one would have a keener appreciation of
this fact than the employing interests of the country. In such a situation, we might be sure that they would shout revolution in all keys,
and try to utilize the government to stampede the workers back to
work in a welter of violence and confusion.

The workers must also be acutely aware of the political character of
the developing mass struggle and, as good strategists, be prepared to
use every political weapon at their disposal. In the great general strike
in England in 1926, one of the worst errors made by the conservative
union leadership was to ignore the obviously basically political character of the movement and to try to keep the struggle restricted to the

economic sphere. This was disastrous, as it prevented the workers from utilizing their many political means of struggle. Such a mistake must not be made in the great struggle that in all probability will develop before the organization of the steel workers is conceded by the steel trust.

Let me repeat: Political action does not consist in relying upon the Roosevelt government to win the workers' fight against the steel trust. On the contrary, the workers must mobilize all their political organizations and sympathizers to reinforce the great economic strike struggle of their unions by bringing mass pressure upon the government, local, state, and national; to prevent the use of troops, injunctions, etc., against the strikers; and to force a strike settlement favorable to the workers. Immediately with the development of such a great strike movement as now appears certain, Labor's Non-Partisan League, the various Farmer-Labor Party groups, the Socialist Party, the Communist Party, the progressive blocs in the national government and state legislative bodies, and other political forces sympathetic to labor, should all connect their forces to mobilize public sentiment and bring determined political pressure against the steel corporations through the government.

The occasion of the strike should also be utilized politically by labor's coming forward militantly with its whole legislative program for the preservation and development of civil rights for the thirty-hour week, improved social security and unemployment relief, the legal right to organize, abolition of company unions, prohibition of scabherding and spy systems, etc. A victory in steel should be accompanied by a general advance of labor legislation in every field.

A great strike in steel, coal, and other industries would also put immediately upon the agenda of the day the question of the political mass strike, and the workers must, from the outset, prepare to use this powerful political force. It is certain that in many localities, especially where the authorities tried to suppress the right to picket and when they used violence against the strikers, local general strike movements would or could result. Also, on a national scale, should the steel trust, supported by organized capital, make a determined effort to defeat the strike by violent measures, the question of a national general strike would almost certainly become a living issue among the ranks of labor, regardless of the efforts of the reactionary trade union officials, the employers, and the government to prevent it. The political mass strike could have as its objectives the withdrawal of troops and the reestablishment of civil rights in the strike areas, the removal of anti-labor government officials, the advancement of important labor legislation thrust up by the strike situation, against the shipment of strike breakers, against evictions of the strikers, for placing of strikers on government unemployed relief, the release of arrested strikers, and for the favorable settlement of the strike.

During the past several years the American working class has gained much experience with the weapon of the mass political strike to add to its previous experience with the historic Seattle and Winnipeg general strikes. It learned very much about this form of political struggle in the great San Francisco strike of 1934, as well as in such local general strike situations as those of Pekin, Terre Haute, Minneapolis, Milwaukee, etc. The many valuable lessons from these struggles must be used if such strikes occur during the approaching labor upheaval. Should the organized employers seriously threaten to beat the strike of the steel workers and the other mass production workers, the masses of American workers generally must defend the right of the steel slaves to organize by using, as the situation may demand, the local or national political mass strike.

STEEL STRIKE ORGANIZATION

In the previous sections I have discussed several major principles of strike strategy and tactics necessary to apply in the event of a great strike in steel and allied industries. It now remains to consider a number of others required to insure the success of such a struggle. These include good strike preparations, thoroughgoing strike organization, democratic strike leadership, mass participation in strike activities, care of the material welfare of the strikers, mobilization of the strike reserves, etc.

In view of the existing very favorable economic and political circumstances a national strike of steel workers, and especially a great strike of steel workers and coal miners combined (and also possibly other industries), would create a situation extremely difficult for the employers to handle, and would probably be of short duration. Nevertheless it would be dangerous simply to place reliance in the prospect of a short, quickly victorious strike. If the employers determine to fight against the unionization of the unorganized workers militantly and with all their power, the consequence might well be a long and bitter struggle, even where such huge masses of workers are involved.

We must remember that the 1919 steel strike of 365,000 workers lasted three and a half months; also that the national railroad shopmen's strike in 1922 of 400,000 workers continued for five months, and that the great coal strike in 1927, involving some 500,000 workers, went on more than a year. In fact, as I write this, we are now seeing the powerful strike of 70,000 maritime workers lasting over two months although it has shipping completely paralyzed on the entire Pacific Coast and badly lamed on the Atlantic and Gulf Coasts. And the glass workers, also, have been on a national strike fourteen weeks already.

In any event, whether the employers intend to resist to the last ditch or not, the best way to bring about a speedy and favorable settlement of the probable 1937 steel strike, which the bosses are forcing on the workers, is to make that strike the biggest, best organized, and most effective in American labor history. The principles of strike organization outlined in this chapter are calculated to help achieve this end. They are based on sound experience and can be applied not only to steel, but also to automobile and such other industries as may be involved in mass strike movements in this period.

Fundamental to the carrying out of a good strike strategy is a thorough preliminary organization for the struggle. This is equivalent to the recruiting and training of an army before the battle. Such preparation is especially necessary in an industry like steel, where the workers have had very little experience in organization and disciplined action, and where the power and ruthlessness of the enemy they have to fight are enormous. Good preparation gives the workers incomparably greater striking power. It is on the same principle that drilled troops are far better fighters than raw recruits.

In strike preparation the first thing to be considered is the building of the union itself. This requires that the present steel campaign be speeded up so that practically the entire body of steel workers are members of the union before the actual strike begins. Nor should the office workers in the steel plants be left out of the steel union in its drive to organization. Under the stimulation of the great strikes in the auto, glass, and other industries, and with the workers' present readiness to organize, this speeding up can be easily accomplished by the application of broader methods of organizing work, that is, the holding of great series of mass meetings, widespread radio broadcasts, vast distribution of literature, etc. It should not be difficult, with the use of such intense organizing methods, soon to have the workers pouring into the union in a great flood. The steel campaign should aim at solidly organizing every worker in the steel towns, including restaurant workers, building trades, retail clerks, etc., into their respective unions.

The extension of the union to include all possible masses of steel workers is the main insurance against the development of the dangerous back-to-work movements that are always organized by the employers in every great strike and which are now so menacing in the automobile strike. It is, of course, vitally necessary to organize the most important key plants, but the work must not be confined to them. It must take in the whole steel industry.

Can the sit-down and stay-in types of local strikes which are now so rapidly organizing the workers in the automobile industry also be used in the preliminary stages of unionizing steel? This remains to be learned. As the steel movement grows, as the workers feel the union becoming strong, as their morale and feeling of power rise, and as they see workers in other industries conducting local strikes successfully, the steel workers, smarting under long years of injustice, may wish to try such strikes themselves, at least in the smaller independent plants. Whether or not they can do so successfully will depend upon whether the employers take advantage of such local strikes to force unprepared and disastrous partial struggles. In any event, the C. I. O. will do well to proceed cautiously in this matter, to guard carefully against untimely local strikes and to continue its present strategy of subordinating all local activities to the development of a great disciplined national movement of steel workers.

It may well be that the method of the stay-in strike will be applied to many steel plants in the event of a general strike call. Whether or not it will be used will depend upon several factors: if the workers consider the experience in the automobile industry was successful, if the government is hostile and will permit the use of gas and other violence against stay-in strikers, if a union feels strong enough to control the plan without staying in, if the prospect is for a long or short strike, etc. It was the steel workers, in Homestead in 1892, who gave the first and most heroic American example of strikers occupying struck plants and it may be followed in the approaching strike.

Besides signing up the workers it is also necessary, as soon as practicable, to set up the new local unions of the Amalgamated Association, and to get them functioning. These locals should be not merely general conglomerations of all the workers from each mill; they should be departmentalized, with sub-locals for the most important mill departments. New officials should be elected throughout the union. The establishment of the locals and new officials will do much to raise the discipline of the men; it will give them more of a feeling of being organized and will increase their confidence in each other and in the stability of the movement. Such solid organization will double the weight of their blow when the strike test comes.

Good strike preparation also requires that the company unions be entirely merged into the Amalgamated Association before the time the probable strike actually takes place. If not, the bosses will attempt to use them as strikebreaking organizations. The company unions, declaring openly for the Amalgamated Association and its demands, should from now on carry on the most active campaign to mobilize their membership into the trade union. And if, when the strike does occur, the company unions are not entirely absorbed by the Amalgamated Association, they should join in its strike call and then formally merge with the trade union. The declaration of the strike must sound the death knell of company unionism in the steel industry, if the workers have not succeeded in killing it even before that time.

Should there be any A. F. of L. craft unions in the steel industry when the strike takes place they should be linked with the Amalgamated Association and should join in its general strike call.

All these organization preparations for the strike should be accompanied by a most thorough education of the steel workers on the tasks and significance of the coming strike. The union demands should be literally plastered over the entire steel industry, and also popularized far and wide throughout the whole country. With myriads of bulletins, leaflets, stickers, posters, etc., as well as broad radio campaigns, newspaper advertisements, etc., the workers and the general public should be taught the meaning of the struggle and be kept advised of its progress. Great mass local, district, and national rank-and-file conferences and meetings of steel workers and, as things approach a head, a great mass strike vote, should be utilized to educate and organize the steel workers for the coming struggle.

The old adage "well begun is half done" applies to strike strategy as well as to other activities. The first blow is often decisive. Usually trade union strikes are badly organized, which weakens them from beginning to end. But this one must be different. It should be thoroughly prepared, organizationally and ideologically. If this is done, then when the steel workers almost certainly strike in 1937, their walkout will be so complete that "no one will be left in the mills even to blow the whistle."

One of the basic means for building a strong strike and for the working out of good strategy is the development of a democratic strike leadership through national and local broad strike committees. Usually A. F. of L. strikes are managed by small and remote committees of bureaucratic officials. These people, whose conservative and slippery policies make it necessary for them to prevent rank-and-file "interference in the strike control," remain quite detached from the working masses. They issue arbitrary commands to the workers, who have practically nothing to say about the whole strike. Commonly the result is that the latter's high qualities of discipline, enthusiasm, and fighting spirit are but little developed. Thus the entire strike is weakened.

The broad democratic strike committee system, which is based on the best strike experience the world over, is vastly superior to the prevailing primitive A. F. of L. system of a handful of dictatorial officials running the strike as they please. The broad strike committee gives the workers the realization that the strike is really their affair. It awakens in them an intelligent discipline and not merely a blind obedience to orders; it raises their morale, avoids the usual mass passivity, and brings about the maximum mass activity. Above all, it provides the means for the strikers to contribute their intelligence to the shaping of strike policy. The broad strike committee system also aids the work of the strike executive leaders by connecting them directly with the masses. It facilitates their knowing what is actually taking place in the strike fields, what tactics the bosses are using, what are the workers' moods, etc.

It also provides the mechanization for the swift mobilization of the workers for a needed defensive or offensive maneuver. This system of broad strike committees has been used to a considerable extent in the A. F. of L. needle trades, and other progressive American unions, but especially by the militant unions, such as the I. W. W., T. U. U. L., etc., and by many unions in other countries. It has always proved highly effective. The coming steel strike, in keeping with the progressive character of the C. I. O. movement, should systematically apply the powerful weapon of the broad strike committee.

The democratization of the strike leadership should start at the top. The national leading committee of the whole strike should consist not only of the national union executives but also of striker representatives from the various striking areas (and industries, if more than steel is involved). This broad committee, with proper departments for publicity, relief, and defense, should deal with major questions of policy. It should meet frequently and have a small executive committee carry on the strike leadership between meetings.

Large departmentalized strike committees, based upon the regular union officials plus a broad representation of mill strikers, should also be organized in the respective steel towns and districts, as local circumstances may dictate. Each steel mill should also have its own broad strike committee. The mill strike committee should conduct their local activities under the leadership of the local or district strike committees; the size of the committees varying according to the size of the mills, the rate of representation ranging from one member for each 25 workers to one member for each 100 workers. Such mill strike committees should be thoroughly representative of all departments, special care being taken also to see that Negroes and foreign-born workers are fully represented and elected to responsible leading posts. The women's trade union auxiliaries should be represented in the strike committees.

The mill strike committees have a maze of functions. Especially complicated are their tasks in the case of stay-in strikes. They have to be organized, through sub-committees, to attend to picketing, discipline, food, sleeping arrangements, medical care, entertainment, defense, liaison with the local strike committee and other struck plants, etc. Consequently, the mill committees must be highly responsive to the needs and control of the strikers.

The strike committees, national, district, local, and mill, should be fully authorized to conduct the strike in all its phases, the various regular trade union organs, such as national executive boards, district councils, local unions, etc., meeting only to transact routine business not immediately connected with the strike. The various strike committees should be elected on the eve of the strike. Before the strike is ended the national strike committee should submit the proposed terms of settlement for a referendum vote by the strikers.

These principles of democratization and departmentalization should also be introduced into the Amalgamated Association structure as the union is built. The Amalgamated Association constitution is obsolete, unfitted for the steel industry and should be completely rewritten.

MASS PARTICIPATION

The working out of a good strike strategy requires the highest degree of mass participation by the strikers in the organized activities of the strike. More than that, it also involves drawing the strikers' families into these activities, for the strikers' women and children are also very effective fighters and morale builders. Only by such a general participation of the whole strikebound population and the development of the highest degree of activity possible by men, women, and children can the maximum striking power of the workers be realized. In this respect again, the coming steel strike must be vastly superior to the ordinary A. F. of L. strike, in which, because the conservative leaders fear the growth of militancy among the rank and file, only a small percentage of the workers, not to speak of their families, actually carry on the strike, the great mass remaining passive.

In previous pages I have discussed various forms of cultivating a high degree of mass strike activity—the holding of democratically elected local, district, and national rank-and-file pre-strike conferences to formulate and popularize the workers' demands and to elect the union officials; the general voting upon all settlement proposals, etc. To these measures should be added the holding of frequent mass meetings during the strike; mass parades of strikers; mass marches of men, women, and children from district to district and mill to mill; the sending of small delegations or flying squads of workers from one area or industry to another; the teaching of the strikers to sing labor songs in their meetings and demonstrations; the development of sports activities for the youth; the holding of social affairs, etc.

But the most important of all forms of mass strike activities is mass picketing. Good picketing is a decisive factor in every big strike —that is why employers are so rabidly opposed to it. Picketing is usually grossly neglected in the ordinary A. F. of L. strike, only a few of the workers carrying it on, and then merely in a desultory fashion. The consequence is a great loss in the holding power of the strike. The best way to conduct picketing is on a mass basis. Not only should all the strikers be mobilized for picketing, but their women and children as well. In addition, prominent liberals and others should be brought into the strike areas from the outside to march in the picket lines. Where one or more industries are striking, joint picketing should be organized. The unemployed can play a most important role in picketing, and the members of non-striking unions should also be systematically drawn into the work. Women's and children's picket lines should be organized on special occasions. This system of broad mass picketing raises enormously the political level, enthusiasm, and resistance power of the strikers. It has been used effectively in many I. W. W. and T. U. U. L. strikes, by the more progressive A. F. of L. unions, and by many unions in foreign countries. When the 1937 steel strike comes, the progressive C. I. O. should adopt the modern, effective system of mass picketing.

The picket line should be well organized, not mere crowds of workers. It should be under the control of the picket committee, which is a section of the strike committee. The picketers should be organized into squads, each squad headed by a carefully selected captain. All strikers should be required to do their bit at picketing. The youth especially should play a big part in the organization of the picket lines. The picket committee must maintain pickets around the mills at all times, whether or not they are trying to operate with scabs. Especially must there be great mass picket lines on Monday mornings and upon all occasions when attempts are being made to bring scabs into the mills. Often the difference between bad picketing and good picketing is the difference between a lost and a won strike.

The question of a well-organized strike publicity is most fundamental to the success of a great strike in steel, or a combined strike of steel, coal, auto, etc. In such a big strike the capitalists will frantically howl that the whole movement is an insurrection, a revolution, and they will throw their entire publicity machine, the newspapers, radio, etc., into the task of terrorizing the public and of driving the workers back to the mills in a welter of violence and confusion. In the 1919 steel strike they used such a red scare effectively, with the help of the Wilson government. In the San Francisco general strike in 1934 they also loudly shrieked revolution and created a hysteria among sections of the population, and they do the same thing to a greater or lesser extent in every strike. We may be absolutely certain, therefore, that their poison gas campaign would be infinitely worse in the case of the prospective nationwide steel or steel-coal strike involving up to a million or more workers.

To combat successfully this vicious strikebreaking propaganda offensive of the employers will be basic for the winning of the strike. In order to create a favorable public opinion it is necessary that the workers develop a great publicity counter-offensive of their own. They must dissipate the charges of revolution by centering the whole agitation around the immediate economic and political demands of the struggle. They should relentlessly expose the vast riches and profits of the employers and the health-destroying, spirit-killing poverty of the workers, the terrorization and suppression of civil rights by the bosses' gunmen, the great significance to American democracy of a victory by the workers, etc. The strikers must know how to dramatize their struggle by sending women's and children's delegations to the state legislatures and to Congress, by securing investigations by government and citizens' committees, by covering the country with a network of sympathetic mass meetings, by staging great mass demonstrations of all kinds throughout the strike areas, by monster mass picket lines, etc.

Not the least of this essential publicity work is the education of the strikers themselves, who will be subjected to the fiercest propaganda barrage from the employers in attempts to stampede them back to work. The striking workers should be systematically taught the meaning and implications of the strike through a plentiful flow of regular bulletins, special leaflets, mass meetings, radio broadcasts, etc. Especially must they be kept informed in detail as to the progress of the strike itself. In this connection, in case of a hard strike, among other such measures to be adopted, rank-and-file delegations should be sent from district to district so that workers may be directly informed as to the status of the strike from personal observation. In 1919, in the later stages of the struggle, one of the most effective strikebreaking methods of the bosses was to have fake delegations of workers visit various strike districts and then start false reports and demoralization among the strikers, both in their home towns and other centers. Neglect of the fundamental task of systematic education could easily result disastrously in a bitterly fought steel strike.

To meet these huge educational tasks of creating a favorable public opinion and of keeping confusion out of the ranks of the strikers, the national strike committee should set up a special publicity section, with an experienced publicity director in charge. This publicity department, in addition to building its own immediate publicity machinery, should systematically mobilize the trade union, militant and liberal press, as well as friendly radio broadcasters and newspapermen working on the capitalist press. All these elements together would constitute a great educational force, one that could make the voice of the strike heard loudly and clearly in every corner of the country.

Strikers, like armies, march on their stomachs, and many are the strikes that have been lost through hunger. In making ready for a great strike in steel it is necessary that all preparations be made to build up a strong system of strike relief, despite the probability of the struggle being of short duration. In the matter of relief work, as in so many other of the phases, American strikes are usually very weak. Strikes which provide relief systems that can serve as examples for the coming strike are the 1919 steel strike and the 1926 Passaic textile strike.*

The strike relief machinery should be in operation not later than two weeks after the strike begins, because from the outset there are always emergency cases requiring attention. The C. I. O. general call for a strike fund ought to go out immediately upon the declaration of the strike. This to be supported by calls from the A. F. of L., individual trade unions, state federations, central labor councils, and other sympathizing organizations. Of course, the reactionary A. F. of L. leaders will either openly or covertly oppose such strike support, but their opposition must and can be broken down by rank-and-file pressure.

The striking union or unions should set up an organized relief department as a sub-section of the general strike committee, with an experienced relief organizer in charge. Strike relief work has two general aspects—collection and distribution—and there must be created special organization for each. On the collection side, the organization should consist of: (a) trade union strike relief committees in various cities and towns; (b) united front relief committees or other workers' organizations in the same localities; (c) special relief committees of liberal professionals, clericals, writers, etc. All these committees are to be co-ordinated through the national relief department of the strike committee. A corps of relief collectors and organizers should be put in the field by the national relief organization. Depots should be established in all important centers for the collection of cash, food, and other strike supplies. National and local relief conferences ought to be held wherever practical. There can be drawn into the relief collection work not only trade unions, but also churches, Y. M. C. A.'s, Negro organizations, fraternal societies, farmers' unions, veterans' organizations, co-operatives, unemployed workers' organizations, and workers' political parties.

The distribution side of the relief is to be handled by special relief

* See William Z. Foster, *The Great Steel Strike and Its Lessons,* 1920; also, Mary Heaton Vorse, *The Passaic Textile Strike,* 1927.

committees of strikers in the strike areas, under supervision of their respective strike committees. The relief committees require sub-committees to investigate needy cases and to check up generally on the distribution of relief. In this sphere, the strikers' womenfolk can do very important work.

At the outset of the strike all efforts should be made to get the strikers on the home relief lists upon the same basis as the unemployed. This can be accomplished in many places with the proper political mass pressure.

Inasmuch as regular strike benefits could not, in all probability, be paid in a national 1937 strike of steel workers, the strike relief necessarily takes three major forms: (a) distribution of cash for the strikers' special expenses; (b) common kitchens where food is prepared for the strikers and their families, with special food for the smaller children; (c) commissaries from which families may carry home groceries, clothing, and other strike relief supplies.

Money. The organizations forming the C. I. O. should place upon themselves heavy strike assessments. Other unions should adopt voluntary assessments. This financial income should be supplemented by tag days, shop collections, social affairs, special milk funds, etc., organized by the strike committees in the various centers.

Food. Great concentration must be made upon the collection of non-perishable foods by the strike committees, house-to-house collections being organized. Special attention should be given to collecting strike relief supplies in the immediate strike areas and surrounding territories. The farmers provide a rich source for food collection in such big strikes and their organizations need to be contacted.

Shelter. This is always a great problem in large strikes. It must be attacked in a variety of ways: by doubling up the evicted families with others, by moratoriums in rent paying in strike-bound towns, by extension of credit to strikers by landlords, by court action and mass pressure to prevent evictions, etc. Where company towns exist, tent colonies and barracks may be necessary to take care of the wholesale evictions. The shutting off of gas, electricity, and water can often be stopped by exerting political pressure upon the local authorities. In some instances cash is necessary to meet rent, water, light, and similar expenses.

Clothing. Systematic collections of all kinds of clothing should be made by the relief committees all over the country. Local clothing repair units can be established in the strike towns by sympathetic women and tailors. Cobblers should be organized to take care of shoe repairs, etc.

Medical Aid. In every strike center medical units of voluntary doctors, dentists, nurses, etc., should be established. Medical units also may be organized outside and sent into the strike areas by the relief committees. In addition, there should be committees of outside doctors to visit and to give publicity on conditions in the strike districts.

Relief collection and distribution must be handled basically as a political question, not as a matter of charity. In the strike districts, strike relief should be so organized as to stimulate mass picketing, each picketer being furnished with a card which is punched to indicate the amount of picketing he has done. The collection of relief in the various cities should be utilized to arouse the class-conscious solidarity of the workers and to draw the broadest masses of workers into active support of the strike. The whole relief apparatus, collection and distribution, must be utilized to popularize the objectives of the strike, to prevent the recruitment of strikebreakers, to defend the strikers' civil rights, and to bring pressure to bear upon the employers and the government for a favorable settlement of the strike. A well-organized relief system can exert a tremendous force in strengthening the strike, both economically and politically.

In every strike the question of defending the civil rights and personal safety of the strikers and the union leaders constitutes an important problem. Especially is this problem acute in a great strike against the lawless and violent steel barons. Defense activities are not only a matter of court action, but especially of mass pressure of the strikers and the widest possible masses of strike sympathizers against the government and the employers. The national strike committee requires a legal department which organizes this branch of strike work. Here the International Labor Defense* can also play an important part. A staff of voluntary attorneys should be recruited nationally and in the respective strike areas.

Attacks on the civil rights of the strikers by the employers, in whatever manner, must be militantly resisted. All the forces of the strikers, the outside labor movement, the strike relief organization and the sympathetic masses generally should be mobilized to protest against such attacks on the democratic rights of the workers, through the holding of mass meetings, sending of delegations to the state legisla-

---

* This old defense organization was absorbed by the Congress of Civil Rights.

tures and Congress. When injunctions are issued forbidding the right of free speech and assembly the strikers should follow the traditional American trade union policy of ignoring such court orders. When troops are brought into a strike area the strikers must not only firmly insist upon the maintenance of their civil rights, but also know how to fraternize with the soldiers and thus win as many as possible of them to the side of the strike.

Vigilant protection must be constantly given to the persons of the strikers and their leaders; when either striker or leader is arrested for strike activities, he should be promptly defended legally and politically. Where there is danger of violent attacks upon the strikers' meetings or upon their leaders by gunmen and vigilantes, these meetings and leaders must be personally defended, such protective measures being organized by the picket committee and being especially the task of the youth. Against the company-controlled violators of civil rights and for the personal safety of strikers and leaders the strikers should make active use of all available political institutions, including the arrest and prosecution of the armed thugs; the securing of injunctions against the violators of the workers' civil rights; the removal, impeachment, and election defeat of lawless city and state officials.

Every good general understands that a basic part of his strategy is carefully to mobilize and utilize his reserves, and the need to do this is no less acute in a strike, especially in the case of a great strike in steel and allied industries. Such a strike would, from the outset, have vast potential reserves, created by the profound sympathy the strike would awaken in the toiling masses. These masses would realize that not only were the strikers' interests involved in the struggle, but also their own living standards and democratic rights. The strike leadership must know how to organize and make the maximum use of this favorable mass sentiment of these great reserves. Usually, this kind of work, like the various other tasks that go to make up a strong strike, are grossly neglected in A. F. of L. strikes. This must not happen in the steel strike, for we may be sure that the steel trust will mobilize every reactionary influence in the United States behind its cause and the workers will need every possible ounce of support for theirs.

The question of mobilizing the reserves of a national steel strike involves not only developing the solidarity of the workers' main forces directly—the support of the unorganized masses of workers, of the members of company unions, of the unemployed, of the non-striking trade unions, of workers' co-operatives, and of the workers' political parties—but also the mobilization of the huge masses of semi-proletarian and petty bourgeois sympathizers who are actively interested in the winning of the strike. This necessitates the development of united front committees of youth clubs, fraternal societies, churches, peace movements, professional guilds, women's clubs, Negro organizations, farmers' co-operatives, veterans' associations, etc., for various strike tasks.

In the preceding pages I have sketched concretely some of the ways in which these very vital petty bourgeois and semi-proletarian strike reserves can be utilized, including their participation in publicity work, technical aid for strikers, defense and relief activities, and general political work. To facilitate the mobilization of these reserves, a national citizens' committee, comprising such liberal strike sympathizers—including politicians, educators, scientists, writers, artists, etc.—should be set up at the commencement of the strike. This committee must work closely with the national strike committee in political activities in support of the strike, and should stimulate the formation of local relief committees of liberal strike sympathizers. Especially in the strike areas is it necessary to build up similar citizens' committees of professionals, small businessmen, clergymen, white collar workers, officers and representatives of various mass organizations, to offset the strikebreaking activities of the ever present and dangerous citizens' committees organized by the employers. A national strike in steel and allied industries must be made a great rallying issue for the major massing of the democratic forces of the United States to win the struggle.

CONSOLIDATING THE VICTORY

It is a fundamental principle of strategy, whether military or labor, to follow up the victory by pushing back the enemy on every front and to capture all possible of his strongholds. In the months ahead the C. I. O. leaders, as well as the progressive forces generally of the labor movement, must give this strategic principle serious consideration.

Lenin once wisely remarked that we never can have real victory unless we also know how to retreat when need be. A good general always bears this thought in mind. In this situation, however, there need be no perspective of retreat. The strategy must be based on the offensive, and animated by a spirit of daring and indomitability. The stage is all set for a great labor victory, provided only that the trade union leadership rises to the occasion, to the height of its tasks. This victory, which can be so readily won, must be realized to the full in all its possibilities and implications. I have already indicated the great importance to the working class of a victory in the steel industry. Now let us look at this whole matter a little more concretely.

When, early in 1936, the workers of France, fighting against the rising menace of fascism and organized in a great united front of Radicals, Socialists, and Communists, defeated the reactionary forces and elected the present Popular Front government, one of the aftermaths of their victory was that within a year the French trade union movement increased its membership from some 1,500,000 to over 5,000,000. This is about equivalent to the American trade union movement (considering the differences in size and industrialization of France and the United States), leaping up from its present low figure of about 3,500,000 to a membership of 15,000,000 or 20,000,000. A victory in steel in the United States, if properly followed up, would undoubtedly give a tremendous stimulation to trade union organization in general in this country. It is a question as to whether there will be as great an advance as that which followed the victory of the Popular Front government in France. But certainly success in the steel industry would throw the door wide open for the organization of many millions of workers. The extent to which the possibilities of the situation will be realized will depend largely upon the ability and farsightedness shown by the trade union leadership.

Even in the very favorable situation after a great victory in steel, the organization of these millions of workers can only happen in the fullest measure if the progressive forces everywhere in the trade union movement make the task of organizing the unorganized all labor's first order of business. Determined drives must be made to begin the unionization of the huge masses of unorganized in all fields, the millions of general metal and electrical workers; the mass of textile workers, the army of truck, bus, and taxi drivers; the great numbers of unorganized packing house, metal mining, building trades, food workers, lumber workers, agricultural workers, etc., as well as those in the auto, rubber, aluminum, oil, glass, and other industries now being organized by the C. I. O. Nor should there be forgotten the masses of white collar workers—teachers, technicians, office workers, and government employes—who are increasingly ready for organization.

Big inroads by the trade unions into these great unorganized millions can be made by the labor movement if the work is gone about with system and decision. Every branch of organized labor must take up the organization work. The C. I. O. should seize upon the event of a victory in steel to redouble its own efforts to organize the mass production industries and to stimulate all sections of the labor movement into the greatest organizing campaign in the history of American labor. The reactionary A. F. of L. Executive Council must be compelled by mass pressure to support the growing organizing campaigns, or at least not to sabotage them. Every international union, state federation of labor, city central body, and local union should begin organizing work in its respective sphere. The whole labor movement must surge with organization work. This is the first task in consolidating a steel victory, by registering it in the fundamental field of organization among the unorganized millions. If this task of organization is well conceived and properly carried out, it will mean incomparably more power and militancy for the labor movement in this country.

1937

27. Organizational Problems of Industrial Unionism

After forty years of intensive educational work by the progressive and militant elements in the trade union movement on the necessity for industrial unionism to organize the workers in the mass production industries of the country, at last it is being applied on a general scale by the Committee for Industrial Organization. The effectiveness of this type of unionism is being borne out in practice by the unparalleled growth of the C. I. O. unions in steel, auto, rubber, oil, radio, shipbuilding, textile, transport, and other industries. Real strides are finally being made toward the organization of the great mass of workers in the basic industries.

The growth of these industrial unions naturally is accompanied by a whole series of new problems, not only in regard to unionizing tactics and strike strategy, but also concerning organizational forms and the methods of conducting the unions' activities generally. In the past there have been a few American trade unions formed on an industrial basis, notably the United Mine Workers of America; United Textile Workers; Paper Workers; Brewery Workers; and (at least on paper) Butcher Workmen; Metal Miners; and Iron, Steel, and Tin Workers, as well as the four semi-industrial needle trades unions. But the new C. I. O. unions are coming into existence under conditions that raise many problems not previously solved by these forerunners of present-day industrial unionism. It is my purpose here to answer the most urgent of these questions, on the basis of broad experience, by many unions in the United States and other countries.

In considering the organizing problems of the new industrial unions, it is necessary always to bear in mind the decisive fact that labor unions are organs of struggle. Unions sign trade agreements with the bosses and carry them out loyally; but behind these agreements a relationship of power always exists. Thus, labor unions are able to secure concessions from the employers in direct ratio to their strength. Hence, all organization forms and practices in the industrial unions must be developed with regard to increasing the fighting power of these bodies.

The basic improvement of the C. I. O. industrial unions over the A. F. of L. craft organizations is that they are more effective organs of struggle against capitalist exploitation. First, instead of splitting the workers of an industry, as the A. F. of L. does, into from ten to twenty-five separate craft unions, all of which are autonomous, pulling this way and that and, consequently, quite incapable of bringing a solid pressure to bear against the employers, the C. I. O. unites all the workers of a given industry into one broad industrial union, thereby enormously increasing the workers' strength. Second, instead of being dominated by arbitrary bureaucracies, such as rule practically every A. F. of L. craft union and thereby paralyze the effectiveness of those organizations, the new industrial unions of the C. I. O., despite some undemocratic hangovers from the past, are developing a new trade union democracy—a real improvement which greatly increases their potentialities in the struggle against the employers.

Behind the basic organizational differences between the A. F. of L. and C. I. O. unions stand two fundamentally divergent conceptions of unionism. On the one hand, the A. F. of L. craft unionism characteristically does not consider or organize the workers as a class or recognize the existence of the class struggle. Instead, it caters principally to the more skilled elements and it does not hesitate to sacrifice the welfare of the broad masses of the semi-skilled and unskilled in order to further the interests of the skilled workers. Upon this general outlook is based the whole policy of the A. F. of L.: its wheedling attitude toward the employers, its subservient policy of class collaboration, its failure to organize the unorganized, its craft scabbery during strikes, its tailing after the capitalist political parties and begging them for minor concessions, etc. We see the general results of such a narrow craft policy in the A. F. of L.'s repeated loss of strikes, its inability to organize the mass production industries, the insignificant percentage of workers (even of the skilled) that it has organized, and the weak position politically of the workers in American life.

On the other hand, the C. I. O. organizes the workers primarily as a class. Although the C. I. O. leadership does not accept the class struggle in theory, the C. I. O.'s very birth, its broad unions, and its strong organizing campaigns and strikes testify eloquently enough to the reality of the class struggle. The basis of the C. I. O.'s industrial unionism is a militant defense of the interests not only of the privileged few skilled workers, but of the great masses of unskilled and semi-skilled as well. With this broader conception and policy of unionism, therefore, it is not to be wondered at that the rise of the C. I. O. unions has been marked by the winning of many strikes against the great trusts, a tremendous strengthening of the trade union movement in the mass production industries and the beginning of a broad political movement of the toilers that is heading in the direction of a Farmer-Labor Party. The A. F. of L. stands for craft unionism, the C. I. O. for industrial unionism. The growth of the C. I. O. implies the consolidation of the American proletariat for the first time as a class.

It is a well-known fact that the political content of an organization's program expresses itself also in the whole structure and organizational practices of that body. In accordance with this principle, the A. F. of L., during its half-century of existence, has built up a whole series of organizational forms and methods corresponding to and flowing out of its basic policy of craft unionism. It is fundamentally necessary that the new C. I. O. industrial unions also adapt all their organic structures and methods of conducting business to fit in with their class conception of unionism.

A firm discipline is a basic essential for the success of industrial unionism, as of labor unionism in general. Good organization and discipline give the workers greater confidence in themselves and in each other and hence increase their fighting capacity. Well-drilled soldiers are far better fighters than loosely organized, poorly trained recruits, and the same principle applies to labor unions. The industrial unions will do well, therefore, in the shaping of their activities, to keep in mind the necessity for creating a good discipline among their membership. With ruthless American capitalism to fight, such a discipline will stand them in good stead and, indeed, is a life and death question for them.

DISCIPLINE, DEMOCRACY, AND EDUCATION

To build up this necessary discipline the prime essential is that the industrial unions conduct their affairs in a democratic manner. Trade unionists are not enlisted men and they cannot be disciplined by mere arbitrary command of their leaders. Their discipline must be essentially self-imposed. And such voluntary union discipline can exist in maximum degree only if the workers feel that they are controlling the union's activities by democratic action.

The A. F. of L. craft union leaders have always grossly violated the principles of trade union democracy. The result is that nearly all A. F. of L. unions are dominated by bureaucrats and dictators who, to enforce their arbitrary will and conservative policies upon the membership, have not hesitated often to use sluggers, stealing of elections, packing of conventions, and other ruthless methods of coercing the rank and file. This violation of democracy has also given birth to racketeering in the unions and has lowered the tone and effectiveness of the whole labor movement.

To the extent that the industrial unions break with the traditional undemocratic methods of craft union leaders and develop a truly democratic life in their organizations, to that degree they will build up a better mass discipline and achieve the added strength that goes with it. But, of course, in establishing trade union democracy it is not necessary to fly to the other extreme and turn the unions into mere debating societies. The correct policy is: first, a thorough discussion of the problem in hand and, then, a firm enforcement of the decision arrived at. Such a procedure at once guarantees a mass participation in policy-making and a good discipline in applying the policy decided upon. The organization principles contained in this whole pamphlet are based on this general conception of democratic centralism, which dovetails with the best trade union practice in all countries.

A good labor discipline necessitates, as we have seen, a thoroughgoing trade union democracy, and such a democracy, in turn, requires an educated rank and file. Discipline, democracy, and education go hand in hand in the building of effective labor unionism, and the new, expanding industrial unions should write this elementary truth plainly in all their constitutions and ways of doing business.

The A. F. of L. unions, with few exceptions, have flagrantly neglected the education of their members to the true nature of the capitalist system and the daily problems confronting them as workers. The "philosophy" of the dominant craft leaders is an open endorsement of capitalism, and their conceptions of many of the workers' problems are only the basic ideas of the employers covered over with a thin veneer of trade union phrases. Most of the craft unions have no organized educational departments whatever, and the educational value of their official journals is just about zero.

The industrial unions should, of course, set up quite a different situation. They must begin earnestly the education of their members and also of the broad masses generally. The C. I. O. needle trades unions have done much valuable work in this vital field, but even this is only a start. Every stage of the labor movement—from the local union to the national labor federation—should have a well-organized, actively functioning educational department, working on a mass scale. In this manner, real progress can be made in offsetting the paralyzing effects of the vast stream of propaganda poison that the capitalists are pouring into the workers' minds, through press, pulpit, radio, movies, etc., etc. The industrial unions will reap rich dividends from such educational work, in the shape of better working and living conditions for their members, and a bigger and stronger organization in every respect.

The most important single educational task confronting the industrial unions is to build up a broad and effective labor press. One of the most disastrous weaknesses of the A. F. of L. unions has always been their miserable papers and magazines. The journals of the international unions are, with few exceptions, dry, uninteresting, saturated with insidious employer propaganda, and closed to progressive thought. The local trade union papers, both official and unofficial, are even worse. Many of them are simply parasitic blackmail sheets, corrupt and rotten to the core. Often they shamelessly take money from employers to fight everything progressive in the labor movement; they sell their columns and "labor's endorsement" to any political faker who wants them. Every important city has one or more such contemptible rags.

And the low tone for all this degraded system of labor journalism is set by the *American Federationist,* national organ of the A. F. of L. The columns of this magazine are packed with reactionary propaganda, advertisements of union-smashing open shop companies, red-baiting, misrepresentations of industrial unionism, lying attacks upon the Soviet Union, etc.

One of the great tasks of the C. I. O. industrial union movement is to free American labor from the tentacles of this disgraceful craft union press and to develop a progressive system of journalism worthy of the labor movement. The new labor press should reflect the great upsurge now developing among the masses; it should make a serious analysis of decaying capitalist society, and teach the workers the way to free themselves from it. It should be a press wide open to the expression of socialism and communism. Each national industrial union should have a first-class weekly or monthly journal that goes to every member; each city central council needs a clean, progressive weekly organ; the national federation ought to publish a great labor daily paper. With such a powerful and progressive press, organized labor would make real progress in the struggle against the employers and their tremendous propaganda machine.

A. F. OF L. PRACTICES

Among the many harmful practices of A. F. of L. unions is the exclusion of large categories of workers from union membership for reasons of their sex, race, politics, etc. Thus various unions specifically bar women from joining; many more, either openly or covertly, refuse to organize Negroes; still others do not take in young workers; and a whole raft of unions, including the national A. F. of L. itself, have clauses in their constitutions which prohibit the membership of Communists.

These narrow practices are nothing more or less than a reflection of the employers' policy of playing off one group of workers against another and thus weakening them all. They have absolutely no place in the labor movement. They violate the most fundamental principle of unionism, the solidarity of all the workers—and they have done incalculable harm to the unions. They must not be allowed to continue on over into the industrial unions. On the contrary, the new unions should throw these contemptible and harmful prejudices into the ashcan of history.

The industrial unions should open their doors wide to all workers (except, of course, those barred for spying, scabbing, and other dishonorable actions) regardless of their sex, color, race, nationality, age, religion, or political opinion. The new unions should extend a warm hand of greeting to the doubly oppressed Negro workers; they should adopt a more liberal apprenticeship and trade school policy for the youth; they should be the special champions of women and their demands; and, above all, they should be alert not to allow themselves or their officials to sink into the practice of red-baiting, which is the weapon of all fascists and near-fascists to attack everything that is progressive and effective in the labor movement.

The industrial unions should also take a more intelligent attitude towards unemployed members than the craft unions do. During the depths of the great industrial crisis of the past several years, the A. F. of L. unions brutally expelled hundreds of thousands of unemployed members. Then they went further along this wrong road by callously neglecting the demands of the starving unemployed and trailing after the infamous Hoover share-the-work scheme. Contrary to all this wrong course, the industrial unions should base their policy upon the unity of interests and organization of the employed and unemployed. This means that they should retain the unemployed in the unions and fight for their demands. In the next industrial crisis, which already even the capitalist economists recognize to be not so far ahead, the employed and the vast armies of unemployed must present a solid front. There are still some 8,000,000 workers unemployed, and the unions should give active support to their demands and also to the Workers' Alliance, the organization of W. P. A. and unemployed workers.

One of the main reasons why the A. F. of L. unions have remained so unprogressive, clinging stubbornly to their horse-and-buggy craft system of unionism in an era of mass production in which this type of organization is hopelessly obsolete, is because they have become heavily encrusted with a conservative bureaucratic leadership that is unresponsive to the needs and interests of the rank and file. To keep themselves in power and to fatten off the unions, these leaders employ a whole series of undemocratic, unproletarian methods that the industrial unions must avoid on pain of a similar stagnation as that which now afflicts the craft unions. Among these harmful practices of corrupt craft officials are: having themselves, by hook or crook, elected to office for life; paying themselves enormous salaries and expenses; handling the union funds as though they were their own personal property; assuming arbitrary power over the membership in various ways; building up executive boards which perpetuate themselves by filling all vacancies through appointment, and by various other democracy-destroying devices that would bring a blush to the face of a Tammany Hall boss. The health and progress of labor unions demand that their officers be the members' servants, not their masters.

Democracy in A. F. of L. craft union conventions is more honored in the breach than in the observance. Reactionary union officials have developed a whole series of corrupt devices to maintain their own control and to prevent the will of the membership from prevailing. This is one of the principal causes for the weakness and unprogressiveness of craft unions. Of these crooked schemes the following are among the most notorious and harmful: (a) narrowing down the convention delegations largely to paid officials; (b) packing the conventions with delegates from "blue-sky" locals; (c) making the conventions so expensive (by high per diem rates) that they cannot be held often; (d) arbitrarily suppressing the conventions altogether (the Retail Clerks have not held a convention for fifteen years), or by having excessively long intervals between them (eight years between the last two conventions of the Carpenters Union); (e) appointment of all convention committees by the union's president; (f) stalling the conventions along and then rushing the important business through in the last hours; (g) the practice of a thousand parliamentary tricks to kill discussion and to thwart progressive legislation, etc., etc.

To help insure democratic, representative conventions, the industrial unions should adopt, among others, the following measures: (a) national conventions should be held at intervals not to exceed two years; (b) have broad rank-and-file delegations in the convention; (c) publication of the convention agenda and officers' reports at least thirty days before the convention date, so that they may be discussed by the membership; (d) strict financial reports as the basis of local union representation, such reports to be available to the convention delegates; (e) all convention committees to be voted on (and amended if so desired) by the convention delegates; (f) no restrictions upon the introduction of resolutions by local unions before or during the conventions; (g) strict prohibition of all direct and indirect proxy delegates and voting; (h) the right of a 30 per cent minority of delegates to secure a roll call vote; (i) the holding of the conventions in important centers of the industry, instead of in remote places where delegates find it difficult to attend; (j) convention expenses of delegates to be split 50-50 between the local unions and the national organization; (k) a reasonable per diem of expense for delegates and thus avoidance of petty corruption and great cost of conventions; (l) only local union delegates should vote; officials, as such, should have no votes; (m) no examination of the political opinions of delegates by convention committees as a condition for their seating; (n) the convention to be adjourned only by majority vote, to prevent officials from arbitrarily closing the convention to stifle democratic rule.

The representation of local unions in the convention should be based upon a principle of modified proportional representation. This means that there should be a minimum of delegates allowed to all locals, plus a diminishing ratio of delegates as the locals increase in size. This system is the best protection against the dangers, on the one hand, of a few big locals dominating the convention, and, on the other, of domination being exercised by a lot of small, weak locals. This general system of representation should also be applied to central labor councils, state federations, and the national labor federation. When convention roll call votes are taken, however, the various delegates should be allowed votes on the basis of, for example, one vote to each one hundred of their actual membership.

Correct constitutional laws alone will not insure a union's being democratic, for in the last analysis this depends upon the alertness and political development of the membership. But such laws are vital, nevertheless, as they place in the hand of the rank and file effective democratic weapons, if they will but use them.

An important democratic system that the industrial unions should develop is the initiative, referendum, and recall. This means that the membership retains the right at all times to initiate new policy, to vote on any proposals that may be before the union or its executive, and to recall any officer from his post by a majority vote. These effective democratic measures have never flourished in the narrow, conservative A. F. of L. unions, although a few unions (miners, machinists, needle trades, etc.), have some traces of them.

The referendum should work thus: the national convention of the union should have full power to act upon all questions. It should elect all general officers, make constitutional amendments, set assessments, decide upon strikes, and generally establish the union's policy. But a substantial minority of the delegates, not less than 30 per cent, should have the right, if they so desire, to have any of the convention's decisions referred to a vote of the general membership.

Certain basic matters, such as important strikes and strike settlements, questions of the union's national affiliation, heavy assessments, etc., should as a matter of settled policy be referred to the membership for a general vote. The national executive board of the union (as well as the convention) should also be required to submit all major matters of policy to a national vote of the members, and a given percentage of the local unions should have the right to demand that any decision of the executive board be referred to a general vote.

The initiative should operate to give the membership the right, especially between conventions, to initiate new policy. Thus, on the demand of a given number of locals, say 10 per cent or so, the national executive board should stand instructed to consider any proposed policy and, if need be, to submit it to a general membership vote.

The recall should be regulated in such a manner that the membership, in a given local union or nationally, should have the right to initiate a vote to recall from office at any time any official—national, district, local, or shop—without formal trial proceedings.

STRIKES, NEGOTIATIONS, AND AGREEMENTS

Strikes are the basic means of a labor union to improve the conditions of the workers. The effectiveness of any given union depends, in the last analysis, upon its ability to bring production to a standstill in its craft or industry and thus to halt the employers' golden stream of profits. And precisely because of their great importance, strikes put the unions, their leaders, and their policies to the acid test.

With the unions confronting the great power of the employers and the state, strikes should not be entered into lightly. Aside from questions of strategy—of seizing upon the right time to strike and of making all essential technical preparations—the most fundamental necessity of a strike is that it have the full backing of the workers involved. This means that the workers must have the decisive say as to whether or not they shall enter into struggle, with all its dangers and hardships. The power to declare strikes and to call them off must rest finally with the workers themselves.

From every angle this democratic control of strikes is necessary to the health of the union. One of the most prolific sources of general weakness and official corruption in the A. F. of L. unions is the usurped power of business agents and other officials to call strikes on or off without consulting the rank and file. Such arbitrary action is the road to defeat of the union, demoralization of the workers, and corruption of the officials.

Before a strike is launched a vote should be taken of the workers involved, and before any settlement is made, either during the strike or prior to its calling, the workers themselves must have the right to decide whether or not it is acceptable. Trade union democracy reaches its highest and most vital expression in the control of strikes, and to assure democracy in this fundamental matter the industrial unions should make all necessary provisions.

But to state that the workers must decide upon striking or not striking does not mean that every local union should have the right to embark indiscriminately upon strikes. Discipline and organized action must prevail or the union will be broken up. The best practice is that minor local strikes may be called by local unions and district councils, but that more important local strikes require the sanction of the national executive board, subject to the referendum procedure of the union. National strike action should only be determined upon after the matter has been passed favorably by a national convention of the union and endorsed by a general referendum vote.

Strikes should not only be democratically called on and off, but also democratically managed. Broad strike committees (on a national, local, mill scale), with a heavy representation of rank-and-file strikers, are incomparably more effective (and democratic) than the narrow little cliques of officials that commonly run A. F. of L. strikes. Where there is more than one union in an industry, all should be represented on the joint strike committee. Likewise, picketing and other strike activities should be carried on upon a democratic, *i.e.,* mass, basis.

Direct negotiations are the most satisfactory method for unions to deal with employers over the workers' demands. Arbitration should not be resorted to except where no other means are available, because employers, with their money and influence, have an uncanny record of winning over to their side the "odd" men on arbitration boards. Such people are usually middle-class liberal elements, who despite their fair-sounding words, in the pinch display employer sympathies. The workers, especially in A.F. of L. craft unions, have lost many a battle by a naive reliance upon slick-tongued arbiters.

Employers are clever enough with their arbitration weapon. Usually their policy is to offer arbitration to strong unions and to refuse it to weak ones.

Before accepting arbitration in a strike situation, the industrial unions should make sure of the following elementary considerations: (a) not to go into arbitration at all unless they are certain that they cannot, by a straight out fight by the union, force the employers to make the needed concessions to the workers through direct negotiations; (b) compel the acceptance by the employers beforehand of as many of the union's proposals as they can, especially the question of union recognition, and thus limit as far as possible the number of demands to be arbitrated; (c) make a last ditch fight to get the best possible composition of the arbitration board; (d) make it clear that an unsatisfactory award will not pacify the workers.

The industrial unions should be on the alert to oppose all forms of compulsory and semi-compulsory arbitration. Craft union leaders, especially of the railroad unions, largely look upon arbitration as a sort of life-saver, and they have openly co-operated with the employers to entangle the railroad unions with practically compulsory arbitration laws. Especially now does the danger of compulsory arbitration become very acute. Many employers, seeing the rapid progress of the C. I. O. in organizing the mass production industries, believe that the halcyon days of the open shop are about over and they think that the best way to cripple the unions would be to force compulsory arbitration and other forms of legal control upon them. This explains the appearance of many bills for state incorporation of unions, for limitation of picketing and the right to strike, etc., all of which tend in the general direction of state-controlled, fascist unions.

Eternal vigilance is the price of liberty. At all costs the unions must defend their right to strike. Under no circumstances should they allow themselves to be hamstrung and paralyzed by anti-strike, compulsory arbitration laws and similar practices.

When the industrial unions sign agreements with the employers they should live up to them. But, at the same time, they should be under no illusions as to the "sacredness" of such contracts, which A. F. of L. leaders are never done harping upon. The plain fact is that employers generally consider agreements with unions as mere matters of convenience; they sign them when they must and violate them when they think they can get away with it. They constantly "chisel" on wage, hour, and working conditions while an agreement is in force, and they do not hesitate to repudiate it altogether if they believe the situation is favorable for doing so. Thus the Pennsylvania Railroad flagrantly violated the national railroad agreement of 1920 and was instrumental in provoking the nationwide shopmen's strike of 1922; the Pittsburgh Coal Company repudiated the U.M.W.A. Jacksonville agreement and caused the national bituminous miners' strike of 1927. Besides these cases, innumerable other instances of the employers' disregard for agreements with trade unions could be cited.

The lesson from this is that trade unions must be alert at all times to enforce their agreements themselves. Within the framework of the agreement they must constantly press for improved conditions. Here a well working shop steward system is vitally important. Any tendency of a union to rely upon the employers' "fairness" and "honesty" in living up to the terms of an agreement is bound to be disastrous to the workers' conditions and the stability of the union.

The industrial unions, especially those in the mass production industries, should strive to secure general national agreements covering their whole industry. Unless this is done, the employers will play off one section of the workers against the others. Thus, for instance, where no national agreement exists, when the workers in a certain plant or company demand better conditions they will be met by the very difficult argument that the employer is paying as much as his competitors. Thus, little can be wrung from him. And the same thing happens when it comes to his competitors' turn to meet the union committee. The craft unions have been up against this situation for years, with the employers playing off one craft or one section of the industry against the others in order to keep the conditions of all as low as possible. The answer to this problem is national agreements covering whole industries. This means that the steel, auto, rubber, textile, and other industrial unions should definitely aim at such general agreements for their respective industries.

In general, union-employer agreements should not run for long periods, especially not in times of rising prices like these. Two years, at most, is long enough, usually. The industrial unions should not go in for the long-term agreements (five to ten years in some cases) that craft unions practice, to their own detriment. Agreements should also contain thirty or sixty day reopening clauses.

In industries when several unions exist (whether C. I. O., A. F. of L., or independent), every effort should be made to bring them all under joint agreements or at least under agreements expiring at the same time. Under no circumstances should one union stay at work while another in the same plant is striking, as we see being done daily by craft unions. Such "union strike breaking" has broken hundreds of strikes and it must be stopped. Good union workers must not walk through picket lines; they should arrange their unions' strategy so that they all move simultaneously in a given industry.

In signing agreements with employers the industrial unions should beware of inserting clauses prescribing financial penalties on the union or its members for unauthorized strikes. Long experience teaches that such clauses exercise a reactionary effect on the life of a union. In handling the question of unauthorized strikes the unions' own disciplinary powers are amply sufficient. Especially now, when the Liberty League pack of ultra-reactionaries are trying to cripple the unions by making them "legally responsible," (that is, by binding them hand and foot with legal restrictions), the unions should be on guard against the insertion of penalty clauses in their agreements. And, especially, the unions should not include in their agreements clauses discriminating against workers because of age, sex, race, or political opinion.

Union recognition in agreements with employers may assume several forms: (a) the collective bargaining right only for the union's own members, as in effect with some new C. I. O. unions, is only of a preliminary character and should be strengthened, as it exposes the union to the rivalry of company unionism under various guises; (b) the collective bargaining right for all the workers of a given company, craft, or industry, is a livable form of recognition in force in many industries and it is essentially the system under which the railroad craft unions operate; (c) the preferential union shop, under which union members are given preference in employment, is a more advanced and effective type of union recognition, and has long been used in some industries; (d) the check-off, by which employers deduct union dues from the workers' pay, is confined mostly to coal mining and it was developed there (after a long struggle by the U. M. W. A.) largely because mine operators had previously established the practice of making deductions from the workers' pay for powder, tools, company store supplies, etc.; (e) the "closed" shop, under which only union members are employed (widely developed in building, printing, transport, etc.), is the most favorable form of recognition for a union and it is the type the industrial unions should strive towards in formulating their agreements. But it must always be borne in mind that even the best form of union recognition by an employer is not of itself sufficient to maintain the union intact; only sound union policies and good organization work generally can do that.

Initiation fees should be moderate, ranging from $1 (or even less) during organizing campaigns, not to exceed $10 or $15 when the union is well established. The industrial unions should never fall into the bad practice of the craft unions of charging enormous initiation fees (sometimes as much as $1,000) in order to keep workers out of the unions. At all times the unions' books must be open to receive new members. "Job trust" policies are one of the reasons for the weakness of craft unionism.

Union dues should also be moderate; not the excessive rates charged in skilled workers' craft unions (sometimes as much as $10 to $15 per month). On the other hand, the industrial unions should not be "cheap dues" organizations; for they must have ample funds to conduct their activities. In most cases $1 dues per month is about right, with lower rates for the poorer paid workers. Care should be also exercised not to load up the membership with needless assessments.

Transfers from local to local and union to union should be free and universal. This correct system should be introduced immediately among the more closely related unions, and then gradually extended to cover other unions. The industrial union should beware of the infamous A. F. of L. craft union permit system, by which regular good-standing members of one local (especially in the building trades) are not allowed to transfer into another local of the same international but must pay a dollar or two a day for a "permit" to work within its jurisdiction. Much of the money raised by this reactionary tax finds its way into the pockets of corrupt business agents and union secretaries.

The trade union movement should have one label to indicate that a given product is union made. The craft unions, true to their spirit of particularism and individualism, have no less than fifty labels. There should be a universal union label and it should be automatically given to all shops that have signed union agreements with their workers, and should be similarly withdrawn from an employer when any union of his workers declares him unfair.

One of the stifling influences in many craft unions is the careless and dishonest way the organizations' funds are often handled by their officials. Time and again it has been exposed how such people help themselves to union dues, initiation fees, permit money, etc., to the tune of thousands of dollars. All such demoralizing looseness should be strictly guarded against in the industrial unions.

The financial department should be highly developed and have business-like arrangements instituted nationally and locally to take proper care of union moneys. Detailed financial reports (not vague general summaries) should be issued frequently by the national office, and standard monthly reports be submitted to all local unions. The union's funds should be deposited in certain designated banks in the union's name (not in the name of some official who then draws the interest). Traveling auditors should periodically check up on the handling of funds by the local unions, instructing them in the use of a standard bookkeeping system, organizing their auditing committees, etc. All national and important local financial reports should be certified by reputable public accountants. All officials who handle funds, locally or nationally, should be adequately bonded by reliable bonding companies, and defaulting secretaries should be prosecuted.

The union should operate nationally (and also as far as possible, locally) on a budget basis, regularly allocating specified percentages of its income into certain designated funds. Thus, special funds should be built up for the union's journal, organization work, educational activities, strikes, sick or death benefits.

Strike funds: Craft unions often depend primarily upon paying relatively large strike benefits for winning their strikes. But industrial unions, because of their larger size and their broader scope of strike action, do not and cannot rely so much on winning strikes by virtue of strong strike benefits, but instead by the paralyzing power of their strikes. Nevertheless, they have a very acute need for funds during strikes (huge strikes of miners have sometimes lasted from six months to a year) and provisions for this financial need should be made by building up strong strike funds.

Sick and death benefits. The industrial unions, in some cases at least, may find it practicable to realize the stabilizing effect that comes from small sick and death benefits. But they must not overload themselves with such fraternal features, as this can then hinder the growth of the unions. The new unions should be militant fighters for social security legislation and active supporters of proletarian fraternal organizations, such as the International Workers Order.

The local unions should pay approximately 50 per cent of their dues to the national office of the union as per capita tax, and about the same proportion of their initiation fees. The remainder, after deductions for regular local expenses, they should be allowed to spend as they may wish. One of the progress-killing measures of craft union leaders is to forbid local unions to expend any funds except for such purposes as reactionary bureaucratic officials see fit to endorse.

1937

28. The Railroad Unions

Ever since its birth about one hundred years ago the railroad industry, heart of the American industrial system, has been exploited for the enrichment of its private owners. The portion of the workers has always been long hours, low pay, unemployment, and bad working conditions; while the owners of the industry, who perform no useful service in its operation, have reaped billions and billions in wealth. The workers have always had to fight for self-preservation against the voracious sharks who own the railroads, and whatever modest successes they have achieved in defending and improving their living and working standards have been won only at the cost of unremitting struggle.

Since the close of the World War in 1918 the railroad industry, which was then already highly efficient, has made further great strides in this respect. But the advantages of this increasing productivity have not gone to the railroad workers. More than ever they suffer from excessive work, mass unemployment, and low standards of living; while into the hands of the owners the rich stream of unearned wealth continues to flow in billions. This one-sided prosperity is the situation that confronts the railroad workers, and the twenty-one standard railroad craft unions, with their ultra-conservative leaders and policies, have not been able basically to alter it.

A MILITANT TRADE UNION POLICY

If railroad workers are to make real headway toward improving their conditions drastic improvements will have to be made in the make-up and conduct of the railroad trade unions. And the first betterment in this respect should be the development of a more militant policy.

Labor unions are fighting organizations. Their effectiveness in winning concessions for their members, in a given political situation, depends directly upon their ability, if need be, to bring production to a standstill. When the employers fear the striking power of a union they make concessions to it, and only then. Unions, therefore, must cultivate their ability to strike effectively, but of course, they should use the strike weapon judiciously. Fancy arguments by leaders, reliance upon arbitration or upon the "good will" of employers, and other such maneuvers can be no substitute for powerful and militant unionism.

The railroad workers, true to this principle, have a long record of militant struggle. Among their many battles for justice were the great national strike of 1877, the American Railway Union strike of 1894 led by Debs, the Illinois Central-Harriman strike of 1911-15, the 1916 strike movement of the four Brotherhoods for the eight-hour day, the "outlaw" shopmen's strike of 1919, the "outlaw" switchmen's strike of 1920, the national shopmen's strike of 1922, and scores of individual craft strikes on various railroads in recent years.

The top leaders of the railroad craft unions seem to have completely forgotten that labor unions are fighting bodies, if they ever knew it. They work on the false theory that the interests of the workers are identical with, or rather subordinate to, those of the railroad owners. Their line of policy is to conciliate the railroad companies, not militantly to defend the interests of the workers.

For many years, with justice, the Communists have been pointing out this situation. And now their assertions are borne out by devastating charges made by President A. F. Whitney, of the Brotherhood of Railroad Trainmen. In the official journal of that organization for July, 1937, he makes the sharpest attack on the policy of the railroad union leaders that has appeared in the official union press for a generation. Says President Whitney:

> In recent years there has developed a philosophy within the Railway Labor Executives Association to the effect that railway labor should surrender its democratic rights to petition the government for just legislation and should circumscribe its activities by carrier limitation.

In other words, this means that the railroad union leaders have been shielding the interests of the railroad owners and not fighting vigorously for the demands of the workers. President Whitney in his article gives many proofs of this fact, and the history of railroad unions for twenty years past (not to go further back) tells the same story. Let us learn a few lessons from that history.

During the World War the railroad workers built up a very powerful organization of some 1,800,000 members. It was militant and progressive. Under the big mass upsurge of that period the railroad unions were developing a greater and greater solidarity through local, system, divisional, and national federations, and, with their Plumb Plan and intensive political activities, they constituted the progressive wing of the whole American labor movement. This situation naturally greatly alarmed the railroad companies, and they proceeded, with the help of their labor leader friends, to undermine the fighting spirit of the powerful railroad unions.

Their aim was especially to take away the strike weapon of the unions; for the companies dreaded the economic power of the strongly organized workers in the key railroad industry. The first long step toward eliminating the strike among railroad workers was the passage of the Transportation Act (with the union leaders' support) in 1920. This law crippled the railroad unions by placing them under the hostile Railway Labor Board, which set about actively to worsen conditions for the workers. The workers rebelled against it and the great national strikes of the "outlaw" switchmen of 1920 and of 400,000 shopmen in 1922 resulted. The union leaders ruthlessly broke the first of these strikes and failed to support the "legal" shopmen's strike solidly, several of the unions remaining at work while the rest were striking. The consequence was a very disastrous defeat which cost the railroad unions several hundred thousand members and gravely weakened their power and progressive character.

The railroad leaders made the effects of this disaster worse by adopting, in 1923, the notorious B. & O. plan of union-management co-operation. The theory of this scheme was that strikes were unnecessary; that all the workers had to do was to speed up production and their steady work and high wages would automatically result. The general consequence was to worsen working conditions, to further destroy the militancy of the unions, to turn them into speed-up agencies of the bosses, and thus to contribute to the general overproduction that caused the great industrial crash of October, 1929.

Together with the disastrous B. & O. plan no-strike policy, the union leaders developed labor banking. This was another cure-all substitute for militant union policies. As every railroader knows, it finally wound up in one of the worst financial scandals in the history of the United States, with the Brotherhood of Locomotive Engineers membership losing some $17,000,000.

Not satisfied with the undermining effect of all these anti-strike tendencies, the railroad companies proceeded (again with the open support of the railroad union leadership) more completely to hogtie the railroad workers by the passage in 1926 of the Railway Labor Act, then popularly known as the Watson-Parker Law. This Act, with its tangle of mediation, arbitration and delay (which six years later was made still worse by amendments) further seriously weakened the strike right of the railroad workers and made arbitration semi-compulsory.

The railroad union leaders hailed the Watson-Parker Law as a great victory, but the Communists denounced it correctly as highly injurious to railroad unionism and they were condemned and expelled from the unions for so doing. In a pamphlet I wrote at the time, I said that this law "virtually fastens compulsory arbitration upon the necks of the railroad workers, it outlaws strikes. . . . The W.-P. law is a blow at the vitals of railroad unionism."

And so it has turned out in fact. Between the effects of the semi-compulsory arbitration of the Railway Labor Act and the non-militant attitude of the union leaders, the twenty-one railroad unions have sunk deeply into a no-strike program. They have also developed other reactionary tendencies. From being the progressive head of the labor movement, as they were in 1920, they have become its tail end. True, the railroad union leaders talk big, adopt radical demands and take strike votes. Such maneuvers may fool some workers but certainly the companies are not deceived by them. The railroad owners know that when they say "no," the union leaders subside. The employers even sneer about it in their trade journals. Said the *Wall Street Journal* recently: "No one supposes that strike votes mean a strike; things don't happen that way in the railroad industry."

SOME RECENT RAILROAD EXPERIENCES

The notorious anti-labor sheet, the *Chicago Tribune* (August 7) scoffs at the no-strike policy of the unions thus:

Twenty years ago the threat of a railway walkout would have been front page news. Business men would have been frantically facing a nation-wide stoppage of industry. It would have been a national crisis equal only to the prospect of war. Today a strike vote is merely a ripple in the course of events, and the membership of the brotherhoods scarcely take it seriously.

In recent labor history there are many more examples to be found of the harmfulness of the railroad union leaders' refusal to fight the employers. Thus, in the depth of the industrial crisis, when millions of workers were on the brink of starvation, the railroad union leaders were even more energetic than the company officials (from whom they took their tip) in denouncing unemployment insurance and substantial work relief programs. Together with President Green and the other reactionary moguls of the A. F. of L., they declared that the establishment of federal unemployment insurance would degrade the American working man and destroy the trade union movement. If, since then, progress has been made toward instituting government unemployment insurance, the railroad union leaders are not entitled to a particle of credit for it. It was the Communists and other militants who made the real fight for this fundamental reform.

Then there was the 1932 wage cut in which the railroad unions led the wage reduction retreat of the general labor movement. President Whitney tells a scandalous story about that. He declares in his article in *The Railroad Trainman* that in the face of the distress then prevailing the union leaders proposed a conference with the companies to provide relief for unemployed railroad workers. But, says Whitney, "The only thing that came out of this conference, which was originally designed by the Railway Labor Executives Association to give relief to employers, was a 10 per cent cut payroll reduction." This constituted a gift of $400,000,000 out of the workers' pockets to the companies before the reduction was eventually cancelled. And this cancellation was brought about not by efforts of the union leaders, but by mass pressure of the workers, a movement in which the rank-and-file Railroad Brotherhood Unity Movement played a big part.

The non-struggle policy of the railroad union leaders was further illustrated in the matter of old-age pensions. It was not they who initiated the pension movement; that was done by the rank-and-file Railroad Employees National Pension Association. The railroad companies frowned upon the idea of a federal pension system; so, of course, the union leaders were also cold toward it. It was only when the railroad workers' sentiment for pensions was almost universal that they came forward with a much inferior bill to that proposed by the R.E.N.P.A. And in the recent amendments to the Railroad Retirement Act (the pension law), so says President Whitney, needless concessions were made to the companies that will cost the workers many millions yearly.

The case of the dismissal wage agreement was another example of the union leaders yielding before the demands of the companies. The owners demanded consolidation principally so that they could knock some 250,000 railroad workers out of jobs. As usual, the union leaders fell in with their plan. Instead of making a last ditch resistance against any loss of employment through consolidation, they (while making much anti-consolidation talk) surrendered to the companies by accepting the miserable dismissal wage in return for throwing large numbers of workers out of work. Then they hailed their retreat as a wonderful victory. This dismissal wage business will return sorely to plague railroad workers when the industry goes slack again and the companies vigorously take up once more their consolidation plans. Chairman Carrol of the Interstate Commerce Commission is now demanding that all the roads be combined into one unified national system. President Roosevelt has also recently strongly advocated consolidation. The whole dismissal wage agreement should be scrapped.

The sham battle conducted by the railroad union leaders around the question of the six-hour day is still another example of their weak policy. To kid the workers, they have talked loudly about this issue, but they have done nothing to realize it in the several years since it was adopted as policy by the railroad unions. And now we have the deplorable spectacle of President Harrison of the Railway Labor Executives Association agreeing with the companies, in view of the then pending wage negotiations, not to insist upon the six-hour bill at this session of Congress. President Whitney is right when he says:

> This Harrison-Phillips philosophy of attempting to surrender the democratic rights of railroad workers to seek desirable legislation in the name of reaching agreements with the carriers, will ultimately lead to the destruction of the organized labor movement if continued.

The union leaders threw overboard the six-hour day and other important legislation presumably in the interests of getting the men a favorable wage increase. But the wage agreement also turns out to be just one more instance of yielding before the powerful railroad corporations' demands. As we have already remarked above, the August, 1937, wage increases were so low that they did not even keep pace with the rising cost of living. They were the very minimum that the workers could be temporarily forced to accept by the combined pressure of the companies and the union leaders.

THE NEED OF A VIGOROUS POLICY

This constant surrender of the union leaders before the companies registers itself in bad wages, hours, and working conditions for railroad workers. It must be stopped. The railroad unions should begin to function again as real labor organizations. The railroad workers are powerfully situated in industry. Their power is tremendous. With a militant policy they can extract many additional concessions from the avaricious companies.

The railroad workers must reconquer the right to strike, which has been surrendered by their leaders. Railroad workers, like all others, may be depended upon to use the strike right intelligently and judiciously. The anti-strike provisions of the Railway Labor Act should be repealed. The railroad union leaders who persist in being so careful of the railroad owners' interests should be supplanted by men who look to their own union membership for instruction.

The whole history of the labor movement proves that the workers get concessions from their employers only to the extent that they are able and willing to fight for them. For example, in 1916, the four Brotherhoods won the basic eight-hour day by a strike movement. Tiring of the companies' opposition and the politicians' delay, they set September 4 as the strike date; but Congress hurriedly passed the Adamson Law on September 2, two days before the strike deadline. Compare this militant policy and its real results with the present empty, endless dilly-dallying over the six-hour day bill.

Or take the question of company unionism. For years, with all their arbitration and other folderols under the Railway Labor Act, the railroad union leaders were quite unable to eliminate company unionism from the railroads. It was only with the development of the great organizing campaigns, strikes, and intensive political activities of the C. I. O., which reflected themselves among the railroad workers and shook some life into the railroad unions, that real progress is finally being made to end the menace of company unionism on the railroads as well as in industry generally. The whole brilliant success of the C. I. O. emphasizes afresh the correctness of militant union policies.

It is high time that the railroad unions wake up and cut themselves loose from the strangling meshes of the Railway Labor Act. This law should be changed to strike out all its semi-compulsory arbitration features. Meanwhile, the railroad unions should adopt a line of vigorous action on both the industrial and political fields. Such a policy will translate itself into higher living standards, better jobs, and greater security for railroad workers, as well as in an enormous strengthening of the whole labor movement.

NATIONAL FEDERATION OF ALL RAILROAD WORKERS

The railroads, as we have pointed out above, are a low-wage industry, despite the tremendous potential economic power of the unions. President Harrison of the Railway Labor Executive Association has stated that the average wage of the members of the fourteen non-train service unions, after the 1937 wage increases, is only 64 cents per hour, as compared with auto 90 cents, steel 82.5 cents, rubber 83 cents, tires and tubes 92.5 cents, etc. (all of the latter being industries where the C. I. O. is strong).

In the previous chapter we have seen the basic cause why this low-wage condition prevails on the railroads, namely, the no-strike policy and subservient attitude of the union leaders toward the railroad companies. Now we shall examine another elementary reason, that is, the horse-and buggy system of twenty-one autonomous craft unions which exists on the railroads and which vastly reduces the strength of the workers.

The railroad companies are powerful, united and ruthless. They are controlled by the greatest combination of capitalists in all the world. In her notable book, *Rulers of America,* Anna Rochester says:

No section of American industrial life has reached a more advanced stage of capitalist development than the railroads. Here we find highly developed monopoly and an open and far-reaching use of the state on behalf of corporations.

. . . There are thirteen major systems . . . controlling, directly or indirectly, nearly 90 per cent of the total mileage in the United States. Concentration of railroad power is even greater than this figure implies. For back of the thirteen major systems and the eight smaller systems is the dominating power of Morgan and Kuhn, Loeb.*

The great House of Morgan, together with its Kuhn-Loeb, Rockefeller, Vanderbilt, du Pont, and other affiliates, dominates not only the railroads, but also many other industries, including steel, automobile, munitions, public utilities, and coal mining, as well as various big banking and commercial enterprises. The gigantic Morgan finan-

---

* Anna Rochester, *Rulers of America,* pp. 223-24, 1936.

cial octopus directly controls capitalist interests of 30 billion dollars; it is closely linked to another 16 billions, has influence over 16½ additional billions and is allied to 15 billions more. Thus the Morgan group either directly controls or actually dominates some 77 billion dollars of capital, or "more than one-fourth of the American corporate wealth."

It is against this monstrous, ruthless, united capitalist aggregation that the union representatives have to contend when they sit down in conference with representatives of the Association of American Railroads. The capitalist wolves may fight among themselves for ownership of the industries, but they present a united front against labor.

And what kind of an industrial organization do the railroad workers possess as against the gigantic power of the banker owners of the railroad industry? The answer is a disgrace and a disaster to the whole labor movement—twenty-one weak, squabbling, autonomous craft unions. It is a mosquito fleet of canoes trying to fight a great battleship. Small wonder, then, that the railroad workers do not get better results from their labor unions.

THE NEED FOR A UNITED ORGANIZATION

For forty years or more the most progressive railroad workers have realized the burning necessity for greater solidarity and a more compact form of organization. They understood the utter folly of single craft unions, or separate groups of such unions, trying to fight the powerful and united combination of railroad corporations. Such a stupid course has led to lost strikes and defeated wage negotiations time after time. Consequently, ever since the days of Debs and the American Railway Union in 1893-94, the progressives have striven to develop a more unified railroad unionism. The companies, of course, have always violently opposed these labor unity tendencies and consequently, inasmuch as it is the union leaders' policy to sneeze every time the railroad owners catch a cold, they, too have set their faces like flint against consolidation of the railroad craft unions and the development of concerted action among them.

Indeed, some years ago, there was the absurd spectacle presented of the railroad union leaders, their own organizations scattered and disunited, carrying on a vigorous campaign for the amalgamation of the railroad companies. Their arguments on how and why the employers should consolidate are contained in a high-priced report sub-

mitted in 1921 to the Railroad Labor Board by W. Jett Lauck on behalf of the Railway Employees Department of the A. F. of L. In this
most untimely report the advantage of unity of the railroad systems
was stressed and opponents of it were condemned as reactionaries
motivated only by "matters of personal advantage." The railroad
union leaders would, instead, have done much better had they planned
the unification of railroad unionism and taken upon themselves the
criticism that they directed to the opponents of unity of the railroad
systems.

At the time of the great strike disaster of 1922, when the running
trades worked while the shop trades struck and thus all were defeated,
the Communist Party and the Trade Union Educational League initiated a broad campaign for the amalgamation of the craft unions into
one industrial union. This timely proposal was endorsed by a majority
of the rank-and-file workers generally in the railroad crafts, but the
union leaders, by reason of their iron-clad, undemocratic grip on the
unions, defeated the movement.

These same railroad union leaders have also castrated and frustrated
the federation movement on the railroads. Federation sprang up on
a large scale several years prior to the war as a result of progressive
rank-and-file activity. It set about linking together the various craft
unions, and the great I.C.-Harriman lines strike of 1911-1915 was
fought over the issue of federation recognition by the companies. The
federation movement prospered, however, in spite of railroad opposition, and it gradually spread all over the country. This resulted in the
organization of the Railway Employees Department of the A. F. of L.,
and, during the war and shortly afterwards, climaxed in various joint
national movements of all the railroad unions and the signing of the
all-inclusive national wage agreement. In many respects it was of a
broad, rank-and-file, democratic character.

The railroad union leaders, with a few notable exceptions, sabotaged the federation movement from the outset. They saw that its
logical result would be to draw the unions closer and closer, until
finally they become a compact organization. And this was precisely
the last thing that the railroads and their friends, the Grand Chiefs,
wanted. So they proceeded to sidetrack the whole federation movement.

Their attack on federation was twofold. Especially following the
1922 defeat, they systematically set about weakening the local, system,
division and national federations by letting some fall to pieces al-

together, and by undermining the rest in various ways. Then they proceeded to develop a substitute for the whole federation movement. This substitute, worthless like most substitutes, is the present Railway Labor Executives Association. This body, consisting nationally of the presidents of the twenty-one railroad unions, has its counterpart in the association of General Chairmen on various railroad systems. Among other things, the Railway Labor Executive Association has gutted the Railway Employees Department and left it virtually without any functions. The R. L. E. A. is a form that reduces rank-and-file control of the railroad unions and the solidarity of the workers to a minimum. It has been a convenient instrument to prevent the workers from making any real struggle against the railroad companies.

The great success of the C. I. O. in organizing the steel, auto, and other industries on the basis of industrial unionism has again caused a new growth of militancy and solidarity among railroad workers. One important manifestation of this is the so-called "local associations movement" now developing in many railroad centers. This movement, despite its similarity of name, is unlike the system of national "associations" of General Chairmen and Grand Chiefs, in that it is a genuine attempt to link all the various crafts on a given railroad system or important railroad center into one broad representative body. It is not a substitute for federation, but a builder and developer of it and a wide path to the solidarity of all railroad workers.

In order to head off this new progressive movement for solidarity of all railroad workers, the leaders of the Railway Employees Department recently issued a leaflet graphically picturing the twenty-one railroad organizations as constituting one great unbreakable chain— the Railway Labor Executive Association. This was a brazen attempt to kid railroaders into believing that they, too, have an industrial union. Such an argument is an insult to the intelligence of railroad workers. What kind of a chain is it in which each link has the power to leave the chain or yield to pressure whenever it sees fit? A chain is no stronger than its weakest link, and the Railway Labor Executives Association is a whole chain of weak links. In fact, its links are not actually joined together at all.

The 1937 wage negotiations showed once again the falsity of the claim that the R. L. E. A. is an "unbreakable cable." Here we saw two quite separate groups of unions, one composed of the five running trades and the other made up of fourteen non-train service organizations, and each carrying on entirely distinct wage negotiations. This separation injured the interests of both groups. Suppose it had turned out that one group had refused to accept the companies' final proposals and declared a strike. Then we would have 1922 all over again, with part of the unions striking and the rest working and helping the employers to break the strike. Railroad workers have had enough of such criminal craft union stupidity. They want a consolidation of their union forces that will bring them into a united front against the powerful railroad combine.

WHAT KIND OF A RAILROAD FEDERATION?

What is urgently necessary is to join together all the railroad craft unions into one well-knit national federation. This federation should be based upon the acceptance of three general principles by the affiliated organizations:

One national wage agreement for all railroad workers.

The federation should finally formulate the workers' demands and be in charge of all negotiations with the railroad companies in support of these demands.

The decision as to whether the workers should strike or not in a given situation to rest solely within the jurisdiction of the federation.

A federation founded upon these three elementary principles would lay the basis for real solidarity and united action among the railroad workers. It would enormously increase their power as a whole. In all other respects, in the beginning at least, the unions affiliated to the industrial federation could retain their autonomy: holding their own conventions, electing their officers, formulating their craft demands, enforcing the agreement in their respective spheres, conducting their insurance systems, collecting their own rates of dues, etc. The effectiveness of this type of organization is shown by the successes achieved in the past four years by the Maritime Federation on the Pacific Coast.

The way to bring about such a national industrial federation of railroad workers is by developing the already existing principle and practice of federation on the railroads. All the international railroad unions should be hooked together nationally in a broad federation; the local, system, and divisional federation should also be expanded to include all railroad unions; and there should be built up all-inclusive railroad councils in every city or town with two or more railroads. Cultivation of the new "local associations movement" is an important step in this general direction. All the leading committees and conventions of the various stages of the national railroad federation should be based on a broad rank-and-file representation, and not be merely little handfuls of officials as in the case of the Railway Labor Executives Association and its associated system chairmen. All the national unions, local, system and divisional organizations, and local railroad councils should send delegates to biennial conventions of the great national industrial federation.

From the workers' standpoint there is every reason why the railroad unions should be joined together in such a federation—it would mean more wages and better working conditions for the workèrs, the certainty of making the railroads 100 per cent union, the making of vast economies in union administration, etc. The only objections against such a federation are the fears of the companies of its great power and the dread of the union officials that it might disturb their too well paid jobs. The old horse chestnut argument that such a broad federation could not properly take care of the interests of all the groups of workers is thoroughly discredited by experience in many industries. It was also shown to be false in the railroad industry itself by the former national railroad wage agreements (1920), which covered all railroad unions and all categories of railroad workers.

In addition to linking the railroad unions in this federated form, there should also be a process started of amalgamating the most closely related unions. This would also lend added great strength to the whole railroad movement. Thus the Order of Railway Conductors, Brotherhood of Railway Trainmen, and Switchmen's Union of North America should be combined into one union—the leaders have been preventing this obviously necessary amalgamation for thirty years. And the same is also true of the Brotherhood of Locomotive Engineers and the Brotherhood of Locomotive Firemen and Engineers, which, but for official opposition, would have naturally fused together a generation ago. Several of the metal trades unions should also be combined, to the benefit of all. The two Negro organizations of Pullman Porters and Dining Car Employees should likewise be combined. In short, by amalgamation the number of unions could, with great profit, be cut at least in half at once. Then the double process of federation and amalgamation should be continued until it reaches its logical conclusion, the eventual development of a great departmentalized industrial union of all railroad workers. With such a united organization the railroad workers would indeed be a power in the land. The

C. I. O. has demonstrated the worth of industrial unionism in the steel, auto, rubber, and other industries; this form of organization will also prove no less valuable in the railroad industry.

The railroad workers, whether in their present craft form of organization, or in later stages of federation and amalgamation, should also enter into close co-operative arrangements with the unions of maritime, truck, bus, trolley, and aircraft workers, with the aim of eventually establishing a great wide federation of all transport workers. The railroad companies are trying to lead railroaders into fighting other transport workers as competitors and enemies; but the railroaders must not be so trapped. All transport workers have interests in common against the great transport capitalists and they should all stand shoulder to shoulder.

MORE TRADE UNION DEMOCRACY NEEDED

Besides federating and amalgamating the railroad unions, they also stand in urgent need of democratization. Such democratization will modernize and strengthen them. Among the more basic measures necessary to this effect are:

1. The shameful discrimination against the large body of Negro railroad workers must be discontinued. There are more than 125,000 Negroes employed in the railroad industry. They are grossly abused by the companies, being forced to accept the worst jobs and the lowest pay. In time of unemployment, they are the first fired and the last hired. Many railroad unions condone and assist this outrageous Jim-Crow system by refusing to allow the Negroes to become union members and to give them organized protection. This condition is a disgrace to the labor movement and a grievous injury to both white and Negro railroad workers. It must be ended, and the hand of democratic union fellowship extended to the doubly-oppressed Negro Workers.

2. A more progressive, democratic, and intelligent attitude must also be taken toward women and young workers in the railroad industry. They should be allowed freely to join the unions, their grievances should be carefully looked after, and special methods to organize and educate them need to be developed.

3. Unemployed railroad workers should also be retained as union members. This will greatly stimulate the unions to fight for their rights. One of the most shameful features of the great industrial crisis

was the ruthless way in which the railroad and other craft union officials dropped the starving unemployed from the membership rolls.

4. The railroad unions also have a crying need for democracy in the conduct of their business. With but rare exceptions, the organizations are dominated by small groups of entrenched officials at the top and the rank and file have little real say in the actual running of the organizations. This was seen once again by the way the recent wage settlements were railroaded through, without the workers being allowed to vote on them and in spite of widespread protest.

The Chicago conference of general chairmen that accepted the recent wage increase of the fourteen non-operating unions was a shocking example of bureaucratic domination. First, the general chairmen were given no previous inkling of the nature of the settlement until they heard Harrison report it at the meeting. Then they were not allowed to discuss the matter in the meeting, as the gathering was at once broken up into crafts, where various means of pressure were used to whip disgruntled chairmen into line. Among these means of coercion were threats to leave out of the settlement altogether any craft that voted against accepting its present terms, lying assertions that the strike vote did not have a majority, etc. By such undemocratic means was the inadequate settlement rammed down the throats of the railroad workers.

To democratize the procedure of the railroad unions the following major proposals are fundamentally necessary: the right of the membership to vote on all wage settlements; their right to recall elected officers by majority vote at any time; more democratically organized conventions, which should be held biennially and the officers' reports published thirty days in advance; election, not appointment, of convention committees; free discussion of all economic and political questions and opinions in the local meetings and official union journals; more strict and business-like system of financial accounts; compulsory retirement of union officials at the age of 65. Especially is it necessary to put an end to the undemocratic and generally harmful practice of paying union officials such large salaries and expense accounts that they live like capitalists and lose all feeling as workers. The practice of looking into workers' political beliefs as a basis for their membership in the union or eligibility for official positions shoud be abolished— true trade union democracy accepts all honorable workers as members without regard to their race, sex, religion, age, nationality, or political opinion.

5. Another important democratic reform necessary to the railroad unions is to broaden out and strengthen the grievance committees along the lines of the new shop steward system of C. I. O. unions. The present grievance and bargaining committees of the unions in the railroad industry are too narrow, too much the affair only of paid officials. This is wrong; every negotiating committee, from the bottom to the top, should be heavily rank and file in composition. The experiences in the auto, steel, and other industries prove the enormous importance of having a well-knit system of shop stewards for each department, shop, plant, etc. Such a shop steward system, adapted to railroad conditions, would greatly strengthen the unions. It would enormously facilitate organization work, would put an end to the harmful chiseling against existing agreements that the companies are carrying on everywhere.

To accomplish these basically necessary measures to strengthen the railroad unions—federation, amalgamation, democratization—it is indispensable that the progressive groups in the unions should campaign vigorously for them among the union members. Of the foregoing proposals there is not one that the broad rank and file would not favor if given a free expression of opinion. But the bulk of the conservative officialdom is against these measures and the unions are so undemocratically run that the will of the leaders, not the membership, is what ordinarily prevails.

This situation can be changed. By raising these questions among the membership, by making them live issues in every local union, in every local and system federation, in every international union convention, by filling the dry-as-dust official union journals with discussions of them—the great rank-and-file membership can be stirred to demand these measures. And once this is done, the conservative officials will either drop their opposition or be supplanted by more progressive leaders. The advance of the railroad unions to a powerful and democratic industrial federation of all railroad workers will come when the progressive elements in the unions set out earnestly to bring it to pass.

1937

TOWARD GOVERNMENT OWNERSHIP

In order that improved conditions should prevail in the railroad industry, regarding wages, rates, service, financing, etc., it is not enough that the present wage-cut be defeated; it is further imperatively necessary that the whole railroad system become the property of the federal government. There must be an end to the absurd and harmful conditions where these great arteries of commerce, vital public services, are owned and exploited by private individuals. The history of private ownership of the railroads is a long story of brutal exploitation of the workers, holding up of shippers and the public for excessive freight and passenger rates, criminal stock gambling and thievery, illegal rate rebating, bribery of legislators, and similar practices. It is a record of corruption and barefaced robbery without parallel in the world. Nationalization—government ownership—will finish off this regime.

In establishing such nationalization it is basically necessary drastically to reduce the present excessive capitalization of the roads. This should be cut in half, at least; for most of it is "water" (and not pure water at that). Just recently the Chicago and Great Western, bankrupt like one-third of the total railroad mileage from financial plundering and mismanagement, went through Interstate Commerce Commission (I. C. C.) reorganization proceedings and consequently the capitalization of the road was slashed from $139,000,000 to $62,000,000, or more than one-half. Approximately the same thing should be done with the railroad systems as a whole. Their fictitious figure of some twenty-four billion dollars capitalization should be reduced to about ten or twelve billions, the actual replacement cost of the roads, and the market value of their securities. The bondholders must also take a reduction in their interest rates, as well as their capitalization; for why should they be paid 5 to 8 per cent, when government bonds draw only 2 or 3 per cent?

Of course, the stockholders will put up a big squawk against this devaluation, but in the real readjustment of the railroads to new traffic conditions—including the many new forms of competition, and general industrial depression—the owners must accept substantial reductions in their profits. The workers, who are least able to stand sacrifices, have suffered to the extent of over one million of them losing their jobs outright and the rest becoming grossly overworked.

Actually, the railroad security holders have only very dubious claims to the ownership of the railroads. In the first place, the roads were built pretty much from public subsidies and land grants. In the early days, for example, the federal government "gave" the railroads (after brazen corruption of Congress members) 160,000,000 acres of rich farm, mineral, and timber lands, or a stretch of territory worth billions and equal in extent to the states of Maine, New Hampshire, Vermont, Massachusetts, Rhode Island, Connecticut, New York, New Jersey, Delaware, Pennsylvania, Ohio, and Indiana. The case of the Central Pacific was pretty typical. Besides gigantic land grants, it received a government subsidy of $86,000,000 to build a road which actually cost but $42,000,000. The original owners put in only $108,987, but up till now they have pulled down about $800,000,000 in profits, or enough to rebuild the road several times over.

Since the beginning of the railroad industry, its private owners have been paid back in dividends and graft many times the value of the roads. Thus, in the last seventeen years they have raked in unearned profits of fourteen billion dollars, or about one and one-half times the actual value of the roads. Yet the railroads still belong 100 per cent to these private owners and they hope to go right on owning them regardless of how many times the people pay for them. In strict justice, the big railroad-owning banks and corporations would be entitled to nothing for surrendering up the railroads to their rightful owners, the people. In the basic financial reorganization, however, care must be taken to protect the interest of the small stockholders who have bought gold brick railroad securities in good faith.

During the industrial crisis years the government has loaned and given the railroads several hundred million dollars, most of which went to fatten interest and dividend rates, and now the roads are clamoring for more. But should any further loans be granted they should definitely be utilized as steps towards government ownership. The government should insist that such funds be used to make work by rehabilitating the badly run-down railroads, that they should be secured by first mortagages, and that the government should have representation on the railroad boards of directors.

When nationalization of the railroads is finally carried through, there are a number of improved labor conditions which the railroad workers should insist upon as part of the new setup. Among them are union representation in the management, the establishment of a standard minimum working force, no consolidations at the cost of workers, jobs, the six-hour day, full crew and train limit regulations, the improvement of the old-age and unemployment insurance laws, the reduction of excessive managerial salaries, better promotion systems, and the working out of a national co-ordinated transportation system to include bus and electric lines, trucking systems, pipe lines, steamships, airplanes, etc., under a federal department of transportation. And the greatest care will have to be exercised to protect the strike right of the workers.

The question of government ownership of the railroads has become a vital question. The railroad unions, the A. F. of L., and C. I. O., and many other organizations favor it. The present critical situation on the railroads caused by the employers' unjustified wage-cut demand stresses afresh its urgency. The railroad unions should push the question with all vigor, as they used to do in the days of the Plumb Plan.

1938

THE RAILROAD UNIONS AND JIM CROW

In the present sharp controversy over the discrimination against Negro workers in the railroad industry there has been a widespread tendency to condemn the trade unions roundly as mainly responsible for the discrimination or, at best, as equally guilty with the railroad companies. But putting the greater responsibility upon the trade unions lends itself easily to anti-union propaganda. Without in the least wishing to excuse the trade unions which practice discrimination against Negro workers, the truth remains, nevertheless, that the railroad corporations themselves are the ones primarily responsible for inflicting this infamous system upon the vast railroad services.

It is an historical fact that the railroad companies introduced Jim Crow upon the railroads as they built them. It is clear that the unions had nothing to do with the original establishment of Jim Crow, because there were no trade unions in existence at that time on the railroads. The railroad unions which now practice discrimination are in the position of having accepted these infamous methods, established long ago by the companies, and then of having, in many cases, collaborated with the companies in making them worse.

The representatives of the railroad companies, at the hearings of the Fair Employment Practice Committee (F. E. P. C.) in Washington a couple of months ago, undertook to excuse away their discrimination against the hiring of Negro workers by stating that in so doing they were merely conforming to a widespread social prejudice which they could not change. By implication, they blamed the unions as the instigators.

That this is all a lie and that the railroads themselves have been a reactionary influence in this whole matter is made obvious by the fact that in the South, where anti-Negroism is the most rampant and where the companies might there be expected to be the most restricted in their employment practices, actually the companies' hiring policies have always been, ever since the railroads were first built, far more liberal than in the North, where Jim Crow is less virulent generally.

Thus, in the South, the railroad companies, from the start, hired numbers of Negro workers in the more skilled trades, including firemen, switchmen, brakemen, shop mechanics, etc.; whereas in the North, these occupations on the railroads, from the earliest days, have been almost completely barred to Negroes.

The explanation of this seeming contradiction is that in the South the railroad companies, in order to meet the labor shortage, were compelled to turn to the great body of available Negroes, the number of immigrants reaching those sections being small. In the North, however, where the railroad companies had huge numbers of white immigrants at their disposal, they, acting in a real Jim-Crow spirit, practically excluded the Negroes altogether from the railroads, save in the Pullman sleeping and dining car services. This was quite in line with the companies' anti-union policies, their playing native-born workers against foreign-born, their pitting whites against Negroes, etc.

When the railroad trade unions began to come into existence and to be a factor in determining railroad working conditions, along in the 1880's and 1890's, they found the Jim-Crow system in full force all over the national railroad network, in the North as well as in the South.

The unions' weakness was that they fell in with this discrimination and, hearkening to the demands of the most backward elements within their own ranks, they have even worsened the existing Jim-Crow practices by denying Negroes union membership and by making discriminatory agreements with the railroad companies against the hiring of Negroes. Such conduct has been absolutely inexcusable on their part.

What the railroad unions have lacked is a leadership intelligent enough to understand the common interest of all workers, regardless of the colors of their skins, and bold enough to smash through the Jim-Crow system, originally established by the companies.

What will the railroad unions do now that the issue of abolishing

Jim Crow has been made acute by the recent decision of the F. E. P. C.? The attitude of the southern railroad companies, in defiantly refusing to obey the anti-discrimination order of the F. E. P. C., is a give-away of the historical anti-Negro position of the railroad companies generally.

It is to be hoped, however, that the railroad unions themselves will not follow this reactionary lead but will finally break with the infamous discrimination system, regardless of the wishes of the railroad companies. Such action is indispensable, in justice to the Negro people, in the best interests of the trade union movement and in the furtherance of our national war effort. The whole labor movement, at this crucial juncture, should give the heartiest support to the F. E. P. C. order and to the elimination of Jim Crowism in all industries and unions.

1943

29. The Communists and the Trade Unions

QUESTIONS AND ANSWERS

Q. What part do Communists play in the trade unions? What is meant by Communist trade union work?

A. Workers organize into trade unions primarily in order to win higher wages, shorter hours, and better working conditions. The Communist Party, as the political party of the working class, always supports the trade unions in their struggles. The Communist Party insists that its members join the unions of their respective industries or trades, that they be the most active fighters for the interests of the workers, that they give their untiring efforts to building and strengthening the unions, that they always protect the unity of the trade unions. The Communist Party educates and organizes the trade union workers into a broad democratic front with the farmers and other toilers in support of their common cause.

But the Communists also look beyond these daily struggles. We believe that a fundamental reorganization of society—socialism—is the only final solution of the workers' problems—unemployment, poverty, war. Not all members of the trade unions accept this socialist viewpoint of the Communist Party, which is based on a scientific analysis of capitalism and on the experience of the workers' struggles the world over. Because of their broad outlook, the Communists are able in every immediate struggle to champion most effectively the interests of the workers. Due to their Marxist-Leninist training, Communists are practical organizers of the workers, know how to estimate the forces of the enemy, and understand what tactics to apply in order to achieve the aims for which all workers are ready to fight at a given time.

We Communists naturally consider it our right to advocate our opinions and win to our viewpoint the workers in the unions. This viewpoint strengthens the fight of the workers today and prepares them for understanding the need for socialism—which can only be brought into existence when the majority of the workers become convinced of its necessity through their own experience.

Q. Is it a fact, as is often charged, that Communists in the trade unions always set out to capture these organizations?

A. This is one of the many false accusations made against the Communist Party by the enemies of a militant and powerful labor movement. The reality is that the Communists join with all other progressives in fighting against the unions being "captured" by any individuals or groups. We believe in democratic unions, organizations in which the membership determines policy, and we work for a broad leadership thoroughly representative of and responsive to the wishes of the rank and file. Communists fight against all clique control and dictatorial tendencies among union leaders, no matter from what direction it comes. As for ourselves, we ask no rights beyond those accorded all other workers. We accept the same responsibilities and duties that non-Communists do.

Communists expect to influence the policies of a labor organization and play a role in its leadership only to the extent that they win the respect and support of the workers. We strive to merit this support by our devoted activities and educational work in the unions, not by acting as an organized group within them. Communists, whether rank and filers or elected officials of a union, have the duty and responsibility to build and improve the organization, work for the realization of its program, and to abide by the decision of the majority, arrived at democratically through the channels of the union. Communists who are elected into leadership of a union are responsible to the membership of that organization, and the Communist Party joins with all workers in calling to account any elected officials, Communist or otherwise, who fail to fulfill the responsibilities and duties entrusted to them by the membership of their trade unions.

Q. Do Communists form factions (organized party groups) within the trade unions?

A. No. In the earlier years of the Communist Party the policy was sometimes followed of the Communist Party members in a given union meeting together to plan educational work in that organization. But this practice has been discontinued, as tending to create possible misunderstanding among the rank and file of the unions. The Communists, like all other members, function through the regular democratic procedures and committees of the unions. We are resolute opponents of factional control of unions, whether by a conservative bureaucratic clique or by some special political group. The Communists have full reliance that the union membership at large, if given an opportunity for a free discussion of the issues before it and the right to decisive, democratic action upon them, will arrive at sound policies. For this reason Communists are everywhere and always the most consistent and determined fighters for trade union democracy.

Q. What is the attitude of the Communists toward unauthorized strikes and toward trade union discipline generally?

A. Communists believe in trade union discipline, based on majority rule arrived at through the democratic processes of the union. Unless there is such discipline the union will be destroyed. Communists are opposed to unauthorized strikes provoked by minorities. Such strikes almost always serve the interests of the employers, not the workers. They commonly result in violent internal conflict within the union, they antagonize middle class sympathizers, and they usually end in defeat. Where a union follows policies really in the interests of the workers and defends actively their grievances, and where trade union democracy prevails, there is no occasion for unauthorized strikes.

Q. Is it true that Communists consider trade union agreements "mere scraps of paper" to be violated at will?

A. It is not true. Communists understand that in modern industry, with all its intricacies, it is necessary for employers and trade unions to put down on paper the complex terms of the workers' employment that they may agree upon. Such agreements, when entered into, should be adhered to by both sides. But Communists do not believe in the illusions of conservative trade unionists that trade union agreements bring about a suspension of the class struggle. The ever-present contest between employers and workers over the product of labor merely takes on new forms under such conditions, with the employers using every trick to violate and chisel upon the agreements. Communists, therefore, are alert to see to it that the employers are compelled to live up to their agreements and that the agreements are interpreted in the interests of the workers. In general, Communists support short-term contracts, not to exceed two years or so. Under no circumstances do Communists consider trade union agreements as justifying one body of workers breaking the strike of another, such as has been done upon innumerable occasions in trade union history by conservative officials using the excuse of inviolable union contracts.

Q. What is the Communist policy on the arbitration of labor disputes?

A. Communists strongly favor direct dealings between unions and employers in the adjustment of labor disputes, as employers with their influence have an unsavory record of winning to their side the "odd" man on arbitration boards. But we are not opposed on principle to the workers accepting arbitration (taking great care of the board's composition) when direct negotiations fail and when a strike is inadvisable. The workers' objective being the attainment of the maximum in living standards (wages, hours, working conditions, etc.), the Communists are willing to use not only direct negotiation, but also arbitration when other means do not get results. We are strongly opposed, however, to compulsory arbitration in whatever form it may take. Under compulsory arbitration the strike right is taken away from the workers and this places them at the mercy of the employers and their representatives.

Q. What about seniority in industry? Do seniority clauses in union agreements constitute a good or bad practice?

A. The Communists endorse seniority provisions in trade union contracts as necessary in order to protect the older workers and also to prevent the arbitrary discharge of militant workers for union activities.

Seniority in industry takes on especially great importance now that there is huge, chronic mass unemployment. But while utilizing seniority practices the unions should also be on guard against serious abuses growing out of them. Thus, on the railroads, because of seniority claims, some workers work the equivalent of thirty or even forty days per month, while others get no work at all. And more serious yet, seniority practices sometimes operate to exclude the younger workers almost entirely from a given industry. This is both unjust and dangerous. The youth have the right to work and to establish a family, and if this right is denied them many may easily become the prey of reactionary demagogues and be used against the labor movement. In working out seniority systems, therefore, ways must be found to check possible abuses and to protect the place of the youth in industry. Seniority rules must not be used to discriminate against the employment of Negroes.

Q. What is the Communist policy on apprentices in industry?

A. The Communists are in favor of young workers being drawn freely into industry, including the skilled trades which require prolonged training. But we oppose the present policies of employers who use the apprentice system to weaken and undermine the unions. We advocate trade schools controlled by the trade unions. We also favor the unions controlling the drawing in and training of youth, jointly with committees of the youth themselves. The young workers should be admitted to membership in the unions upon the beginning of their "apprenticeship." Communists demand payment of fixed wages on the basis of "equal pay for equal work" for the type of work that the apprentice performs. We oppose all tendencies toward "job trust" unionism through undue restriction of apprentices, excessive initiation fees, etc.

Q. What is the Communist attitude toward sick and death benefits and other fraternal features in trade unions?

A. The Communists favor the adoption by unions of sick and death benefits and other benevolent provisions. They tend to stabilize the unions. But it is important that such undertakings be so organized and administered that the funds are properly protected, that the workers exercise full control, and that they get the maximum service at a minimum cost. Often it is advisable for a union to operate through an existing, well-recognized workers' fraternal organization, such as, for example, the International Workers Order. Care should be taken that union benefit funds are not used for ventures into labor banking or real estate speculation. The insurance service should be optional, so that workers who cannot afford it shall not be deprived of full union membership. Unions cannot meet this whole problem by themselves, however, and should, therefore, actively support old age, unemployment, sickness, accident and other forms of social insurance by the federal and state governments.

Q. I often hear it said: "Communists always bring politics into the unions." What's the answer?

A. "Politics is concentrated economics," said Lenin. Politics is always present in the trade union, but not always working class politics. Frequently, as we all know, conservative trade union leaders misuse the unions in the political interest of themselves and the bosses. Communists give a working class character to trade union politics. The nature of the struggle of the workers under the present conditions of capitalist development makes political action more and more necessary.

The unions are concerned with wages, hours, and working conditions. These questions have all become political issues. Just to recall the Wages and Hours Laws or the Wagner Act makes this clear. Or take unemployment relief and insurance; these are also vital political matters. Likewise the workers are interested in the preservation of peace. This, too, is political. So is the fight against lynching, injunctions in labor disputes, use of police against workers, as well as the election of the city, state and national legislative bodies. All these are political issues of basic importance to labor; and all trade unions, including the A. F. of L. Executive Council and not only the C. I. O., are compelled to deal with them regularly. Even the old, outworn A. F. of L. policy of "reward your friends and punish your enemies," though harmful politics, is politics nevertheless. The Communists put trade union politics on a working class basis and advocate the organization of the workers solidly, politically, in a broad democratic front with the farmers and professionals, thereby enabling them to defend themselves effectively on every field of the class struggle.

Q. Can craft unions exist as parts of a general progressive labor movement?

A. Yes. In many countries craft and industrial unions are to be found side by side, working peacefully and constructively in the same national trade union federation. While unquestionably the industrial form of unionism is the superior type, still in a number of industries in this country, especially railroads, building trades, printing trades and amusement trades, experience teaches us that craft unions can exist and defend the interests of their members. These craft unions develop a measure of the necessary industrial solidarity through various types of federation (Railroad Employees Department, Building Trades Councils). But, on the other hand, in such industries as coal, chemical, steel, auto, textile, metal mining, electrical manufacturing, and generally where modern methods of mass production are in operation the industrial form of unionism is necessary. There is no valid reason whatever why craft and industrial unions, each confining itself to its proper sphere, cannot live harmoniously together in one national federation.

Q. Why do Communists so insistently demand the admission of Negroes into trade unions?

A. First, because refusal to grant trade union membership to Negroes is a gross insult and serious injury to them, by tending to bar them from working in various industries and by depriving them of all organized protection in their wage, hour, seniority, promotion, and working conditions. Free admission of Negroes into all trade unions, with full right to hold union office and to enjoy all union privileges, as is becoming the case with many unions, will go far toward smashing the whole shameful Jim-Crow system.

Second, because close working relations between Negro and white toilers is fundamentally necessary for the development of the democratic front of all progressive forces and the achievement of its demands; for the defense of American democracy against its reactionary foes. The question is, therefore, one of basic political significance. Karl Marx truly said, "Labor with a white skin cannot be free while labor with a black skin is branded." The degree of political understanding and power of the labor and progressive movement can be pretty accurately gauged by the extent to which it extends the hand of brotherly cooperation to the doubly oppressed Negro people.

Q. What is there to the common contention of reactionaries that high wages are the cause of economic crises?

A. Nothing. It is a false argument used by spokesmen for Wall Street as an excuse for cutting wages and maintaining and increasing profits. Contrary to it, one of the main reasons for the economic slump of 1937 was precisely that the real wages of the workers—what they can actually purchase with their pay—did not keep up with the rise in the cost of living. Higher wages have a lessening effect upon the crisis by increasing the purchasing power of the masses and enabling them to buy back a larger portion of what they have produced.

The industrialists deliberately mislead the workers when they claim that higher wages cause curtailment of production and the shutting down of factories. The big trusts increased the prices of their products far more than the small raises they were forced to give the workers. The steel trust, for example, after giving a small raise to its workers in 1937, boosted the price of steel by a margin ten times as much as the wage increase. Not high wages, but exorbitant monopoly prices were one of the main factors which brought on the crisis. High wages expand the market for commodities and make for industrial activity; low wages and high monopoly prices sharply reduce consumer demand and make for economic crises.

Q. How do Communists raise the demand for the right to work?

A. The Communists support the demand of organized labor for the right to work. Practically, this involves the government taking responsibility, when private industry cannot or refuses to provide jobs, to guarantee adequate relief and jobs for workers. This is why the Communists propose that, for instance, the government should launch a huge program of socially needed public works, which will give employment to all able-bodied workers at trade union wages and working conditions, and will wipe out such public sorespots as slums and sub-standard living conditions in the rural areas. This is why the Communists further propose the immediate enactment of federal legislation providing for a five-day week, six-hour day in all industries and the establishment of a minimum annual wage guaranteeing an American standard of living. Similarly the Communists call for suitable amendments to the Social Security Act, which will create a unified national system of social insurance covering such hazards as unemployment, old age, maternity and sickness.

Q. *What is the Communist stand regarding employers' share-the-work policies?*

A. The Communist Party is opposed to employers' share-the-work plans, which in reality mean sharing the misery among the workers. Adequate relief and public works jobs should be furnished the unemployed. However, in certain seasonal industries, like the needle trades, the trade unions have developed a method called "equal division of work," a plan for sharing all available work during the slow seasons. This is an important demand and is supported by the Communists, because the peculiarities of these industries make equalization of work a practical necessity. Likewise, in the maritime industry, the Communists support the proposals of the unions of the seamen and longshoremen for establishing a rotation system of employment under the supervision and control of the unions themselves.

1939

PART FOUR

30. The Trade Unions and the War

The workers constitute by far the biggest, most progressive and most solidly anti-fascist section of our population. They are the vitalizing force that gives life to the national unity of workers, farmers, professionals, small businessmen, and capitalists, which stands behind the government for the winning of the war against Hitlerism. The workers furnish a huge portion of the armed forces, and they have the main task in carrying on production. Furthermore, their fullest political participation in the war effort is indispensable in order to offset business-as-usualism and fifth-column activities; to strengthen generally the anti-Hitler policy of the government; to develop the resolute type of armed struggle necessary to smash the Axis, and to provide guarantees for a just and lasting peace at the conclusion of the war.

Within the framework of national unity it is the duty of the workers—the class which has the most to lose by a Hitler victory and the most to gain by a Hitler defeat—to set a patriotic example for the rest of the population.

The workers have to take the lead in accepting willingly every sacrifice necessary to prosecute the war; they must be tireless in carrying out the multitudinous tasks of the war; they must make the defense of the nation in this crisis their supreme lodestar in all their activities.

At the same time, in building national unity and strengthening the war effort, the workers must protect their own living standards and safeguard their trade unions. Only healthy workers can give the best results, whether it be in industry or in the armed forces; and a strong and vigorous trade union movement is indispensable for the maintenance of American democracy and the successful prosecution of the war.

It is the supreme task of the trade unions, with their 11,000,000 members, to mobilize and lead the working class in performing its unflinching anti-Hitler role in the war. This task is doubly that of the trade unions because there is no broad farmer-labor party in the United States able to command the allegiance of the great masses of the working class. Nor is the Communist Party, despite its extensive influence, in a position of decisive political leadership. The masses of workers still look very much to the trade union leadership for political guidance.

The responsibility for developing the maximum war activities of the working class is not one that the trade unions may assume or reject as they see fit. It is a categoric *must,* placed upon them by history. The fulfillment of this big task is imperative, not only for the achievement of the greatest possible national war effort, but also for the health and progress of the trade unions themselves. In this crucial period, with the very life of our nation at stake, the trade union movement can be strong and grow vigorously only if its leadership is clearly conscious of the unions' historic responsibility as the war organizers of the working class.

THE TOTAL MOBILIZATION OF LABOR

Total war against Hitlerism requires that our people be organized and mobilized on a war basis more completely than ever before. To meet the present life-and-death national war crisis the government, despite entrenched defeatist elements, is straining itself to develop the utmost war power of our people; industry is being pushed to the accomplishment of a production program so great as to have been called "fantastic"; energetic steps are being taken to create a powerful army, air force, and navy; the financial strength of our nation is being developed on an unprecedented scale; entire local populations are being united for civilian defense; the whole lives of our people are being drastically changed and reshaped.

Therefore the trade union movement, which plays such a vital war role, must also be thoroughly mobilized, from top to bottom, so that it, too, can throw its maximum possible strength into the national war effort.

As things now stand, the trade unions are making a tremendous contribution to the nation's fight against Nazi Germany and its allies.

In industry, in the armed forces, in civilian defense, in the raising of war funds, everywhere that the war effort is taking shape, the workers and their trade unions, without fanfare or publicity, are to be found in the very forefront of our warring people's activities.

Nevertheless, considering the urgency of the war's relentless demands, there is still room for a vast improvement in the war work of the trade unions. Their total war mobilization remains far from complete. They have not yet risen to a full sense of their leading responsibility in the war; of the need for them to develop their own initiative to the utmost. There are still too many hangovers of trade-unionism-as-usual practices of pre-war days.

Labor as a whole especially needs a broad win-the-war program, covering all phases of the war effort, as indicated by the C. I. O. Steel Workers, New York Industrial Council, and other bodies. The unions' war work is going ahead too scatteredly. What is necessary is for the whole trade union movement to plan and to carry out its work far more systematically and with a better utilization of all its resources.

To this end it would be a highly advisable step for the A. F. of L., the C. I. O., and the Railroad Brotherhoods to call a broad national conference, as the C. I. O. Executive Board has already suggested, and there to work out their national war program and plan of action. Such a national conference, assembling together hundreds of delegates from all industries and all localities, would give an enormous stimulus to the war work of organized labor everywhere.

Such a national conference should be followed by local conferences in all the industrial centers of the country. These would further concretize the national win-the-war program on a local scale and organize the local forces to realize it. Already numerous localities have shown initiative along these lines.

Local joint committees, as proposed by the C. I. O. in its recent national conference, should be set up everywhere as the basis of labor's war work in the various communities. These local committees, formed by A. F. of L. and C. I. O. delegates on a broad and democratic basis, and establishing contacts with other pro-war groups and movements, could become powerful organizing forces in their respective spheres. They would give a real push to the local war work in all its phases. The present rudimentary war committees in many local unions could be strengthened and their work regularized; production could be stimulated, as could civilian defense, morale building, bond selling, war relief, etc.

A better mobilization of labor's forces for war can and should be brought about. To give the main push for this is primarily the job of the national leadership; but the unions in the localities should also use their own initiative. Labor, by the total mobilization of its forces for the war, must set the pace for our whole people. In doing so, labor will greatly strengthen the national war effort and also improve its own position in the country.

During the past few months reactionaries of all stripes—business-as-usual-ists, open shoppers, fifth columnists—taking advantage of the war situation and the fact that the trade unions have agreed not to strike during the war, have been delivering a ferocious offensive against the workers and their organizations. Proposals to wipe out the forty-hour week and eliminate overtime pay, to freeze wages, to outlaw the right to strike, to register the trade unions, to abolish the union shop, to do away with the right to organize, etc., etc., have literally flooded Congress.

The National Association of Manufacturers, the United States Chamber of Commerce, notorious anti-labor politicians such as Reynolds, Byrd, Hoffman, Hobbs, Smith, Vinson, etc., together with reactionary newspaper columnists and radio commentators of the kidney of Pegler and Kaltenborn, have all joined in the anti-labor drive.

If successful, this anti-labor drive would sharpen the class struggle, weaken national unity, and undermine the whole war effort. This is precisely what most of the professional open shoppers and defeatists have in mind. In fighting against this anti-labor drive, therefore, the unions are fighting for national unity and for the successful prosecution of the war.

Labor's best protection against such reactionaries is to intensify greatly its war work on every front, to become an ever more dynamic force in our national unity.

Labor, far more than at present, should stand out clearly to the nation as the great mass force working to win the war. Wherever war work is going on, there the trade unions should be found in the very forefront. Then the open shoppers and defeatists will find it virtually impossible to attack them successfully.

The trade unions should get out of their present defensive position. Once organized labor gets its forces fully lined up in a maximum all-out drive in war work, then, instead of being the object of such dangerous attacks as at present, it will move into a period of growth and popular prestige such as it has never before known.

THE BATTLE FOR PRODUCTION

In the production of the war materials so vitally needed to smash Hitler and his Axis, organized labor, especially the C. I. O., is making a splendid showing. The whole trade union movement, to insure continuous production, has laid aside the use of the strike for the duration of the war and, in order to increase production to the maximum, the unions are working in close collaboration with the government and the employers. If Donald Nelson, chief of the War Production Board, was able to say that the President's gigantic Victory Production Program would be achieved, or even surpassed, the American people have the loyal work of the trade unions largely to thank for it.

In the great battle for production the C. I. O., displaying outstanding leadership, has stood far in the forefront of the whole labor movement. With its Murray Industrial Councils plan and its specific production plans for the auto, steel, electrical, metal mining, maritime, farm equipment, communications, and various other industries, it has blazed the trail for both the government and the employers. Mr. Nelson's labor-management committees, which are securing fine results by increasing production in some 700 key war plants, are obviously suggested by the much more elaborate Murray Industrial Councils.

The A. F. of L. also has thrown itself wholeheartedly into the battle for production, calling upon its millions of workers to extend themselves in turning out the necessary war materials. The A. F. of L. unions, however, save in a few localities, do not occupy such key positions in the basic war industries as do the C. I. O. unions, nor have they shown an equal energy, planfulness, and militant leadership in the adaptation of their industries to war production.

Despite the generally excellent showing of the trade unions in war production there are, nevertheless, some weak spots which require improvements. First, regarding the many railroad unions. These organizations still seem to be going along pretty much on a trade-unionism-as-usual basis. The railroads, allowed to run down badly by their owners and now heavily overloaded with traffic, are perhaps the most serious bottleneck in the whole war production program. Yet, so far, the railroad unions, whose main spokesman is the Railway Labor Executives Association, have not come forward with plans for the adaptation of the railroads to the war situation and for government operation. There is a burning need for them to prepare a railroad program, and to play an active part in the railroad reorganization that the government and the employers are now putting through while the unions sleep on.

Another union weak spot in production is the United Mine Workers of America, headed by John L. Lewis. It is significant that this great organization of 600,000 miners, situated in a key industry, is the only basic union in the C. I. O. which has not developed a production plan. Lewis, who is busy "organizing" the farmers and trying to split the C. I. O., is not bothering his head over coal production. This is a reflection of his thinly disguised opposition to the war and his open hatred of the Roosevelt administration.

Organized labor as a whole has need to unify its efforts in production. This would greatly improve its work. To this end, a national production conference of the C. I. O., A. F. of L. and Railroad Brotherhoods would be very much in order. The conversion of the industries to a maximum war production is creating a host of problems for the unions. Among them a few are: the training and distribution of manpower, the entry of large masses of Negroes and women into war industry, the matter of incentive pay for higher production, questions of seniority, the modification of certain trade union rules, the problem of organizing the unorganized during war conditions, the preservation of the workers' health under the present industrial strain, the re-examination of apprenticeship regulations, etc., etc.

The wartime production and union problems in industry should not be allowed to accumulate or to find offhand local or sectional solutions. Nor can they be adjusted through separate actions by the A. F. of L. and C. I. O. top councils. The necessity for speeding the war production program, as well as the immediate welfare of the unions themselves, demands that these vital general problems be tackled in a basic, united and systematic way by the whole trade union movement. The best manner to do this would be through a national production conference, at which all branches of the labor movement were represented.

THE ANTI-INFLATION PROGRAM

The seven points presented to Congress recently by President Roosevelt are designed to avert the rapidly growing danger of inflation. They should be supported by organized labor, with insistence upon the necessity for periodic adjustments of wage rates by collective bargaining. Failure to do this is a big mistake.

A comprehensive anti-inflation program was long overdue to check soaring prices and skyrocketing profits. Experiences in England and Canada indicated the general direction it should go. Nevertheless, the trade unions were slow to formulate anything approaching an adequate broad economic program, although they support various price and profit control measures. And the unions are in the main still not fully alert to the great need for supporting President Roosevelt's seven points.

The failure of organized labor to speak out quickly and concretely on the vital economy question had bad consequences. With the cost of living going up daily and with popular unrest rising, the reactionaries were quick to try to put the responsibility on the trade unions. They shouted that it was all due to rising wages, and they delivered a slashing attack against the unions' rules calling for double time for Sunday work and against the federal forty-hour-week law, with its time and a half for overtime. The Peglers, Kaltenborns, and Hoffmans howled that the trade unions cared nothing for the war effort and paid attention only to their own economic interests. Many of these reactionaries demanded that the unions be curbed in various drastic ways. This violent campaign definitely put the unions on the defensive.

Now if the trade unions had promptly worked out a comprehensive war economy program and actively presented it to the nation, as they could have done, a quite different picture would have resulted. Organized labor would have been able to show, to vast numbers if not to all the people, that the rising cost of living was due basically to rising commodity prices and increasing profits, and also that raises in wages, including the application of the overtime provisions, were lagging far behind the advance in the cost of living.

This whole economy plan situation emphasizes a vital wartime lesson which organized labor should learn thoroughly. It is that the trade union leaders, freeing themselves completely from lingering trade-unionism-as-usual hangovers, must think and act boldly in terms of the entire nation and not only of the labor movement.

WARTIME WAGES, HOURS AND WORKING CONDITIONS

In approaching questions of wages, hours, and working conditions the trade unions' policy is necessarily based upon the national interest of winning the war. Our nation's present supreme needs call for a powerful armed force and a maximum munitions production; hence all trade union policy should be directed toward developing the workers' greatest productive and fighting efficiency.

Respecting wages, this means that the workers' present real wages should be essentially maintained, with improvements in those of the masses of workers now being paid substandard rates.

The President's seven-point anti-inflation program will, if adopted, check but not entirely halt the rising cost of living. Therefore, wage adjustments will be necessary, as in England, where even more drastic economic controls are in effect. Such adjustments are already overdue in several industries. While the President's anti-inflation program correctly tends toward a relative stabilization of wages, the workers should oppose rigid wage freezing in the face of rising living costs. In making wage proposals, the workers should propose adjustments to offset the increased cost of living, the greater strain placed upon the workers by intensified production, and to improve the at present excessively low wage levels of many workers. To keep the workers well-fed, healthy, and strong is a major requisite for winning the war, even as is the production of the physical well being of our fighting forces.

In all their handling of wages, working conditions, production problems, etc., the unions should insist upon the maintenance of the health of the workers as the minimum basis for stabilizing the economic standard of the workers.

Regarding hours, the goal for the unions to aim at should be the maximum possible production that will at the same time permit the workers to maintain their health and their maximum efficiency. But, while seeking to increase production, the trade unions should also be on the alert to defeat attempts by unscrupulous employers to extend unduly the work-day and work-week. Therefore the trade unions should insist resolutely upon the maintenance of the legal forty-hour week.

In the matter of working conditions, the trade unions need to show real flexibility. Some unions, especially in the A. F. of L., may have to modify certain of their working rules to facilitate increased production. Required modifications will become evident through the workings of labor-management committees. In making such changes the unions should guard against subtle attempts by the bosses to break their working standards, and they should also secure guarantees that the alterations made shall be continued only for the duration of the war. Where changes in working rules are obviously necessary they should be made boldly and quickly. Thus, in the recent case of the controversy over double time for Sunday work, organized labor would have fared much better if it had handled the matter promptly, before it became a national issue and put the unions on the defensive.

The workers should insist uncompromisingly upon the maintenance of collective bargaining during the war. They should also defend their right to organize and to establish the closed shop. Likewise, although temporarily giving up the strike in the war period and accepting decisions of the War Labor Board, the unions should protect their legal right to strike. The unions must not surrender their primary right to settle wages, hours, and working conditions in direct negotiations with the employers. The British unions have not given up such rights, nor should ours. The labor movement, during the war, must be on guard against open-shoppers, defeatists, and fascists who would hamstring and destroy it by robbing it of its power for collective bargaining.

In defending the economic standards of the workers during the war the trade unions should be especially keen to checkmate those elements, such as Lewisites, Trotskyites, Coughlinites, Thomasites, etc., who are urging the workers to grab what they can in the matter of wages. Such a policy would be doubly unwise. It would both militate against the winning of the war and would bring severe condemnation down upon the unions from the workers, the public, and the government. Also organized labor must now, as never before, be disciplined regarding strikes. It must not tolerate wildcat local walkouts and it must keep its eyes wide open to detect the pro-fascist elements who are seeking to provoke strikes in war industries. To sum up, in matters of wages, hours, and working conditions the trade unions should set a national example of patriotism, being guided constantly in their policy by a determination to win the war. This is the road to the maximum national war effort, to the greatest possible well-being of the workers, and to a strong and vigorous trade union movement.

THE UNIONS AND THE CLOSED SHOP

One of the most striking developments of the war is the extreme virulence of the reactionaries' fight against the closed shop.

Behind this fight there is a belief (and a hope) that the war has undermined the basic economic functions of the trade unions and that without the closed shop the unions cannot maintain themselves. With the agreement by the workers that sacrifices must be made to win the war; with their acceptance of wage stabilization, lengthening of the work week, and slackening of trade union shop conditions; and with their laying aside of the strike weapon for the duration—all these things made trade unions unnecessary, say these people, and the workers will, therefore, not continue to pay union dues without some form of compulsion. One hears this argument echoed in the press and on the radio, and even in some labor official circles.

Actually never were the unions more necessary to the workers or called upon to play a more vital role in our national life than now. Never were their tasks and responsibilities so heavy. The closed shop, the check-off, and the War Labor Board's new device of the "maintenance of membership," and similar member-holding plans are important and the unions should insist upon their establishment wherever possible; nevertheless they are by no means the life-and-death necessities that they have been painted both by some friends and many enemies. The health and growth of the trade unions must derive primarily from a fulfillment and active carrying out of the tasks that devolve upon the trade unions in this war period. These tasks all revolve within the wider framework of our nation's task of winning the war and smashing the Axis forces.

Among the trade unions' war tasks is the necessity to protect the welfare, health, and productive efficiency of the workers in the new war economy that is now taking shape. This involves keeping wages up to satisfactory levels, preventing undue extension of the work-week, insisting upon the maintenance of sound safety and housing conditions, working for the establishment of a just and effective system of rationing, price control, taxes, bond-buying, and other economic factors affecting the workers' living and working standards. In all these matters the intervention of the trade unions is of paramount importance.

Also, the trade unions in wartime are the very bulwark of our democratic liberties. They safeguard the American people's historic rights of free speech and free assembly, defend the body of social legislation from reactionary attack, and defeat the attempts of those who would try to make the United States into a fascist country while it is fighting Hitler. They see to it that centralized war controls over labor and industry are carried through democratically by the government.

Next there is the vital matter of achieving maximum war production. Here, too, through labor-management committees and otherwise, the trade unions have a most important function to fulfill. The workers appreciate this role, for no class in society is as anxious to defeat Hitler as they are.

Then there is the fundamental matter of helping shape the general war policies of the government. In this, as the very backbone of national unity, the trade union movement has influence of great weight, despite the fact that the unions are as yet very lacking in direct representation in the various war committees and boards, from the Cabinet on down. The stronger the trade unions, the stronger the nation's fight against Hitler.

There are a host of other war tasks which fall upon the trade unions, including the fight against the fifth column, an active participation in the vast network of civilian defense, the sale of government bonds, etc., etc.

The fact that these activities in defense of the workers' interests, in support of the war, are carried on mostly by political means, rather than by strikes, in no sense detracts from the role of the unions. These varied functions clearly furnish the groundwork for a vigorous trade union movement based upon voluntary membership.

There is no basic reason, therefore, why both the C. I. O. and A. F. of L. trade unions should not continue to make real growth during the war period. According to the latest figures of *Labour,* February, 1942, official organ of the British Trade Union Congress, the British trade unions increased in membership from 6,230,000 at the end of 1939 to 6,542,000 at the close of 1940. American trade unions can very easily do much better in strengthening themselves numerically.

To maintain and extend the trade union membership it would be folly simply to rely upon such measures as the closed shop, check-off, maintenance of membership clauses, etc., necessary though these may be. Three further major considerations are more important. The first of these is for the unions to prosecute vigorously their new wartime tasks; the second is for them to carry on wide educational work among the toiling masses to explain the role of the unions; the third is for them to unfold vigorous campaigns of membership recruitment. If these things are done systematically the American trade union movement will grow swiftly in numbers and influence during the war.

If the trade unions are to be able to mobilize their large membership and vast body of sympathizers for the fullest possible support of the war they need to be thoroughly represented in the government and in all its war committees, nationally and locally.

LABOR IN THE GOVERNMENT

As things stand organized labor is very poorly represented in the various stages of the government, from the top down. It has no members in the Cabinet; it is not heading a single one of the various new national war agencies, such as the War Production Board, the Office of Price Administration, the Selective Service Administration, the Office of Civilian Defense, the Office of Defense Transportation, nor is it to be counted among various industrial "bars." Only in the National War Labor Board is labor well represented. Only here and there does a trade union official hold a secondary or third-line post in the war set-up. The weakness of labor in the war apparatus of the government is further emphasized by the fact that the trade unions, because they have not built a labor party, are almost destitute of substantial and reliable representation in Congress and in the various state and local legislative bodies. The Roosevelt administration generally follows a liberal attitude toward the trade union movement, but not in the respect of entrusting it with decisive executive positions.

Why should not organized labor in this country, with its 11,000,000 members, who with their families constitute about one-third of the nation, have several posts in the President's War Cabinet, as is the case in Churchill's Cabinet in Great Britain? Who will assert that skilled trade union executives are not as competent for Cabinet war posts, for example, as the lawyers and business men who now fill them? Or that a labor man would not do a good job as head of some of the new national boards—say the Manpower Commission? Organized labor could furnish representatives who would do as well as, or better than, the present members. But conservative capitalist forces in the United States have not yet got around to the point where they are willing to make such concessions to the trade unions, and their hold-back influence is still decisive with the administration in the matter.

Organized labor itself is also partly to blame. It is altogether too modest in demanding government representation and responsible executive posts in the war administration. It is amazing how weak is the trade union demand for posts in Roosevelt's Cabinet, and also how calmly labor accepts third- or fourth-line war positions, while the decisive offices are handed to lawyers and business men, who are often quite without experience for their vital war functions. This all goes to show that the trade union movement, despite its great numerical strength, is not yet mature politically, nor is its top leadership fully conscious of the fundamental role that must be played by the working class and its main mass organizations, the trade unions, in this decisive moment of history.

Not long ago President Roosevelt organized the Victory Labor Board (sometimes called his War Labor Cabinet), composed of three representatives each from the A. F. of L. and the C. I. O., with himself as chairman. This represented an advance in the government's recognition of organized labor, as it enabled the trade union leadership to reach the President quickly and often with their proposals. But this board has neither legislative nor executive power; it is only advisory in character. This board should not be considered by organized labor as a substitute for posts in the President's Cabinet, nor for decisive executive leadership in the various war boards.

In pre-war days it would have been correct for organized labor not to accept appointive Cabinet positions in the capitalist government, as this would have circumscribed its independence and hindered its defense of the workers' interests. But today organized labor is supporting the war against Hitlerism, and it must be allowed its full weight in the government's organization of the national war effort. In insisting upon the fullest representation in the President's Cabinet and in the various war boards, organized labor is not merely asserting its right of democratic representation; it is especially advocating a fundamental measure vitally needed to strengthen national unity and to win the war.

THE WORKERS AND FOREIGN POLICY

One of the major responsibilities thrust upon organized labor by the war is to use its great influence in shaping every phase of the government's foreign policy. Yet, of all the widespread war work of the trade unions, this is perhaps the weakest. The trade unions have endorsed the war against the Axis and are giving the government their hearty support. But that is about as far as they go in the matter of foreign policy. Seldom do top trade union leaders (especially those of the A. F. of L.) speak out definitely on important international questions of policy; such as, for example, relations among the powers constituting the United Nations; the status of India and China; the government's attitude toward Vichy France, Finland, and Spain; the question of establishing a Western Front in Europe; the statement of our war aims, etc. Exceptions to this general rule were the recent splendid meetings of the United Steelworkers of America and the C. I. O. Executive Board.

This failure of the trade unions to interest themselves more positively in the shaping of American foreign policy is a great weakness, and at the same time it is an expression of their lack of an alert spirit of internationalism. This is a people's war, and such basic people's organizations as the trade unions must play the utmost possible active role in formulating international policies. The recent splendid convention of the C. I. O. steel workers showed a great advance in this respect.

Moreover, the war situation imperatively demands that the American and British trade union movements not only exercise vigorously their democratic strength in helping shape the policies of their own governments, but that they also co-operate actively with the other big democratic forces of the world, including the colonial and semi-colonial countries (India, China, Latin America, etc.), the peoples of Nazi-occupied Europe, and the Soviet Union—that is, in every way to influence democratically the international policies of the United Nations.

The democratic forces of the world must help shape the course of the war if the war is truly to accomplish its anti-fascist purposes. In all the capitalist countries of the United Nations there are powerful reactionary forces, saturated with fascist tendencies, who are ceaselessly trying to twist the war to serve their predatory interests. In the United States we have plenty of these fifth-column and near-fifth column elements, in the Hoovers, Lindberghs, Hearsts, Byrds, Reynoldses, Dieses, Pattersons, Hoffmans, Howards, Kaltenborns, Peglers, Coughlins, Smiths, Norman Thomases and John L. Lewises, etc. Such people have a background of Munichism and appeasement of Hitler. They try to force upon their governments the "defense" strategy which led from one defeat to another; they would gladly support a negotiated peace with Hitler which would give him victory and they can be counted upon to do everything possible to reconstruct the post-war world on a fascist model.

To win this war and to establish a just and lasting peace it is imperative that the world democratic forces overcome the sinister influence of the reactionary elements who are trying to shield fascism from overwhelming defeat. The trade union movements of the United States and the British Empire must become decisive forces in outlining the foreign policies of their governments; the representatives of the peoples of the occupied and colonial countries should come forward militantly in the making of world policy; the United Nations must grow from its present status of a narrow United States-British controlled body into a full-fledged military alliance between the United States, Great Britain, the U.S.S.R., China, India, and the rest of the co-operating nations.

The meaning of all this for the American trade union movement is that it must interest itself far more than at present in questions of foreign policy. A general endorsement and support of the war are not enough. The trade union movement, top and bottom, should speak out quickly and act vigorously regarding every aspect of the rapidly changing world situation. Organized labor needs to liquidate the last remnants of isolationism and become truly international in its outlook and activities.

The most vital single question now before the American and British peoples is that of establishing a Western Front this spring in Europe to catch Hitler in the trap of a two-front war. Organized labor should join its strength with those broad popular forces who are demanding this new front against Nazi Germany. Unfortunately, however, seldom do we hear the voice of a top labor official or of a strong union in the widespread debate that is now taking place in the press, on the radio, and in the legislative halls upon this most important issue. The action of the Steel Workers' convention, in endorsing a second front, showed the growing union sentiment on this question.

LABOR AND THE U.S.S.R.

One of the most basic tasks put upon the shoulders of the American trade union movement by the war is to cultivate the closest possible fighting relations between the United States and the Soviet Union. To win the war these two great countries must become allies, friendly and co-operative, in the fullest sense of the word. They should be equal partners in a powerful United Nations military alliance. To accomplish this the great trade union movement in this country can contribute greatly.

Today the U.S.S.R. is carrying the main burden of the struggle against the chief foe, Hitler. The fate of world humanity, including our own national independence and freedom, rests upon the Soviets' ability to hold off Hitler's armies. The Red Army is magnificently fulfilling the great historic task that has fallen upon it, of defending world democracy from the fascist barbarians. President Roosevelt recently said: "On the European front, the most important development of the past year has been the crushing offensive on the part of the great armies of Russia against the powerful German army." In the same vein Lord Beaverbrook stated: "The Russians kill more Germans every day than all the Allies put together." And General MacArthur put it correctly when he declared: "The hopes of civilization rest on the worthy banners of the courageous Russian Army." Former Ambassador to the U.S.S.R., Joseph E. Davies, hit the nail of American public opinion squarely on the head when he declared recently: "We say to the government, Red Army and Soviet people, 'Hold the fort, for we are coming.'"

The need for close understanding and working relations between the U.S.A. and the U.S.S.R. is now particularly urgent. Hitler and his friends and dupes in this country, using the divide and conquer strategy, are trying to drive a wedge between this country and the Soviet Union, on the lying basis that the Soviet government intends to make a separate peace; that Japan, not Nazi Germany, is our main enemy; that co-operation with the U.S.S.R. means a tacit acceptance of communism; that the Russians do not need our help, and many similar representations. Especially are these fifth-column elements trying to prevent the United States and Great Britain from establishing a great Western Front in Europe which could, in collaboration with the Red Army, smash Hitler this year.

Both the C. I. O. and the A. F. of L. have endorsed our government's policy of extending munitions aid to the U.S.S.R., and recent news dispatches inform us that Presidents Green and Murray of the A. F. of L. and C. I. O., and President Whitney of the Railroad Trainmen have become members of the Board of Directors of Russian War Relief, Inc. Nevertheless, the top leadership of our labor movement has been slow in this whole question. There is need for strengthening trade union official policy in respect to solidifying the bonds between the U.S.A. and the U.S.S.R.

Especially is it necessary for the A. F. of L., C. I. O. and Railroad Brotherhoods to link themselves with the Anglo-Soviet Trade Union Committee, as the recent steel workers' convention proposed. Our trade union leaders should feel honored to clasp hands in international solidarity with the representatives of the heroic Soviet working class, and the membership of their unions would applaud them for doing so.

The Anglo-Soviet Trade Union Committee has great potentialities —to tighten the relations between the three respective governments, to increase war materials production in the respective countries, to help keep the war on a truly anti-Hitler basis, to help provide guarantees that the eventual peace will be a just and lasting one.

American organized labor is becoming increasingly conscious of its responsibility to help bring about a betterment of relations with our great Soviet neighbor. This is shown by the growing number of C. I. O. and A. F. of L. unions that are speaking out upon the matter. Our trade union movement, casting off its swaddling clothes of isolationism like the rest of our people, is moving toward playing its proper international role. This can be done adequately only in fraternal affiliation with the British and Russian unions in the Anglo-Soviet Trade Union Committee.

WARTIME DEMOCRACY

To conduct total war effectively against Hitlerism it is imperative that the government set up, as it is doing, a whole series of strongly centralized wartime controls. Among these are: conscription for the armed forces, general registration of manpower, rationing of everyday necessities, priorities in industry, the compulsory conversion of plants to war purposes, the seizure of incompetently operated plants, the establishment of industrial "tsars," price control, restrictions upon the press to guard military secrets, the imposition of vast financial burdens, etc., etc. Such necessary centralizing measures need not, however, be anti-democratic in their effects.

Powerful reactionary forces—in the government, in industry, in public life generally—are seeking to take advantage of the war situation by attacking American democracy fundamentally. Their spokesmen argued before the war that if we fought Hitler we must become a fascist country ourselves, and they are trying to make this lying statement come true. They are especially attacking the trade unions, trying to abolish their right to strike, to organize and to function in behalf of the workers, they are assailing such vital social legislation as the Wagner Act, and the Wages and Hours Act; they are vilifying and persecuting the Negroes and the foreign-born. They hope, by thus undermining democracy, to sabotage the war and to move toward fascism in this country.

This makes it necessary for organized labor, in conjunction with other popular forces, to use actively its vast influence for the preservation and strengthening of American democracy in these crucial war times. First, there is the whole group of tasks connected with making the new wartime government controls work democratically. The unions must help see to it that press restrictions are directed only against defeatists and betrayers of military secrets, and that the right of constructive criticism is maintained; that the price control regulations are carried out vigorously and without fear or favor; that labor's right of collective bargaining is carefully guarded; that the rationing of necessities is fairly administered; that the distribution of manpower within the industries is democratically regulated; that the tax burden and the sale of war bonds are justly distributed; that no social legislation is sacrificed to the defeatists; that the economic standards of the workers are protected so as to insure our nation's health and war efficiency.

Then there are the vital tasks indispensable for directly combating the fifth column, the defeatists and the appeasers; including the liquidation of the Christian Front, Ku Klux Klan, and other definitely fascist, war-sabotaging movements; the jailing of such pro-fascist elements as Coughlin, Smith, Deatherage and Dennis; the impeachment of Martin Dies and the liquidation of his fake committee; the political defeat of such reactionary figures as Reynolds, Nye, Byrd, Wheeler, Hoffman, Vinson, Cox, etc.; a careful and thoroughgoing check-up of saboteurs in industry; the cleansing from the radio of such defeatist types as Kaltenborn, Boake Carter and Norman Thomas; the complete suppression of the fascist press and the public condemnation of the defeatist Hearst, Patterson, McCormick, and Scripps-Howard newspapers; the breaking of the influence of John L. Lewis, W. L. Hutcheson, and others of their like in the labor movement; the refusal of responsible war posts to the Lindberghs, Kennedys, Bullitts, and others of their stripe.

The spokesmen of labor, in the press, over the radio, on the public platform, should be the leaders (which they are not yet, save in a few instances) in the struggle against every move, ideological or otherwise, made by the fifth column. The fight against the appeasers and defeatists is not simply the affair of the federal government; it is most of all the task of the masses of the people themselves, which means, in first line, of the trade union movement.

Finally, there is the whole maze of problems relating to the positive strengthening of our democratic institutions; such as the further building up of the trade unions; the securing of full representation of organized labor in the Cabinet and all war boards, national, state, and local; the broadest possible extension of labor-management co-operation in industry; the democratic development of the people's organizations of civilian defense; the infusion of a democratic spirit and regime into all branches of the armed services; the ready acceptance of women in all branches of industry; the accordance of full economic, political and social rights to the Negro people; the establishment of trade union unity; the close co-operation of all people's organizations—economic, political, cultural, national, etc.—for the prosecution of the war; the creation of a broad network of local committees to organize the great masses of the people for war work.

If this war is to be won and the peace to be a satisfactory one the United States must fight the war on a democratic basis and come out of the war a more democratic country than before. This requires that the labor movement, far more than it has done up to date, must pay close attention to the democratic tasks connected with the war. Hitler can be defeated only by peoples democratically inspired and organized. Let the United States, and especially its great trade union movement, not be wanting in this vital qualification for winning the war.

LABOR AND JOHN L. LEWIS

The most serious obstacle within labor's ranks against an all-out effort of the trade union movement in support of the war is John L. Lewis and his organized henchmen. Lewis' line is to make a feeble pretense of endorsing the war and then to hinder it in various ways. His policy is detrimental to the national war effort, to the economic well-being of the workers, to the welfare of the trade union movement.

Lewis' "endorsement" of the war, mere lip-service, is essentially the anti-war line of his Republican friends, Hoover and Landon, and it merges into that of the Trotskyites and Thomasites. The fascist Father Coughlin knew what he was doing when, in *Social Justice,* he gave Lewis a flaring endorsement. Lewis, like Lindbergh, has formally "accepted" the war, but he has never even made a speech for it; he is a bitter-ender opponent of the Roosevelt administration, and he has done virtually nothing (outside of some bond buying which he could hardly escape) to mobilize his great union in support of the war. Hitler could not be beaten in a thousand years were the country to undertake the job in the spirit of Lewis' milk-and-water "support."

As before December 7, Lewis is an isolationist, an opponent of the war. If he does not speak out his real sentiments more frankly it is because if he did he would be swept out of office at once by the patriotic miners.

Lewis' opposition to the war takes the form, besides his hostility to the Roosevelt administration, of a series of disruptive activities which tend to weaken the war effort of organized labor generally. First there is his bizarre attempt to organize the farmers into the United Mine Workers. The farmers belong not inside the trade unions, but in organizations of their own, which should work in collaboration with the labor movement. The general effects of Lewis' efforts to organize the farmers are to strengthen reactionary forces among them (as in New York State); to throw the labor movement into inner strife over the question; to create bad blood between the organized farmers and the trade unions, and to weaken national unity.

Next, there are Lewis raids upon A. F. of L. unions through his Construction Workers and his nondescript District 50 of the U. M. W. A., headed by his brother and his daughter, respectively. These disruptive activities make unity more difficult between the A. F. of L. and the C. I. O., thereby lessening their combined war effort and to that extent undermining national unity. They show that his present proposals for unity between the A. F. of L. and the C. I. O. were based on false pretenses.

Then there is Lewis' effort to split the C. I. O. Here we have the spectacle of a labor autocrat, who has suppressed democracy in his great union and has the bulk of the membership living under "provisional government" arbitrarily appointed by himself, deliberately trying to pull the Miners' Union out of the C. I. O. contrary to the will of the working miners. To prepare for this union-splitting and anti-war step, Lewis is doing his best to discredit the leadership of Philip Murray and to throw the whole C. I. O. into confusion. His removal of Murray from his office of vice-president was the action of an autocrat.

Finally, there is Lewis' avowed intention to "clean house" in the United Mine Workers by eliminating those officials—Murray, Van Bittner, Fagan and others who are loyally and actively supporting the war—a disruptive move which has created a sharp factional situation in that union and greatly weakened it as a constructive force within the anti-Hitler national unity. It is sinister that Lewis is covering up this anti-war move by vicious red-baiting against Murray.

The workers will do well to understand clearly the anti-war policies of John L. Lewis and the danger they present to labor and the
union. His refusal to dissociate himself from such America First elements as Lindbergh, Landon, Hutcheson and company; his failure to
mobilize his union for active war work; his embroiling of the farmers
against the workers; his efforts to drive a wedge between the A. F.
of L. and the C. I. O.; his attempt to split the C. I. O.; his maneuvers
to plunge the U. M. W. A. into internal turmoil; his relentless opposition to the Roosevelt administration—all show conclusively that
Lewis is against the war and that his pretended endorsement of it is
only to shield himself from the wrath of the anti-fascist miners. Lewis'
anti-war activities disqualify him for labor leadership. The sinister
portent he holds for the future is evidenced by the fact that he is the
favorite labor leader for many appeasers, defeatists, and fascists.

THE UNIONS AND THE NEGRO PEOPLE

It has long been a national disgrace the shameful way the Negro
people are discriminated against—in politics, in industry, in the armed
forces, in social life. The treatment accorded them is more in line
with Hitlerite race oppression than in the tradition of a free people.
In this war the Negro question is coming to a head and is insistently
demanding attention from our people and the government, and especially from the trade union movement.

During recent years the Negro people have grown enormously in
political strength. They are no longer, and justly so, in a mood to
tolerate the discriminatory abuses which are constantly visited upon
them. This war has dramatized the evils from which the Negroes
suffer, and it is stimulating them to demand redress. Especially so
since reactionaries and defeatists, eager to weaken the war effort however they can, are redoubling their efforts to discriminate against Negroes in the war industries, in housing projects, in the armed forces,
and everywhere else.

The question of Negro discrimination has become an issue of
grave national importance. At a time when complete unity of our
people for the struggle against Hitler is so urgently needed, it is a
matter of the utmost concern that among the 13,000,000 Negroes, considerable sections are in doubt that this is really their war. Moreover,
the matter also takes on an international significance; for the Nazis
working among the Arab peoples and the Japanese working among

the Asiatics have made wide, and not ineffective, use of the fact that Negroes in this country are so barbarously discriminated against.

The Roosevelt administration recognizes the present great importance of the Negro question and it has taken some steps to alleviate it. There was President Roosevelt's order to admit Negro workers to employment in the war industries and also Secretary Knox's ruling to permit the regular enlistment of Negroes in the navy. But there is still too much concern in government circles for the tender feelings of the poll-tax Congressmen of the South and for Negro-baiters in general. Discrimination against Negroes remains rampant in the industries, in the army and navy, and elsewhere.

For this situation, which is a disgrace to American democracy, the trade union movement bears a heavy share of responsibility, both by sins of commission and of omission. Many craft unions have long barred Negroes from membership and have also objected to their employment in industry. Particularly are the railroad unions guilty of such reactionary Jim-Crow practices. The A. F. of L., while adopting liberal resolutions regarding Negro discrimination, has dodged about and never taken real action to scourge the cancer of Jim Crowism from its affiliated organizations. It is only since the rise of the C. I. O. unions that the Negroes have been able to get real consideration in broad sections of organized labor.

The need for national unity demands that discrimination against the Negro people be discontinued. The Negroes must be granted full citizenship in every sense of the word. Above all, the trade union movement should free itself quickly and completely from all traces of Jim Crowism in its ranks and use actively its great political and economic influence in behalf of Negro rights. The fight for democratic justice to the Negro people is one of the major tasks of the trade unions in this people's war.

WOMEN WAR WORKERS

In great and rapidly increasing numbers women are engaging in industry, in war relief work, in civilian defense, and now they are even being inducted into the armed forces. In the United States women are beginning to perform the vital war role that they have long since been doing in England and, above all, in the U.S.S.R.

Especially important is the entry of women in large numbers into the war industries. Already many thousands are employed in the aircraft and other war plants. The *American Federationist* for March estimates that "several million women will be brought into war production." Also, the government is contemplating registering all women up to 65 for war services.

Women in war industries are doing many kinds of work which were hitherto considered to be impossible for them. Their industrial capacities are coming as a big surprise to conservative labor leaders and industrial managers alike. But really to see what women are capable of industrially one has to look to the U.S.S.R., where, it has been recently reported in press dispatches, the majority of workers now in industrial production are women, and that agriculture is being carried on overwhelmingly by them.

The big influx of women workers into American industry presents many important problems to the trade union movement. They must be trained for their jobs; they must be unionized, educated for union leadership, be given the fullest union protection regarding equality of pay, etc. As yet, however, the trade unions seem only vaguely aware of the new problems. So far, neither the C. I. O. nor the A. F. of L. has developed any program.

Traditionally the trade unions in this country have held very conservative positions regarding women workers generally. Save in the garment trades, the textile industry, and a few other occupations, there has been a widespread tendency to look upon women workers as rivals for the all too few jobs, instead of as fellow workers. In many instances unions have vigorously objected to women entering their trades.

A striking manifestation of the traditional trade union neglect and underestimation of women workers is the almost complete absence of women in top trade union leadership. Neither the A. F. of L. nor the C. I. O. has found it necessary to include even one woman representative in its executive council. And women are as rare as white blackbirds in the decisive committees of all but a very few of the national unions in both federations of labor. The C. I. O., true to its generally more progressive trend, has shown increasing concern about women workers, but even here there is a great lack.

Organized labor should take up promptly and energetically the burning problem of women in war industry. This it ought to do, not only to strengthen the national war effort, but also from the standpoint of trade union organization and practice. After this war women are going to be a far greater factor in industry than ever before. Large numbers of those now working in plants will remain there after the war—which will be one of the democratic achievements of the war. The trade unions must incorporate these women workers within their ranks. Under no circumstances, therefore, can the question of the woman worker in war industry be slurred over or neglected on the grounds that it is only a temporary, wartime problem.

What is necessary is a national trade union conference on the question of women workers in industry and agriculture. Such a conference, made up of delegates from both the C. I. O. and A. F. of L., could work out a comprehensive program to meet the situation. The gathering, representing all localities and industries, could take up every angle of the problems of the new women war workers and give organized labor a clear lead on them. The woman worker is now here in vastly larger numbers than ever before and she is going to stay; hence her problems must be attended to and her voice heard in the highest councils of the trade union movement and the government.

THE WAR AND THE YOUTH

The war against Hitlerism has developed a host of youth problems —new, vast, and pressing. These relate to the building and functioning of the armed forces, the mass of which are made up of the youth, the entry of huge numbers of young people, especially girls, into industry, and the big role being played by the youth, and children, in a wide variety of civilian war activities.

It is imperative that the trade unions interest themselves closely in all these new youth activities, for two vital reasons. The first and main one is that only thus, with the help of the unions, will our nation be able to develop to the fullest the tremendous fighting and working power of the youth, upon whom falls the chief burden of winning the war. The second reason is the need for the unions to establish the closest liaison with the youth in all their war activities, for already we can see the reactionaries, who hope for a post-war youth violently anti-union, trying to drive a wedge between the young men in the armed forces and the trade unions. As yet, however, the trade unions do not realize the great importance of the new youth problems and they are but scatteringly working for their solution. I can give here only a bare indication of the line trade union youth activities should now take.

The trade unions should develop the closest possible relation with the armed forces. They should insist upon the maintenance of a democratic spirit and an efficient leadership in the army and navy. They should fight there against Jim Crowism. They should make all efforts so that dependents of soldiers and sailors are properly taken care of. Trade union influence should be actively present in all the educational and entertainment work carried on among the troops. Members in the service should be kept in good standing in the unions, furnished with trade union journals, and corresponded with regularly by local union officials and members. The jobs of workers now in the service should be guaranteed them upon demobilization. At every point the fraternal, co-operative bonds between the trade unions and the armed forces should be cultivated and strengthened.

In industry the trade unions should see that the vast numbers of new young workers are properly trained; each union should have a job-training program. The crafts must be opened to the youth. There should be an easing of union initiation fees and apprenticeship regulations. Particular attention should be paid to the special problems presented by young Negro workers and girls. Every effort should be made to unionize the new armies of young workers and also to invigorate the trade union officialdom by entrusting to the youth responsible leading posts.

In civilian war activities, also, the trade unions should pay special attention to the youth. They should take the initiative in establishing Youth Auxiliaries in Civilian Defense. In war bond and stamp selling, in the salvage of waste materials, and in a host of other ways, the youth, including even small children, are a very important factor. The trade unions should see to it that their youth participate in all these civilian war activities, in full strength, in an organized manner, and under trade union leadership.

The trade unions are doing a tremendous service to the youth in the armed forces by helping furnish them a great flood of munitions with which to fight the enemy. They are also co-operating deeply with the youth by defending American democracy and maintaining the economic standards of the workers during wartime, so that the youth, when the war is over, may find democratic freedom in the country and some measure of job protection. But such general activities, important though they may be, are not enough. The trade unions need to take up every angle and detail of the problems of youth in wartime and devote the closest attention to them. The unions should set up youth committees in their organizations and apply themselves to youth activities including mass sports, educational activities, etc. Only in this way can the full strength of the patriotic American youth be organized for the war, can the trade union movement derive the benefit of a great influx of youthful vitality, and can there be adequate safeguards erected against the attempts of fascist-minded reactionaries to mislead the youth in the post-war world. The potentialities are here for a great patriotic youth movement in which the unions can be a decisive factor.

TRADE UNION UNITY

The question of unity of action between the C. I. O., A. F. of L., and Railroad Brotherhoods is of national importance as a war necessity. It is indispensable to secure the fullest and most effective mobilization of the workers in the total war effort of the nation; hence it has much more significance than the immediate interest of the labor movement itself.

Since Pearl Harbor much progress has been made toward labor unity. In a great number of localities joint actions have been developed between the A. F. of L. and C. I. O. organizations around war issues. Also, the head officials of both federations have come into closer co-operation in the War Labor Board and in the Victory Labor Board; by their agreement amicably to settle jurisdictional disputes; by their co-operative work in national radio broadcasts; by the joint appearance of Presidents Green and Murray on the same platform in Pittsburgh, etc.

Nevertheless the progress toward trade union unity has been somewhat slow and hesitant in high trade union official circles. The tempo of developing labor's co-operation should be speeded up. What is needed is greater boldness and planfulness. At all stages the A. F. of L., C. I. O. and Railroad Brotherhoods should link up for war work. In every locality there should be joint labor committees, as proposed by the recent C. I. O. national conference, which could develop a whole program of energetic war activities. The state federation and state industrial councils of the A. F. of L. and C. I. O., which are now generally holding their conventions, could exchange delegates and establish joint state committees for war work. Similar action might be taken by the various national unions in the given industries. In the same spirit, it would be timely for the executive councils of the A. F. of L. and C. I. O. to exchange at least fraternal delegates, or, better yet, to hold a joint meeting; or, still better, to call a broad C. I. O.-A. F. of L. national conference to work out labor's win-the-war program. At the coming national conventions of the two federations, too, delegates could be exchanged and a broad all-labor war committee established.

Joint labor action carried on upon such a broad and intensive scale as this would greatly increase labor's war efforts on all fronts. It would also add to labor's prestige throughout our nation. The first and hardest steps toward labor unity have already been taken; the labor movement, animated by an eager win-the-war spirit, has broken through the factional walls developed during the big split. What remains to be done is to give real expression to the powerful unity spirit prevailing throughout all sections of the labor movement.

Within the scope of the developing trade union unity, with its accompanying internal constructive criticism, there is also the need to cultivate the spontaneous war activities of the great membership masses. The workers are enthusiastically supporting the national war effort, and their role is not simply to wait for detailed instructions from above. Every local union, every central labor body, every state council, every national union, of both the C. I. O. and A. F. of L., should be animated with a sense of responsibility for the war effort and encouraged to take the initiative in war work. In cultivating this sense of spontaneity and initiative in war work by the local labor bodies, all pro-war forces, including the Communists, have a very important task.

If the trade union leadership bears a heavy responsibility in the present war situation, so, too, do the Communists and other left wingers, whether they are union officials or not. They must know how to organize collaboration with leaders and forces with whom they had long been in opposition; they must learn how to make their criticisms and programs non-factional and non-sectarian; they must develop the initiative of the masses without antagonizing leaders who are genuinely supporting the war. In sum, they must at all times keep their eyes upon the main task of winning the war and of mobilizing to the utmost labor's unity and strength to this end.

The present trend of the A. F. of L., C. I. O. and Railroad Brotherhoods to co-operate together in support of the war is also the most practical path to eventual full trade union unity. It is unlikely that the trade unions will again try to achieve unity by the virtually impossible route of first settling all their jurisdictional overlapping by formal conferences, as some are now urging. Such an attempt could end in an impasse and a deepening of the split, as it did before. Far better would it be for the two groups of unions to continue to develop their present co-operative relations, leaving jurisdictional disputes to be taken care of piecemeal and with their complete settlement not to be posed as a condition for national joint labor co-operation as proposed by the C. I. O.; a combined C. I. O.-A. F. of L. committee could be set up to deal with general matters of interest to each group of unions. This course could soon lead to joint conferences or even conventions of both organizations, and otherwise lead toward organizational trade union unity.

1942

31. The Political Maturing of Labor

Beginning about ten years ago, the relatively weak and primitive trade union movement in this country took a great step forward in the broad campaign of the C. I. O. to organize the unorganized workers. The general result was that today industrial unionism is solidly established, most of the basic industries have been organized, and the numerical strength of all the unions has leaped from about 3,000,000 in 1934 to over 13,000,000 at the present time.

Now the trade unions are in the midst of another tremendous stride forward. This is a rapid politicalization of the labor movement; a much more active and extensive intervention of the working class in the political life of our country and the world. This movement of labor politicalization will prove not less important than the organization of ten million workers during the past decade. It signifies that our vast labor movement is now entering into a new and higher stage of political understanding, strength and responsibility.

The first decisive sign of the new political status of American organized labor was seen in the greatly extended activity of the C. I. O. and of many A. F. of L. organizations during the recent political campaign. And the significance of the new political activities of labor is that, instead of the trade unions allowing their political movement to fall to pieces now that victory has been won by the progressive forces, the unions will go on to develop new and intense forms of political action. This was the meaning of the decision of the C. I. O. convention to continue and expand the Political Action Committee. Some of the more progressive A. F. of L. bodies, including the Pennsylvania Federation of Labor, have also decided to continue their political action committees.

Organized labor, in collaboration with its progressive allies, will henceforth take on increased interest in politics that will be something new in the American scene. The unions will be far more active factors in the constantly recurring local, state, and national elections; they will also pay much closer attention to the legislation that comes before Congress and the various state legislatures and city councils.

At least four major reasons may be listed as to why organized labor is now making its historical advance into the field of politics.

First, practically every important question that now confronts the trade unions is political in character. Wages, hours and working conditions, questions which not long ago were matters solely for negotiation between employers and workers, are now political matters of first rank. So, also, are a host of other questions of social security, price control, employment, and the maintenance of high levels of production. War conditions accentuate the need for the government to keep its hand in such matters; but it is certain also that even after the war is over the extent of the government's control over these questions will be so great that the workers will be unable to defend their interests without carrying out an organized policy of political action.

A second basic reason for labor's increased political activity from now on is the fact, well realized by the workers, that in this country there is a strong and ruthless opposition which, if victorious, would not only lower the workers' living standards and undermine their unions, but would also open the road to a World War III. Hence, in rapidly increasing measure, the workers are concluding that they must enter the political arena and make their great weight count for progress.

Thirdly, organized labor's politicalization is coming at this time because the unions have become numerically strong enough to be a very potent factor in politics. This they demonstrated in the recent elections. So long as the trade unions counted only two or three million members their political influence was potentially not great; but now that they have 13,000,000 members, they constitute a stupendous force which can be readily organized.

Lastly, an important contributing element in labor's present expanding political activities is the progressive character of the C. I. O. leadership. The reactionaries at the head of the A. F. of L. Executive Council and of many of its affiliated unions are seriously hindering the political growth of the labor movement; but, as against this reactionary force, the C. I. O. leaders are definitely stimulating politically all sections of labor, including the advanced sections of the A. F. of L. and Railroad Brotherhoods.

To further this political development of labor is of the most vital importance. Here we confront many serious problems. One of the most basic tasks is for the unions to learn that their programs must be formulated not only in the class interest of the workers, but in the general interest of the nation as well. Unless labor takes this broad stand the workers and the people as a whole will never be able to cope with the grave national and international problems of this wartorn world. The C. I. O. convention especially distinguished itself by acting in this national, patriotic sense, in contrast with the narrow line of the A. F. of L. convention.

Besides this, there is the grave need for trade union unity, both nationally and internationally. The historic importance of the C. I. O.'s participation in the London world trade union conference and also of President Murray's offer of political co-operation with the A. F. of L. lies in the fact that these two lines of action are entirely in tune with, and indispensable for, the great politicalization development now taking place in the ranks of American labor. Only by such co-operation on a national and world scale can organized labor meet the heavy political responsibilities that have been placed upon it by the whole course of military, economic, and political events.

Lastly, the progressive forces in the A. F. of L. must not allow themselves to be hamstrung politically by the reactionaries and dead wood in the Executive Council. They must give a strong political lead to the workers, jointly with the C. I. O., as was done in the Presidential elections. The political advance of the American working class cannot be blocked by A. F. of L. reactionary leaders.

It is of the utmost importance that the leaders and the most advanced sections of the labor movement should realize fully the character and significance of the broad politicalization that is now taking place in the ranks of the labor unions. Only by understanding this political movement can one grasp the meaning of the new period that American labor unionism is now entering into and be prepared to carry out the great tasks connected with this new status of our trade unions. With this present entry into politics on a mass scale as never before, a whole new horizon of responsibility and achievement opens up before the labor movement. Let us do our part to see that these glowing possibilities are realized speedily and in full.

1944

32. Trade Unions in the Soviet Union

In the Soviet Union, where the workers and farmers rule, the trade unions play a most vital part. Gigantic in size, comprising before the war some 26,000,000 members, or about 85 per cent of all workers, they are a mainspring of Soviet life. Lenin, at the Fifth Trade Union Congress in 1919, indicated their role as follows:

Precisely because political power has passed over into the hands of the proletariat, it is necessary for the trade unions to come forward on an increasing scale *as the architects of the new society.*

The Soviet political system rests upon broad, democratic mass organizations of the people, formed for every conceivable purpose: economic, political, military, cultural, etc. Stalin has listed the main great foundation organizations in the order of: trade unions, local Soviets, collective farm organizations, and the Communist Party. As the basic organization of the working class, the trade unions' chief task is to concern themselves with all questions affecting the immediate welfare of the workers, including wages and working conditions, production, labor protection, social insurance, cultural matters, housing, etc. They are a basic factor in the development of industry. They also play a vital role in all other issues affecting the general welfare of the Soviet nation. Especially since the U.S.S.R.'s involvement in the war have their responsibilities become heavy and involved. No major question of policy is decided by the Soviet government without trade union consultation. In no other country in the world is the influence of the trade unions anywhere near so great as in the U.S.S.R.

Are the Soviet trade unions free, in the sense of leading an autonomous existence within the U.S.S.R.? The answer to this question is that they are far more independent than the trade unions in any capitalist country. But let us see first just what is meant by "free" trade unions. In all capitalist lands, including the United States, trade union freedom is limited indeed. Facing capitalist controlled governments, hostile employer organizations, reactionary newspapers, and restrictive legislation that barely gives them room to breathe, the trade unions in the capitalist countries, without exception, are constantly menaced with attack by class enemies. They always run the danger of being forced into illegality or of being actually wiped out, notwithstanding such formal "recognition" as they may have achieved after many decades of hard struggle. Under the Weimar Republic the German trade unions enjoyed a far greater "recognition" than American or British unions now do, and the world knows their fate. That the life of the American trade unions is anything but secure is obvious from even a glance at the mass of reactionary, anti-labor legislation now piling up in Congress and in many state legislatures. In such conditions, with the trade unions hedged about by restrictive laws and constantly under attack from powerful and ruthless enemies, it is stretching matters quite a bit to boast of their freedom.

In the Soviet Union, the reverse of all this is true. The trade unions find themselves in quite a different and altogether freer situation. There are no enemy class forces to attack them. The workers and their farmer allies are in complete control of the government; in the Supreme Council of the U.S.S.R. workers, both of factory and office, which means trade unionists, are in a big majority. N. M. Shvernik, head of the Soviet trade unions, is president of the Council of Nationalities, one of the two equal Chambers of the Supreme Council of the U.S.S.R.* Worker majorities prevail in the Soviets of all the industrial centers, and in the country areas the Soviet majorities are composed of friendly collective farmers. In the Communist Party the bulk of the membership is also made up of workers who are, of course, nearly if not all trade unionists, and the party top committees contain many trade unionists. Naturally, too, the Soviet press and radio are 100 per cent favorable to trade unionism.

While the Soviet labor organizations enjoy a high degree of independence, at the same time they work in the closest collaboration with the Communist Party, the Soviet government, farmer collectives,

* N. M. Shvernik is now President of the Soviet Union.

industrial organizations, press, radio, etc.—as integral parts of the people's great social organism. They all work unitedly together under the world's most advanced system of national planning for the building of socialism, a type of society whose central and sole purpose is to advance the welfare of the workers and toilers.

In this friendly and co-operative environment the Soviet trade unions function with a freedom and effectiveness hardly even dreamed of by trade unions in capitalist countries. As for the right to organize, which is constantly under attack in capitalist lands, this is so much a basic feature of Soviet life that no one would even think of assailing it. The Soviet Labor Code, which is the most advanced in the world, crystallizes into law many rights that trade unions in other countries are either still trying laboriously to achieve or have not yet even ventured to formulate. The right to organize is written into the very constitution of the U.S.S.R., which is named after Stalin:

Article 126. In conformity with the interests of the working people, and in order to develop the organizational initiative and political activity of the masses of the people, citizens of the U.S.S.R. are ensured the right to unite in public organizations—trade unions, co-operative associations, youth organizations, sport and defense organizations, cultural, technical and scientific societies.

The Soviet trade unions are organizationally independent of both the Soviet government and the Communist Party. The assertion of the Wolls and other Soviet-baiters that the Soviet labor organizations are not free is a deliberate falsification. The relation of the trade unions to the Soviet state was the subject of a big controversy between Lenin and Trotsky in 1920-21, a basic dispute which agitated the whole Soviet people for many months. Lenin insisted upon the independent role of the unions, whereas Trotsky wanted to make them organs of the state. Trotsky was overwhelmingly defeated and Lenin's conception was endorsed. It remains Soviet policy today.

As for all the allegations that the Soviet trade unions are dominated by the Communist Party, this is simply a straw man. How baseless such charges are was illustrated by Shvernik, who says that "Among the members of the trade union committees of factories and other establishments, 80 per cent are non-party. . . ."[*]

As to how the Communist Party influences the decisions of the Soviet trade unions, Beatrice and Sidney Webb state:

[*] *The Land of Socialism, Today and Tomorrow*, p. 405, 1939.

If the party influences or directs the policy of individuals or public authorities, it does so only by persuasion. If it exercises power, it does so by "keeping the conscience" of its own members, and getting them elected by the popular vote.*

On the basis of their independent position, the Soviet trade unions work out their policies within the general framework of the socialist program of the Soviet nation. They elect such officers and adopt such organizational forms as they see fit. They dispose of their funds as they wish. Membership in the unions is not compulsory, but voluntary. This is demonstrated by the fact that only about 85 per cent of the workers belong to the unions. Members are attracted to the unions by the many special advantages they offer, as in other countries; except that in the U.S.S.R. the trade unions have a whole series of additional benefits to offer, including the use of their vast health and recreational institutions. There is no compulsion to join the unions, not even in the form of the check-off or the closed shop, both of which are unknown in the Soviet Union.

The 192 national Soviet trade unions, based upon the industrial union principle of all the workers in an enterprise belonging to one union, are highly democratic in character. Their dues and initiation fees are moderate, amounting usually to about 1 per cent each of a month's wages. There is no discrimination against women or against people of dark skins, a factor that disgraces many A. F. of L. and railroad unions. Their broad leading committees, in which the rank and file are heavily represented, and their wide discussion of all trade union policies, would, from the standpoint of democracy, put to the blush such unions as the carpenters and coal miners, which are autocratically ruled by tsars Hutcheson and Lewis. It is an insult to the Russian workers to compare their splendid unions, as the Wolls and Dubinskys do, with the employer-ridden German Labor Front or the Italian Corporations. Instead of throwing rocks at the Russian unions, the top A. F. of L. leadership could well take lessons from them.

COLLECTIVE BARGAINING IN THE U.S.S.R.

Carrying out their main function of attending to the immediate economic interests of the workers, the Soviet trade unions practice collective bargaining nationally in all the individual industries. "Far

* Beatrice and Sidney Webb, *Soviet Communism, A New Civilization*, p. 340, 1936.

from there being less collective bargaining in the U.S.S.R. than in Great Britain or the United States, or in Germany before the Hitlerite dictatorship," say the Webbs, "there is actually very much more than in any other country in the world."* And collective bargaining is practiced by the Soviet trade unions under conditions incomparably more favorable to them and the workers than those of capitalist nations.

In the U.S.S.R., where there are no capitalists, no hostile government, no antagonistic press to fight against the workers' proposals, the situation is totally different from that in the capitalist countries. The whole matter of establishing the workers' wages and working conditions is worked out on a co-operative basis between the workers and the representatives of their Soviet state. "The economic and political contradictions between workers, peasants, and intellectuals are disappearing, becoming obliterated," states the resolution of the Eighteenth Congress of the Communist Party of the Soviet Union. Indeed, the wage negotiation process in the U.S.S.R. can hardly be called "bargaining" at all, in so far as that term implies bickering and struggling. This is so because the Soviet government's industrial and other representatives, who are also workers, farmers, or professionals, are no less interested than the union leaders themselves in seeing to it that decisions are arrived at that will conserve the interests of the workers and the nation. In the ninth general convention of the Soviet trade unions, Shvernik, the general secretary, put the question of collective bargaining this way:

In capitalist countries collective agreements are the armistice terms of two hostile forces. In the negotiations the employers strive to force the worst conditions on the workers. . . . Here there is no enemy. No one tries to give as little as he can for as much as he can.†

In the U.S.S.R. the basic wage negotiations are carried on between the All-Union Central Council of Trade Unions and the leading state economic authorities and representatives of the Council of People's Commissars, as part of the general task of establishing the national Five-Year Plan and its subsidiary one-year plans. The allocation of the whole nation's income is taken as the basis of the negotiations. In determining the total amount to be set as wages for the workers as a whole, the needs of the government for administration expenses, for national defense, expansion of industry, education, social insurance,

* Beatrice and Sidney Webb, *op. cit.*, p. 183.
† *Report of the Ninth Trade Union Congress*, pp. 64-65, 1933.

and other necessary expenditures have also to be provided for. The draft plan thus arrived at is then sent out to the masses for discussion, after which it is reconsidered for necessary changes. This equitable, democratic and scientific adjustment of the wage question is quite impossible in any capitalist country.

After the basic wage rates have thus been established, generally and for the respective industries, the individual unions, through their national and local committees, enter into negotiation with the representatives of the various industries and factories in order to work out detailed wage and other conditions for their specific situations. These national and local agreements, besides adjusting time and piece rates, the matters of vacations, overtime, etc., also deal with a host of other questions, many of which are quite beyond the scope of American and British trade union agreements. A very important matter in trade union agreements is that of housing the workers. The English trade union experts, Beatrice and Sidney Webb, say:

> The foreign observer is surprised to find the safety and amenity of the places of work, the provision of hospital and sanatorium beds, the measures taken for the prevention of accidents, the provision of additional or better dwelling accommodations for the persons employed, the establishment of crèches and kindergartens for the young children; the workmen's clubhouse and the technical classes provided to enable them to improve their qualifications—and many other matters of importance to the workmen's daily life, dealt with in the detailed agreement (*kol-dogovor*) drawn up annually in March between the management and the various workmen's committees.*

All these trade union agreements—national, industrial, local—are subjects of the most intense discussion by the workers before they are finally formulated and put into effect. General Secretary Shvernik in 1932 described a condition which remains typical:

> The attendance of workers and employees at the meetings where drafts of the new collective agreements were discussed has in a number of enterprises been as high as 95 or 100 per cent.

Naturally, relatively few wage controversies occur in the U.S.S.R. Those that do come up are adjusted by an elaborate system of joint dispute committees, by conciliation and arbitration, and in the labor sessions of the people's courts. All these bodies, like every Soviet practice and institution, operate in the socialist spirit of advancing the

* Beatrice and Sidney Webb, *op. cit.,* p. 188.

workers' interests to the maximum possible under the circumstances. Heads of factories who violate trade union agreements, which have the force of law, may be severely punished. The extent to which the workers' interests are conserved under these agreements may be indicated by the fact that *the body having the last word in their interpretation and application is the All-Union Central Council of Trade Unions itself.*

Strikes are not prohibited in the Soviet Union, but they seldom occur. The fundamental reason for the lack of strikes is the equitable way of establishing the workers' wages and working conditions, coupled with the efficient and just methods of handling of their grievances. In the early days of the revolution, however, there were numerous strikes, Maurice Dobb listing 505 in 1922-23, affecting 154,000 workers.* These strikes were usually caused by bureaucratic neglect, by inexperienced factory managers. Of course, there are no absurd jurisdictional strikes in the U.S.S.R., with one union fighting another over which shall control this or that type of work. In recent years, with the strengthening of Soviet industrial organizations generally and the swift rise in the workers' standards, stoppages have naturally grown fewer and fewer. During the war, with fascist hordes overrunning large sections of the country, stoppages would, of course, not be tolerated by the workers themselves, nor by their party or government.

Under Soviet collective bargaining, the living and working conditions of the Soviet workers made spectacular advances, but these were temporarily checked by the outbreak of the war. The shortest workday of any country prevailed—seven hours generally and six hours in heavy and dangerous trades, with time-and-one-half, or double time, for overtime. Huge progress had been scored, too, in developing the elaborate system of social insurance. The average annual wage of Soviet workers made an unparalleled increase from 703 rubles in 1928 to 4,360 rubles in 1941. Although the Soviet workers are unavoidably undergoing many hardships under the Hitler attack, the protection of their health and working efficiency is recognized as a major necessity for winning the war. Collective bargaining has not been abandoned. The workers in the U.S.S.R. are not afflicted with profiteers seeking to exploit them ever more intensely and to throw the war's economic burdens onto their shoulders, as we now see happening in our industries and in the American Congress. *Trud,* the daily paper of the

---

* *Organized Labor in Four Continents,* p. 296, 1939.

Soviet trade unions, expressed the fundamental policy of the Soviet system when it declared recently:

The drive for improved living conditions of the working people during wartime is a matter of great military, economic, and political importance. The Soviet government pays great attention to this matter.

SOVIET PRODUCTION AND THE TRADE UNIONS

American workers are commonly penalized for increasing production because such increases operate to bring more profits to the employer and lowered wage rates and the menace of unemployment to the workers.

In the Soviet Union a totally different situation prevails than that which exists throughout the capitalist world. With no capitalists to exact their destructive profit toll from the workers, the more the latter produce the greater they benefit, and the more the nation as a whole prospers. This explains, also, why there are so few strikes in the U.S.S.R.—for it is evident that by halting production the workers would only be injuring themselves.

From the outset of the Russian Revolution in November, 1917, the Soviet trade unions have played a vital role in production, especially in cultivating an efficient and comradely labor discipline. This role has been greatly enhanced during the present war emergency. In every local and national union, and in the trade union movement as a whole, there are special departments of production. For over twenty years, in every state industry, nationally and locally, there exist committees of the unions and the managements for working out specific production problems. Between the All-Union Central Council of Trade Unions and the economic apparatus of the Soviet government there is the closest working together in every phase of production. C. T. McAvoy tells us:

The State Planning Commission, composed of technicians, industrial experts, economists and representatives of the All-Union Central Council of Trade Unions, draws up a preliminary plan covering all of Soviet industry for five years, broken down into schedules for each year.*

The Webbs explain how this preliminary plan is then referred for amendment to the workers of the nation:

* *The Trade Unions of Our Soviet Ally,* The American Council on Soviet Relations, p. 12, 1942.

Gosplan [the government planning agency] now submits it for consideration, through the several commissariats and other centers, to all the enterprises and organizations whose proceedings for the ensuing year it will govern. . . . In each factory or office the part of the Plan relating to that establishment is not only exhaustively examined by the directors and managers and heads of departments, but also submitted to the whole of the workers concerned, through their various factory or office committees, production conferences and trade union meetings. . . . All sorts of suggestions and criticisms are made, which are considered by the foremen and managers, and finally transmitted to Gosplan. . . . Very often, during the last few years, the workmen's meetings have submitted a counter-plan, by which the establishment would be committed to a greater production than the Provisional Plan had proposed.*

This is industrial democracy on a scale and in a degree that the trade unions of the United States and Great Britain, despite their wartime labor-management committees (which the employers look upon with mean and jaundiced eyes), do not even remotely approach. It is one of the most basic factors responsible for the spectacular advance of Soviet industry, which from 1929 to 1940 increased its output five times over, a rate of growth totally unknown in any capitalist country in all history. In a few years the industrially backward Russia became the second industrial country in the world. And since the war began, even greater marvels of production have been achieved, as we shall note later on. These accomplishments could not possibly have been made without the wholehearted co-operation of the trade unions.

Precisely because there is no capitalist exploitation in the U.S.S.R. the trade unions of that country freely adopt incentive systems of various sorts, many of which are difficult for American trade unionists, living in a totally different, capitalist environment, to understand. The basis for the general work and wage policy of the U.S.S.R. is laid down in that country's national constitution, as follows:

Art. 12: In the U.S.S.R. work is a duty and a matter of honor for every able-bodied citizen, in accordance with the principle: "He who does not work shall not eat."

The principle applied in the U.S.S.R. is that of socialism: "From each according to his ability, to each according to his work."

This means that under Soviet socialism, according to the principles long ago enunciated by Marx, Engels, Lenin, and Stalin, the workers are paid upon the basis of what they produce. Those who argue that

* Beatrice and Sidney Webb, *op. cit.,* p. 645.

equality of wages is a feature of socialism speak either from ignorance or a desire to deceive. In the U.S.S.R. there are different scales of wages, a system which, under socialism, constitutes a powerful incentive to production and for workers to fit themselves for more skilled and better paid work. The higher communist work principle of "From each according to his ability, to each according to his needs" can be achieved only later in the U.S.S.R., when the question of production ceases to be a serious problem, through the necessary broad expansion of industry and agriculture, the development of a highly skilled and efficient working class, and the decline of the need to maintain big armed forces.

The most basic form of incentive wages in the U.S.S.R. is the piece-work system, which is widely prevalent in the industries. But piece-work in the U.S.S.R. has been systematically misrepresented for years by enemies of the Soviet Union, such as Matthew Woll, who have claimed that it causes exploitation of the workers. Soviet trade union leader Shvernik, speaking of pre-war conditions, thus explains it:

Here, where the state is exercising the maximum degree of care in the protection of labour, and where we have a working day lasting seven hours, the piece-work system accelerates the tempo of socialist construction, increases the productivity of labour, and guarantees the improvement of the material and general living conditions of the workers.*

Accordingly, in the U.S.S.R. [say the Webbs], there are none of the clever piece-work systems by which, in capitalist industry, the workers are made to gain less per unit the faster they work. Under Soviet communism, the piece-work rates are never digressive. They are, in some cases, even progressive, the rate rising by stages for output beyond the norm."†

In Soviet industry there are a host of additional incentive methods, all of which can be understood only in the light of the socialist system of the U.S.S.R., in contrast to the exploitation in effect in capitalist countries. Among these methods may be cited the famous Stakhanovite movement, created by the rank-and-file workers themselves to devise more efficient methods of production; socialist competition between workers, shops, industries, and cities for better and greater production; shock brigades of *udarniki,* or best workers, who improve the output of whole plants and industries; cost-accounting brigades, which find

* Quoted by Beatrice and Sidney Webb, *op. cit.,* p. 704.
† *Ibid.,* p. 706.

means for reducing production costs; the policy of the best-working departments and shops "towing" the weaker ones by helping them directly; "comradely courts" in the factories, which give praise or blame to competent or neglectful workers; the conferring of Soviet Orders upon heroes of labor, and upon extra efficient industries, etc. These many methods have been expanded and various new ones developed as the trade unions have bravely tackled the gigantic industrial problems thrust upon them by the war. In all this work of carrying on and improving production great care is used to protect the health and strength of workers, for which purpose the U.S.S.R. has enacted and diligently applies the best and most elaborate system of labor protection laws and shop practices of any country.

SOCIAL INSURANCE, LABOR PROTECTION, CULTURAL WORK

The Soviet trade unions, in addition to their wage and production activities previously indicated, carry on normally in peacetime three other major mass functions: in the fields of social insurance, labor protection and cultural work. In all these matters they operate on a scale and with an authority quite unknown in any other country. As in the case of wages and production, the labor unions, from the All-Union Central Council of Trade Unions down to the factory committees, have special commissions which organize these activities.

The Soviet Union, true to its socialist character, is far and away the world leader in all forms of social insurance. The right of the workers to this protection is established in the Stalin Constitution of the U.S.S.R., which states:

Art. 120: Citizens of the U.S.S.R. have the right to maintenance in old age and also in case of sickness or loss of capacity to work.

Accordingly, the government spends huge sums annually for its elaborate system of social insurance. Neither the proposed Beveridge Plan in England nor that of the National Resources Planning Board in the United States reaches anywhere near the level of the Soviet social insurance system. In their book on the U.S.S.R. the Webbs say:

As with Public Education, the sums allocated to all these services have been increasing year by year, by leaps and bounds, calculated to reduce to despair the Finance Minister of any capitalist community.*

* *Ibid.*, p. 639.

The Soviet 1941 national budget provided no less than 49,000,000,000 rubles for the network of social insurance, education and cultural projects.

At all stages of their lives the Soviet workers are financially protected from every possible hazard: sickness, old age, accidents, permanent disability, maternity, death, etc. The insurance benefits range from 50 to 100 per cent of the workers' regular wages. The funds are provided by payroll assessments against the state industrial enterprises, the workers making no direct contributions. The only "hazard" not covered by insurance is unemployment; for there is no unemployment in the socialist system which constantly permits the full productive capacity of the people. Soviet workers are entirely free of the dread of joblessness, because their scientific economic system has completely abolished industrial crises and other causes of mass unemployment. The Constitution of the U.S.S.R. provides:

Art. 118: Citizens of the U.S.S.R. have the right to work, that is, are guaranteed the right to employment and payment for their work in accordance with its quantity and quality. The right to work is ensured by the socialist organization of national economy, the steady growth of the productive forces of Soviet society, the elimination of economic crises, and the abolition of unemployment.

The vast social insurance system of the U.S.S.R. has, since 1933, been under the direct administration of the trade unions. In any capitalist country the exploiters would be frantic at a proposal to turn over even their scanty social insurance systems to the management of the trade unions; yet in the Soviet Union, where capitalism has been abolished, to put the unions in charge is deemed perfectly natural and proper. The All-Union Central Council of Trade Unions manages the funds generally, the various national trade unions take care of insurance matters in their respective industries, and the actual distribution of benefits to the workers is handled by the local factory committees. For this purpose each factory committee has a broad social insurance council, elected by direct vote of the workers. These factory insurance councils decide upon the amount of compensation in each case, and they also check to see that the state enterprises keep their assessments paid up.

In the field of labor protection, too, the Soviet trade unions exercise great powers, such as unions in capitalist countries would hardly dream of. It is their right and task to administer the whole body of labor laws in the U.S.S.R. These laws, guaranteeing the seven and six-hour day, time-and-one-half and double pay for overtime, the fullest rights of trade union organization and collective bargaining, complete protection of women and young workers, thoroughgoing health and safety measures, paid vacation provisions for all workers, etc., are without their equal anywhere.

In 1934 the government abolished the existing national department of labor and turned its functions over to the All-Union Central Council of Trade Unions, it being taken for granted in a socialist regime that no group in the country is more competent or trustworthy to administer the nation's labor laws than those persons most directly concerned, the workers themselves. But imagine what a wild outcry such a proposal in the United States would wring from the reactionaries. The Soviet trade unions, in protecting the rights and welfare of the workers in the industries, have the power to issue regulations having the binding force of law, and for whose infraction careless or bureaucratic factory managers may be punished. To supervise the country's great labor protective service the trade union movement has its own system of factory inspectors. Each factory council has a commission to attend to problems of local enforcement in the plant, mine, office or railroad.

In the broad field of education and general culture of mind and body the Soviet trade unions also carry on immense activities and bear unique responsibilities. One great program in the gigantic work of educating the Soviet people that the government is now working on, is, as Shvernik puts it, "towards the realization of the historic task of raising the cultural and technical level of the working class in the U.S.S.R. to the level of engineers."* This is a concept utterly unthinkable in any capitalist educational system. The scope of the unprecedented educational work going on just prior to the war, in spite of the government's necessity to devote a huge share of the national production to building the industrial system and to strengthening the armed forces, may be gathered from the statement of Molotov in 1939 at the outset of the Third Five-Year Plan: "The student body in our institutions of higher learning," he said, "is greater than the combined total of Germany, England, France, Italy and Japan." He added, "Our libraries contain seventy-five books for each 100 inhabitants of the Soviet Union, which is over three times as many as Germany had in 1934."† In 1932 the production of books in the U.S.S.R.

* *The Land of Socialism, Today and Tomorrow*, p. 442.
† *Ibid.*, p. 108.

(surpassed by far in later years) reached the vast total of 500,000,000 copies, which, the Webbs estimate, "probably exceeds the output for the year of all the publishers in the rest of the world."*

Every open-minded, honest observer of what is taking place in the U.S.S.R. is enthusiastic about that country's tremendous mass cultural work. In every sphere of Soviet life scientific principles are assiduously applied in raising the national economy and the people to higher levels. In this respect the Webbs say:

> It is, we think, clear that the Soviet government, inspired and guided by the Central Committee of the Communist Party, has, during the past decade, manifested a greater devotion to science than any other government in the world. Not only does it spend more on the teaching of science and on the promotion of scientific research, but it habitually defers more, in its policy and practice, to the lessons of science.†

The trade unions are deep in the whole great Soviet cultural advance. Their representatives are playing decisive roles in state and voluntary educational movements and institutions of all sorts, to an extent hardly dreamed of by British and American labor organizations. They work in closest collaboration with the Departments of Health and Education. They are also carrying on a very extensive educational work upon their own score, sometimes with government social insurance monies, but often with the unions' funds. Shvernik says that from 1933 to 1938 the trade unions conducted classes for 5,000,000 illiterates and semi-literates, and he further declared that the total number of trade union members who are members of cultural circles—political, general educational, defense, dramatic, music, singing, sports, etc.—increased from 4,730,000 in 1935 to 6,573,000 in 1938. In trade union libraries of more than 1,000 books each there were, in 1938, 6,343,000 subscribers, who read an average of eighteen books yearly.

Add to such activities some eight hundred trade union sanitoriums and rest homes, innumerable child care institutions, workers' clubs, moving picture houses, dancing, art and literary circles, physical culture groups, organized excursions, etc., and one gets at least a faint idea of the vast cultural and recreational work being done by the Soviet trade unions.

* Beatrice and Sidney Webb, *op. cit.*, p. 920.
† *Ibid.*, p. 988.

The A.U.C.C.T.U., among its many other activities, gives national leadership to the labor movement on all these questions through its highly specialized Sanatoriums and Health Resort Department, Tourist Department, Sports Bureau, Engineers and Technical Workers Bureau, Proletarian Students Bureau, Trade Union Academy, Institute of Scientific Research, Trade Union movement, etc. In short, wherever the interest and welfare of the workers are to be promoted—in wage standards, social security, working conditions, housing, education, health—there the Soviet trade unions are tirelessly active and are exercising a profound influence.

1943

33. The New World Federation of Labor

The gathering in London during February 1945, of the representatives of some sixty million trade unionists from all parts of the democratic world, climaxed in a brilliant success by the unanimous adoption of a proposal, made by Sidney Hillman, head of the C. I. O. delegation, to establish a new world federation of labor "at the earliest practicable date," and to commission the Continuations Committee of 41 members to take all necessary measures to accomplish this end. Thus the workers of two score countries took the most decisive step in labor history to unify the international labor movement and to make its influence count on a world scale.

Naturally, such a great advance by the workers was not made without serious resistance from the hold-back and obstructionist forces within their own ranks. Especially the reactionary clique now controlling the A. F. of L. Executive Council was conspicuous by its active opposition to the formation of the new world labor federation. Indeed, this clique is the spearhead of the whole opposition. These A. F. of L. leaders had the insolence to denounce the great London conference as a "rival, dual" movement and a Communist "plot." They refused to send delegates to it. They are obviously determined to wreck the new world federation at any cost, if they can. In this work of obstruction and destruction they are counting upon obtaining the help of certain conservative leaders of the British unions, as well as of numerous continental Social-Democrats. Their game is to revive the practically defunct International Federation of Trade Unions (I. F. T. U.) and then use this organization as a means for struggle against the new world federation of labor now being born.

But this splitting maneuver of the reactionaries, led by Woll, Hutcheson, Lewis, Meany, Dubinsky and company, will not succeed. The whole weight of the international situation is against it.

The new world federation of labor, which has the backing of every important national trade union center in the world except the A. F. of L., is being called into existence by the workers precisely because the I. F. T. U. has failed to function effectively as the world organization of labor. This is not to say, however, that the A. F. of L. leaders cannot do much harm by their attempts to breathe the breath of life into the I. F. T. U. and therewith to split world labor.

The I. F. T. U., even in the years when, numerically speaking, it could make a pretense of representing a great part of the world's trade unions, was a narrow, ineffective organization.

During the period between the two world wars, this body, controlled by conservative and reactionary Social-Democrats, kept the world labor movement divided along "right" and "left" lines. So deeply was it interested in instigating this destructive factional struggle that it refused to make a united front with the anti-fascist trade unions of the U.S.S.R. and other countries to crush Franco in Spain, and to defeat the first steps of the hordes of Hitler and Mussolini in their unfolding campaigns to conquer the world. By this reactionary course the I. F. T. U. showed that it was unfit to serve as the world center for organized labor.

By its narrow, sectarian composition, the I. F. T. U. disqualified itself from being the international federation of labor. It refused to admit into its ranks the great Soviet trade unions; it ignored and neglected the struggling labor unions of the colonial and semi-colonial countries, and it had a restrictive rule in its constitution admitting only one trade union center from each country, a device which barred the American C. I. O. and progressive unions in various other countries.

Even as late as May 1944, on the very eve of the great London World Trade Union Conference, the I. F. T. U. refused to change its constitution so as to admit the great new labor forces all over the world which were clamoring for international organization. Through this short-sighted action, dictated by the A. F. of L. leaders, the I. F. T. U. virtually committed suicide.

As though to make it triply clear to the workers everywhere that it was unfit to be a real world labor center, the I. F. T. U. failed utterly to give a lead in the international labor movement during the bitter crises of this great world war. All through the struggle it has remained quite dead. Although there were a hundred issues demanding the workers' international action, the I. F. T. U. took no steps to bring the forces of world labor together and to work out methods for mobilizing labor's strength behind the war efforts and national-economic programs of the United Nations.

Nor does it now, as victory looms in the offing, make any attempt whatsoever to map out peace and postwar policies for world labor. To all intents and purposes the I. F. T. U. is politically dead so far as being the spokesman of the world trade union movement is concerned.

The new world federation launched at London corrects the many glaring and basic weaknesses and narrownesses of the old I. F. T. U. In step with the great movement for national and international unity now sweeping the peoples of the United Nations, the new federation has thrown its doors wide open to both "rights" and "lefts" in the labor movement and has already assembled all the genuine trade unions throughout the democratic world, including all those in the I. F. T. U. except the A. F. of L. It is a real world organization in its composition and its scope of affiliations. And equally significant, the new organization is already highly active politically, in the spirit of the Moscow, Teheran and Crimea conferences. Among other activities, the Continuations Committee is now preparing labor's program to present to the coming meeting of the United Nations in San Francisco beginning on April 25. From now on, it is safe to predict, labor's influence internationally will increase rapidly.

The A. F. of L. leaders' plan of galvanizing the obsolete I. F. T. U. into life and of pitting it counter to the new world federation of labor is nothing short of a crime against the workers of this and every other country. It is also a threat to the whole program of the United Nations. Such a policy could originate only in the minds of the Wolls and Hutchesons, men who are tied up with the most reactionary sections of big business and who, like these fascist-minded employers, are mortally afraid of the new democratic upsurge that is taking place all over the world under the flags of the United Nations and of which the new world labor federation is such an outstanding manifestation.

In the difficult years ahead the United Nations will have to face many hard problems, in the winning of the war, in the complete uprooting of fascism, in the establishment of a durable peace, and in the economic rehabilitation of the war-torn world.

To solve these terrific problems will require united action by organized labor on a world scale. The implied slogan of the United Nations—Peoples of the World, Unite—must be reinforced by realizing the great slogan—Workers of the World, Unite—in the trade union field. Therefore the little band of reactionaries and saboteurs now controlling the A. F. of L. Executive Council should not be allowed to jeopardize the whole perspective of our people by their irresponsible attacks against world labor solidarity.

This means that if the wrecking activities of the Wolls, Hutchesons, etc., are to be prevented, the progressive forces within the A. F. of L.—the great rank and file and lower officialdom—must speak out. They, together with the C. I. O. and the Railroad Brotherhoods, must put the whole American working class on record for the new world labor organization.

There can be no doubt whatever but that the overwhelming majority of the A. F. of L. membership will favor the program and movement launched by the London conference. They should see to it, therefore, that their wishes are carried out by their official leaders. The A. F. of L. Executive Council clique must be told in no uncertain terms to drop their war against the new world federation and to affiliate the A. F. of L. to this great and promising organization.

The new world trade union body is scheduled to meet in Paris next September (at the same time as the I. F. T. U.), in order to further consolidate its organization and to advance its program.* At that time the I. F. T. U. which, with all its unions already in the new world federation, could maintain even a weak semblance of life only by A. F. of L. plotting, should accept the verdict of history by merging its identity (for that's about all it has left) with the new international federation. The I. F. T. U. will so merge if enough A. F.

* The conference, which was held September 25–October 8, 1945, representing 66,700,000 members, organized the World Federation of Trade Unions. In the autumn of 1946, the W. F. T. U. reported a membership of 71 million in 56 countries. In the United States only the C. I. O. is affiliated to the new world trade union body.

of L. local unions, city central bodies, state federations and international unions demand that their leaders quit trying to keep that phantom organization alive.

World labor unity, as never before, can now be achieved; the reactionary Wolls and Hutchesons must be swept out of its path.

1945

34. Wage and Job Strategy

In this early postwar period the workers throughout the United States are demanding wage increases, generally running to about 30 per cent. This is one of the broadest wage movements in American history, involving many industries — steel, auto, machine building, radio-electric, railroad, oil, marine transport, building, lumber, coal, textile, printing, motion pictures, etc. — and it is being led by A. F. of L., C. I. O., and independent unions.

The basis of the present huge wage movement is the workers' resistance to the general slash in take-home pay that has occurred since the ending of the war — through the elimination of overtime, the down-grading of pay rates, etc. During the war the workers' wages lagged far behind the rise in living costs. By applying the "Little Steel" formula, which restricted basic wage rate increases to not more than 15 per cent above the rates in effect on January 1, 1941, the War Labor Board ignored the fact that the cost of living had actually advanced about 50 per cent during this period, as the figures of both the A. F. of L. and C. I. O. clearly demonstrate. And, of course, the workers' wages failed to keep pace with the gigantic war-time profits of the employers which, after paying taxes, averaged three times higher than the pre-war year 1939. The bosses have been indulging in a regular orgy of profit-grabbing while labor was making war.

In order to carry through their wage demands, which are inextricably bound up with the problems of furnishing jobs and relief to the unemployed, it is indispensable that the workers proceed along the lines of a definite strategy calculated to mobilize the maximum of support behind their proposals. This pamphlet indicates some of the major lines necessary to such a strategy.

THE UNITY OF ORGANIZED LABOR

It is becoming increasingly clear that the Truman administration, in spite of its pledges to carry out the Roosevelt policies, is yielding to the pressure of the bosses and is sacrificing the most elementary economic needs of the workers. Therefore, the workers must look, in first line, to the strength of their own organizations, particularly the trade unions, to put through their wage demands. This especially emphasizes the need, in this critical postwar period, for the greatest possible unity within the ranks of the workers.

First, in this respect, it is necessary to soften, or to do away entirely with, the warfare that the top leaders of the A. F. of L. and the U. M. W. A. are waging against the C. I. O. The attempts of such men as William Green, Matthew Woll, W. L. Hutcheson, David Dubinsky, John L. Lewis, etc., to destroy the C.I.O. in the postwar period are a crime against the whole labor movement. Their hopes that the C. I. O. will fall to pieces after the war (with them helping to destroy it) are apparent. Were the A. F. of L. to succeed in breaking the C.I.O. it would ruin not only labor's hard-won organization in the trustified industries, but it would also undermine the whole position of the A. F. of L. itself. One can hardly imagine anything more suicidal to the workers' interests than the fight of the A. F. of L. reactionaries against the C. I. O., a fight from which only the employers can benefit and which dovetails exactly with the union-smashing program of the National Association of Manufacturers.

The lower bodies of the A. F. of L.—the international unions, state federations, city labor councils, and local unions—should take a hand in this situation and insist upon a co-operative policy being followed by their top leaders toward the C. I. O. During the present wage movements many fine examples of A. F. of L.-C. I. O. collaboration have developed in various industries and localities. These are steps in the right direction, and they should be followed through vigorously. Such local and industrial co-operative movements should be forerunners of a general get-together policy by the A. F. of L. and C. I. O. If the rank and file of labor will take a determined stand in this unity matter, even the hardest boiled reactionaries in the A. F. of L. Executive Council will have to pay attention.

A second vital consideration in the present big movement to protect wages and to provide jobs is the need to extend trade union organization still further into the vast ranks of the unorganized. There are still many millions of workers outside the labor unions— especially workers in the manufacturing industries, white collar workers, agricultural workers, and workers in small towns. These workers all feel the need for higher wages and will readily respond to trade union organizing campaigns. The question of organizing the unorganized, therefore, should now be made a central issue throughout the labor movement. Organized labor will make a big mistake if it does not utilize the present wage movement greatly to strengthen itself by drawing several millions of new workers into its ranks. Such increased trade union strength is deeply needed for the big tasks ahead in protecting the workers' and the nations' interests in every sphere of our economic and political life.

Thirdly, in order to solidify its own ranks, organized labor must also pay special attention to defending the interests of Negro workers, particularly in connection with their right to work. This is a solidarity question of the highest order. As matters stand now, the Negro workers, usually the lowest on the seniority lists, the last to be hired and the first to be fired, are being literally swept out of the war plants, and, with few honorable exceptions, the unions are doing very little to protect the Negroes' rights to jobs. Aside from the injustice to the Negroes in this, the danger is that such a situation might enable the employers to drive a wedge between the white and Negro workers, a split which would be a major setback for the entire labor movement. This, the unions must avoid at all costs. If organized labor understands its true interests it will pay triple attention to the burning question of defending the Negroes' right to work and see to it that a due percentage of them are kept in the plants. This will require certain local variations of the seniority system.

Fourthly, under the general head of unifying labor's forces, the A. F. of L. should affiliate to the newly formed World Federation of Trade Unions, which now has some 70,000,000 members. Such an action would greatly help the workers everywhere in all their fights for better economic and political conditions, including those of American workers. The isolationist attitude of the A. F. of L. top leadership in standing aloof and warring against the W. F. T. U. is intolerable. Their refusal to participate in this great international labor federation because the C. I. O. and the Soviet trade unions are affiliated to it is a scandal and a disgrace. The new W. F. T. U. will be a great buttress to the United Nations and the whole cause of world peace; hence, the organized workers should compel their reactionary leaders to affiliate the A. F. of L. to it.

THE QUESTION OF STRIKES

Throughout the war the workers submitted to the injustice of the "Little Steel" formula being enforced against them, to the detriment of their living conditions. In a high spirit of patriotism, and being determined to win the war at all costs, the workers loyally lived up to their no-strike pledge and kept the industries in full operation in spite of every provocation from the employers and profound neglect by the government. Their no-strike record was splendid. The total loss of time by war-time strikes was so small that it was more than offset, for example, by the extra time put in by the workers in working on one single holiday, and they worked on many such holidays during the war.

Now, however, the war is over and labor's no-strike pledge is no longer in force. This does not mean, of course, that the workers should rush helter-skelter into strikes to secure their wage demands. Strikes are very serious actions for workers and should not be undertaken without serious consideration. Workers understand this very well. It is true that a number of strikes have occurred during the present wage movement, provoked by stubborn capitalist resistance to justified wage demands, but the number and extent of these have been grossly exaggerated by the reactionary capitalist press in order to poison public opinion against the labor movement.

One very important thing that the workers should bear carefully in mind in the present wage movement is the need for the broadest and best disciplined solidarity, particularly where strikes are involved. In the face of the highly organized employers, the unions should generally follow an industry-wide, national wage strategy instead of attempting to concentrate against this or that individual employer. Also, groups of industries, on the basis of unified demands, should act together. Indeed, the best wage strategy would require that the A. F. of L., C. I. O., Railroad Brotherhoods, Coal Miners, and independent labor unions should come together in a national conference and prepare demands for general wage increases for the entire working class.

Where strikes become unavoidable, due to an intransigent attitude on the part of the employers and the administration, they should be conducted in a resolute and disciplined manner. They should be well-organized, for the trade unions face the most powerful capitalist class in the world. Jurisdictional strikes should be ruled out as sheer poison, for nothing hurts the trade unions more, internally and in public opinion, than these destructive inner controversies. Wildcat strikes should also be avoided wherever possible. In this respect, however, it must be said that when wildcat strikes occur they are almost always the result of extreme employer provocations and the failure of conservative union leaders to move to protect the interests of the workers concerned. Our labor history has many such "unauthorized" strikes, some of them national in character. The recent New York rank-and-file strike of longshoremen was typical in this respect of employer provocation and official union inaction. Once in a while, however, as in the recent Hayes-Kelsey auto parts strike in Detroit, Trotskyite and other disrupters managed to pull out workers in conflict with their own interests and with the union's wage policy.

The trade unions must, in this situation, pay close attention to the question of company unionism. Despite the Wagner Act, there are still many company unions in the industries, and the employers, to combat the spread of real trade unionism, will undoubtedly organize many more. Often the workers have illusions about such organizations being helpful to them. In dealing with such unions, therefore, it is not adequate merely to make head-on attacks against them. Particular attention must be paid to winning them from the inside. Recent American labor history is full of instances when company unions were either won over to the labor movement or broken up by the efforts of workers within them to use them as the instruments for achieving their economic demands.

In this period, when the country is anxious to get back to peacetime production, the unions necessarily have to give serious consideration to the question of arbitration as a means of adjusting their demands. But here a sharp warning is very necessary. The workers must be alertly on guard against every attempt to force compulsory arbitration upon them, whether by law, by the pressure of the administration or by the weight of the reactionary press. The workers must watch out that arbitration does not become just a convenient means for the employers to defeat the demands of the workers. These few words of caution about arbitration must therefore be sounded. First, arbitration must, when entered into, be purely upon a voluntary basis; second, the workers involved should look very carefully at the composition of the arbitration board; and, third, it is a good practice to secure as much as possible of their demands beforehand by direct negotiation, referring only the remaining unresolved questions to arbitration.

To facilitate its movement for better wages, the labor movement should insist that the wartime controls over wage increases be removed. Legal limitations on the right to strike, as incorporated in the notorious Smith-Connally Act, should also be done away with. The war is over, and there is no need for the continuance of such restrictive limitations upon the basic rights of the workers.

Labor should insist, however, that price controls must be maintained. This is indispensable. For if the purchasing power of the masses is to be maintained, the highly organized employers must not be allowed to boost prices as they see fit. In years past, when the national interest imperatively demanded it, the government took away from the railroads the right to jack up freight and passenger rates, and it turned the control of such matters over to the Interstate Commerce Commission. In line with this same general principle, the national interest now demands that prices generally shall be kept as low as possible and wages raised to as high levels as are practicable (if we are to avoid the most devastating effects of future economic crises). Hence, a larger government control over prices than has ever existed before in peacetime must be developed. But, of course, this price control will have to be operated far more in the public interest than has ever been the case with the Interstate Commerce Commission which has always been heavily under the influence of the great railroad kings.

UNITY IN STRUGGLE FOR WAGES AND JOBS

One of the most important lessons that organized labor must fully grasp in the postwar period we are now entering into, if it is to protect the workers' interests successfully, is that the struggle for better wages and the fight to create more jobs for the workers are inseparable. They are both part of one broad general struggle to protect the economic interests of the workers. This is not as simple a proposition as it appears on the surface, and labor must consciously strive to keep the two phases of the general struggle constantly in mind. For if either is neglected, both will suffer.

During many years, in the recurring economic crises, it was a great weakness of A. F. of L. unions to concentrate their attention almost exclusively upon protecting the conditions of the employed workers and to allow the unemployed to shift pretty much for themselves. Indeed, it was as late as 1934 before the A. F. of L. top leaders even began seriously to demand relief and insurance for the unemployed. Such a one-sided policy of short-sightedly neglecting the welfare of the unemployed of course, in turn, reacted also against the interest of the workers who held jobs.

In the present situation there is definitely a danger of such unwise policies being followed by some unions. Thus, in the big attention being now paid to the burning question of wage increases, there is a distinct tendency to neglect the no less vital matter of the struggle to provide jobs and relief for the unemployed.

This is a great weakness. We are now entering into a period of mass unemployment, with the danger of a major economic crisis looming not far ahead for us; hence, at all costs, we should secure the "full employment" legislation now pending in Congress, in the shape of the Murray Bill and President Truman's recommendations. Therefore, as the workers press on for improved wages they must also imperatively demand the enactment into law of the principles of President Roosevelt's Economic Bill of Rights. If this is not done, the future will show that the present wage increases will be largely cancelled out by the pressure of the unemployed upon the labor market.

In this linking together of the fight for better wages and for more jobs, there must also be an organizational tie-up between the trade unions and the unemployed. Under no circumstances should the mistake be made that the unemployed be allowed, as in other times of mass joblessness, to drift away from the trade unions. To prevent this the unions should keep their unemployed members in good standing; they should set up committees to look after their unemployed workers; they should cultivate all necessary forms of organizations of their unemployed; they should participate in all demonstrations and other actions in support of the "full employment" program. The trade unions, breaking sharply with conservative policies of the past, must constantly be conscious of their great task to defend the economic protection of the unemployed and to fight for the maintenance of employment at the highest possible levels.

UNITY OF THE ECONOMIC AND POLITICAL STRUGGLE

In carrying through their present fight for better wages and more jobs the workers must understand, as never before, the need to carry on their struggle upon both the economic and political fields simultaneously. This is a lesson of supreme importance to the workers. Their whole future depends upon the extent to which they grasp it.

The day is gone when the workers could settle their economic and other demands simply by negotiating with the employers, with the government playing only a minor, if any, part at all in these negotiations. Today all important economic questions concerning the workers—wages, hours, prices, production, etc.—have become largely political issues of the first magnitude. This was true, not only in the war period that we have just been through but it will also be the case, under different conditions, of course, in the peacetime perspective ahead of us. The unions therefore must combine political action with strike action and collective bargaining. The old Gompers slogan "No politics in the unions" is hopelessly out of date. It is not only obsolete, but highly dangerous. Now the workers, on pain of disaster to themselves, must become organized and active politically.

In their political activities the workers must also concern themselves not only with matters dealing directly with their own economic conditions, but also with our whole national and international political life in general. Today the capitalist system of the world is in a deepening crisis, and this crisis gives birth to a host of vital political problems which the workers, along with other democratic forces, must actively help solve. Failure to do this would mean to bring down disaster upon the heads of the workers and the whole people.

The great monopolists, the mainspring of reaction in the United States, are determined to still further tighten their grip upon Congress in the elections of 1946. They also want to cripple the trade unions by hostile legislation, of which the Burton-Ball-Hatch Bill is a current example. This situation lays the imperative task upon the shoulders of organized labor to mobilize politically all its own forces and those of its natural allies—farmers, professionals, small businessmen, veterans, etc.—so that the 1946 elections may be made into a great democratic victory for the whole American people.

Organized labor must also bring its great forces politically to bear to block the present drive of American imperialistic forces to dominate the world. This imperialist drive, which has behind it the great monopolies and trusts of this country, is manifest in every phase of our foreign policy—in our failure to take drastic steps to root out fascism in Germany and Japan, in our attempts to dominate the trade of the world, in our maintenance of a gigantic military, naval, and air force, including the atomic bomb, in our policy of "getting tough" with the U. S. S. R., etc. Such policies are full of danger to the American people and the world. They point the way to fascism, economic chaos, and another world war. Organized labor, therefore, has the historic task of balking the imperialists' plans and of influencing our foreign policies in the direction laid down at the famous conferences of Moscow, Teheran, Yalta, San Francisco, and Potsdam.

A further, especially urgent reason why labor must pay particular attention to organized political action is the sharp tendencies of the Truman administration to surrender to the forces of reaction and imperialism. Although President Truman has pledged himself to carry out the policies laid down by former President Roosevelt, obviously he is not doing so. More and more his policies yield to reaction, both on the domestic and international fields. It is a dangerous fact that today in Congress the voice of Herbert Hoover is much more hearkened to than is that of President Truman, regarding both domestic and international policies. Organized labor, therefore, must bestir itself to defeat reaction and to have the broad policies associated with the name of Roosevelt carried into effect. And clearly, from the strength of the drive of the reactionaries, it will require the full strength of labor and its friends to accomplish this purpose.

In the 1944 elections, organized labor, in such organizations as the Political Action Committee of the C. I. O., legislative committees in the A. F. of L., etc., worked out the general forms along which the political struggle should be prosecuted. But, with reaction on the offensive, organized labor must organize its forces far better and be much more active than it was during the great election struggle of 1944.

Finally, the trade unions must sharply oppose the Rankin House Committee on un-American activities, the resurrected Dies Committee. This committee is a combination of Hitlerian red-baiting, Japanese "dangerous thought" persecution, and Salem witch-hunting. Its purpose is, by creating a fascist-like red scare, to provide a smokescreen behind which the power greedy monopolists can carry on their program of reaction in this country and of imperialist aggression abroad. The Rankin Committee, in the Hitler tradition, starts out by attacking the Communists, but it soon develops its real program, which is to undermine the trade unions and to weaken everything progressive in the United States. Organized labor must not, as often in the past, stand aside and let this imitation Gestapo carry on its activities unmolested. The unions must realize that it is a bread and butter question, involving their whole struggle for wages and jobs, that it is, in fact, a life and death matter for them generally, to defeat and to force the dissolution of the fascist-breeding Rankin Committee.

UNITY OF LABOR AND NATIONAL INTERESTS

One of the most basic phases of organized labor's wage and job strategy is the necessity of making the people at large realize that the demands of the workers for better wages and adequate jobs are not merely the concern of the workers, but are in the most fundamental interest of the whole nation. For only if the purchasing power of the workers is maintained by providing the workers with jobs and good wages can the country's great industrial machine be kept in operation.

Of course, organized labor for many years past has always tried to win the support of the public behind its demands for better economic conditions for the workers. But this was done largely upon a humanitarian basis. Now, however, the approach must be fundamentally different. The people at large must be made to understand that the demands of organized labor for jobs and better wages are vital to their own interests, and that the alternative is chronic mass unemployment, wholesale prostration of industry, and hard times for everybody. By the same token, organized labor must also show the people that its democratic proposals generally are in the national interest.

Very much of organized labor's success in the future will depend upon the degree to which it manages to convince "public opinion" that its program is in the national interest, and to which it succeeds in mobilizing the people generally behind its demands. Unfortunately, however, many labor leaders, particularly those at the top of the A. F. of L., grossly underestimate masses of the American people.

The necessity for winning the broad masses of farmers, professionals, veterans, small businessmen, etc., to support its program entails certain heavy responsibilities upon the trade union leadership. For one thing, these leaders will have to think and act more in terms of the national interest, giving particular attention to the specific demands of the other democratic strata of the population. They must also work out practical forms of political co-operation with all these elements in a great national democratic coalition. Local and national conferences with these forces are very much in order. Organized labor must break down the spirit of isolation which has characterized many of its conservative leaders up till now.

Above all, the trade unions must establish good working collaboration with the ex-servicemen and women. The trade unions must become the ardent champions of the legitimate demands of these decisive forces, and work out every practical means of collaboration with them. Especially, the workers must establish labor posts in all the veterans' organizations. Under no circumstances should the N. A. M. and other reactionary employer forces be allowed to succeed in their nefarious scheme of driving a wedge between the war veterans and the workers. That would be a menace to our American democracy, whereas a good working alliance between organized labor and the veterans would be the best guarantee of success in the fight to secure full employment, to strengthen this country's democracy, to maintain world peace, and to defeat American reaction's attempt to dominate the world.

The trade unions, in order to tie the workers' interests in tightly with those of other democratic segments of our population, must especially become active in the fight of the masses against rising living costs. They must convince the people at large that the employers are well able to meet the present wage demands of the workers out of their fabulous reserves and current profits, without raising prices. They must also convince the "public" that the adoption of a full employment program would in itself bring about a huge reduction in production costs, and would enable the granting of still higher wages. In short, the people must be convinced not only that the better utilization of our great industrial machine will allow of higher wages, shorter hours, and lower prices, but also that to achieve these objectives is in the vital interest of the whole American people, save a small minority of monopolists and other exploiters who seem to believe that America was created simply for their private enrichment and to satisfy their love of power.

All this means, necessarily, that the trade unions will have to carry on far more elaborate campaigns of public enlightenment than they have ever done before. The employers fully understand the vital importance of winning public opinion; hence their elaborate campaigns on the radio, in the press, in Congress and elsewhere in support of their reactionary programs. This should be a signal to organized labor to revamp completely its obsolete methods of reaching the people's mind and to adopt modern methods of publicity on a huge scale. Labor must "sell" its case to the people at large as never before.

TASKS IN PERSPECTIVE

The foregoing are some of the most urgent tasks needful to accomplish if organized labor is to win its fight for better wages and more jobs—that is, there must be more unity in the ranks of labor itself, there must be a linking of the wages and job struggles, there must be a tying together of the economic and political struggles of the workers, and there must be an identification of the demands of labor with the interests of the nation as a whole, and the building up of a great democratic coalition upon the basis of these common interests. The success of organized labor in the present and the period ahead, the extent to which it achieves better living standards and job protection, will depend upon the measure in which it grasps these elementary lessons of the present situation.

But organized labor must needs go beyond the confines of these immediate tasks. The time is now at hand when the trade unions of this country will have to analyze far more basically the system under which we live than they have ever done before, and to adopt from their analysis, far-reaching social programs of progress.

The world capitalist system is sick, very sick. Proof of this is the fact that capitalism, during the past generation, has given birth to two devastating world wars, to a shattering world economic crisis, and to the deadly disease of fascism. And now, although we have just finished a war that has laid Europe and a large part of Asia in ruins, already the reactionaries are talking glibly of a new world war ahead of us. And the peoples of the capitalist world, famished and destitute, are now looking with terror towards new economic crises and mass unemployment in their war-ravaged countries.

The tortured and impoverished masses of Europe and Asia, in the midst of wrecked cities, ruined industries and collapsed political systems, are taking emergency methods to protect themselves under the tottering capitalist system, by nationalizing the banks and basic industries, by breaking up the big landed estates, and by democratizing their governments. But more and more they are getting their eyes fastened upon the real social evil, the capitalist system itself. Nor will they rest content until they have finally abolished capitalism altogether, and, through the establishment of socialism, bring about the socialization of the great means of production and the abolition of the exploitation of man by man for profits' sake. For socialism is the only means by which peace, democracy and prosperity can be guaranteed, both on a national and international scale. The existence of the U. S. S. R. has demonstrated this great historical fact.

The American social system, despite all its present seeming strength, is a blood brother to the decaying capitalist system of Europe and Asia, and it is subject to the same basic laws of economic and political development that have flung the old world capitalism into its present ruinous plight. Our country, too, is involved in the deepening general crisis of capitalism. American workers, therefore, must necessarily start to study our capitalism through and through and, in the light of Marxist-Leninist science, begin to orientate upon the socialist perspective that is becoming so obviously needed in the rest of the world.

The United States is very rich in natural resources, in great industries, and in trained manpower, the wealth-producing capacity of which will be enormously increased by the development of atomic power. But the greed of the monopolists—with their program of low wages and restricted production—stands in the way of realizing the potential well being of the masses that our national wealth and industrial development make possible. By organizing their forces thoroughly, the workers and their allies can, under capitalism, win for themselves a measure of well being, a degree of protection against the recurrent economic crises. But only under socialism, with the social means of production owned by the whole people, will America realize its great historical dream and become truly an unsurpassed land of liberty, peace and well being.

1945

35. The Historic Necessity of Trade Union Unity

As the workers and the people generally in this country face the many difficult domestic and foreign problems of the postwar period the split in the American labor movement looms more and more a menace to their hopes and aspirations. Whichever way one looks there are to be seen evidence of the harm and folly of permitting the internecine struggle between the A. F. of L. and the C. I. O. to continue. It has become a most urgent necessity, therefore, not only to organized labor, but to the whole nation that the rupture in the ranks of the trade union movement be healed as promptly and as thoroughly as possible.

There is no sane reason why the A. F. of L. and the C. I. O. should not get together at once either in one all-inclusive federation or, as a step in that direction, linking their forces in a whole series of collaborative movements for immediate objectives. The main reason why such unity has not been brought about is the obstructive policies in the top leadership of the A. F. of L., who are putting their own personal interests above the welfare of the labor movement as a whole.

It was these same elements who caused the split in the first place, ten years ago. They were quite willing then to see the basic industries remain unorganized rather than to risk their own positions by bringing great new masses of workers into A. F. of L. unions. So they caused the split which forced the C. I. O. to become an independent movement. And now it is these identical bureaucrats who, for the same selfish reasons, are preventing unity between the A. F. of L. and C. I. O. and who indeed, would like nothing better than to have the C. I. O. unions broken up altogether.

The split, by dividing the ranks of labor, drastically weakens the whole democratic cause. There we see the A. F. of L. leadership nationally and in various states at cross-purposes with the C. I. O. on legislation vitally needed. Characteristically too, in the recent Detroit mayoralty elections Richard Frankensteen, the labor candidate, could have been elected had it not been that the local A. F. of L. leadership, headed by Frank Martell, opposed him and supported the reactionary candidate, Jeffries. Similar situations are constantly occurring in local elections.

The split is also compromising the present big campaign of labor for wage increases. Not only is there no common program of demands and no unity of action between the two national labor federations, but the A. F. of L. leaders seem to be more anxious to defeat the C. I. O. which is leading the general movement than they are to secure wage advances for their own members.

The split is also provoking a whole series of jurisdictional quarrels and strikes of the two groups of unions against each other with the A. F. of L. on the offensive. Such internal strife literally poisons public opinion against the labor movement generally, and it is highly provocative of hostile, anti-trade union legislation.

The split likewise interferes with the organization of the millions of still unorganized workers, what with the various unions, instigated by the top A. F. of L. leadership, fighting over the control of the workers who are already organized. Nothing is more harmful to organizing work than just such internal squabbles.

The split, too, is having a disastrous effect upon labor's position in the current Labor-Management Conference. For the A. F. of L. leaders, aided by John L. Lewis, do not hesitate in their war against the C. I. O. to line up with the employers in order to defeat the progressive measures proposed by the C. I. O.

The split also extends its deadly influence out upon a world scale, as witness the A. F. of L. refusal to affiliate with the C. I. O. to the New World Federation of Trade Unions, and its shameful attempts to disrupt this vitally needed world labor organization.

It is about time that the workers took this dangerous split situation in hand and remedied it. The reactionary trusts and monopolies of this country are now on the march. They are determined not only to cripple organized labor in this country, but also to reduce the whole world under their imperialist sway. World reaction now has its most powerful center right here in the United States. And American labor cannot solve all the big problems involved in this situation with its own forces split right down the middle. If organized labor, facing this difficult situation, does not heal its internal split it will be inviting a major disaster to itself and to American democracy in general.

It is necessary, therefore, that the A. F. of L. membership wake up to the danger presented by their reactionary leaders and bring about unity with the C. I. O. in spite of them. It is absolute folly to expect that the Greens, Wolls, Lewises, Hutchesons, Dubinskys, and similar reactionaries will do anything to bring about labor unity, for their whole aim is to keep labor split. The unification process must be advanced by the rank and file and by the lower officials among whom a strong unity spirit exists.

A. F. of L. leaders opposed to this splitting policy of the Wolls and Hutchesons must be encouraged. Only a strong and organized pressure by the rank and file and pro-unity forces in the A. F. of L. can free the A. F. of L. Council to abandon its labor-splitting policy.

The present big wage movement, the fight for full employment legislation, and the establishment of the New World Federation of Trade Unions have brought about many local movements of direct co-operation or of parallel action between A. F. of L., C. I. O. and railroad unions. These are steps in the right direction. Such spontaneous movements of unity at the bottom should be encouraged in every way possible. They must be extended to include such demands as the removal of American troops from China and the internationalization of the atomic bomb. For it is an obvious fact that unity between the A. F. of L. and the C. I. O., when eventually it is achieved, will be brought about by A. F. of L. rank and file pressure notwithstanding the resistance of the top A. F. of L. leadership.

The question of labor unity is not one that will wait indefinitely. The host of great problems pressing for solution forbid delay. And one of the most vital of these urgent problems relates to the Congressional elections of 1946. In these elections the reactionaries are going to make a most determined effort to foster their deadly grip more tightly upon an already dangerously reactionary Congress. For organized labor to go into these elections divided into two warring camps, with one camp, the A. F. of L., going along with the enemy, would be suicidal folly.

For ten long years the American trade union movement has suffered from the present great split. It cannot tolerate it any longer without running a serious danger. The split must be healed, and it can be healed when the progressive forces in the A. F. of L. wake up and take the job in hand.

Organic unity of the A. F. of L. and C. I. O. or co-operation movements between them would be a tremendous step forward for the workers. It would give the whole democratic movement in the United States a great new strength for the stupendous tasks now confronting it.

1945

36. The Peril of Red-Baiting

A serious disease in the labor movement, and one that must be combated, is the widespread practice of red-baiting. Thus, in many A. F. of L. and some C.I.O. unions, various leaders are carrying on a violent campaign of denunciation against the Communists, accusing them of all sorts of vicious anti-union, anti-democratic, and anti-American practices. In many instances Communists are specifically prohibited from holding official union positions or even from being members of the union. Usually this red-baiting is accompanied by reckless attacks upon the U.S.S.R. and often by ill-concealed anti-Semitism, anti-Negroism, anti-Catholicism, anti-foreignerism, and the like. It is employer poison in the ranks of the labor movement.

Red-baiting is not political criticism; it is political persecution, just as anti-Semitism and Jim-Crowism are persecution. It is a weapon of reaction, taken straight from the arsenal of the late, unlamented Adolph Hitler. Its purpose is to develop an ideological terrorism, first against the Communists, next against all the progressive forces and eventually against the unions themselves. Red-baiting opens the way for the most dangerous attacks by employers against the labor movement.

Although workers are not so easily deceived by red-baiting as they used to be, since they have heard men like President Roosevelt, Philip Murray, and Sidney Hillman denounced as "Reds" by Thomas E. Dewey in the 1944 election campaign, nevertheless it would be a big mistake to underestimate its destructive effects in the unions. Red-baiting seeks to weaken the effectiveness of the most clear-headed and devoted workers in the labor movement by singling them out for vicious attacks; it works to undermine the co-operative relations between that progressive combination of forces, the left wing and the center, upon which all advances of the labor movement depend; and it also serves as an effective cover-up for the agents of the imperialists and the war-mongers in the labor movement. Red-baiting and reaction go hand in hand. The union that tolerates red-baiting leaves itself wide open to the assaults of the worst forces of reaction.

Among the worst red-baiters in the labor movement are the Social-Democratic trade union leaders. These people, who have nothing Socialist about them, cover up their alliances with the Wolls, etc., and also their own reactionary policies, by delivering fierce tirades against the Communists. Their "hate Russia" campaign is no less virulent than that of the Hearst press. They are eager supporters of every move of reaction looking towards a war against the U.S.S.R. The Trotskyites and the Social-Democratic leaders who presume to speak in the name of labor and socialism, make attacks upon the Communists and the U.S.S.R. their chief stock in trade. Their whole line furnishes material to those reactionary elements who are seeking an anti-Soviet war. Typically, Norman Thomas, a so-called Socialist, all through the war saw not Hitler, but Stalin as the danger. Red-baiting has become a well-paid journalistic profession among such pseudo-left elements as the Social-Democrats and Trotskyites.

Although the charges made by the red-baiters against the Communists are without foundation, they are nevertheless not without effect among the masses because of the Hitler "big-lie" technique that is used to put them across; their constant reiteration with every means at hand.

Communists are charged, for example, by reactionary A. F. of L. leaders as trying to "break up the labor movement." This, notwithstanding the patent fact that Communists attach the very greatest importance to the trade unions (more, in fact, by far than do the A. F. of L. leaders themselves) both in the defense of the workers' interests under capitalism and as the main force for bringing about socialism. Such charges are made in spite of the facts, too, that the Communists have labored devotedly through the years to build up the American labor movement, and that Communists are the most decisive leaders in the present-day, rapidly growing labor movements in many European countries. American Communists were ardent supporters of unemployment insurance, for example, when the leaders of the A. F. of L. were telling the workers that it would destroy the labor unions and American democracy. They have long been militant pioneers for industrial unionism, the organization of the unorganized, the improvement of trade union democracy, the trade union rights of

Negroes, the elimination of gangsterism, for labor unity, and every other progressive trade union issue.

Another stupid argument of red-baiters charges that Communists are irresponsibly in favor of strikes and do not care whether they are won or lost. The absurdity of this is demonstrated by two basic facts: First, the Communists, being part of the working class, have the same need as all other workers to win the economic advantages that come from victorious strikes; and, second, only if the Communists prove themselves to be successful leaders of the workers' everyday struggles under capitalism can they hope to win the workers for the incomparably greater task of establishing socialism. No element in the labor movement, therefore, has a more responsible attitude towards strikes than the Communists. None are more careful about launching strikes, and none are more determined to win them once they are called. The Communists are opposed to wildcat strikes and stand firmly for united, disciplined action. During the late war the Communists stood second to none in loyally carrying out organized labor's no-strike pledge.

Charges by red-baiters that the Communists, supposedly directed by outside forces, seek to grab control of the unions, are equally contrary to the facts. Communists, unlike the Lewises, Dubinskys, and others of their kind, have no machines in the unions. Their role as Communists is to teach the workers the principles and policies of Marxism-Leninism. Once the decision of the union is made in a given problem, they follow out loyally the trade union discipline. As for trying to "grab" leadership in the unions, the Communists understand full well the folly of such a course. Communist policy everywhere, in the unions and on the political field, is to work jointly with progressive, non-Communist forces. Obviously such a co-operative policy cannot be successful on the basis of the Communists "grabbing" for control. The fact is that today in the trade union movement generally the Communists, instead of being over-represented in leading committees and councils, are very much under-represented, considering the size of their following in the unions. But it is in line with the Hitlerian "big-lie" technique of red-baiting to shout that any union or political organization that has even one Communist or supposed Communist on its executive committee is "Communist-dominated," or is a "Communist-front" organization.

Red-baiters also assert that Communists are "totalitarians" and anti-democratic. Communism is the most democratic movement in the world, economically, politically, and socially. Communist principles call for the ultimate establishment of the most democratic society yet conceived by man, one in which there will be no social classes, no exploitation, and no state, and where everyone will produce according to his ability and receive according to his needs. In line with this fundamental democracy, Communists all over the world, including those in the United States, are front-line fighters for every democratic reform under capitalism. They are also the most resolute fighters against fascism, and they are the mainspring in the new democratic governments of Western and Central Europe. In the Soviet Union, where Communists lead the nation, the greatest democratic advances in the history of mankind have been achieved. These include the conquest of political power by the workers and farmers, the socialization of industry and the collectivization of the land, the abolition of capitalist exploitation, the doing away with economic crises and mass unemployment, the adoption of the most elaborate system of social insurance in the world, the establishment of complete social and national equality of all the peoples within the U.S.S.R., the full emancipation of women, the liquidation of illiteracy, etc., etc. To call Communists anti-democratic in the face of all these democratic achievements and struggles is a Hitler "big lie" of the first water.

Communists are also often accused by red-baiters of persecuting Catholic workers. This is a monstrous falsehood, too. Communists recognize that Catholic workers have the same economic and political interests as all other workers—they want peace; they want democracy; they want prosperity. So the Communists hold out the hand of solidarity to Catholics for the joint accomplishment of these democratic objectives. The Communists spare no efforts in fighting against religious bigotry, holding that in these critical days it is especially disastrous to engage in religious quarrels, from which only reaction can profit. At the same time, the Communists consider it politically necessary to condemn the clerical-fascist policies now being followed by the Vatican and by the many powerful figures in the Catholic hierarchy in the United States.

Lastly, the red-baiters never tire of shouting that the Communists, because of their friendly attitude toward the Soviet Union, are un-American and "agents of a foreign power." This is the greatest of all the Hitlerian "big lies" of the professional red-baiters and reactionaries. In reply to it, the attitude of the Communists towards the U.S.S.R. may be stated under two heads:

First, the Communists are ardent supporters of friendship between the great American and Soviet peoples. They refuse to take "no" on this question, because collaboration between the U.S.A. and the U.S.S.R. is the key to the progress of world democracy and the maintenance of world peace. Thus, if during the middle 1930's the United States had joined with the U.S.S.R. in its proposed international front of the democratic powers to maintain world peace, as the Communists urged, Hitler's fascism would have been choked in its cradle and World War II could have been prevented. During the great war against Hitlerism, American-Soviet collaboration, supported by the far-sighted Roosevelt, was actually achieved, and victory in the war was the result. And now, if the peace is to be won and another world war avoided, there absolutely must be American-Soviet collaboration. In fighting for such collaboration the Communists, therefore, are defending our people's most profound national interest. This is Americanism of the highest order. Those red-baiters and Soviet-haters who are now so busily sowing seeds of dissension between the U.S.A. and the U.S.S.R. are, on the contrary, betraying our country, even though they wrap themselves around with a million pseudo-patriotic phrases. Soviet-baiters are imperialist warmongers, and they would have millions of American soldier boys and hosts of civilians die in a fruitless war to advance Wall Street's profits at the expense of the American, Soviet, and other peoples.

Second, the U.S.S.R. is a socialist country. Socialism represents a vast democratic advance over the present social system of capitalism. It indicates the path by which the peoples of the world will finally emancipate themselves from the jungle of present day society, the breeder of fascism, imperialism, and war. Naturally, Communists, who advocate socialism, as the first stage of communism, have a friendly attitude towards this new regime of the U.S.S.R., the harbinger of the glorious future of mankind. Their attitude in this respect is very much like that of democrats all over the world in the years when the American Republic was young. The democrats of those times understood that the new republic being so painfully reared in our country was a great step forward over the prevailing reactionary feudalistic monarchies. Regardless of the red-baiters of those days, these democrats considered it no act of hostility to their own nation to recognize the advanced character of the very promising new American Republic and to give it their blessing. The Communists today take the same position towards the world's most advanced republic of our times, the U.S.S.R.

The red-baiters, for all their violent attacks, will not succeed in killing Communist influence in the trade unions. The message of the Communists is much too vital for that. The Communists, with their Marxist-Leninist analysis of capitalism, their practical everyday economic and political policies, their matchless loyalty to labor, their indomitable fighting spirit, their long record of support of progressive labor policies, and their ultimate goal of a socialist America, will grow, not decline, in influence. All over the world the Communist parties, responding to the burning needs of the peoples, are expanding rapidly, in spite of the frantic red-baiters. The Communist Party of the United States, with the help of vast numbers of new trade union members, will travel the same victorious path. American labor and the American people need and must have a strong Communist Party.

Labor leaders who indulge in the dangerous, fascist-like practice of red-baiting are playing the game, whether they realize it or not, of the most reactionary big monopolists, the bitterest enemies of trade unionism and of every other phase of American democracy. It's about time, therefore, that red-baiting be knocked on the head in the American labor movement. This Hitlerian slander campaign should be recognized for what it is, the spreading of employer-inspired, imperialist warmonger propaganda in the ranks of the workers, in order to destroy their fighting spirit and organization. Trade union progressives (including those who sometimes do a little red-baiting themselves in the vain hope of warding off reactionary attacks) should take up the cudgels against the red-baiting menace. Red-baiting must be eliminated from the trade unions. This is a major necessity for the further strengthening of the labor movement.

1946

37. The Trade Unions and Socialism

To meet the ever more complex problems of the post-war period, organized labor must, as we have pointed out, improve its domestic and foreign policies, build a broad new political party, organizationally strengthen the trade unions, unify its forces nationally and internationally, and cleanse its ranks of fascist-like red-baiting. But above all, American labor needs to modernize its political conceptions. It must cease worshipping an outworn capitalism and turn its hopes and efforts to the building of a new system of society worthy of the understanding and resources of modern man, socialism.

In its earlier competitive stage, capitalism was a progressive system. Under it modern industry was built, the working class was born, democracy developed, and science made great strides. But now capitalism has become monopolistic; it is in its imperialist period and has grown obsolete and reactionary. The capitalist system is full of incurable contradictions—between the social mode of production and the private ownership of industry, between the great producing power and weak purchasing capacity of the workers, between the antagonistic interests of the working class and the capitalist class, between rival imperialist powers, between the imperialist states and the colonial countries, between the capitalist and socialist parts of the world, etc., etc. These contradictions are constantly sharpening and deepening. World capitalism is today in general crisis, and its continued operation produces one disaster after another for tortured humanity.

Capitalism, as Marx pointed out long ago, is causing a spreading mass pauperization. This is shown by the terrible poverty of China, India, Latin America, and war-torn Europe, and by the awful fact that today at least a billion people throughout the world are facing famine conditions. All this misery (none of which is necessary) has been produced by the workings of capitalism in its period of decay.

Capitalism is causing an increasing economic chaos throughout the world. Before the war the periodic economic crises, which are an inevitable result of capitalism, were constantly growing sharper and more prolonged—the 1929-33 crisis being the most severe ever known. And now, particularly in the United States, the stage is being set for another world economic smash-up, once the war boom is over, that will make the terrible crisis of sixteen years ago seem like prosperity in comparison.

Capitalism today also automatically generates fascism. The great trusts and monopolies find that, with ever sharpening problems, they cannot continue to rule at home and carry out their program of imperialist aggression abroad without weakening or destroying the democratic organizations and liberties of the people. That is why fascism came to Germany, Italy, Japan, and other countries, and that is the great menace of fascism in the United States. Trusts are born enemies of democracy.

Capitalism today also systematically causes wars of unprecedented extent and devastation. The big imperialist states, intent upon world rule for themselves, collide with each other and the result is war. Twice in one generation wars have resulted from this basic cause, and now preparations are being hurried for a third and even more terrible world war. Imperialist war is a fundamental expression of the general crisis of capitalism.

The capitalist system in the United States is subject to the general economic and political laws that govern capitalism everywhere. It has within it the same basic, destructive contradictions that are undermining world capitalism in general. American capitalism, however, has been favored by history. The United States is a land of vast natural resources; the growth of capitalism here was not seriously hindered by hangovers of feudalistic institutions; the country had literally to be built from the ground up almost within the memory of living man, and instead of being seriously injured by the two world wars, which have wrought such havoc with capitalism elsewhere, this country actually fattened on them. For the past thirty years this country's "prosperity" has largely depended on furnishing war munitions, and in repairing the ravages of war. These, and other factors, have tended to prolong the life and vigor of American capitalism. But the structural weaknesses that have so enfeebled European capitalism will also eventually drag down the seemingly impregnable American capitalism, for both of them are cut from the same cloth. It is absurd to expect, as many do, that the capitalists of this country can instill the breath of life again into the decadent capitalism of the various other nations. And it is equally idle to believe that American capitalism can prosper as a sort of island in a wide sea of sick world capitalism.

The world forces of democracy can, by close organization and determined struggle against the monopolists, somewhat lessen the disastrous effects upon the masses of the reactionary tendencies of capitalism. The workers and their allies can win some degree of protection against mass unemployment through social insurance; they can lessen the severity of the inevitable economic crisis by "full employment" public works programs; they can check the menace of fascism by determined measures of democracy, and by united action they can postpone the outbreak of new wars. It is the task of the workers to fight for as many as possible of these ameliorations under capitalism, but at the same time they must realize that only under socialism can the gross evils produced by capitalism be finally done away with.

The establishment of socialism will eliminate these fast-growing evils by striking at their basic root: the private ownership of the social means of production. By the workers and other democratic forces winning political power, and by socializing the industries and the land, abolishing capitalist exploitation, and carrying on production for use instead of for profit, the basis will be laid for a peaceful, democratic, and prosperous world. The root cause of mass poverty is thereby eliminated; order is introduced into industry; economic crises and mass unemployment become things of the past; fascism is uprooted, once and for all, and the groundwork for imperialism and war disappears. Socialism supplies the sole answer to poverty, economic chaos, fascism, and war. It is the next higher rung on the social ladder that man has been ascending for ages. And mankind must climb up to socialism or sink into even greater calamities than those which for the past generation have plagued the world.

The discovery of atomic energy emphasizes afresh the obsoleteness of capitalism. The monopoly capitalists, alarmed that this new and great power will create havoc among their industries by increasing economic crises and by rendering huge amounts of investments useless, are already moving to stifle the development of atomic energy. About the sole use they are looking forward to for this tremendous source of power is to make it into atomic bombs. Only a socialist system, based on production for use and not for personal profit, can make full use of the revolutionary discovery of atomic energy.

The Soviet Union has proved the workability of socialism. It has made an end of capitalist exploitation and laid the basis for the general democracy and prosperity of its peoples; it has done away completely with economic crises and mass unemployment that are such terrible scourges under capitalism; it has abolished the capitalist bankers, industrialists, and landlords, who are the poison source of imperialism, famine, and war. And these great democratic achievements were accomplished by the U.S.S.R. in spite of a hostile capitalist world, which tried by armed intervention, civil war, economic blockade, political isolation, and imperialist invasion to smash the Soviet system. The capitalists of the world hate and fear the U.S.S.R., not because they dread an attack by the Red Army upon their countries, but primarily because they are afraid of the effects the example of a successful socialist system will have upon the oppressed millions of the earth.

The vast majority of the workers in Europe are now socialist in outlook. They are drawing the needful elementary lesson that the recurring economic crises, fascism, and wars take place because capitalism is obsolete and reactionary, and they are looking forward to the abolition of that system altogether. Today, although often under untrustworthy Social-Democratic leaders, such as the Attlees and Bevins in Great Britain, they are carrying through far-reaching programs for the nationalization of basic industries, and tomorrow they will take up more definitely the building of socialism itself.

The great body of American workers, unlike their European brothers and sisters, have not yet, however, adopted a socialist perspective. This is, as we have seen, because of the relatively more favorable position of capitalism in the United States. But the American workers are also on the march ideologically. The Hoover economic crisis and the reforms of the Roosevelt regime made them think deeply and caused them to lose much of their old-time faith in so-called free enterprise—a concept that means to leave the economic system to the tender care of the capitalists and all will be well. The workers now know that only if the government intervenes with public works programs, farm subsidies, and the like, can industry be kept going. This is a big stride forward ideologically. It means that the American working class, with its faith in capitalism weakening, is taking its first hesitant steps on the road toward socialism. Nor can there be any doubt but that the next big economic crisis will cause among the mass of American workers widespread demands for the nationalization of basic industries, and, on the part of the more advanced workers, for socialism.

A socialist perspective has now become an urgent necessity for the American working class. For only when the workers and their leaders begin to grasp the principles of Marxism-Leninism can they understand what is happening to world capitalism, and only then will they be in a position to take the necessary measures, now and in the future, to protect themselves and the world from the disasters of poverty, fascism, and war caused by the decaying capitalist system. It is indeed time that the leaders of the trade unions stop parroting the "free enterprise" slogans of the capitalists. The acquirement of a socialist outlook by the labor movement will be the greatest step forward it has ever taken. It will register the maturity of the American trade unions.

Our country has before it a glorious future, but not under capitalism. The capitalist system can bring us only more and deeper tragedies, until finally the workers and their political allies see fit to put an end to it. Socialism will come when the majority of our people demand it. The workers of the world are marching forward to socialism. The American labor movement must take its proper place in their invincible ranks.

1946

38. Summary and Conclusions

During the half century traversed by this book the American trade union movement has made great progress. From an organization of less than 2,000,000 members, which was constantly fighting a life and death struggle for survival, it has grown into a vast, well-established labor movement of 15,000,000 affiliates. From a narrow organization chiefly of skilled workers, it has now become representative of the whole working class. In doing so organized labor has also achieved substantial improvements in program, leadership, and social outlook. In the course of this evolution many of the progressive fights of the left wing were definitely victorious; but there are still many more big battles to be won if the labor movement is to be able to stand against the powerful, fascist-minded monopoly capitalists now arrayed against it.

LEFT-PROGRESSIVE COOPERATION

One of the major lessons of this book, developed in terms of practical struggle, is the important role that has been played in the development of the American labor movement by the working united front between the Communists and the center progressive forces in the trade unions. This left-center combination, expressing a common program of action has been the driving force of progress in the labor movement. Those times when for some reason the lefts and progressives did not work together and when the right wing had a free hand, were periods of stagnation and defeat for the trade unions. At the present time, when labor is faced with many difficult problems, the co-operation, between the Communists and the progressives, is more important than ever for the labor movement. A major objective of the current red-baiting campaign, which is a key weapon of reaction both outside and inside the unions, is to drive a wedge between the left wing and the center progressive group. Should this attempt succeed it could only result in making the right wing union leadership supreme, thereby crippling the labor movement.

INDUSTRIAL UNIONISM

Ever since the days of Daniel DeLeon and Eugene V. Debs, from about 1893 onward, the left wing has been an indefatigable advocate and fighter for industrial unionism. With the growth of large-scale industry and the trusts, and particularly after the loss of the Home-stead steel strike in 1892, which demonstrated the inability of craft unions to organize the basic industries and to protect the living stand-ards of the workers, the left wing has tirelessly worked for the estab-lishment of industrial unionism. This was true of the Communists, no less than of the Socialist Laborites, Socialists, and Syndicalists who preceded them.

The notable success of the C. I. O., beginning in 1935, in unionizing the trustified industries, was a dramatic justification of the left wing's generation-long struggle for the organization of the unorganized into industrial unions. However, the cause of industrial unionism, despite these successes, is not yet fully won in the labor movement. For there are labor leaders who are still strongly opposed to industrial unionism. Indeed, the Executive Council of the A. F. of L. would even now criminally break up into crafts the industrial unions in steel, automo-bile, radio and electric, rubber, metal mining, and other basic industries if they could do so. The need, therefore, still exists for the hard-won C. I. O. industrial unions to defend themselves not only against the trusts, but also against the craft-splitting, A. F. of L. reactionaries.

MILITANT UNIONISM

The Communists also have always been inveterate opponents of the "harmony-of-interests-between-capital-and-labor" conception of labor leaders of the Gompers school (of whom unfortunately many are still with us). As vigorous advocates of a unionism based upon the realities of the class struggle, the left has continuously propagated the truth that in order to wring concessions from stiff-necked employers the unions must be both strong and also willing, when need be, to fight stubbornly.

Present-day American labor organizations, including those in the C. I. O., have by no means freed themselves of the class collaboration illusions of the old-style unionism. The unions generally have, nevertheless, made considerable strides forward. Today many unions, also in the A. F. of L., use mass picketing, joint wage and strike strategy, industry-wide strikes, planned organizing campaigns, and other militant forms of trade unionism that once were exclusively used by left wingers. There is need still, however, to continue the struggle against class collaborationism, ideologically and practically, in all its insidious forms. Especially is this true at the present time when the employers and their conservative labor-leader stooges, realizing that the unions are very strong, would like to circumvent, and eventually to rob them of their power by inveigling them into various tricky schemes of no-strike policies, semi-compulsory arbitration, industrial speed-up, labor courts, and other enervating industrial practices.

TRADE UNION DEMOCRACY

Nothing is more necessary to the health of the labor movement than democratic practices and a democratic spirit. Unfortunately, this has been greatly lacking in the American labor movement. Indeed, the want of democracy, especially up to the time of the formation of the C. I. O. in 1935, was a decisive source of trade union weakness. Rank discrimination against Negroes regarding membership and employment, refusal to organize women and young workers, persecution and expulsion of left wingers, union election frauds, convention packing, financial corruption, and collusion with employers against opposition elements are only some of the principal undemocratic procedures that sapped and weakened A. F. of L. unions almost from that federation's inception.

The Communists and progressives, throughout the years, as is evidenced by the on-the-spot writings in this book, waged increasing warfare against the would-be labor dictators and for trade union democracy. Nor has this fight been fruitless. Today there is a much higher degree of democracy in the unions than ever before. The greatest advance in this respect is the improved attitude towards Negro workers. Not only have large numbers of these doubly oppressed toilers been admitted into the unions and given at least some protection on the job, but the doors of leadership are also being opened to them. Thus is being gradually removed the most shameful stain on the banners of the American labor movement—Jim Crow discrimination against Negroes.

The rise of the C. I. O. with its progressive leadership, plus the generally liberal political climate that prevailed during the Roosevelt regime, dealt a blow to grafting officials in the labor movement. Although the corruption evil has by no means been fully eradicated from labor unionism, nevertheless substantial progress has been made. The shameless "strike insurance," selling out of strikes, and raiding of union treasuries that were so prevalent in A. F. of L. unions in earlier periods, have decreased markedly during recent years. Much of the corruption of old-time A. F. of L. local labor papers has also gone.

The C. I. O. has reached the highest level of democracy of any section of the labor movement. But there are many Social-Democratic union leaders and old-time trade union bureaucrats in C. I. O. organizations who are gradually undermining the democracy that has been set up in their unions by the millions of basic industry workers. As for the A. F. of L., while it, too, has felt the surge of the workers for democracy in the trade unions, it still has many labor autocrats dominating it. Lack of trade union democracy explains, in the main, why dictatorial A. F. of L. top leaders dare to work hand-in-glove with the National Association of Manufacturers, the Republican Party, and reactionary Democrats, although their affiliated workers are largely opposed to these reactionary forces. Although the American labor movement in recent years has made much progress towards more rank and file expression, a continued fight for trade union democracy remains a major necessity.

NATIONAL TRADE UNION UNITY

An endless struggle of the progressive forces throughout the years has also been carried on to establish closer unity among the forces of labor—economic unity of all the workers in a given craft or industry, organic unity of the labor movement as a whole, political unity of the working class with the poorer farmers, the Negro people, and other democratic forces. It has been an unceasing fight against conservative labor officials, who have sought to keep labor divided in order to serve their own narrow, selfish purposes.

With labor divided into two great, often hostile camps, the A. F. of L. and the C. I. O., plus the independent railroad unions, labor unity never was more urgently necessary than at the present time. Faced by the powerful post-war offensive of big business, which, in foreign policy aims at world domination, and in domestic policy aims at reducing the living standards of the workers, weakening the whole labor movement and undermining American democracy in general, the trade unions imperatively need to unite their forces.

The practical approach to unity at this time is along the lines of united action to advance labor's economic and political demands and interests. It is decidedly practical to expect the A. F. of L. and the C. I. O., along with the Railroad Brotherhoods, to enter into joint agreements to support this or that legislation, wage movement, or political slate. That united labor action of this character is possible is evidenced by the many cases in which it has already been practiced and also by the insistent rank and file and lower officials' demand for it. The task is to make united labor action on a national scale the established policy of the labor movement, in spite of the resistance of ultra-conservative labor leaders.

Such united labor action, besides giving organized labor immediately a strong united front in the face of its powerful employer enemies, also offers the long range means by which eventual organic labor unity can be brought about. That is, the three big groups of unions—the A. F. of L., the C. I. O. and the Railroad Brotherhoods— by working together on practical economic and political tasks, will gradually bring all these sections of labor closer and closer together, breaking down factional antagonisms, harmonizing conflicting jurisdictions, and setting up joint committees, until finally an amalgamation has been accomplished. Communists never cease to struggle for labor unity.

INTERNATIONAL LABOR UNITY

World labor unity has long been a goal of the more advanced workers in all countries. And never was this unity more urgently needed than right now. Wall Street imperialism is on the rampage. Many powerful reactionaries and fascists in this and other countries accept the idea that war with the Soviet Union is inevitable and they are preparing for such a war. A great trade union international federation can be of gigantic importance in holding these warmongers in check. The long fight of the Communists and progressives in this country for a world organization of labor, which is reflected in this book, has reached fruition in the recent formation of the World Federation of Trade Unions.

The W. F. T. U. is a true global federation of unions, which its predecessor, the International Federation of Trade Unions, was not. The W. F. T. U., embracing some 70,000,000 workers in 60 countries, includes the big unions of Soviet Russia and also the huge labor organizations of Asia and Latin America. The I. F. T. U., which was principally a European organization, never attracted to itself these big labor movements and it never reached more than a third of the total membership of the W. F. T. U. Moreover, the I. F. T. U. was practically limited to unions led by Social Democrats, while the W. F. T. U., true to the broad principles of labor unity, includes Socialist, Communist, Catholic, and "pure and simple" trade unions.

The refusal of the A. F. of L. to affiliate to the W. F. T. U. is a demonstration of the reactionary character of the men at the helm of the former. Cut from this same cloth also is the A. F. of L.'s present attempt to break up the Latin American Confederation of Labor and to supplant it by a puppet organization working under reactionary A. F. of L. control.

The fight for world labor unity, therefore, must be pressed with redoubled vigor, especially here in the United States. Today in our country only the C. I. O. is affiliated to the W. F. T. U. There must be no cessation of effort until the A. F. of L., in spite of the professional world labor disrupters, has also become part of the great world organization of labor.

INDEPENDENT POLITICAL ACTION

Throughout this book's account of many years of Communist union activities the question of independent working class political action is a never-ending theme. While seeking to build the Marxist-Leninist Communist Party, the Communists have also tirelessly fought against "no-politics-in-the-unions" fallacies and urged the masses to organize a broad party, composed of the labor movement, farmers, Negro people, professionals, small businessmen, and other democratic elements.

This long fight now appears about to bear fruit. Many powerful economic, political, and social factors are pushing the workers and their political allies to break out of the capitalist two-party system and to move towards the formation of a great new mass people's anti-monopoly, anti-fascist party. Among these factors, on the *negative* side, are the ruthless offensive of big capital against the living standards and democratic rights of the people and the peace of the world, the surrender of the Truman administration to pressure of big capital, and the dangerous expansion of fascist ideas and organizations in this country. And on the *positive* side are the tremendous growth of the labor unions, the politicalization of all the major problems that the workers have to face, the vast political experience which the workers and other democratic forces gained under the Roosevelt administration, and the growing feeling among the masses that both the Democratic and Republican parties are employer-controlled and do not represent their interests. These combined factors are making for the reconstitution of the pro-Roosevelt national democratic coalition on a higher political level, in the shape of a third, people's party.

The time is now at hand when the trade unions, grown powerful numerically and ripening ideologically, should end their political tutelage to the old capitalist parties. This action will represent a gigantic step forward for the American labor movement. It will also be the realization of one of the objectives for which the Communists and other progressive forces have long struggled. After World War I the American labor movement, because its conservative leaders refused to adopt the most elementary reforms in trade union organization, programs and tactics, suffered a crushing defeat at the hands of the militant employers. But after World War II (let us hope) the labor movement (if not its A. F. of L. leaders) will show better judgment than it did after the last war in order to repel the attacks of the employers. The most urgent thing it must do in this respect is to establish a broad mass party of the democratic people.

ANTI-COMMUNIST SLANDERS

Even a casual reading of the material in the book, which was written on the firing line of the class struggle, makes it quite clear that every progressive movement in the trade unions finds ardent pioneers and tireless champions in the Communists. It raps on the head the anti-Communist slanders of the red-baiters.

First, it refutes in practice the absurd charge that Communists are "foreign agents." For all the struggles and programs dealt with in this book are obviously American in content and direction. They are based exclusively upon American needs and conditions. Only those who are hopelessly prejudiced can deny the progressive role of the Communists, and ignore the patent fact that the Communists and their left-wing forbears have always been keenly American in their proposals and struggles.

Second, the history embodied in these writings shatters also the contention of red-baiters that Communists are callous to the interests and sufferings of the masses and that they advocate strife for strife's sake. The contrary is true. The Communists stand out as indefatigable fighters for the best interests of the workers and the whole people. It could not be otherwise, for two very good reasons: (a) the Communists, being flesh and blood of the working class, suffer all the hardships of the workers and have the same urgent interest as other workers to abolish or alleviate these hardships, and (b) only when the Communists, by loyal service in the class struggle, prove to the workers that they are the best and most trustworthy fighters in the daily struggle against capitalist abuses, can they win the workers' understanding and support for their larger objective of socialism. This is why, all over the world, Communists are the most responsible leaders in strikes and other struggles.

Third, this book also explodes the red-baiters' myth that the Communist Party, for narrow partisan purposes, "interferes" in the internal life of the trade unions. Incidentally, people making such charges conveniently forget that all capitalist parties, as well as the Catholic Church, the capitalist press, and various other non-working class institutions, interfere actively in the trade unions. The difference is that whereas the Communists who are themselves workers and as such are active trade union members, work and fight for the best interests of labor, the other institutions noted are basically hostile to the labor movement. Indeed, the Republican and Democratic parties participate far more extensively and aggressively in trade union life than the Communists have ever done. They look upon the trade unions as if they were their very own, for political exploitation. Not only have these two parties succeeded in winning the open political allegiance of the vast bulk of trade union members and leaders, but they have also definitely stamped their capitalist ideology upon the workers' organizations.

By showing the constructive activities of Communists in the unions, this book exposes the reactionary spirit of those who, falling in line with the boss-inspired, Hitler-like red-baiting, would either prohibit the Communists from holding union office or would exclude them from union membership altogether.

THE QUESTION OF SOCIALISM

The aspiration for socialism is not a new idea in the American trade union movement. Growing out of the struggle for the organization of the workers and the improvement of their conditions, the aim of socialism was an active force in the trade unions for at least two generations prior to the formation of the Communist Party. As far back as 1912, fully one-third of the delegates to the United Mine Workers convention carried Socialist Party cards, and actively campaigned for socialism. Many unions were then led by exponents of socialism, however reformist. In the conventions of the A. F. of L. itself the Socialist Party vote against the Gompers reactionaries ran as high as 40 percent. But what is the situation today? Outside of the handful of Communist union officials, there is practically no acceptance of socialism in the top trade union circles, even in the progressive C. I. O. Significantly also, official support for the nationalization of individual industries, which used to be widespread in the unions, has very greatly subsided.

This phenomenon of a reduced acceptance of socialism in American trade unions during the past generation contrasts drastically with what has happened to the workers in Europe. Today the great bulk of the European working class is overwhelmingly Socialist and Communist. The basic explanation for this contradiction is that American capitalism, which has fattened upon two world wars, has occupied a relatively sheltered position, whereas European capitalism has suffered the full force of both devastating wars. Consequently it is experiencing the sharpest forms of the deepening general crisis of the world capitalist system, more than is the case with American capitalism.

With American capitalism in this relatively favorable position, there has been a tendency for our trade union leadership (also the workers) to look away from socialism, or from even the nationalization of industry under capitalism, and to fall victims to the capitalist illusions so assiduously cultivated during recent decades in the United States. During the 1920's economic boom period, for example, the trade union leadership swallowed hook, line and sinker the N. A. M.

propaganda to the effect that the workers could solve all their economic problems through class collaboration and increased production. The Social-Democrats and Liberals literally became intoxicated with these prosperity illusions. The 1929 economic crash was a heavy blow to these illusions, but soon they were replaced by others. During the economic crisis years of the 1930's, the trade union leadership succumbed no less completely to the new Keynes reformist theories, advocated and applied by Roosevelt. The substance of these theories is that capitalism can overcome its periodic economic crises and provide full employment through government make-work plans. Obsessed by such illusions, intensely propagated by capitalist writers and speakers, trade union leaders and members found little need for socialism or even for the nationalization of specific industries under Roosevelt. Hence, from these various factors, we find the almost incredible situation of even "progressive" labor leaders almost universally propagating the absurd capitalist slogan of "free enterprise."

Despite their slowness in accepting anti-capitalist Marxist slogans and ideology, American workers, nevertheless, have been making definite political progress, especially during the past fifteen years. They are militant in strikes. They are becoming politicalized in their outlook. They are heading towards the formation of an independent mass political party. They are rapidly losing confidence in so-called free enterprise, which is shown by their almost universal conviction that state intervention is indispensable in order to keep industry going, to furnish them jobs, and to provide them with social security.

This ideological growth of the American workers is bound to continue, and its ultimate end is a socialist viewpoint. The world capitalist system, of which American capitalism is an organic part, is sinking deeper and deeper into insoluble contradictions. Outside of the Western Hemisphere that system is now in most difficult straits. Nor can the seemingly all-powerful United States escape the general capitalist decay, with its increasing economic chaos, fascist-like reaction, and atom-bomb war preparations. Once it passes through the present post-war industrial boom, which is based upon repairing the ravages of the war, it, too, will sink into grave economic and political difficulties. The workers and their political allies, in order to cope with these problems, will have to apply not only Rooseveltian economic reforms. They will be compelled to go far beyond and, as the peoples of Europe are doing, to begin to nationalize industry. Nor can the people stop short of eventual socialism. In the process the workers will build a strong mass Communist Party. The fight for a socialist ideology for the American working class is a good fight, and it is not in vain.

References

The following is a list of writings by William Z. Foster from which the selections in this volume have been made. Where selections are from more than one book or pamphlet, the references follow the sequence in the chapter. No reference is given for chapter 38 since it was written especially for the present volume.

Chapter
1. From Bryan to Stalin, 1936, pp. 11-73
2. From Bryan to Stalin, 1936, pp. 90-104
3. From Bryan to Stalin, 1936, pp. 105-26
4. From Bryan to Stalin, 1936, pp. 43-47
5. From Bryan to Stalin, 1936, pp. 133-36
6. Misleaders of Labor, 1927, pp. 53-61
7. Bankruptcy of the American Labor Movement, 1922, pp. 19-24, 30-42
8. Bankruptcy of the American Labor Movement, 1922, pp. 49-56
9. From Bryan to Stalin, 1936, pp. 171-73
10. Labor Herald, July 1923, pp. 11-12
11. From Bryan to Stalin, 1936, pp. 185-87
12. Misleaders of Labor, 1927, pp. 62-95
13. Wrecking the Labor Banks, 1927, pp. 8-17, 55-57, 59-60; Misleaders of Labor, 1927, pp. 222-24
14. Misleaders of Labor, 1927, pp. 124-26, 194-96, 271-74, 286-305
15. From Bryan to Stalin, 1936, pp. 191-92, 177-84
16. From Bryan to Stalin, 1936, pp. 195-209
17. Organize the Unorganized, 1925, pp. 5-29
18. From Bryan to Stalin, 1936, pp. 209-12
19. From Bryan to Stalin, 1936, pp. 216-20
20. The Daily Worker, May 16, 1929
21. From Bryan to Stalin, 1936, pp. 192-94
22. From Bryan to Stalin, 1936, pp. 220-29
23. From Bryan to Stalin, 1936, pp. 245-47, 251-54, 277-81
24. Industrial Unionism, 1936, pp. 25-33, 35-36, 38-42

25. The Communist International, June 1937, pp. 397-402
26. What Means Strike in Steel?, February 1937, pp. 11-51
27. A Manual of Industrial Unionism, August 1937, pp. 5-6, 38-58
28. Railroad Workers Forward!, October 1937, pp. 5, 18-39; Halt the Wage Cuts and Layoffs on the Railroads, October 1938, pp. 9-12; The Daily Worker, December 16, 1943
29. Your Questions Answered, June 1939, pp. 68-76, 79-80, 86, 59, 63-64
30. The Trade Unions and the War, April 1942, pp. 3-22, 24-29, 31-40, 44-47
31. The Worker, December 31, 1944
32. The Soviet Trade Unions and Allied Labor Unity, June 1943, pp. 17-21, 23-37
33. The Daily Worker, March 4, 1945
34. The Strike Situation and Organized Labor's Wage and Job Strategy, November 1945, pp. 5-23.
35. The Daily Worker, November 14, 1945
36. Problems of Organized Labor Today, 1946, pp. 34-41
37. Problems of Organized Labor Today, 1946, pp. 42-48

Index

A. F. of L. Committee for Unemployment Insurance and Relief, 191

Amalgamated Association of Iron, Steel, and Tin Workers, 12, 33 *f.*, 41 *f.*, 85, 231 *f.*

Amalgamated Clothing Workers of America, 151 *f.*; militants in, 78 *ff.*

Amalgamation of trade unions, 61 *f.*, 75 *f.*, 164, 269 *f.*; results of 1922 campaign, 82 *f.*; T. U. E. L. drive for (1922); 81 *f.*, 130

American Alliance for Labor and Democracy, 58

American Federation of Labor, bureaucracy in, 57; campaign against T. U. E. L., 140 *ff.*; and capitalist rationalization, 90; and corruption, 119 *ff.*; and economic crisis, 186 *ff.*; fight for industrial unionism at 1935 convention, 205 *f.*; founding of, 10; and "higher strategy of labor," 107 *f.*; history of reactionary role of leaders of, 211; and independent unions, 160 *ff.*; and international trade union unity, 304 *f.*, 333 *ff.*; membership growth in World War I, 59; membership of (1937), 215 *ff.*; and Negroes, 249 *f.*; and 1919 steel strike, 33; 1934 convention of, 205 *f.*; and 1937 steel strike, 221 *f.*; offensive against Communists (1923), 140 *f.*; and organization of unorganized, 84 *f.*; and packinghouse campaign, 26 *f.*; policy in World War I, 24 *f.*; Portland convention (1922), 142; progressive forces in, 318 *f.*; rejects T. U. E. L. program, 61 *f.*; split in, 213 *f.*; and steel campaign, 34 *f.*, 37 *f.*; and trade union unity, 338 *f.*, 352; undemocratic practices of, 247 *f.*, 251; and unemployed, 343; and "union-management cooperation," 101 *f.*; wage policy of, 100 *ff.*; weakness of, 200 *ff.*; and World War I, 57 *f.*

American Federationist, 249.

American Railway Union, 10 *f.*

Amsterdam International. See International Federation of Trade Unions

Amter, Israel, 192

Anglo-Soviet Trade Union Committee, 304 *f.*

Apprenticeship, 284

Arbitration, Communist position on, 283; dangers in, 254 *f.*, 341 *f.*; in packinghouse campaign, 28

Atomic energy, 361

Baltimore and Ohio plan, 97 *ff.*, 262 *f.*

Banking. See Labor banks

Brady, Peter, 104

Bribery, 121

Brotherhood of Locomotive Engineers, 102 *ff.*; 111 *ff.*

Brotherhood of Railway Carmen, 142

Building trades unions, 121 *f.*

Bull Moose campaign (1912), 18

Bureaucracy, in A. F. of L., 57 *ff.*; and organization of unorganized, 158 *f.*; in trade unions, 124 *ff.*, 250 *f.*

"Business unionism," 91 *ff.*

Butcher Workers Union, 22 *f.*, 30

Capitalism, corruption by, 183 *f.*; decay of, 348, 359 *ff.* See also Imperialism

Capitalist propaganda, in Coolidge period, 89 *f.*

Carpenters Union, 128

Carver, Thomas Nixon, 89 *f.*, 92 *f.*

Catholic Church, 125 *f.*

Catholic workers, 356

Check-off of dues, 257 *f.*

Chicago Federation of Labor, 20 *f.*; and amalgamation campaign (1922), 82; and steel campaign (1919), 32

Chicago Railroad Council, 21

Chicago Stockyards Council. See Stockyards Labor Council

Civil rights, of strikers, 240 *ff.*

Class collaboration, 57 *ff.*, 90 *f.*, 98, 101, 136 *f.*, 185, 365; of A. F. of L., 107; in unions (1920's), 96; after World War I, 60 *f.*

Workers Party. See Communist Party
Workers' Ex-Servicemen's League, 192
Working class. See Trade unions; Un-
employed; Names of organizations
World Federation of Trade Unions, 333 *ff.*,
339 *ff.*, 368 *ff.*

World War I, A. F. of L. and, 57 *f.*;
trade union growth in, 59
World War II, trade unions and, 289 *ff.*

Youth, organization of, 172; trade unions
and, 312 *ff.*